WEB BROWSERS AT-A-GLANCE

DOWNLOADING INFORMATION	PLATFORMS	PRICE		
Download via ftp: ftp.ncsa.uiuc.edu; directory path: web/mosaic/windows	Windows, Macintosh, X Windows	No charge... available for downloading and upgrading via the Internet.		Mosaic
Evaluation copy: http://www.spry.com/sp_prod/airmos/amosdown.html	Windows	$49.95	Internet access on a single disk. Installs the software to connect to the Internet, and establishes an account with an Internet service provider.	Spry's Air Mosaic™
Evaluation copy: http://www.qdeck.com	Windows	Call (800) 354-3222 for pricing.	Powerful, feature-rich Web browser; includes many tools to help search the Internet and ships with several supporting applications.	Quarterdeck Mosaic™
Not available via the Internet	Windows, Macintosh, X Windows	Price varies depending upon the version and distributor.	Simple installation and menu structure make it easy to get started. Includes support for several security modules.	Spyglass® Mosaic™
Evaluation copy: ftp://ftp.mcom.com/netscape/	Windows, Macintosh, X Windows	$39.00	Security features protect your account and credit card numbers. Safely use financial services and shop online.	Netscape® Navigator

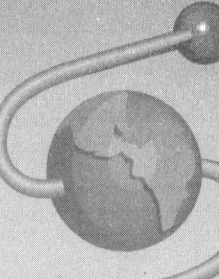

The Mosaic Roadmap

ROBIN MERRIN

SYBEX®

San Francisco • Düsseldorf • Paris • Soest

ACQUISITIONS MANAGER: Kristine Plachy
DEVELOPMENTAL EDITORS: Steve Lipson, Brenda Kienan
EDITOR: Armin Brott
PROJECT EDITOR: Michelle Khazai
TECHNICAL EDITOR: Peter Stokes
BOOK DESIGNER: Helen Bruno
DESKTOP PUBLISHER: Dina F Quan
PRODUCTION ASSISTANT: Ron Jost
INDEXER: Matthew Spence
POSTER DESIGN: Seventeenth Street Studios
COVER DESIGNER: Seventeenth Street Studios

NCSA Mosaic is a registered trademark of the National Center for Supercomputing Applications.

Air Mosaic is a registered trademark of Spry Inc.

Quarterdeck Mosaic is a registered trademark of Quarterdeck Office Systems, Inc.

Spyglass Mosaic is a registered trademark of Spyglass, Inc.

Netscape Navigator is a registered trademark of Netscape Communications Corp.

Chameleon ™ Sampler is a trademark of NetManage, Inc.

SYBEX is a registered trademark of SYBEX Inc.

TRADEMARKS: SYBEX has attempted throughout this book to distinguish proprietary trademarks from descriptive terms by following the capitalization style used by the manufacturer.

Every effort has been made to supply complete and accurate information. However, SYBEX assumes no responsibility for its use, nor for any infringement of the intellectual property rights of third parties which would result from such use.

Copyright ©1995 SYBEX Inc., 2021 Challenger Drive, Alameda, CA 94501. World rights reserved. No part of this publication may be stored in a retrieval system, transmitted, or reproduced in any way, including but not limited to photocopy, photograph, magnetic or other record, without the prior agreement and written permission of the publisher.

Tables 8.1 and 8.2 have been reprinted with permission from *The Internet Roadmap*, by Bennett Falk, copyright 1994 SYBEX Inc.

Library of Congress Card Number: 95-69358
ISBN: 0-7821-1698-1

Manufactured in the United States of America

10 9 8 7 6 5 4 3 2 1

SOFTWARE SUPPORT

On the enclosed disk is a copy of NetManage's Chameleon Sampler software. This software and any offers associated with it are supported by NetManage. NetManage can be reached by calling (408) 973-7171.

Should the manufacturer cease to offer support or decline to honor the offer, SYBEX bears no responsibility.

DISK WARRANTY

SYBEX warrants the enclosed disk to be free of *physical defects* for a period of ninety (90) days after purchase. If you discover a defect in the disk during this warranty period, you can obtain a replacement disk at no charge by sending the defective disk, postage prepaid, with proof of purchase to:

> SYBEX Inc.
> Customer Service Department
> 2021 Challenger Drive
> Alameda, CA 94501
> (800) 227-2346
> Fax: (510) 523-2373

After the 90-day period, you can obtain a replacement disk by sending us the defective disk, proof of purchase, and a check or money order for $10, payable to SYBEX.

DISCLAIMER

SYBEX makes no warranty or representation, either express or implied, with respect to this medium or its contents, its quality, performance, merchantability, or fitness for a particular purpose. In no event will SYBEX, its distributors, or dealers be liable for direct, indirect, special, incidental, or consequential damages arising out of the use of or inability to use the medium or its contents even if advised of the possibility of such damage.

The exclusion of implied warranties is not permitted by some states. Therefore, the above exclusion may not apply to you. This warranty provides you with specific legal rights; there may be other rights that you may have that vary from state to state.

COPY PROTECTION

None of the programs on the disk are copy-protected. However, in all cases, reselling or making copies of these programs without authorization is expressly forbidden.

To Douglas Robert Merrin

Acknowledgments

MANY people contributed talent, time, and energy to see this book to completion and I thank them for their hard work and dedication.

Most importantly, I'd like to express my gratitude to my husband, business partner, and perennial technical expert, Thomas Merrin, for helping to plan and organize the material and for testing and retesting every word I wrote to make sure it was accurate. He suggested improvements along the way when he thought I'd overlooked some detail and also captured every figure and graphic.

Our daughter Cecile Merrin generously loaned us her computer so we could run five products simultaneously.

Thanks also to Steve Lipson for offering me this project and for his dauntless support during our alliance together at Sybex. Finally, I'd like to thank Brenda Kienan for guiding the book's development, Michelle Khazai for painstakingly managing all the details, Armin Brott for meticulously editing it, Peter Stokes for providing the final level of technical quality assurance, Lorrie Fink for designing the eye-catching new cover and poster, and Dina Quan and Ron Jost of the Sybex production department for putting all the pieces together.

Roadmap QuickKey

Starting Out

What Is the Internet?	2
What Is Mosaic?	3
The Many Forms of Mosaic	3
Getting Connected	13
Getting Help Online	20
Downloading NCSA Mosaic	35
Installing and Configuring NCSA Mosaic	41
Handbook	133
Help Menu	133
Starting Mosaic	251
What's New Page	286

Getting around the Web

Looking at Mosaic: A Guided Tour	16
The NCSA Windows Mosaic Home Page: Start Here	16
Browsing with Hypertext Links	19
Browsing the Internet	22
Back	67
Cancel, Cancel Current Task	71
Demo Document	89
Forward	121
Global History	127
Go To	129
History	135
Home	137
Link	167
Link Tree	169
Local History	173
Location	173
Mosaic Help Page	189
Moving Backward and Forward	191
Online Documentation	197
Open	197
Open File, Open Location	198
Open Local File, Open	199
Start With	250
Starting Points	251
Stop	253
URL Helper	270
URLs	272
View History	278

Changing Your Display

As Icons, Icon List, Text List or Tree	63
Browser Window	69
Cascade	72
Change Cursor over Anchors	72
Customizing the Mosaic Window	83
Document Display Area	94
Document View Window	96
Duplicate	97
Kiosk Mode	165
Mosaic Window	190
Presentation Mode	205
Refresh	225
Reload	226
Show Annotations	242
Show Browser Margins	242
Show Current URL	243
Show Directory Buttons	243
Show Document Title	244
Show Document URL	244
Show Location	245
Show Page Turners	245
Show Status Bar	246
Show Toolbar	246
Show Toolbar As	247
Show URL Field	247
Show URL Helper	248
Show URL in Status Bar	248
Status Bar	252
Tile	263
Toolbar	264
Toolbar Icon Settings	266
Toolbar Style	267
Toolbars at Startup	267
URL Bar	270

Modifying, Saving, and Printing Web Pages

Annotating Documents	57
Annotate Menu	57
Autoload Home Page	64
Copy	79
Creating Lists of URLs	80
Cut	84
Delete this Annotation	85
Document Info	94
Document Source	94
Edit this Annotation	99
Home Page	138
Home Page Location	142
Load Home Page	170
Load to Disk	172
Local Files	172
Page Setup	201
Paste	202
Print	206
Print Margins	207
Print Preview	208
Print Setup, Printer Setup	209
Save	229
Save As	229
Save As Text	230
Select All	233
Selecting Text	234
View Source	278

✪ Roadmap QuickKey

Changing the Look of Web Pages

Anchors	56
Auto Load Images	63
Background Color: Pick Color	68
Bullet Style	70
Choose Font	74
Display Inline Images	91
Followed Links Expire	115
Fonts	117
Fonts: Scheme	118
Fonts Styles	116
GIF Images	127
HTML Commands	148
HTML Documents	149
HTML Tags	149
HTML Viewer	150
Hypertext Link Style	152
Images	153
Images: Colors	153
Images: Display Images	156
Indent Width	158
Inline Images	159
JPEG Images	165
Link Color	167
Link Styles	169
Load Images	170
Load Images Automatically	171
Load Missing Images	171
Numbered Lists Style	196
Paragraph	201
Round List Bullets	227
Style Sheet	253
Styles	254
Visited Link Color	283
When Loading Images, Redraw Every	286

Customizing Hotlists

Add Bookmark	48
Add Current To Hotlist	49
Adding to a Quicklist	55
Archives	62
Bookmark File	68
Bookmarks	69
Changing a Hotlist	73
Creating a Hotlist	79
Deleting a Hotlist	85
Deleting Items from a Hotlist	87
Deleting Items from a Quicklist	89
Exporting a Hotlist	102
Folders	112
Hotlist	142
Hotlist Manager	145
Import NCSA Menu as Hotlist	156
Modifying Bookmarks	181
Modifying Hotlists	185
Properties	210
Quicklist	217
Save To Current	231
Set As Current	242
View Bookmarks	278

Customizing Menus

Adding to a Menu	51
Creating a Menu	81
Deleting a Menu	86
Deleting Items from a Menu	88
Modifying Menus	189
User Configurable Menus	273

Sending and Receiving Mail and News

Electronic Mail	99
E-mail Address	100
Extended News Listing	104
Go To Newsgroups	129
Internet Address	160
Internet Newsgroups	160
Mail Document	175
Mail/News	177
Mail Server	178
News	194
News RC File	194
News Server	194
Newsgroups	195
NNTP Server	195
Reading News	221
Send Mail	234
Sending Mail	236
SMTP Server	249
Signature File	248
Subscribing to Newsgroups	255
Subscriptions	259
Usenet Newsgroups	273
Your E-mail	291
Your Name	291

Roadmap QuickKey

Searching, Finding, and Retrieving

Anonymous FTP	59
Archie	60
Archie Request Form	60
Find	108
Finger	110
Finger Gateway	111
FTP	122
Gopher	130
Gopher Servers	130
GopherSpace Overview	131
Retrieving a WAIS Document	227
Searching for Information in a Document	232
Searching Indexes	232
Telnet	261
Telnet Applications	262
TN3270 Application	264
Veronica	275
WAIS	285
WAIS Proxy	285

Configuring Your Browser

Action	48
Audio	63
Cache	71
Cache Enabled	71
Cache Timeout	71
Cached Documents	71
Configuration	77
Console	79
Data Engine	85
Directory and File Locations	90
Disk Cache	91
Disk Cache Directory	91
Document Caching	91
Documents in Drop Down	97
Extensions	104
FTP Proxy	122
Gopher Proxy	130
Helper Applications	134
Helpers	134
HTTP	151
HTTP Proxy	151
Initial Window Placement	158
Interlace Method	160
Launch Application	167
Max Cache Size	179
Memory Cache	179
MIME	180
MIME Type	180
News Proxy	194
No Proxy On	196
Preferences	203
Proxies	211
Save Last Window Position	231
Save Options	231
Security Alerts	233
Security Proxy	233
Services	239
Show a Popup Alert Before	242
Supporting Applications	259
Table	261
Use Browser as Viewer	272
Use Extended FTP	272
Use Internal (8-bit) Sound	273
Use Current Window Position	272
User Name	273
Viewers	278
Wait for Images	285
Wipe Interval	287
Window Styles	287

Contents

Introduction xxv

PART I

⊛ The Big Picture

What Is the Internet? 2
   What Is the World Wide Web (WWW)? 2
What Is Mosaic? 3
   What Can You Do with Mosaic? 3
   What Can't You Do with Mosaic? 3
The Many Forms of Mosaic 3
   NCSA Mosaic 5
   Comparing Web Browsers 6
   Quarterdeck Mosaic 8
   Spry's Air Mosaic 9
   Spyglass Enhanced NCSA Mosaic for Windows ... 10
   Netscape Communications Corporation's Netscape Navigator ... 11
   What About Mosaic for the Macintosh and X Windows? ... 13
Getting Connected 13
   How Can You Get Connected? 13
   What Connections Do You Need? 13
   What Hardware Do You Need? 13
   What Software Do You Need? 14
   What is a TCP/IP Protocol Stack? 14
   What are SLIP and PPP? 15
Getting Started 15
Looking at Mosaic: A Guided Tour 16

The NCSA Mosaic Home Page: Start Here	16
Browsing with Hypertext Links	19
Going Back and Forth	20
Getting Help Online	20
The Online User's Guide	21
A Quick Approach to Online Help	22
Browsing the Internet	22
What's New on the Internet?	22
Browsing for Something that Interests You	23
Using the History Window	26
Changing Options	27
Are You Looking for Something Specific?	29
Using Uniform Resource Locators (URLs)	30
You're on Your Way	33
Exiting Mosaic	33
Downloading NCSA Mosaic	35
Using the Chameleon Sampler	35
Installing the Chameleon Sampler Software	36
Establishing Your Internet Account	37
What Other Software Must You Download?	37
Downloading NCSA Mosaic with Windows FTP	37
Installing and Configuring NCSA Mosaic	41
Installing Win32s	42
Installing and Configuring NCSA Mosaic	43

PART 2

✪ Web Browsers A to Z

A

About Mosaic	47
Accelerator Keys: NCSA Mosaic	47
Action: Quarterdeck Mosaic and Netscape	48
Add Bookmark: Netscape	48
Add Current to Hotlist, Add Document to Hotlist	49
Add Current to Hotlist: NCSA and Spyglass Mosaic	50
Add Document to Hotlist: Air Mosaic	50
Add Document to Hotlist: Quarterdeck Mosaic	50
Adding a URL to a Hotlist: Quarterdeck Mosaic	50
Adding from the History to the Hotlist: Quarterdeck Mosaic	51
Adding to a Menu	51

Adding to a Menu: NCSA Mosaic	52
Adding to a Menu: Air Mosaic	52
Adding an Item to the Starting Points Menu: NCSA Mosaic	54
Adding an Item to the SPRY Menu: Air Mosaic	55
Adding to a Quicklist: NCSA Mosaic	55
Anchors: NCSA Mosaic	56
Animate Logo: Air Mosaic	56
Annotate Menu: NCSA Mosaic	57
Annotating Documents	57
Annotate: NCSA Mosaic	57
Annotation: Quarterdeck Mosaic	58
Viewing an Annotation: NCSA Mosaic	58
Viewing an Annotation: Quarterdeck Mosaic	58
Editing an Annotation: NCSA Mosaic	58
Editing an Annotation: Quarterdeck Mosaic	58
Deleting an Annotation: NCSA Mosaic	59
Deleting an Annotation: Quarterdeck Mosaic	59
Editing the Annotations Items in the NCSA MOSAIC.INI File	59
Anonymous FTP	59
Applications and Directories: Netscape	59
Archie	60
Archie Request Form: NCSA Mosaic	60
Archives: Quarterdeck Mosaic	62
As Icons, Icon List, Text List, or Tree: Quarterdeck Mosaic	63
Audio	63
Auto Load Images, Autoload Inline Images	63
Autoload Inline Images: Air Mosaic	64
Auto Load Images: Netscape	64
Autoload Home Page: NCSA Mosaic	64

B

Back	67
Back: Air Mosaic, NCSA Mosaic, Spyglass Mosaic	67
Back: Netscape	68
Back: Quarterdeck Mosaic	68
Background Color: Quarterdeck Mosaic	68
Bookmark File: Netscape	68
Bookmarks: Netscape	69
Browse: Netscape and Quarterdeck Mosaic	69
Browser: Quarterdeck Mosaic	69
Browser Window: Quarterdeck Mosaic	69
Browsers	69
Bug List: NCSA Mosaic	69
Bullet Style: Quarterdeck Mosaic	70

C

Cache: NCSA Mosaic	71
Cache Enabled: Quarterdeck Mosaic	71
Cache Timeout: Quarterdeck Mosaic	71
Cached Documents: Air Mosaic	71
Canceling	71
Cancel Current Task: Air Mosaic	71
Cascade: Quarterdeck Mosaic, Spyglass Mosaic	72
CERN	72
Change Cursor Over Anchors	72
Change Cursor Over Anchors: NCSA Mosaic	72
Change Cursor Over Anchors: Quarterdeck Mosaic	72
Change Fixed or Proportional Font: Netscape	73

Changing a Hotlist	73
Changing a Hotlist: NCSA Mosaic	74
Changing a Hotlist: AIR Mosaic	74
Choose Font: NCSA Mosaic	74
Clear: Spyglass Mosaic	76
Close: Quarterdeck Mosaic, Spyglass Mosaic	76
Color: Netscape	76
Configuration: Air Mosaic	77
Console: Air Mosaic	79
Copy	79
Creating a Hotlist	79
Creating a Hotlist: AIR Mosaic	79
Creating a Hotlist: NCSA Mosaic	79
Creating Lists of URLs	80
Creating a Menu	81
Creating a Menu: NCSA Mosaic	81
Creating a Menu: Air Mosaic	81
Adding a Cascading Menu	82
Adding a Cascading Menu: NCSA Mosaic	82
Adding a Cascading Menu: Air Mosaic	83
Customizing the Mosaic Window	83
Customizing the Window: Air Mosaic	83
Customizing the Window: NCSA Mosaic	84
Customizing the Window: Netscape	84
Customizing the Window: Quarterdeck Mosaic	84
Customizing the Window: Spyglass Mosaic	84
Cut: Netscape, Quarterdeck and Spyglass Mosaic	84
Cyberspace	84

D

Data Engine: Quarterdeck Mosaic	85
Delete: Quarterdeck Mosaic	85
Delete this Annotation: NCSA Mosaic	85
Deleting a Hotlist	85
Deleting a Hotlist: NCSA Mosaic	86
Deleting a Hotlist: Air Mosaic	86
Deleting a Menu	86
Deleting a Menu: NCSA Mosaic	86
Deleting a Menu: Air Mosaic	87
Removing a Menu from the Menu Bar: Air Mosaic	87
Deleting Items from a Hotlist	87
Deleting Items from a Hotlist: NCSA Mosaic	88
Deleting Items from a Hotlist: Air Mosaic	88
Deleting Items from a Menu	88
Deleting Items from a Menu: NCSA Mosaic	89
Deleting Items from a Menu: Air Mosaic	89
Deleting Items from a Quicklist: NCSA Mosaic	89
Demo Document	89
Demo Document: NCSA Mosaic	90
Demo Document: Air Mosaic	90
Demo Document: Quarterdeck Mosaic	90
Demo Document: Netscape	90
Demo Document: Spyglass Mosaic	90
Directory and File Locations: Netscape	90
Disk Cache: Netscape	91
Disk Cache Directory: Netscape	91

Display Inline Images 91
   Display Inline Images: NCSA Mosaic 91
   Display Inline Images: Quarterdeck Mosaic 91
Document Caching 91
   Document Caching: NCSA Mosaic 92
   Document Caching: Air Mosaic 92
   Document Caching: Netscape 92
   Document Caching: Quarterdeck Mosaic 94
Document Display Area 94
Document Info: Netscape 94
Document Source 94
   Document Source: Air and NCSA Mosaic 96
   Document Source: Quarterdeck Mosaic 96
   Document Source: Netscape 96
   Document Source: Spyglass Mosaic 96
Document Title 96
   Document Title Bar: Air Mosaic 96
Document View Window 96
Documents in Drop Down: Air Mosaic 97
Doorkey Icon: Netscape 97
Duplicate: Quarterdeck Mosaic 97

E

Edit Menu 99
Edit this Annotation: NCSA Mosaic 99
Electronic Mail (E-mail) 99
   Electronic Mail: NCSA Mosaic 99
   Electronic Mail: Air Mosaic 100
   Electronic Mail: Quarterdeck Mosaic 100
   Electronic Mail: Netscape 100
E-mail Address 100
   E-mail Address: NCSA Mosaic 100
   E-mail Address: Air Mosaic 101
Error Messages 101
Exit 101
Exporting a Hotlist 102

Exporting a Hotlist: Air Mosaic 102
Exporting a Hotlist: Spyglass Mosaic 103
Extended News Listing: Air Mosaic 104
Extensions 104
   Extensions: Air Mosaic 104
   Extensions: Quarterdeck Mosaic 104
   Extensions: Netscape 105

F

FAQ Page, Frequently Asked Questions: NCSA Mosaic, Netscape 107
   FAQ Page: NCSA Mosaic 107
   Frequently Asked Questions: Netscape 107
Feature Page: NCSA Mosaic 107
File Menu 108
Find 108
   Find: NCSA and Quarterdeck Mosaic 108
   Find: Netscape 109
   Find: Air Mosaic 109
   Find: Spyglass Mosaic 110
Finger 110
Finger Gateway: NCSA Mosaic 111
Firewall 112
Folders: Quarterdeck Mosaic 112
   Add a Document to Folder: Quarterdeck Mosaic 113
   Adding a URL to a Folder: Quarterdeck Mosaic 113
   Adding from the History to a Folder: Quarterdeck Mosaic 114
   Creating New Folders: Quarterdeck Mosaic 114
   Deleting Folders: Quarterdeck Mosaic 114
   Renaming Folders: Quarterdeck Mosaic 115
Followed Links Expire: Netscape 115
Fonts Styles: Quarterdeck Mosaic 116

Fonts	117
Fonts: Air Mosaic	117
Fonts: NCSA Mosaic	118
Fonts: Quarterdeck Mosaic	118
Fonts: Scheme: Quarterdeck Mosaic	118
Creating a Font Scheme	118
Choosing a Different Scheme	119
Removing a Font Scheme	119
Forms	119
Forward	121
Forward: Air Mosaic, NCSA Mosaic, Spyglass Mosaic	121
Forward: Netscape	121
Forward: Quarterdeck Mosaic	121
FTP	122
Downloading Files with FTP	122
FTP Proxy: Netscape	122
FTP Sites: NCSA Mosaic	122

G

Gateway	125
General: NCSA Mosaic	125
General: Quarterdeck Mosaic	125
GIF Images	126
GIF Viewer: Quarterdeck Mosaic	127
Global History: Quarterdeck Mosaic	127
Displaying the Global History: Quarterdeck Mosaic	127
Changing the Global History Options	128
Go: Netscape	128
Go To: Quarterdeck Mosaic	129
Go To Newsgroups: Netscape	129
Gopher	130
Downloading Files with Gopher	130
Gopher Proxy: Netscape	130
Gopher Servers: NCSA Mosaic	130
GopherSpace Overview: NCSA Mosaic	131

H

Handbook: Netscape	133
Help Menu	133
Helper Applications: Netscape	134
Helpers: Spyglass Mosaic	134
History	135
Using the History Window: Air Mosaic, NCSA Mosaic	135
Using the History Window: Spyglass Mosaic	136
Using the History Window: Netscape	137
Home	137
Home: Air Mosaic, NCSA Mosaic, Spyglass Mosaic	138
Home: Netscape	138
Home Page	138
Home Page: Air Mosaic	140
Home Page: NCSA Mosaic	140
Home Page: Spyglass Mosaic	140
Home Page: Quarterdeck Mosaic	141
Home Page Location: Netscape	142
Hotlist	142
Using the Hotlist: Air Mosaic	142
Using the Hotlist: NCSA Mosaic	143
Using the Hotlist: Spyglass Mosaic	144
Hotlist Manager: NCSA Mosaic	145
Creating a Hotlist	146
Deleting a Hotlist or Menu	146
Adding to a Hotlist or Menu	146
Adding an Item To the Current Hotlist: NCSA Mosaic	147
Changing the Current Hotlist	147
Removing Items from a Hotlist or Menu	147
Placing Hotlists on the Menu Bar	148
Importing a Hotlist	148

HTML Commands	148
HTML Documents	149
HTML Tags	149
HTML Viewer: Quarterdeck Mosaic	150
HTTP	151
HTTP/0.9: Air Mosaic	151
HTTP Proxy: Netscape	151
Hypermedia	151
Hypertext	151
Hypertext Link	152
Hypertext Link Style: Quarterdeck Mosaic	152

I

Images	153
Images: Netscape	153
Images: Colors: Netscape	153
Images: Display Images: Netscape	156
Import NCSA Menu as Hotlist: Air Mosaic	156
Indent Width: Quarterdeck Mosaic	158
Initial Window Placement: NCSA Mosaic	158
Inline Images	159
Interlace Method: Quarterdeck Mosaic	160
Internet Address	160
Internet (Usenet) Newsgroups	160
Internet Relay Chat (IRC)	161

JK

JPEG Images	165
Kiosk Mode: Air Mosaic	165

L

Launch Application: Netscape	167
Link	167
Link Color	167
Link Color: Air Mosaic	167
Link Color: Spyglass Mosaic	168
Link Styles: Netscape	169
Link Tree: Quarterdeck Mosaic	169
Load Home Page: Quarterdeck Mosaic	170
Load Images: Netscape	170
Load Images Automatically: Spyglass Mosaic	171
Load Missing Images: Spyglass Mosaic	171
Load to Disk: Air Mosaic, NCSA Mosaic	172
Local Files	172
Local History	173
Displaying the Local History: Quarterdeck Mosaic	173
Location: Netscape	173

M

Mail and News: Netscape	175
Mail Document: Netscape	175
Mail/News: Quarterdeck Mosaic	177
Mail Server: Netscape	178
Mail Technical Support: NCSA Mosaic	178
Max Cache Size: Quarterdeck Mosaic	179
Memory Cache: Netscape	179
Menu Editor: NCSA Mosaic	179
Mime	180
Mime Type: Netscape	180
Modifying Bookmarks: Netscape	181
Displaying Bookmarks: Netscape	182
Removing Items from Bookmarks: Netscape	182
Renaming Bookmark Items: Netscape	183
Reordering Bookmarks: Netscape	183
Importing Bookmarks: Netscape	184
Exporting Bookmarks: Netscape	185
Modifying Hotlists	185
Modifying Hotlists: Air Mosaic	185
Modifying Hotlists: NCSA Mosaic	187
Modifying Hotlists: Spyglass Mosaic	187

Modifying Menus	189
Modifying Menus: Air Mosaic	189
Modifying Menus: NCSA Mosaic	189
Mosaic Help Page	189
Mosaic Window	190
MOSAIC.INI File: NCSA Mosaic	190
Movies	191
Moving Backward and Forward	191
Moving between Documents Using Links	191
Moving between Documents Using URLs	191
MPEG Movies	191
Multimedia Files	192

N

Navigate Menu	193
Navigating the Web	193
NCSA	193
Network: Quarterdeck Mosaic	194
News: NCSA Mosaic and Netscape	194
News Proxy	194
News RC File: Netscape	194
News Server	194
Newsgroups	195
NNTP Server	195
NNTP Server: NCSA Mosaic	195
NNTP Server: Quarterdeck Mosaic	195
News (NNTP) Server: Air Mosaic	195
News (NNTP) Server: Netscape	195
No Proxy On	196
Numbered Lists Style: Quarterdeck Mosaic	196

O

Online Documentation	197
Open: Quarterdeck Mosaic	197
Open File, Open Location: Netscape	198
Open File	198
Open Location	199
Open Local File, Open URL: Air, NCSA, and Spyglass Mosaic	199
Open Local File	199
Open URL	200
Options Menu: NCSA and Air Mosaic, and Netscape	200

P

Page Setup: Spyglass Mosaic	201
Paragraph Spacing	201
Paste: NCSA, Quarterdeck and Spyglass Mosaic, and Netscape	202
Pop-up Menus: NCSA Mosaic, Quarterdeck Mosaic, Netscape	203
Preferences	203
Preferences: NCSA Mosaic	203
Preferences: Quarterdeck Mosaic	204
Preferences: Spyglass Mosaic	204
Preferences: Netscape	204
Presentation Mode	205
Print	206
Print Margins: Air Mosaic	207
Print Preview: NCSA, Air and Quarterdeck Mosaic, Netscape	208
Print Setup, Printer Setup	209
Program Icon	210
Properties: Quarterdeck Mosaic	210
Proxies: Netscape	211
Proxy	212
Proxy: NCSA Mosaic	213
Proxy: Quarterdeck Mosaic	214
Proxy Server: Spyglass Mosaic	214
Proxy Servers: Air Mosaic	215

QR

Quicklist: NCSA Mosaic	217
Quicktime Movies	217
Reading Mail: Quarterdeck Mosaic	219

Reading News	221	Services	239
Reading News: Air Mosaic	221	Set as Current: Quarterdeck Mosaic	242
Reading News: NCSA Mosaic	221	Show a Popup Alert before: Netscape	242
Reading News: Netscape	222	Show Annotations: Quarterdeck Mosaic	242
Reading News: Quarterdeck Mosaic	224	Show Browser Margins: Quarterdeck Mosaic	243
Reading News: Spyglass Mosaic	224	Show Current URL: NCSA Mosaic	243
Refresh: Netscape	225	Show Directory Buttons: Netscape	244
Reload	226	Show Document Title: Air Mosaic	244
Retrieving a WAIS Document	227	Show Document URL: Air Mosaic	245
Round List Bullets: NCSA Mosaic	227	Show FTP File Information: Netscape	245
		Show Link URL(s): Qdeck Mosaic	245
		Show Location: Netscape	245

S

Save	229	Show Page Turners: Quarterdeck Mosaic	245
Save As	229	Show Status Bar: Air Mosaic, NCSA Mosaic	246
Save As Text: NCSA Mosaic	230	Show Toolbar: Air Mosaic, NCSA Mosaic, Spyglass Mosaic, Netscape	246
Save Last Window Position: Air Mosaic	231	Show Toolbar As: Netscape	246
Save Options: Netscape	231	Show URL Field: Quarterdeck Mosaic	247
Save To Current: Quarterdeck Mosaic	231	Show URL Helper: Quarterdeck Mosaic	248
Searching Indexes	232	Show URL in Status Bar: Air Mosaic, NCSA Mosaic	248
Searching for Information in a Document	232	Signature File: Netscape	248
Secure and Insecure Documents	232	SMTP Server	249
Security: Spyglass Mosaic, Netscape	232	SMTP Server: Air Mosaic	249
Security: Netscape	232	SMTP Server: NCSA Mosaic	249
Security: Spyglass Mosaic	233	SMTP Server: Netscape	249
Security Alerts: Netscape	233	SMTP Server: Quarterdeck Mosaic	250
Security Proxy: Netscape	233	SOCKS	250
Select All: NCSA Mosaic and Spyglass Mosaic	233	Source: Netscape	250
Selecting Text	234	Start With: Netscape	250
Send Mail: NCSA Mosaic	234	Starting Mosaic	251
Sending Mail: Air, Quarterdeck Mosaic	236	Starting Points: NCSA Mosaic	251
Sending Mail: Air Mosaic	237	Status Bar: Quarterdeck Mosaic	252
Sending Mail: Quarterdeck Mosaic	237		

Stop	253
Stop Current Read: Quarterdeck Mosaic	253
Stop Loading: Netscape	253
Interrupt Current Operation: Spyglass Mosaic	253
Style Sheet: Spyglass Mosaic	253
Styles: Netscape	254
Subscribing to Newsgroups	255
Subscribing to Newsgroups: NCSA Mosaic	256
Subscribing to Newsgroups: Netscape	256
Subscribing to Newsgroups: Quarterdeck Mosaic	258
Subscriptions: NCSA Mosaic	259
Supporting Applications: Netscape	259

T

Tables: NCSA Mosaic	261
Telnet	261
Telnet Application: Air Mosaic, Netscape, NCSA Mosaic	262
Temporary Directory: Netscape	262
Terminal Program: Air Mosaic	263
Tile: Quarterdeck Mosaic, Spyglass Mosaic	263
TN3270 Application: Air Mosaic, Netscape	264
Toolbar	264
Moving the Toolbar: Quarterdeck Mosaic	265
Toolbar Icon Settings: Quarterdeck Mosaic	266
Toolbar Style: Air Mosaic	267
Toolbars at Startup: NCSA Mosaic	267
Trash: Quarterdeck Mosaic	268

U

Underline Links	269
Underline: Quarterdeck Mosaic	269
Underline Hyperlinks: Air Mosaic	269
Underline Links: Spyglass Mosaic	269
Underlined: NCSA Mosaic	269
Underlined: Netscape	269
Undo: Netscape	270
URL Bar	270
URL Helper: Quarterdeck Mosaic	270
URLs	272
Use Browser as Viewer: Netscape	272
Use Current Window Position: NCSA Mosaic	272
Use Extended FTP: NCSA Mosaic	272
Use Internal (8-bit) Sound: NCSA Mosaic, Air Mosaic	273
Usenet Newsgroups	273
User Configurable Menus: Air Mosaic, NCSA Mosaic, Netscape	273
User Name: Quarterdeck Mosaic	273

V

Veronica	275
Performing a Veronica Search	275
View Bookmarks: Netscape	278
View History: Netscape	278
View Source: Spyglass Mosaic	278
Viewers	278
Downloading Viewers	280
Associating Viewers: Air Mosaic	280
Associating Viewers: NCSA Mosaic	282
Associating Viewers: Quarterdeck Mosaic	283
Visited Link Color: Spyglass Mosaic	283

W

WAIS	285
WAIS Proxy	285
Wait for Images: Quarterdeck Mosaic	285
What's New Page	286
When Loading Images, Redraw Every: Air Mosaic	286
Window Styles: Netscape	287
Wipe Interval: Quarterdeck Mosaic	287
World Wide Web	287
WWW	287

XYZ

XBM Images	291
Your E-mail: Netscape	291
Your Name: Netscape	291

Index **293**

Introduction

BASED on what you've heard and read, does exploring the Internet—though appealing—sound complicated to the point of being overwhelming? It really isn't, so don't let anyone intimidate you if you are ready to get started. Using Mosaic or any similar Web browser to access the Internet is easier than revising a spreadsheet, managing a database, or desktop publishing a brochure. We'll show you how and why.

This book can help you decide which Web browser is for you, get started using it, and continue to learn as you become proficient.

You have the software you need on the disk and the instructions you need in this book. To minimize the hassles, we've also included a chart that tells you where to get each product, showing which you can acquire for free or on a trial basis.

As you progress, or if you've already started with a particular form of Mosaic, the book will help you decide when—and if—you should switch. For example, when you think you've outgrown your Web browser, or if you started with more features and complications than you really need, this book can help you find something more appropriate.

WHO ARE YOU?

We're assuming you're intelligent enough to learn from a book, or you wouldn't have wasted your money buying one. You are competent in other Windows applications. You have diverse interests. One of these three descriptions probably fits you:

- You are curious about what's out there.
- You already know what's out there and want to find it more quickly and easily.
- Quite frankly, you don't want to know all this, but you need to know it to do your job.

If you fit into the third category, we'll try to make this book as painless as possible. For everyone else, though, it'll be pretty exciting.

WHY FIVE DIFFERENT PRODUCTS?

Guess what? The developers of every Web browser claim their product is the fastest and most powerful tool you can use to travel the Internet. Several manufacturers claim their product is also the most widely used. No single product has been declared clearly superior by any objective third party, but all the products in this book are reasonably priced (or free) and have a strong user base. They'll all help you search for information, save what you find, and record where you found it—essentially what you want to do as you travel the Internet.

You'll like one of the five products—or all of them—and the great thing about Web browsers is that you can easily use more than one without making a commitment. The investment is minimal.

By the way, this book really covers more than five products, since some of the products are distributed under more than one name. For example, Spry's Air Mosaic, described in this book, is essentially the same software as the CompuServe NetLauncher.

HOW TO USE THIS BOOK

This book is written in plain English without computer—or even worse, Internet—jargon. It explains how to do just about everything you can do with Web browsers, while skipping over the unnecessary. For example, you don't have to configure the dozens of options you'll find in these products in order to get started, but when you are ready to customize your browser, you'll find the details you need succinctly presented.

There are enough illustrations to keep you on track. The figures will also help you *see* the similarities in and differences between the products, in addition to reading about them. If there is a button you can click to speed up a task, we'll show you that. In fact, we'll try to show you the fastest way of doing everything.

Throughout the book, there are plenty of cross-references to minimize repetition and to help you locate material easily. The Roadmap QuickKey we've included supplements the detailed Table of Contents and the Index, so you can quickly track down the answers to your questions.

The book is organized into two parts: an overview and an alphabetical reference.

Part One: The Big Picture

Part One covers the basics of the Internet, the Word Wide Web, and how to find your way around. We tell you how to use the software on the disk that comes with this book to download NCSA Mosaic for free. If you've already installed a Web browser, you can skip the sections you don't need, and read the parts that you find helpful.

Part Two: Web Browsers A to Z

Once you get started, use the alphabetical listings in Part Two to find out how to do everything else (after installation). If you are browsing the Web in your spare time, you'll appreciate the speed with which you can find a topic, read it, and apply what you've read. You'll also learn, gradually, how each topic fits into the big picture you saw in Part One.

What's in the Boxes?

Throughout this book, various pieces of text will be highlighted with boxes.

This is a note, emphasizing some information that might interest you, like how a different browser approaches a similar task or feature.

············· Tip ·····················

This is a tip, highlighting a technique or feature that will help you navigate the Web with speed and ease.

This is a warning, alerting you to a possible problem. Happily, there aren't many warnings in this book. Web browsing isn't usually harmful to you or your computer.

This Might Interest You

This is a sidebar, which contains some background or other relevant information on a particular topic. It's included because we thought many readers might find it interesting. It's set aside in a box because you don't have to read it to understand how to accomplish something. You can read it whenever you have time, if you want.

Tables and Charts, Too

The Mosaic Roadmap also has some tables and an overview chart (in the front) that help you compare products and summarize information in an easy-to-look-up format. There's a detailed, feature-by-feature comparison table of the browsers in Part One. And there's a table of interesting Web pages on an assortment of topics in Part Two. All in all, you'll have some great starting points—whatever your interests.

A Few Conventions

We also use a few conventions to make the directions easy to follow. When we give you directions for something that you might type, it looks just like the text you're reading now. Certain keys on the keyboard are shown with familiar symbols. For example, the Enter key looks like ↵.

Internet addresses and any text strings you need to type in are written in a font `that looks like this`.

I'd Like to Hear from You

Once you're on your way, please let me know what you learned from this book and what you'd like to see more of in the next edition. And tell me what needs fixing, and I will. My e-mail address is `rsmerrin@callamer.com`. You can also write to me:

Robin Merrin
c/o SYBEX
2021 Challenger Drive
Alameda, CA 94501

PART I

the Big Picture

....

MOSAIC

This book is about different forms of Mosaic and other Web browsers and how you can use them to find your way around the Internet. Not surprisingly, the five different products covered in detail in this book have a great deal in common: they are all based on the underlying principle that it should be easy to browse around the graphical universe of the World Wide Web, if you are already using the graphical user interface provided by Windows.

Of course, since Web browsers all have their strengths and weaknesses, how do you know which will be best for you? We think this book will help you decide. As you are learning to use one product, you'll be exposed to similar or superior features in the other products, and you'll acquire a basic understanding of all of them. If you don't have Mosaic yet, you can use the Chameleon Sampler that comes with this book to download NCSA Mosaic (at no cost) and get started. Or, if you already have a form of Mosaic or another Web browser, you can jump right in with the information in this book. Later, you'll be able to move on to a product with more of the features and power you'd like. We'll show you how to make the most of what you have and how to upgrade when you're ready.

See Browser; What Is the Internet?; What Is the World Wide Web?

WHAT IS THE INTERNET?

If you were interested enough in Mosaic to buy this book, you probably have some idea what the Internet is. But just to remind you, the Internet is made up of more than two million computers which are linked, or networked, to each other with physical connections and software, in order to freely share and transfer information.

See Getting Connected

What Is the World Wide Web (WWW)?

The World Wide Web (usually referred to as the Web or WWW) is a system on the Internet that supports documents that are linked to other documents—as well as formatted text, graphics, sound and movies—which you can view with Mosaic. The Web helps facilitate the distribution of information over the Internet by presenting documents which are formatted for easy—and often entertaining—viewing and by guiding your search for information with familiar point-and-click actions. Remember, the Web is not the entire Internet, just the graphical portion—the portion you can access with the Web browsers covered in this book.

Home pages, which you'll see in a few minutes, help organize the whole process of searching the Web by giving you a convenient and logical starting point.

See   **Home Pages; World Wide Web**

WHAT IS MOSAIC?

Mosaic is an application that runs under Microsoft Windows and lets you search for information. It lets you access the Internet without having to learn a series of UNIX commands and the syntax that those commands require. If you are already using other Windows applications—for word processing, spreadsheets, e-mail or entertainment—you'll find that Mosaic offers you the quickest approach to browsing around the Internet to see what's on it for you. In fact, that's what Mosaic is—an Internet *browser* which makes the Web graphical, like Windows, instead of non-graphical like the UNIX (or DOS) command line.

See   **Browsers**

What Can You Do with Mosaic?

With Mosaic, you can find, read, print and save information that is stored on computers all over the world. The information can be contained in documents containing text, graphics, audio, and even movies. You can search through large numbers of documents to find something specific. Or, when you are first getting started, you can simply browse around for something to read, in much the same way as you channel surf with a TV remote control.

What Can't You Do with Mosaic?

Although there are thousands of computers available to you on the Internet, there are also many others you cannot access. For example, you can't send and receive e-mail or subscribe to newsgroups with all forms of Mosaic; you'll need to use different applications for comprehensive mail and news support. But don't worry: mail and news are also described in this book.

See   **Electronic Mail; Newsgroups**

THE MANY FORMS OF MOSAIC

The first Mosaic, NCSA Mosaic version 1.0, was developed by the National Center for Supercomputing Applications. The current version of NCSA Mosaic, version 2.0x beta, is shown in Figure 1.1.

In 1994, NCSA licensed Mosaic version 1.x to software manufacturers who modified it or added their own user interface with different menus, button bars and other tools. These manufacturers offer a number of enhancements, described on the next few pages. They also offer their own customized starting points, known as *home pages*. And they ship with additional software for connecting to the Internet and accessing other Internet capabilities such as e-mail and newsgroups. What's best for you depends on what you want or need to

4 THE MANY FORMS OF MOSAIC

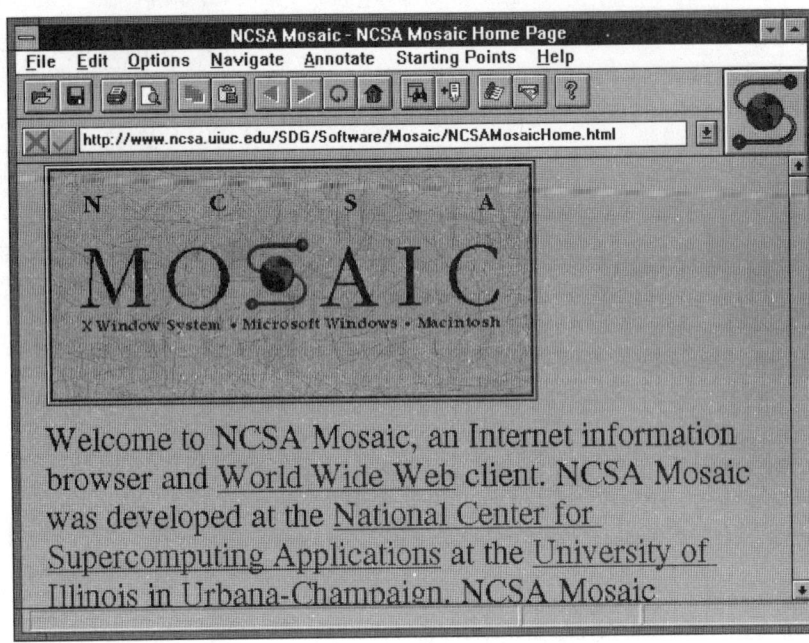

Figure 1.1

NCSA Mosaic for Windows, version 2.0x beta

do, and the intangibles which define how you like to use your computer.

> **Each manufacturer has created a home page that is highly creative, visually appealing and very useful. But home pages are not reserved for software manufacturers; any company or individual can create a home page—you can even create your own.**

The Web browsers covered in this book include NCSA Mosaic and four of the most popular commercial Web browsers. Three are enhanced forms of NCSA Mosaic (the first three in the list below):

- Quarterdeck Mosaic
- Spry's Air Mosaic
- Enhanced NCSA Mosaic for Windows from Spyglass
- Netscape Communications Corporation's Netscape Navigator

See **History; Home Pages; Link; Save**

THE MANY FORMS OF MOSAIC 5

Mosaic: What's in a Name?

For simplicity throughout this book, we refer to each product by an abbreviated and easy-to-recognize name (listed below on the left) <u>not</u> by the complete manufacturers' name (below, on the right).

Air Mosaic	Spry's Air Mosaic
NCSA Mosaic	NCSA Mosaic for Windows
Quarterdeck Mosaic	Quarterdeck Enternet Q/Mosaic
Spyglass Mosaic	Enhanced NCSA Mosaic for Windows from Spyglass
Netscape	Netscape Communications Corporation's Netscape Navigator

Much of their functionality is the same; for example, they all:

- Display a customized home page so you have a starting point for your Web exploration.
- Let you download and display documents by clicking on a link you see on your screen.
- Maintain a *history*—a list of documents you've looked at during the current session.
- Let you save documents on your own computer when you come across something really important.

NCSA Mosaic

NCSA Mosaic is free. And now that you have the Chameleon Sampler (which came with this book) you can download NCSA Mosaic and get started just as soon as you establish an account with a service provider. All the instructions you need are found later in Part 1 (in the section "Downloading NCSA Mosaic").

Although NCSA Mosaic is free, there are advantages to using one of the other forms:

- You have to spend some time downloading the NCSA Mosaic software, as well as other software that is required to run NCSA Mosaic, such as Win32s.
- If you are paying connect charges, you have to pay for the time you spend downloading. On the other hand, if you purchase a different form of Mosaic, all the software you need *may* be provided on the diskettes you receive. (*See the note at the end of this list.*)
- NCSA does not provide technical phone support for those with a problem. You'll have to send an e-mail to them and wait for a reply. With

commercial forms of Mosaic, technical support is available by phone.

- NCSA Mosaic 2.0 is still under development and not every feature works or has been thoroughly tested. For example, as of this writing, the Preferences dialog box has tabs that are being reorganized and options that are being renamed. Other forms have already passed through the development and testing phases.

- Context-sensitive online help is not currently available for NCSA Mosaic. It is available with several of the commercial enhancements.

- Enhanced forms provide features which are not available with NCSA Mosaic. These are described in the next few sections.

If you acquire a form of Mosaic on disk; for example, the Mosaic which comes with several O'Reilly and Associates books, you'll need to also purchase SLIP/PPP software elsewhere, paying yet again. We don't cover their Mosaic form in our book. However, the Mosaic-on-a-disk that comes with both Mosaic in a Box and SYBEX's Mosaic Access to the Internet does not require you to get SLIP/PPP; it comes preconfigured with everything you need.

If you've already purchased a different form of Mosaic because you didn't realize you could obtain NCSA Mosaic free of charge, you'll definitely realize some benefits. And if you haven't purchased anything yet, NCSA Mosaic is a good place to start. With a minimal investment (the price of this book), you'll be able to see whether the Internet is what you were expecting it to be. And you can always purchase another product at any time later. Besides, the current version of NCSA Mosaic probably has 90% of the features you'll want initially.

See   **Downloading NCSA Mosaic**

Comparing Web Browsers

If you are starting out with NCSA Mosaic, you may want to purchase another Web browser sometime down the road. Table 1.1 compares the key features of the Web browsers covered in this book. Use this table to help you understand the strengths and special features of each.

These features are covered in detail under the alphabetical listings. Some may jump out at you. For example, Netscape's security features will appeal to you if you plan on shopping online. Other features may be of little interest until you read about them in detail or need them for some specific purpose.

Table 1.1
Web Browser Feature Comparison

Name	NCSA Mosaic	Air Mosaic	Q/Mosaic	Spyglass Mosaic	Netscape
Version number	2.00	3.09	1.0	2.0 enhanced	1.1N
Document cache	No	Yes	Yes	No	Yes
Custom Hotlist	Yes	Yes	Yes	Yes	Yes
Download status displayed	Yes	Yes	Yes	Yes	Yes
Drag and drop documents	No	No	Yes	No	No
Editable URL box	Yes	Yes	Yes	Yes	Yes
Forms support	Yes	Yes	Yes	Yes	Yes
Hierarchical Hotlists	Yes	Yes	Yes	No	Yes
History list	Yes	Yes	Yes	Yes	Yes
Displays as documents load	No	No	Yes	No	Yes
Kiosk mode	Yes	Yes	No	No	No
Select and copy text	Yes	No	Yes	Yes	Yes
Proxy support	Yes	Yes	Yes	Yes	Yes
Document security	No	No	Yes	Yes	Yes
Toolbar with shortcut buttons	Yes	Yes	Yes	Yes	Yes
Find text	Yes	Yes	Yes	Yes	Yes
Turn on/off image display	No	Yes	Yes	Yes	Yes
Context-sensitive online help	No	Yes	Yes	No	No
Read news	Yes	Yes	Yes	Yes	Yes
Post to a newsgroup	Yes	Yes	Yes	No	Yes
Subscribe to a newsgroup	Yes	No	Yes	No	Yes
Send e-mail	Yes	Yes	Yes	No	Yes
Receive e-mail	No	No	Yes	No	No
FTP	Yes	Yes	Yes	Yes	Yes
Gopher	Yes	Yes	Yes	Yes	Yes
Telnet	No	No	Yes	No	No
WAIS	No	No	Yes	Yes	Yes
	17	18	25	15	21

THE MANY FORMS OF MOSAIC

Some special features of each Web browser are described in the next few sections.

Quarterdeck Mosaic

Quarterdeck Mosaic ships with a complete package of Internet tools called Quarterdeck Enternet. Quarterdeck Mosaic, shown in Figure 1.2, displays the first page of a document with improved speed, while the document is still being downloaded. (This means that you can start reading right away, instead of waiting for the entire document to be retrieved.) Multiple folders can be created for storing lists of documents, called *hotlists* in the other products. Multiple document view windows can be opened at one time. A history of all the documents you have retrieved from all your Mosaic sessions is maintained, not just a history of the current session. The Mail and News application is a related product which can be launched through Quarterdeck Mosaic. You can modify the toolbars and display. Finally, context-sensitive online help is available.

This is the perfect product for you if you want Mosaic, e-mail and newsgroup subscription capabilities all within one product, if you plan on accessing and downloading multiple documents which you want to organize in personalized folders, and you want drag-and-drop document management capabilities. Quarterdeck Mosaic is an application designed for Windows power users.

Figure 1.2
Quarterdeck Mosaic

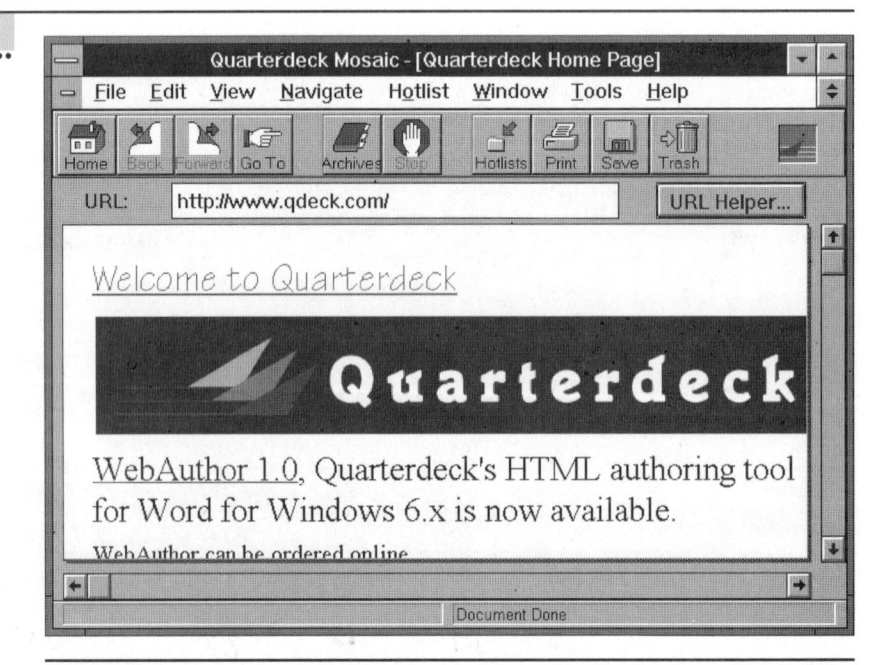

THE MANY FORMS OF MOSAIC

See Document View Window; Folders; History; Hotlists; Menu Editor; NCSA; Online Documentation; Toolbar

Spry's Air Mosaic

Air Mosaic, shown in Figure 1.3, is included in Spry's Mosaic in a Box and Internet in a Box packages, and as part of its AIR Series product. It's also available in SYBEX's *Mosaic Access to the Internet*, a book/disk package available for just $26.99. Both packages include other software for connecting to and working on the Internet. Air Mosaic's features include the ability to create multiple folders for storing hotlists and a document title drop-down list for quickly selecting documents you've browsed before. Air Mosaic also lets you display only the document view window by hiding everything else that's usually on-screen (menus, toolbar, etc.), so you have the largest possible area for reading documents.

Mosaic in a Box provides instant Internet access on a single disk, and is currently the only product to offer this complete approach. Not only does Mosaic in a Box provide Air Mosaic, but it includes and installs the software necessary to connect to the Internet, and establishes

Figure 1.3

Air Mosaic

Mosaic in a Box's All in One Setup

If you want to minimize your efforts, in terms of finding a service provider, setting up the communications software on your computer, and downloading software, you might want to purchase Spry's Mosaic in a Box. Mosaic in a Box's setup program:

- Installs the communications software you need.
- Provides you with a list of local telephone numbers with service providers in your neighborhood.
- Sets up your account and registers you with the service provider you choose.
- Installs Air Mosaic.

Mosaic in a Box's setup program does everything for you in a few minutes, and guides you with clear, onscreen instructions and prompts.

However, their hourly connection charge may be higher than the amount charged by other service providers in your area. If it is, you can still use Air Mosaic with another service provider while enjoying the easy installation procedures.

---

an account for you with an Internet service provider. This is also true of SYBEX's *Mosaic Access to the Internet*.

The version of Air Mosaic that comes with Mosaic in a Box (or with the Sybex package) is the perfect product for you if you want the fastest, easiest installation and setup possible, especially if you don't already have an Internet SLIP or PPP account. See "Mosaic in a Box's All-in-One Setup" for more on this.

See **Document Title; Document View Window; Folders; Kiosk Mode**

Spyglass Enhanced NCSA Mosaic for Windows

Spyglass's Enhanced NCSA Mosaic for Windows, shown in Figure 1.4, is available as an OEM product. If you have a copy, you probably received it when you purchased your computer, modem, or another book about the Internet.

Spyglass Mosaic includes a Cyberspace Sampler with over 30 home pages you can retrieve in 10 different categories. You can't annotate documents and there are fewer menus than in NCSA Mosaic. Nevertheless, Spyglass Mosaic does have one significant advantage over NCSA Mosaic: all its features were fully tested and debugged before its release. Online documentation is included, but there is no context-sensitive help.

Figure 1.4

Spyglass's Enhanced NCSA Mosaic for Windows

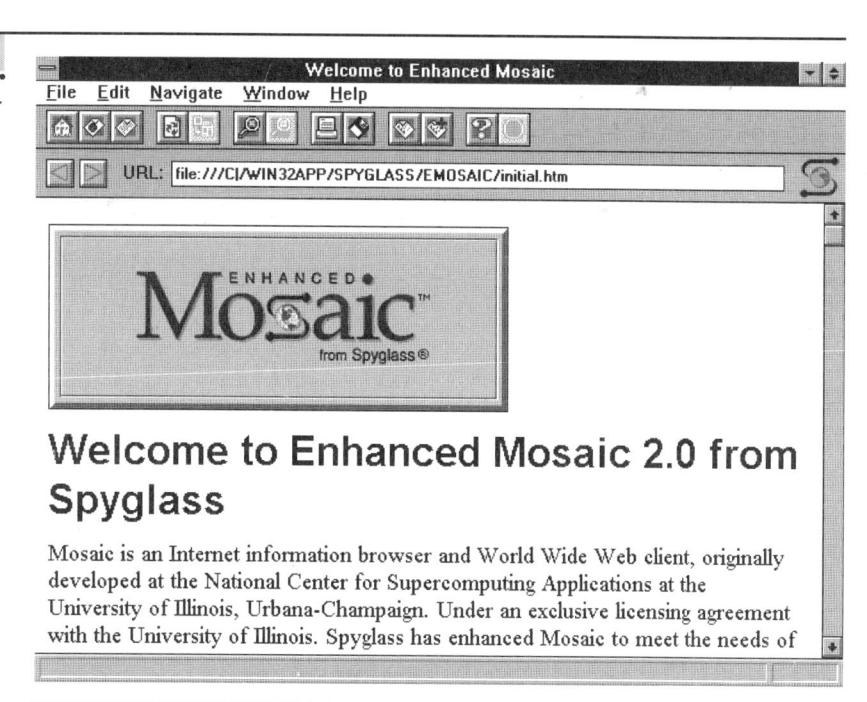

Although not as feature-rich as other Web browsers, if you already have Spyglass Mosaic and an Internet service provider, there is no reason to switch to another product yet. Spyglass Mosaic is easy to use and offers you full access to all the documents on the Web. What it doesn't offer is some of the more advanced document management capabilities of other products. If you find you need these features, you can easily make the switch later.

See **Cyberspace; Document View Window; Home Pages; Starting Points**

Netscape Communications Corporation's Netscape Navigator

Netscape Navigator's (see Figure 1.5) most significant improvement—security—is one you won't see on the screen. Netscape includes security features that protect your private financial information such as account and credit card numbers. You can safely use financial services and shop online, and take advantage of other features that require that sensitive information be exchanged.

Figure 1.5

Netscape Navigator's Web browser

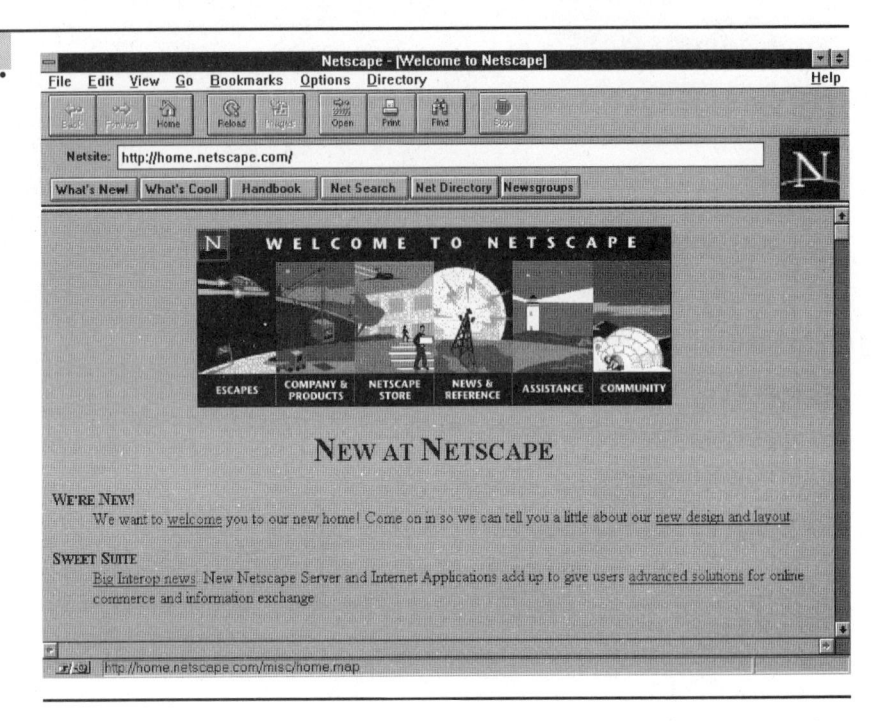

Unlike the Web browsers from Quarterdeck, Spry and Spyglass, Netscape is not an enhanced form of NCSA Mosaic 1.0. It was designed and developed by the same person who led the original NCSA Mosaic development team—after he left NCSA and co-founded Netscape—but as an entirely separate effort. Because it is so similar to NCSA Mosaic in functionality, and, therefore, destined to be a widely used Web browser, we've included it in this book.

Other improvements include multiple document windows and the ability to choose links in documents while the documents are still loading. Netscape also has added a Bookmark feature that lets you save lists of documents and add the lists to a menu. You can also browse and post to newsgroups without relying on another application.

Is Netscape for you? If you are going to be shopping online (using credit card information), or exchanging any other sensitive or confidential information, the answer is *yes*. Netscape's security features are the deciding factor, and, as of this writing, superior to those found in the other forms of Mosaic we discuss.

See Document View Window; Bookmarks; Newsgroups; Security

What About Mosaic for the Macintosh and X Windows?

The Web browsers we discuss in this book run under Microsoft Windows.

Forms of Mosaic for the Macintosh and X Windows also exist and are very similar in look and function to the Mosaics you'll see pictured throughout these pages. If you have or choose to acquire Mosaic for the Macintosh or X Windows, you will still be able to use this book to find your way around both the Internet and Mosaic.

GETTING CONNECTED

Getting connected to the Internet can be as simple as asking your computer support person at work, or a local service provider, to set you up. For those of you who are doing it yourself, we've included all the software and information you need with this book. Read on for details.

How Can You Get Connected?

If you are at a government site, a university, or a large company you may already be on the Internet. Check with your local MIS support person for details for connecting at your location.

If you are on your own, don't be discouraged. It is incredibly easy to get connected. There are hundreds of service providers with local and 1-800 numbers. There's also a list of service providers on the Chameleon Sampler disk in the file PROVIDER.TXT. Simply pay for the service and the provider will help you set up the connection using Chameleon Sampler.

> **If you already have an Internet connection established with a service provider and a form of Mosaic installed, just skip ahead to the section "Looking at Mosaic: A Guided Tour."**

What Connections Do You Need?

As you might imagine, there is more than one way to connect to the Internet—services offered and software requirements vary greatly. When you sign up, make sure you get either a SLIP or PPP connection (described in the next section), as these are necessary to run any form of Mosaic for Windows or Netscape.

What Hardware Do You Need?

Check the documentation for the program you choose for the specifics. And make sure

GETTING CONNECTED

you have the necessary hardware and peripheral devices *before* you begin installing any form of Mosaic. In general you'll need:

- An IBM PC or compatible computer with a 80386 processor or better and at least 4 MB RAM.
- A hard disk drive with 4 MB of available disk space.

In addition, you'll need one of the following:

- A SLIP or PPP Internet account via a modem (9600 baud minimum) and phone line.
- A computer on a network that is already connected to the Internet.

What Software Do You Need?

The specifics will vary, but for most Mosaic-type Web browsers, you'll need:

- Microsoft Windows 3.1 or higher, Windows for Workgroups 3.1, or Windows NT.
- Win32s version 1.20 with OLE support (if you aren't running Windows NT).
- SLIP or PPP software if you are connecting to the Internet via a modem and phone line (found on the Chameleon Sampler disk that comes with this book).
- A TCP/IP protocol stack running on your computer if you are going to connect through a SLIP or PPP account (also found on the Chameleon Sampler disk).

For the version of Air Mosaic you'll find in SYBEX's Mosaic Access to the Internet and Spry's Mosaic in a Box, you'll just need Windows and the software on the install disk.

···········Tip···················

If you are connecting to the Internet through a networked computer, the TCP/IP software does not have to be run on your individual computer.

What is a TCP/IP Protocol Stack?

A *TCP/IP protocol* (Transmission Control Protocol/Internet Protocol) *stack* is a program that handles the communication between your computer and the Internet, including the special requirements of downloading data from and uploading data to the Internet.

Chameleon Sampler includes the TCP/IP protocol stack software, and the examples later in Part 1 show you how to use it to download NCSA Mosaic.

GETTING STARTED 15

What are SLIP and PPP?

SLIP is the abbreviation for *Serial Line Internet Protocol*. PPP is the abbreviation for *Point-to-Point Protocol*. Both are software that makes it possible for your computer to communicate with the Internet through a modem connected to your computer's serial port and a phone line. This software is also included as part of Chameleon Sampler. A SLIP or PPP account is simply an account with a service provider who supports SLIP/PPP access to the Internet, making it possible for you to run Mosaic and have complete access to all Internet offerings via modem. A list of service providers who offer SLIP or PPP accounts is also included on the Chameleon Sampler disk.

Other Software from Sybex

You may have already obtained and installed the software you need to connect to the Internet if you have purchased another book from Sybex. *Mosaic Access to the Internet* by Daniel A. Tauber and Brenda Kienan includes a plug-and-play version of Air Mosaic. *Surfing the Internet with Netscape* by Tauber and Kienan, again includes Chameleon Sampler and complete instructions for getting, installing and using NetCruiser. *Access to the Internet* by David Peal includes Netcom's NetCruiser on disk.

GETTING STARTED

If you have an Internet account set up, and any Web browser already installed, turn to the next section, "Looking at Mosaic: A Guided Tour."

If you need to install the Chameleon Sampler, set up an Internet account, and/or download NCSA Mosaic, we recommend that you take these steps now, before starting the Guided Tour.

NCSA Mosaic is free and can be downloaded from the Internet. To learn how, turn to the section "Downloading NCSA Mosaic" later in Part 1. The step-by-step instructions for installing Chameleon Sampler are there as well.

Tip

If someone you know offers you a copy of **NCSA** Mosaic, it's okay to accept it. That is because Mosaic was developed by the **National Center for Supercomputing (NCSA)** with government (taxpayers') money for use by the public and is intended to be used by *anyone*, free of charge, to help you interact with the Internet more easily.

See Downloading NCSA Mosaic

LOOKING AT MOSAIC: A GUIDED TOUR

This section tells you how to get started with each form of Mosaic and Netscape. Pay close attention to the additional information specific to the Web browser you are using, found in the sidebars, as you go through the steps.

Before you start Mosaic, your Internet connection must be established. This means that you have to start your communications program if you are using a SLIP/PPP account. These steps show you how to start if you are using Chameleon Sampler.

If you are using the current version of Air Mosaic, you do not have to connect to your account before you launch Mosaic.

1. Double-click the Custom icon in the Chameleon group window. The Custom window and the NEWT icon (which actually looks like a newt) are displayed.
2. Click Connect in the Menu bar. The Connect dialog box is displayed with the status. Once the connection is made, the dialog box disappears.

····················Tip······················

Remember that you'll always have to establish your Internet connection before you launch Mosaic, if you are using a dial-up account.

To launch Mosaic once you are connected to the Internet:

1. Double-click the Mosaic icon of the product you are using (see Figure 1.6).

You'll see the Mosaic window. Inside the window you'll see the *home page* for NCSA Mosaic for Windows (or the form of Mosaic you're using).

THE NCSA MOSAIC HOME PAGE: START HERE

To see just how Web browsers work and what happens in a Mosaic session, we'll use NCSA Mosaic as our example. The process is basically the same for all Web browsers, so if you haven't installed NCSA Mosaic, you can follow along with the one you're using.

The first thing you might notice about the Mosaic window, as shown in Figure 1.7, is that the document in it has text which is highlighted; it is either displayed in blue, is underlined, or maybe both. If you don't

Figure 1.6

Each form of Mosaic installs with its own Group window and program icon.

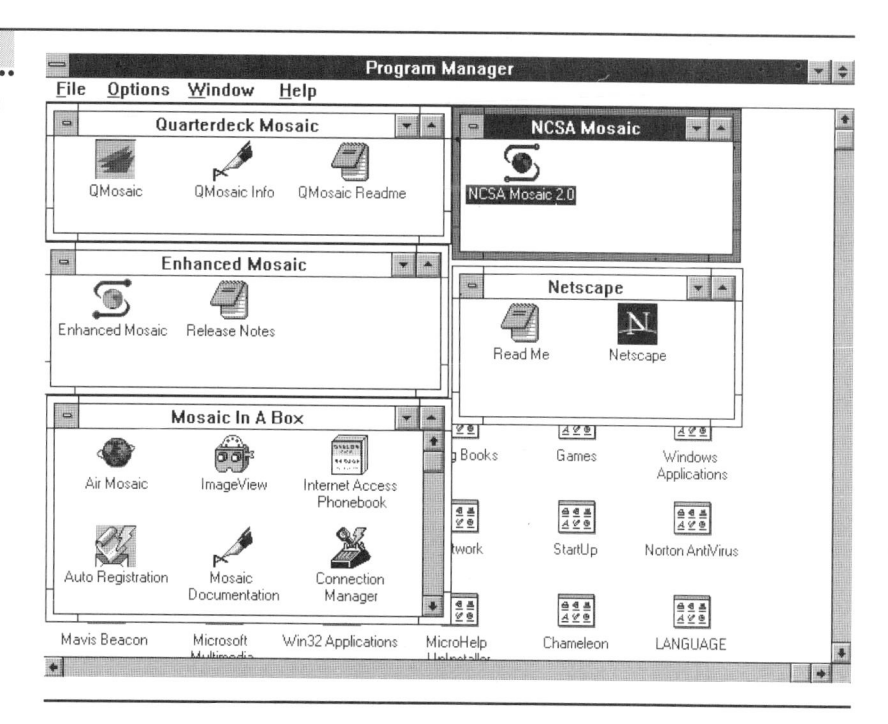

see any highlighted or underlined text, scroll down the page. These text items are *hypertext links* which will display another document or resource when you click on them. In fact, the way you browse through a Mosaic document is very similar to the way you browse through a Windows online help file—just click on the links.

> **Because home pages are easy to update, they seem to change pretty regularly. So don't be concerned if the home pages you see on your screen look a little different than the ones shown in the Figures.**

Notice that as you move the cursor over each hypertext link, the cursor changes to a hand. When you see the hand, you can click the text under it to jump to another document.

Here's what the components are of the Mosaic window:

Title bar Displays NCSA Mosaic, which is the title of the application, and the title of the document you are currently viewing in the window.

Menu bar Displays the names of the Mosaic menus, from which you can

Figure 1.7

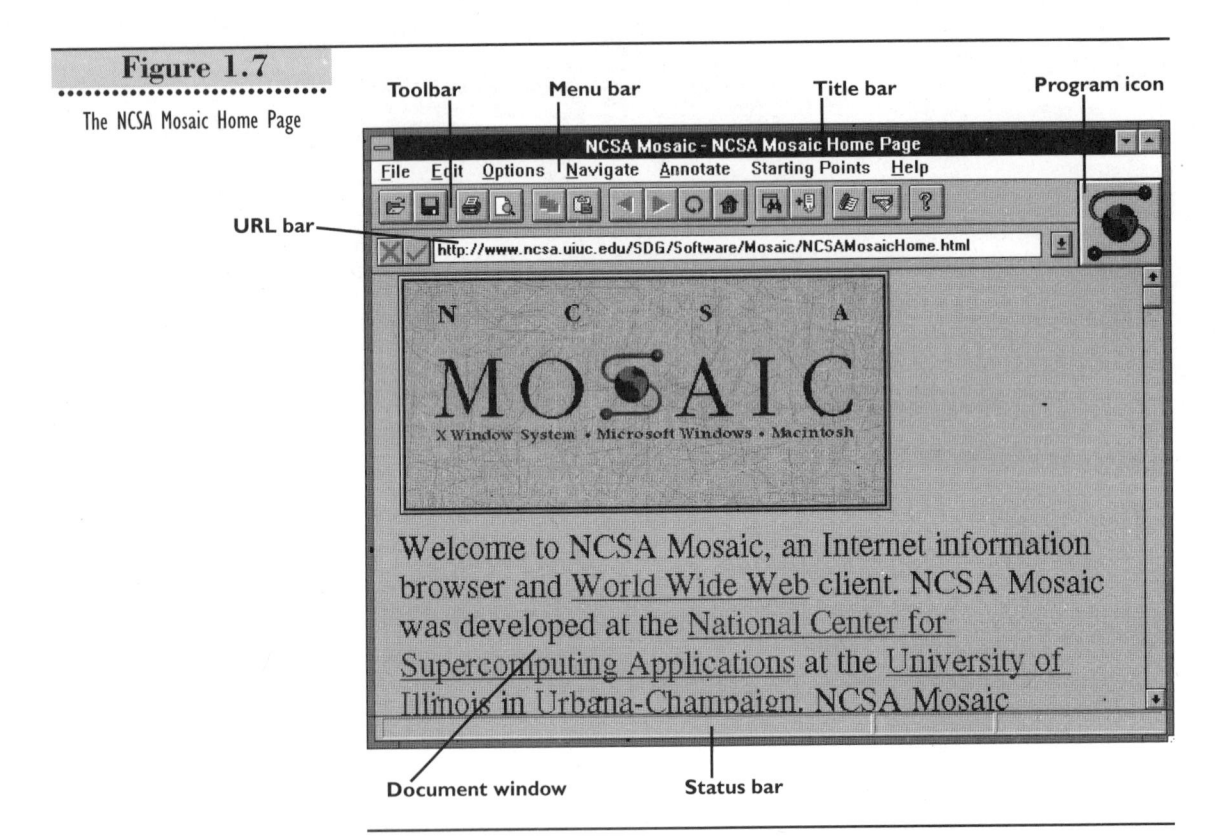

The NCSA Mosaic Home Page

Labels on figure: Toolbar, Menu bar, Title bar, Program icon, URL bar, Document window, Status bar

access all Mosaic commands and features. The commands are described in depth in the alphabetical listing, and you'll have a chance to try out some of the commands in this tour.

Toolbar Provides buttons which can be used as shortcuts to execute the most frequently chosen commands. Buttons are displayed for the Open, Save, Back, Forward, Reload, Load Home Page, Add to Hotlist, Copy, Paste, Find, Print, Read Newsgroups, Send E-mail, and About Windows Mosaic commands.

URL bar Displays the *Uniform Resource Locator* for the current document. The Uniform Resource Locator is the name of the file combined with its location; for example, the server it is located on and the directory path it can be found in. The URL bar also contains the Mosaic program icon, which rotates or moves as a document is being retrieved. (Keep this in mind if there seems to be a long delay as a document is being retrieved for you.)

Document window Displays the name of the selected document. You may also choose to start Mosaic without displaying a document automatically, in which case this area will be blank.

Status bar Displays information about each document as it is being retrieved. When you move the cursor over a link (but don't click on it), the status bar shows the URL of the document associated with the link. The position of the Caps Lock, Number Lock and Scroll Lock keys is also displayed to the right; when one is on, CAPS, NUM or SCROLL is displayed.

See   Document View Window; Links; Menu Bar; Status Bar; Title Bar; Toolbar; URL; URL Bar

BROWSING WITH HYPERTEXT LINKS

The quickest way to understand what Mosaic and the Internet offer is to start using them. The hypertext links on your screen can provide a great overview. In fact, that is exactly what they were intended to do.

Other Application Windows and Home Pages

Each Web browser ships with its own home page or Introduction page designed to help you learn about the Internet and the product.

Begin with one of the following starting points, if you aren't using NCSA Mosaic. All of the forms have many similarities and we include directions along the way, where you might get confused.

- **On the Quarterdeck Mosaic home page (refer back to Figure 1.2), start by clicking on the Internet Navigation System item, then look at the What's New Page, and any topics which interest you. Each topic in this list leads you to additional documents.**

- **On the Air Mosaic home page (refer back to Figure 1.3), start by exploring Spry City or Hotland. Just click on it to see additional topics.**

- **On the Spyglass Mosaic home page (refer back to Figure 1.4), start by clicking on the Cyberspace Sampler or Starting Points item, then look at What's New with Mosaic and the WWW, College and University Home Pages, and any topics which interest you.**

- **On the Netscape home page (refer back to Figure 1.5), start by exploring the What's New, Escapes, and News and Reference. You can click on the Welcome, What's New, What's Cool and Net Directory buttons to start your browsing.**

If you are using NCSA Mosaic, begin by reading the first section, "NCSA Mosaic Flavors," which you'll see when you scroll down the page. Then click the item NCSA Mosaic for Microsoft Windows.

Going Back and Forth

Every form of Mosaic has buttons which let you go back and forth between documents you have jumped to with links. After you jump to a document by clicking on a link, read the information on the page you displayed, then click the Back button in the toolbar to display the previous document.

Once you return to the previous document the Forward button is also available. You can then move back and forth between the two documents, if you wish.

The next document you should read in NCSA Mosaic is listed under Starting Points. Click on the NCSA Mosaic Demo Document link. This document will give you an opportunity to try out the embedded graphics, audios and movies. Take some time to read the information and click on the highlighted items—they'll most likely be surrounded by a blue box on your screen.

When you are finished, click the Home Page button in the toolbar to display the first document again.

> **Tip**
>
> If you are using any other form, click the links you see on your screen to browse around and learn to navigate.

See Back; Demo Document; Forward; Home Page; Hypertext

GETTING HELP ONLINE

Obviously, Mosaic is pretty easy to use. Since you probably won't want to have this book in your lap all the time, it's a good idea to know how to find the online help.

NCSA Mosaic has an online User's Guide, but as of this writing, it doesn't have the context-sensitive Windows help that you are probably used to.

> Air Mosaic and Quarterdeck Mosaic **do** have context-sensitive help and each has some online documentation. The Online Documentation sidebar explains what is available.

Online Documentation

Each product has documentation somewhere online, in some form, although it may be a bit different from what you are accustomed to for Windows applications. Instead of including a full Windows online help system, several products include a Web document.

Air Mosaic Choose Contents from the Help menu or press FI at any time to open the Help Contents. Click the Help button in every dialog box for context-sensitive help.

Netscape Choose Handbook from the Help menu to display an online user's guide.

Quarterdeck Mosaic Choose any item from the Help menu, click the Help button in every dialog box or press FI at any time for context-sensitive help. A full Windows help system is included.

Spyglass Mosaic Choose Help Page from the Help menu to see a list of help topics available online.

The Online User's Guide

There is a long and a short way to display the online User's Guide for NCSA Mosaic. Let's start with the long way first, so you see what else is available.

1. On the NCSA Mosaic Home Page, scroll down to the bottom of the Starting Points section again near the bottom of the Home Page.

2. Click on Index in the item "An index to Mosaic documents and tutorials" (see Figure 1.8). The NCSA Mosaic Web Index is displayed.

3. Scroll down to the NCSA Documentation by Platform section.

4. Under Mosaic for Microsoft Windows, click on Online Documentation. The table of contents for the Online User's Guide is displayed. Scroll the page to see the contents of this document.

Figure 1.8

Click on Index to retrieve the NCSA Mosaic Web Index.

5. Click on any highlighted words that interest you right now, or just make a mental note of what's available.

6. When you are finished, click the Back button to go back through the documents you just displayed until you reach the home page again.

    As you do, take some time to read anything that interests you, and click on any highlighted words that arouse your curiosity. Since you are learning to use Mosaic to find and acquire information, browse through the information at your own pace, and don't stop until you've read everything you want to.

7. When you are ready to move on, choose Home Page from the toolbar to return to the home page.

    See   Print; Save

A Quick Approach to Online Help

Now let's try the quick method for accessing the online documentation.

- Open the Help menu and choose Online Documentation. Again, the table of contents for the Online User's Guide is displayed. This is obviously the method you'll use most often to access the online documentation, but look what you learned by taking the scenic route first.

BROWSING THE INTERNET

There are a variety of different reasons for wanting to connect to the Internet, but most people fall into one of two basic categories:

- You're looking for some specific information on one or more topics.
- You're just plain curious and you're browsing to see what's out there and what might be of interest to you.

Whatever your reason is for being on the Internet, the following sections contain some pointers that can help you get to know the neighborhood.

What's New on the Internet?

The most exciting pages you can browse through as a new user might be found under the What's New topic. Why? Because every day, new people and organizations try to create pages that are more exciting, innovative, and appealing than yesterday's. The example in Figure 1.9 may be old news by the time you read this book, but the steps will be the same.

1. From the home page, click on What's New with NCSA Mosaic and the Internet under the Starting Points section.

2. Scroll the pages until you find a document description that interests you and click on the link.

BROWSING THE INTERNET 23

Figure 1.9

The NCSA Mosaic What's New Page

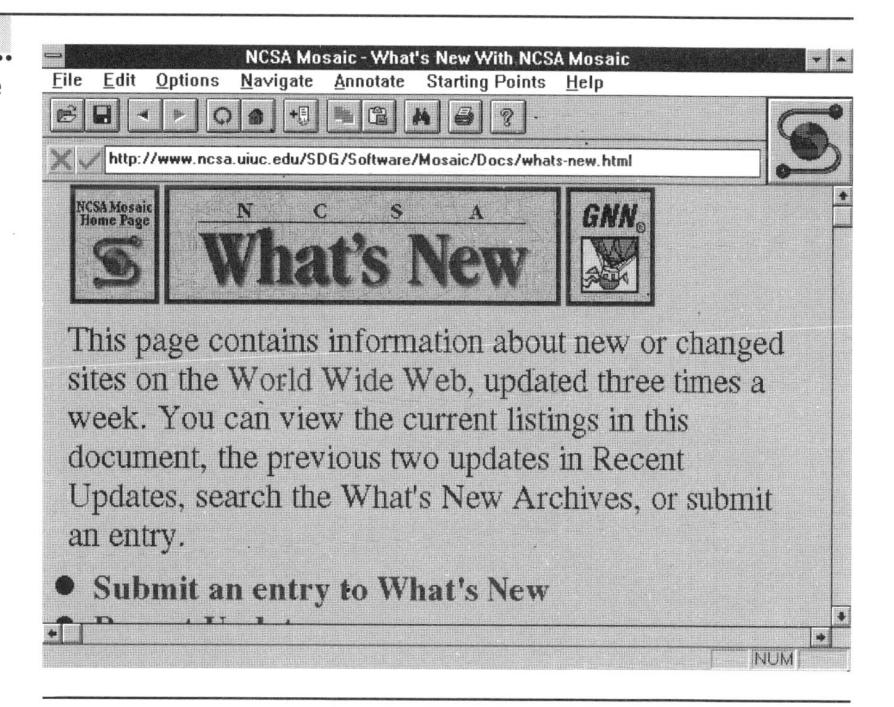

> **Tip**
>
> The Pick of the Week is always worth a look.

Just remember to use the Back button on the toolbar to get back to this What's New document and use the Home Page button to redisplay the home page when you are ready. Refer to the sidebar if you are using a different Web browser.

Browsing for Something that Interests You

NCSA Mosaic's Starting Points menu is the best place to start browsing. It offers you the opportunity to access a number of servers at different sites and display their home pages. Those home pages offer hypertext links to documents on a vast assortment of topics. The menu also duplicates some of the items in the NCSA Mosaic Home Page that you saw when you logged on, providing an alternate access method.

> ## *What's New from Anywhere*
> . . . .
> There is a way to get to the *What's New* section from every form of Mosaic.
>
> **Air Mosaic** On the Spry Home Page, click on Spry City, then click on Internet Source. Scroll down to the section titled Other Lists of Web Sites and then click on What's New to Visit? New Web Pages in the list below.
>
> **Netscape** On the Welcome to Netscape page, click the What's New button.
>
> **Quarterdeck Mosaic** On the Quarterdeck Home Page, click on Internet Navigation System, then click on NCSA What's New Page at the bottom of the list.
>
> **Spyglass Mosaic** On the Welcome to Enhanced NCSA from Spyglass page, click on either Starting Points or Cyberspace Sampler. Scroll down to the section titled Directories and Indexes and then click on What's New with Mosaic and the WWW.

Each item on the Starting Points menu will take you in a different direction. Display some of them yourself to get a first hand look.

1. Choose Home Pages from the Starting Points menu. A cascading menu with additional choices displays (see Figure 1.10).

2. Click Honolulu Home Page. The NCSA icon in the upper right corner of your screen begins to spin, letting you know a document is being retrieved. In the status bar at the bottom of the screen you'll see a series of messages updating the progress of the retrieval process, with the number of bytes (the amount of information) retrieved thus far. When the document is retrieved, you'll see it displayed in the document window, as shown Figure 1.11. In the URL bar, you'll see the URL for the document.

The document turns out to be the Home Page for Honolulu Community College, with links to information both about the college and Honolulu. If you'd like to browse through the information it offers, click on any link. Remember to use the Back button to get back to the previous page.

Before you move on to the next section, spend as much time as you like selecting other home pages from the Home Pages cascading menu.

Refer to the sidebar if you are browsing with another form of Mosaic.

See   **Home Pages**

Figure 1.10

The NCSA Starting Points menu includes a Home Pages cascading menu with some interesting Home Pages around the world.

The University of Illinois at Urbana-Champaign
NCSA Home Page
CERN Home Page
UNC-Chapel Hill home page
ANU Bioinformatics
Data Research Home Page
British Columbia
BSDI Home Page
Carnegie Mellon
Cornell Law School
Cornell Theory Center
DESY Home Page
ECE WWW Page
Honolulu Home Page
Indiana Home Page
Lysator ACS Sweden
National Center for Atmospheric Research
Northwestern Home Page
CICA's WWW Server
Ohio State Home Page
SSC Home Page

Figure 1.11

The Honolulu Home Page

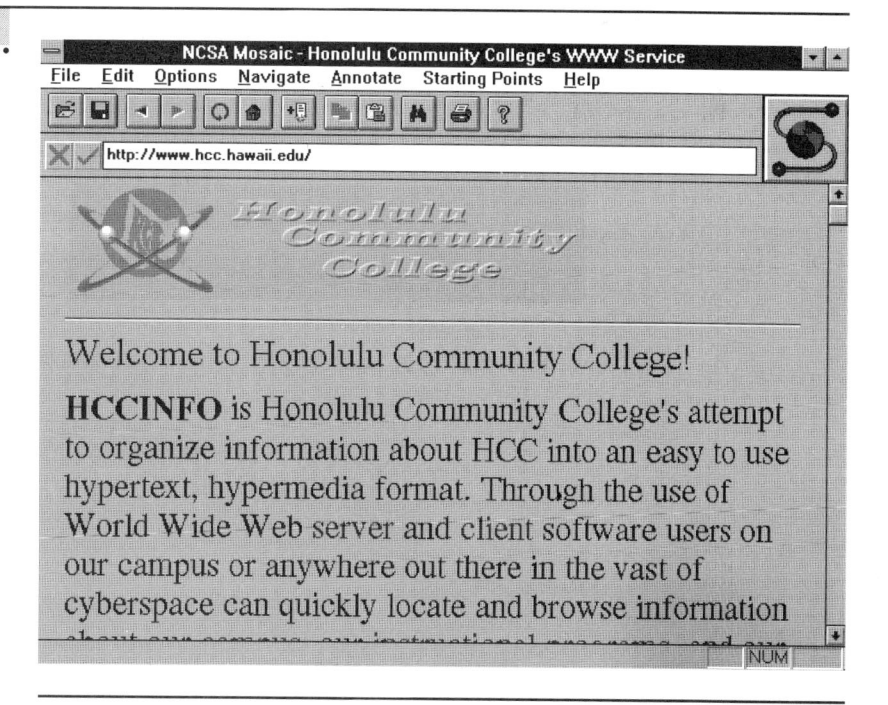

NCSA Mosaic - Honolulu Community College's WWW Service

File   Edit   Options   Navigate   Annotate   Starting Points   Help

http://www.hcc.hawaii.edu/

Honolulu Community College

Welcome to Honolulu Community College!

HCCINFO is Honolulu Community College's attempt to organize information about HCC into an easy to use hypertext, hypermedia format. Through the use of World Wide Web server and client software users on our campus or anywhere out there in the vast of cyberspace can quickly locate and browse information

Browsing with Mosaic

Every commercial form of Mosaic retrieves a customized home page the first time you start it, and each subsequent time you start it until you choose not to see it. Each home page is designed specifically to help you browse the World Wide Web (and usually to learn more about each company's products). So click on any text or graphic link that interests you, and keep using the Back and Home buttons to find your way back to the home page if you lose your way.

Using the History Window

If you've been browsing around the Internet, you've already found how easy it is to lose your sense of direction and not be able to find your way back to a specific document. You can use the Back command to go backwards, but if you've looked at a number of documents, Back won't help much. Fortunately, there's a shortcut: the History window.

Each Web browser handles the History window in a different way. Refer to the sidebar for specific instructions.

1. Choose History from the Navigate menu. The History window (see Figure 1.12) opens with a list of all the pages you've displayed since you started the current Mosaic session. The bad news is that the names of the pages are not displayed. Instead, the URLs are displayed. The good news is that you can go back to any page you've displayed thus far. See if you can recognize a URL.

2. Click on it, then click the Load button or double-click the URL in the list.

Figure 1.12

The History window shows the URLs for every page you've looked at in this session.

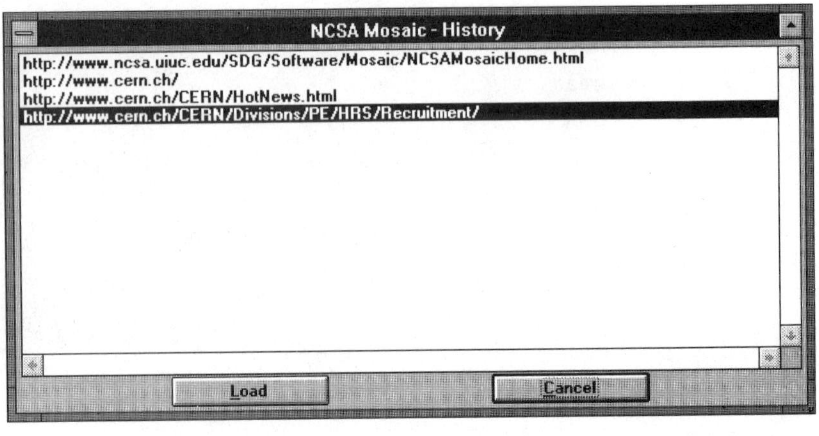

The page associated with that URL is displayed. You might try to recognize other URLs in the list and display other pages, if you wish.

3. When you are finished, click Dismiss (or Close, depending on the form) in the History window.

See **History**

Finding the History

Each product includes a history window which is similar to the one included with NCSA Mosaic. Here's where to find it:

Air Mosaic Choose History from the Navigate menu. Then double-click any item in the list or highlight an item and click the Load button.

Netscape Choose View History List from the Go menu. Then double-click any item in the list or highlight an item and click the Go To button.

Quarterdeck Mosaic The History Window may already be displayed on the left side of the application window. If not, choose Local History from the window menu and double-click any item in the list.

Spyglass Mosaic Choose History from the Navigate menu. Then double-click any item in the list or highlight an item and click the Go To button.

Changing Options

As with all Windows programs, you can change some of Mosaic's options to suit your work style and needs. You can increase the document view window and speed up the document retrieval process by turning off some of the default options.

For example, now that you've had an opportunity to see many pages with their graphic contents, you might want to turn off the automatic display of graphics. Documents will be retrieved and displayed faster, and you can display individual graphics if and when you want to.

1. Choose Preferences from the Options menu.
2. Click Display Inline Images to remove the check.
3. Click OK to close the dialog box. Now retrieve an item with several graphics.
4. Choose NCSA Mosaic's What's New Page from the Starting Points menu. You've looked at this document before, so you should be able to notice how much faster documents are retrieved when their graphics are not displayed. The icon shows what the graphics in this document look like now. They are replaced with a placeholder—simply an icon and the word "image."

🖼 Image

5. Place the mouse over the first image's icon and click the *right* mouse button. A popup menu displays.
6. Click on Load Images. You can see the image.
7. Place the mouse over the second image's icon and click the *left* mouse button. The document associated with that link is retrieved. Note that a graphic does not have to be displayed in order for its link to function properly.

For the illustrations in this book, we'll turn the Display Inline Images option back on by selecting it again. You can do the same or leave it deselected, depending on the improvement in retrieval speed you see and how important the graphics are to you.

Now change one of the display options to increase your document view window.

1. Choose Show Toolbar from the Options menu. The check is removed from the item and you have a slightly larger document view window.
   You could also choose Show Status Bar and then Show Current URL from the Options menu to increase the document view window even further, but wait until you've used Mosaic for a while longer before deciding whether or not you need these items displayed. If you want to turn the toolbar display back on now, go ahead.
2. Choose Show Toolbar from the Options menu.

Use these display options at any time to increase the viewing area for documents; they won't affect anything else you are doing at the time.

See **Document View Window; Kiosk Mode; Options**

How Much Do You Want to See?

Each product lets you turn off the downloading of graphics, in order to save time and, if you are paying for your connection by the hour, money.

Air Mosaic Choose Autoload Inline Images from the Options menu to remove the check.

Netscape Choose Autoload Images from the Options menu to remove the check.

Quarterdeck Mosaic Choose Preferences from the Tools menu, then click the HTML Viewer tab. Click Display Inline Images to remove the check.

Spyglass Mosaic Choose Preferences from the Edit menu, then click Load Images Automatically to remove the check.

Toolbars Take Up Room

Since toolbars use some of the room you'd otherwise dedicate to displaying documents, you might want to work without a toolbar. Here's how to turn it off:

Air Mosaic Choose Configuration from the Options menu, then click Show Toolbar to remove the check.

Netscape Choose Show Toolbar from the Options menu to remove the check.

Quarterdeck Mosaic Choose Toolbar from the View menu to remove the check.

Spyglass Mosaic Choose Preferences from the Edit menu, then click Show Toolbar to remove the check.

Are You Looking for Something Specific?

If you have a particular area of interest or if you're looking for information on a specific topic, there are two methods you can use:

- Find the document with that information by using a series of links.
- Type in the URL for a document and retrieve it immediately.

Finding precisely what you are looking for the first time you browse around the World Wide Web is probably the most frustrating part of getting started. So we've provided some additional places to look for specifics.

You've already seen some ways to search, whichever product you are using. Look back to the sidebar titled "Browsing With Mosaic" if you need a reminder.

1. Choose World Wide Web Info from the Starting Points menu. A cascading menu with additional choices displays.

2. Click Information by Subject.

The WWW Virtual Library is displayed with a catalog of information by subject. All the highlighted items in this document are jumps to other information sources.

> Documents on the Web are in a constant state of change—new documents are always popping up and existing ones are changing. This is part of what keeps the Web interesting. Unfortunately, documents also cease to exist sometimes. So if you can't find a document mentioned here, or if it looks different, you aren't doing anything wrong. It is just a sign of the changing times.

BROWSING THE INTERNET

Using Uniform Resource Locators (URLs)

You've already mastered the process of following links, and you can figure out how to retrieve documents via the menus. Now let's try using URLs to retrieve a document.

If you are interested in finding information pertaining to the U.S. Federal Government, for example, entering their URLs is the best way.

1. Choose Open URL from the File menu. The Open URL dialog box is displayed as shown in Figure 1.13.

2. In the URL text box, type http://iridium.nttc.edu/gov_res.html.

3. Click OK. The U.S. Government Information Sources is displayed as shown in Figure 1.14.

More than one source for looking up information is usually available. Try this alternative.

1. Choose Open URL from the File menu. The Open URL dialog box is displayed.

Finding the URL Text Box

Each Web browser includes a dialog box where you can enter a URL, but in an effort to make the whole matter less cryptic, the abbreviation URL isn't always used. Try this:

Air Mosaic Choose Open URL from the File menu.

Netscape Choose Open Location from the File menu.

Quarterdeck Mosaic Choose Open from the File menu.

Spyglass Mosaic Choose Open URL from the File menu.

2. In the URL text box, type http://www.fie.com/www/us_gov.htm.

3. Click OK. The WWW Servers of the U.S. Federal Government is displayed as shown in Figure 1.15.

Figure 1.13

You can type the URL directory in the text box in the Open URL dialog box.

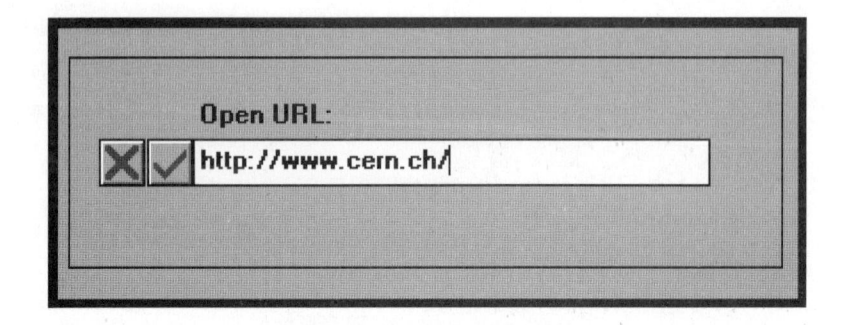

Open URL: http://www.cern.ch/

Figure 1.14

The U.S. Government Information Sources page

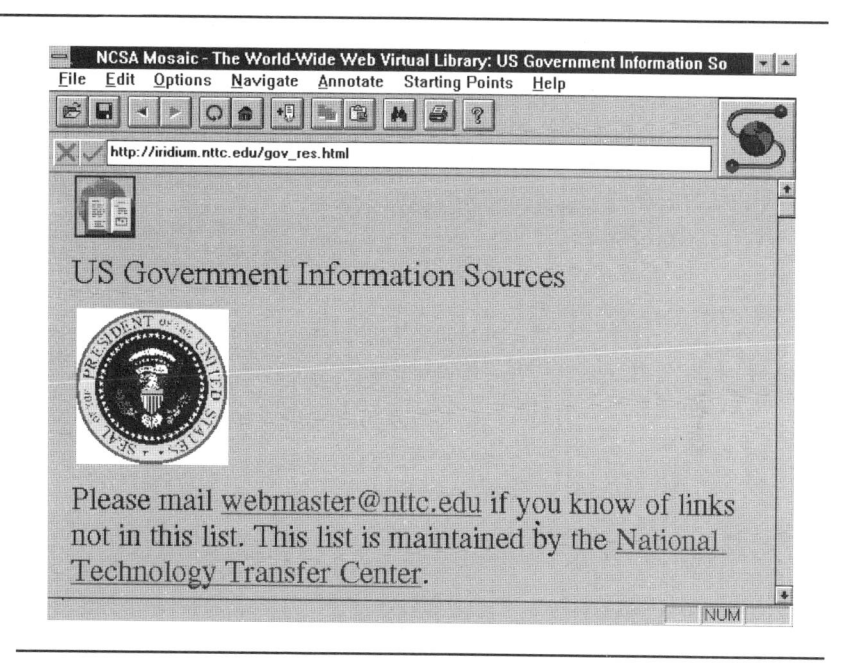

Figure 1.15

WWW Servers of the U.S. Federal Government page

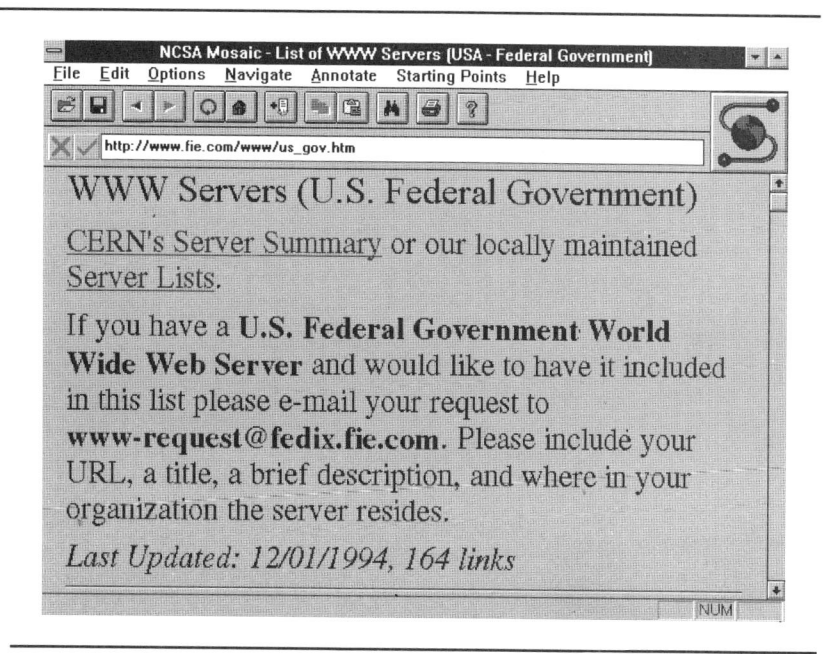

If you'd like to see information specific to the CIA, take a look at the CIA's World Fact Book. If you are displaying the current URL in the application window, you can use a shortcut to enter the URL.

1. Delete the URL currently shown in the URL box and type http://www.ic.gov. You can highlight the entry and press Delete or click in the box and press Backspace to delete part of the entry.

2. Click the Check button or press ƒ.

The CIA's World Fact Book is displayed as shown in Figure 1.16.

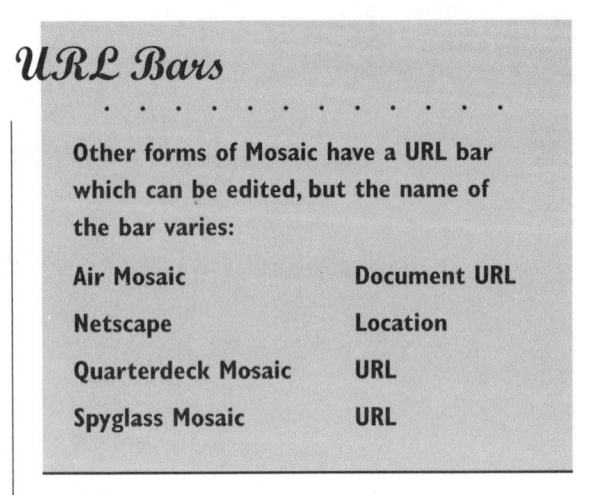

URL Bars

Other forms of Mosaic have a URL bar which can be edited, but the name of the bar varies:

Air Mosaic	Document URL
Netscape	Location
Quarterdeck Mosaic	URL
Spyglass Mosaic	URL

Use the Open URL command to retrieve the Virtual Tourist home page (Figure 1.17) and see the world. The URL for it is http://wings.buffalo.edu/world.

Figure 1.16
CIA's World Fact Book page

Figure 1.17

Virtual Tourist home page

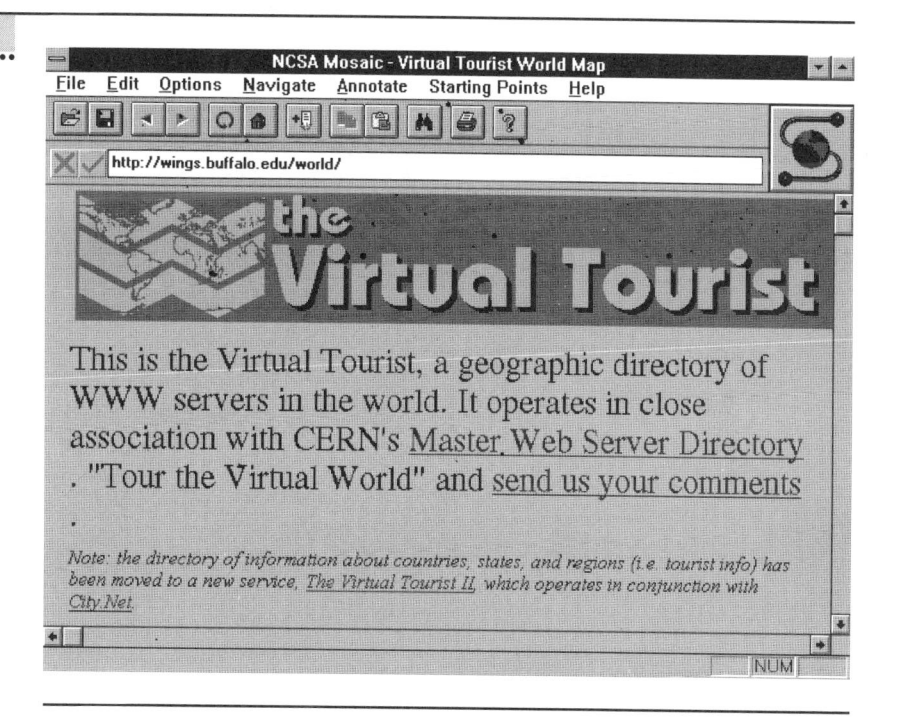

You can also travel the world by starting with a list of W3 Servers arranged alphabetically by continent, country and state as shown in Figure 1.18. The URL for this is http://www11.w3.org/hypertext/DataSources/WWW/Servers.html.

An excellent source of business information is CommerceNet. To retrieve their home page (Figure 1.19) use their URL, http://www.commerce.net.

Let's try one more. Retrieve the World Wide Yellow Pages page (Figure 1.20), a different source of business information. The URL for it is http://www.yellow.com/.

YOU'RE ON YOUR WAY

You now have the skills to begin exploring the Internet on your own. The Roadmap on the following pages provides additional directions for moving along.

Exiting Mosaic

You can exit Mosaic as you do any Windows program.

1. Choose Exit from the File menu or double-click the Control box in the upper left corner.

Figure 1.18

A list of W3 Servers arranged alphabetically by continent, country and state

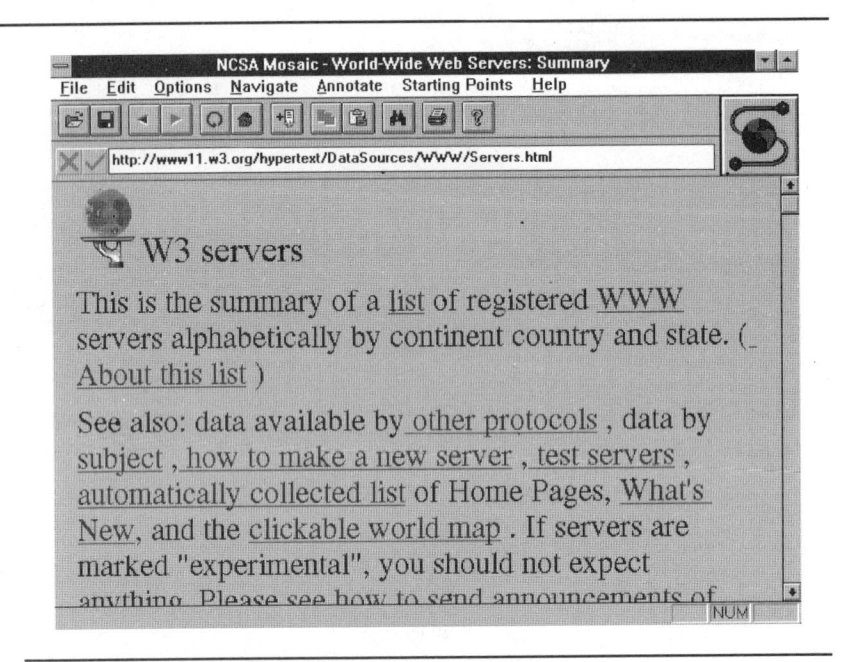

Figure 1.19

CommerceNet home page

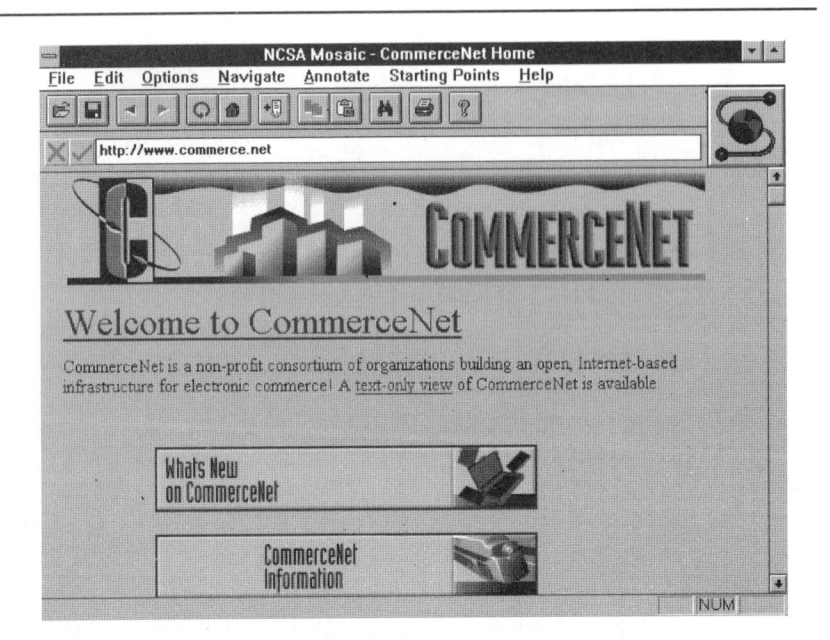

DOWNLOADING NCSA MOSAIC   35

Figure 1.20

The World Wide Yellow Pages

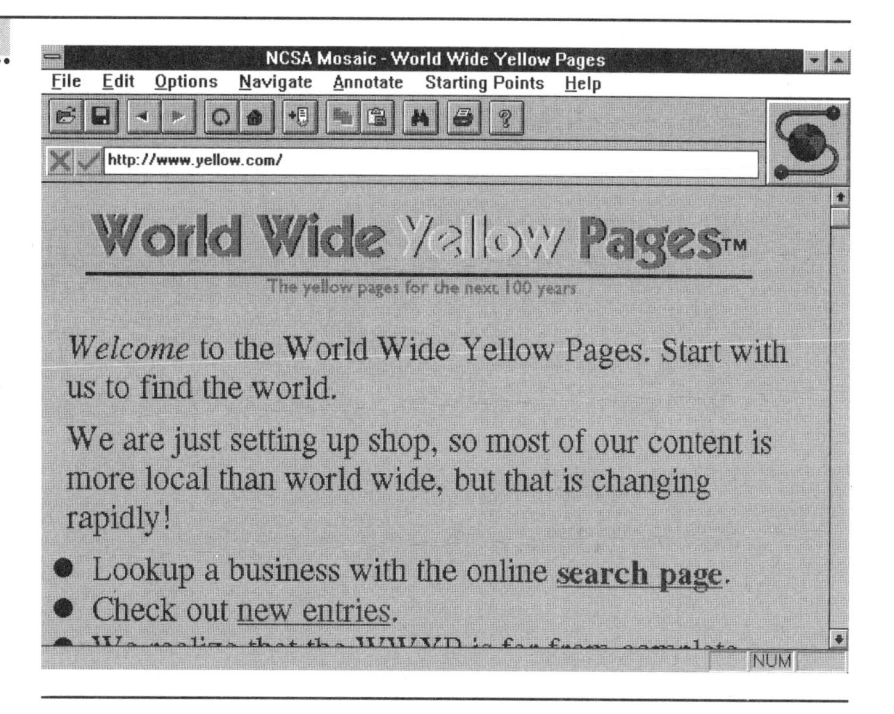

2. Close your connection if you are connected to the Internet via a SLIP or PPP account over a modem.

DOWNLOADING NCSA MOSAIC

You can download the NCSA Mosaic software with FTP (an Internet file transfer program) which is part of Chameleon Sampler. The steps are included here.

See **FTP**

Using the Chameleon Sampler

The Chameleon Sampler disk contains the software you need to set up an Internet account and download NCSA Mosaic. It also includes a list of service providers you can contact to set up your account. You'll want to:

- Install the software.
- Print several of the text files for additional information.
- Set up your Internet account.

Installing the Chameleon Sampler Software

To install the software, place the disk in your disk drive and follow these simple steps:

1. Choose Run from the File menu in Program Manager.
2. Click the Browse button to open the Browse dialog box.
3. Select the A: or B: drive in the Drives drop-down list box, then click the SETUP.EXE file in the File Name list box. Then click OK. The filename is displayed in the Run dialog box.
4. Click OK in the Run dialog box and follow the onscreen prompts to install Chameleon Sampler.
5. Click Continue when you see the information about installing over other networks.
6. Accept the directory path as shown and click Continue again. When the installation process is complete, you'll see a message confirming this.
7. Click OK. A new program group is created for Chameleon Sampler as shown in Figure 1.21.
8. Double-click on the Readme icon to open the Readme file. This usually opens the Windows Notepad text editor, unless you have changed your file associations so another text editor is opened instead. The contents of README.DOC are displayed in the window.

Figure 1.21

The Chameleon Sampler group window

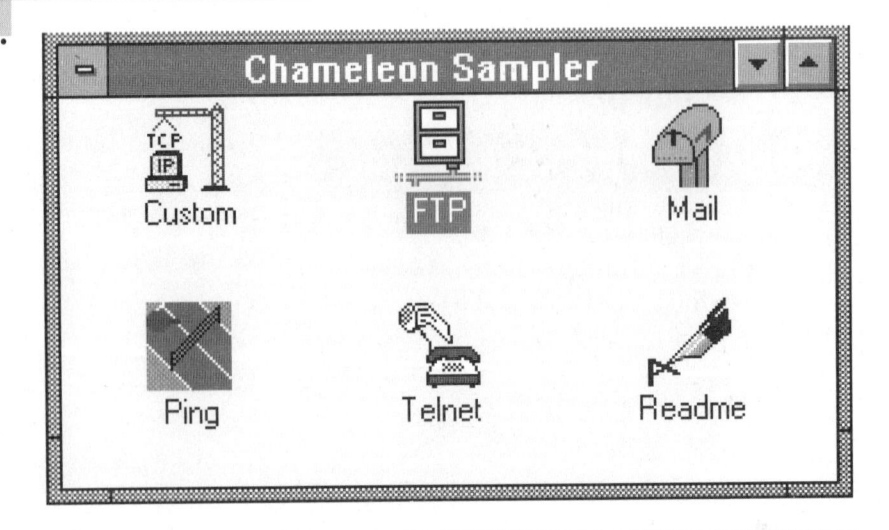

9. Choose Print from the File menu to print this file and then read it.
10. Choose Exit from the File menu to close the Notepad.

Establishing Your Internet Account

Now that the software is installed, you'll need to establish an account with an Internet service provider in order to use the software. Print the file titled PROVIDER.TXT, which is in the NETMANAG directory, and read it. (You can use File Manager for this.) This file contains a list of providers, with addresses and phone numbers. Select a provider that covers your area, and call them to set up your account. Then go on to the next section.

What Other Software Must You Download?

You may also need to download the Win 32s software; the filename is W32SOLE.EXE.

Mosaic is a 32-bit application, designed to take advantage of the power of Windows NT. So, if you aren't running Windows NT, you'll need to run Win 32s in order to run Mosaic. Win 32s is simply an application you can run under Windows that lets you then run 32-bit applications. If you install it once, you'll never have to think about it again.

···············Tip······················

Before you go to the trouble of downloading this file, see if you have it already installed. It will be in a subdirectory named WIN32S in your WINDOWS\SYSTEM subdirectory. You might have installed it in order to run another application, or someone might have installed it for you when setting up another application.

Downloading NCSA Mosaic with Windows FTP

Follow these steps to download NCSA Mosaic with Chameleon's FTP program. The steps assume Windows is already running, and Chameleon has been installed. You also have to have your SLIP software installed and your Internet account set up.

When you download Mosaic, it will be a ZIP (compressed) file. Files are compressed so they take up less room on the server, and less time to transfer. Because the files are compressed in a self-extracting ZIP file, you don't need any special software to decompress them.

First, use File Manager to create a TEMP directory for the files you will download, if you don't already have one. Here's how to do this:

1. Double-click the File Manager icon to run File Manager.
2. Highlight the C: drive at the top of the directory tree. You can substitute another drive if you like.
3. Choose Create Directory from the File menu. The Create Directory dialog box is displayed, as shown in Figure 1.22.
4. Type TEMP in the text box and click OK. The new directory is created and shows in the directory tree.
5. Click the Minimize button in the upper right of the File Manager window to minimize File Manager for now. You'll use it again later.

Now, begin downloading the files.

1. Double-click the Custom icon in the Chameleon group window.

The Custom window is displayed (Figure 1.23) and the NEWT icon is also displayed with any other minimized icons. When NEWT is displayed, it means that the TCP/IP stack has been loaded.

2. Click Connect in the Menu bar. There's no Connect menu, so clicking Connect selects the command. The Connect dialog box is displayed with the status. Once the connection is made, the dialog box is no longer displayed.
3. Double-click the FTP icon in the Chameleon group window. The FTP window is displayed.

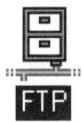

4. Click Connect in the Menu bar to select the Connect command. The (FTP) Connect dialog box (Figure 1.24) is displayed.
5. In the Host text box, type ftp.ncsa.uiuc.edu. This is where you'll find a copy of Mosaic to download.

Figure 1.22

Create a TEMP directory to store the files you download.

Figure 1.23

The Custom window is where you'll start the Internet connection.

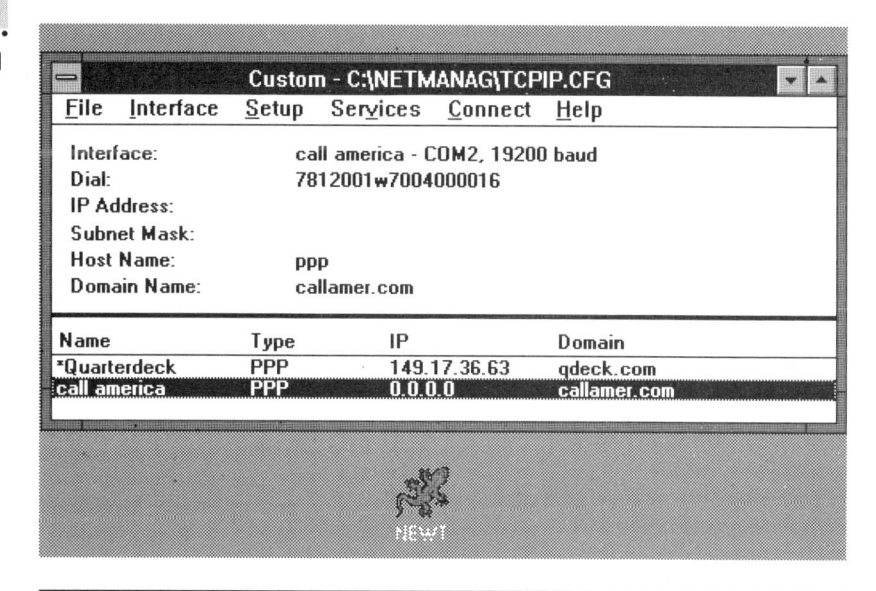

Figure 1.24

Use the FTP Connect dialog box to log on to the server.

6. In the User text box, type anonymous.

7. In the Password text box, type your user name and Internet address; for example, merrin@callamer.com.

8. In the System drop-down list, select Auto.

9. Click OK. You'll be connected to the NCSA server and logged in as an anonymous user. Now you'll have to find the Mosaic file to download.

10. In the upper right of the FTP window (see Figure 1.25), double-click on the directories until you display the WEB/MOSAIC/WINDOWS directory. The files in the WEB/MOSAIC/WINDOWS directory are displayed in the Files list box below.

11. Double-click on the first file you need, MOS20BX.EXE or MOS20X.EXE, the current version of Mosaic for Windows. The file is displayed in the Files text box at the top of the list.

Figure 1.25

Use the FTP window to select the files you'll download.

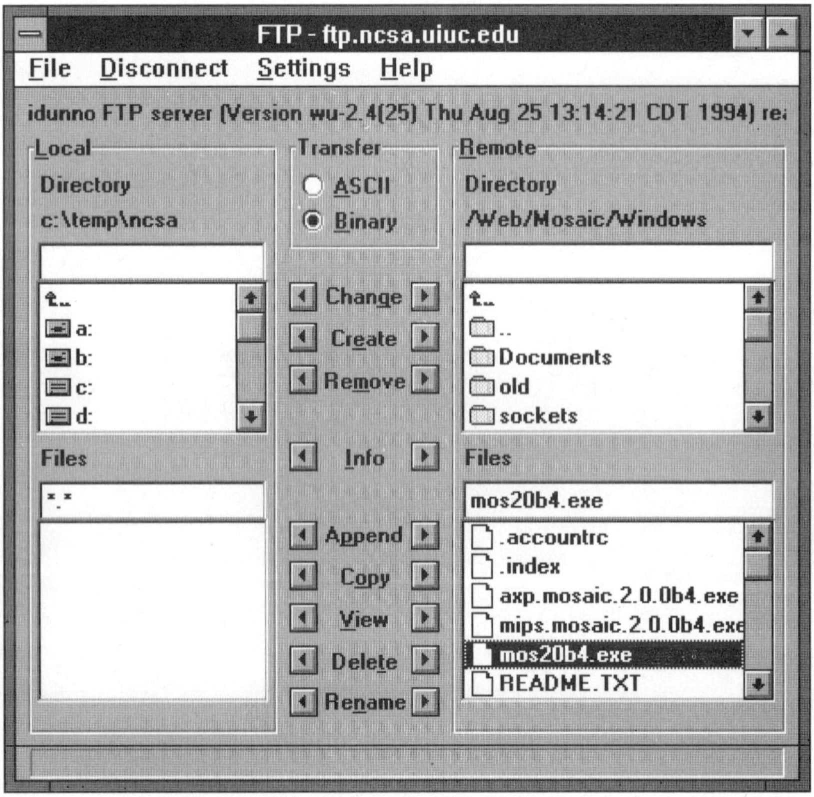

> **If a more recent version has been released by the time you read this book, you will be downloading MOS20B10.EXE, the Beta 10 version, or a release version.**

12. Click the Binary option in the Transfer box.

13. Click the button to the left of Copy.

> **Tip**
>
> You can also drag and drop a file from the Remote (right) Files box to the Local (left) Files box to copy a file to your hard disk. This transfers the file from the directory shown on the right to the directory shown on the left.

The file transfer process begins and a progress box is displayed. Once it is completed, you can download the Win32s file if you need to. Otherwise, skip to Step 16 to disconnect.

14. Double-click on the next file you need to download, W32SOLE.EXE. The file is displayed in the Files text box at the top of the list.

15. Click the button to the left of Copy to transfer this file to your hard disk.

16. Click Disconnect in the Menu bar to select the Disconnect command. The confirmation dialog box is displayed. Click Yes. This disconnects you from the FTP server but does not disconnect you from the Internet.

17. Click Disconnect. Now you are disconnected from the Internet and you have the files you need on your hard disk. Go on to "Installing and Configuring NCSA Mosaic" to see what you need to do next.

See **FTP**

INSTALLING AND CONFIGURING NCSA MOSAIC

Most Windows users are accustomed to installing new products by inserting a disk in the floppy disk drive, running Setup, and following screen prompts. You'll be happy to know that you can install both Win32s and NCSA Mosaic with Setup programs. But you will have to extract these files before you can install them.

> **To extract or unzip files means to copy all the individual files from the large single file you downloaded and to return them to the original, useable state they were in before they were compressed or zipped.**

Depending on what you have already loaded, you'll need to do the following:

1. Extract the Win32s files and run setup to install Win32s.
2. Extract the Mosaic files and run setup to install NCSA Mosaic.

All the steps you need to take are included in order—just leave out the ones that don't apply. For example, if you already have the Win32s software installed on your hard disk, just skip the steps.

Installing Win32s

To install Win32s, you'll extract the files from the one file you downloaded, then run the Win32s setup program.

1. Double-click the MS-DOS Prompt icon to display the command line.

MS-DOS Prompt

2. Type CD\TEMP and press f. The prompt will show as C:\TEMP>.
3. Type W32SOLE.EXE and press f. The file extraction process begins, and several files are extracted. When the extraction process is completed, the C:\TEMP> prompt is displayed again.
4. Type install and press f. The file extraction process begins again. When the extraction process is completed, the C:\TEMP> prompt is displayed again.
5. Type exit to return to Windows.
6. Choose Run from the File Menu in Program Manager.
7. Click the Browse button to open the Browse dialog box. You'll notice that you now have additional subdirectories in the TEMP directory named DISK1, DISK2 and so on. These were created when you extracted the files a minute ago.
8. Select the TEMP\DISK1 directory in the Directories list box, then click the SETUP.EXE file in the File Name list box as shown in Figure 1.26. Then click OK.
9. Click OK in the Run dialog box and follow the onscreen prompts to install Win32s. You will have the opportunity to install Freecell, a game that lets you confirm that Win32s is properly installed. Choose OK to install it.
10. When the installation process is complete, you'll be prompted to restart Windows. Choose Continue.

When Windows restarts, move on to the next section.

Figure 1.26

Use the Browse dialog box to select DISK1, then select the file SETUP.EXE.

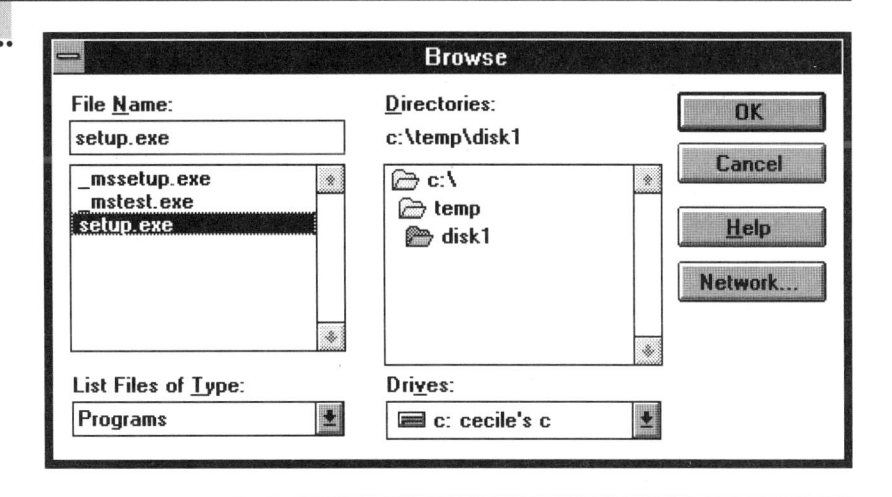

Installing and Configuring NCSA Mosaic

Now you are ready to install NCSA Mosaic. This part is easy. You'll extract the files from the one file you downloaded, then run the Mosaic setup program.

1. Double-click the MS-DOS Prompt icon to display the command line.

2. Type CD\TEMP and press ƒ. The prompt will show as C:\TEMP>.

3. Type MOS20B4.EXE or the exact name of the file you downloaded, if it was different, and press ƒ. The file extraction process begins. When the extraction is completed, the C:\TEMP> prompt is displayed again.

4. Type exit to return to Windows.

5. Choose Run from the File Menu in Program Manager.

6. Click the Browse button to open the Browse dialog box.

7. Select the TEMP directory in the Directories list box, then click the SETUP.EXE file in the File Name list box. Then click OK. The filename is displayed in the Run dialog box, shown in Figure 1.27.

8. Click OK in the Run dialog box and follow the onscreen prompts to install Mosaic.

When the installation process is complete, you'll see a new program group for NCSA Mosaic, with the program icon for NCSA Mosaic.

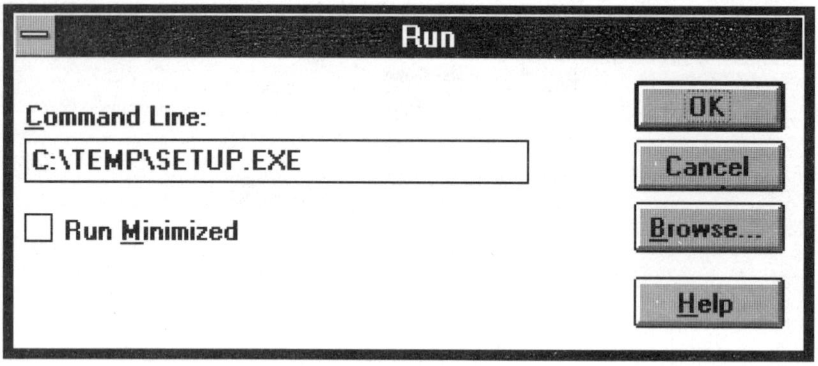

Figure 1.27

The Windows Program Manager Run dialog box

> After you install both Win32s and Mosaic, you'll want to delete all the files and subdirectories you extracted to the TEMP directory since you no longer need them. You can use the Delete command in File Manager to do this.

Now start NCSA Mosaic by double-clicking on the NCSA icon and return to the section titled "Looking at Mosaic: A Guided Tour."

See MOSAIC.INI

PART 2

Web Browsers
A to Z

MOSAIC

A

ABOUT MOSAIC

Whatever form of Mosaic you are running, you can always determine which *version* you have by clicking on the About Command on the Help menu. The About box which is displayed holds the version number for the product, as well as some copyright information and the programmers' names.

1. Choose About from the Help menu. (Each form's command is slightly different, so pick the one you need from the list below.)

Air Mosaic	About Air Mosaic
NCSA Mosaic	About Windows Mosaic
Netscape	About Netscape
Quarterdeck Mosaic	About Quarterdeck Mosaic
Spyglass	About Mosaic

> **Netscape doesn't use a dialog box. Instead, it displays the text on a full screen. To return, click the Back icon.**

2. Click OK to close the dialog box.

In NCSA Mosaic you can also click the About button in the toolbar to open this dialog box.

ACCELERATOR KEYS: NCSA MOSAIC

NCSA Mosaic provides several accelerator keys to speed up the entering of URLs. These keys move the cursor into the URL bar and enter a prefix in one step, so there is less for you to type in.

Keys	Enter
Ctrl + F	ftp://
Ctrl + G	gopher://
Ctrl + H	http://
Ctrl + M	mail:
Ctrl + N	news:
Ctrl + U	Moves the cursor only, doesn't enter anything

> **Quarterdeck Mosaic's URL Helper also enters a prefix for you so you don't have to type it in.**

See Also URL Bar; URL Helper

ACTION: QUARTERDECK MOSAIC AND NETSCAPE

The Action options found in the Quarterdeck Preferences dialog box and the Netscape Preferences dialog box (Figure A.1) let you specify how each viewer or Helper Application should be used.

Select one of the following options:

- **Use Browser as Viewer** and **Quarterdeck Viewer** display the downloaded file in the document view window within the browser.

- **Save** and **Save to disk** open the Save File dialog box where you can save the downloaded file under any name you enter.

- **Launch Application** and **External Viewer Application** open the associated application and load the downloaded file in the application. Enter a directory path and filename in the text box below. You may use the Browse button to select the filename.

- **Unknown: Prompt User** displays a dialog box which prompts you to take an action. You can decide what to do for each individual file.

See Also Extensions; Helper Application; MIME Type; Preferences; Viewers

ADD BOOKMARK: NETSCAPE

In Netscape, you can add the document currently displayed in the document view window as a Bookmark so you can locate it again quickly and easily. To better help you recognize the document, its title will be added to the Bookmark menu as well as to the list in the Bookmark window. Netscape will also save the URL so it knows the document's location.

To add a document as a Bookmark:

- Choose Add Bookmark from the Bookmark menu.

To see the document again at any time:

- Click on it in the Bookmark menu.

Figure A.1

The Action options are found by choosing Helper Applications from the drop-down list.

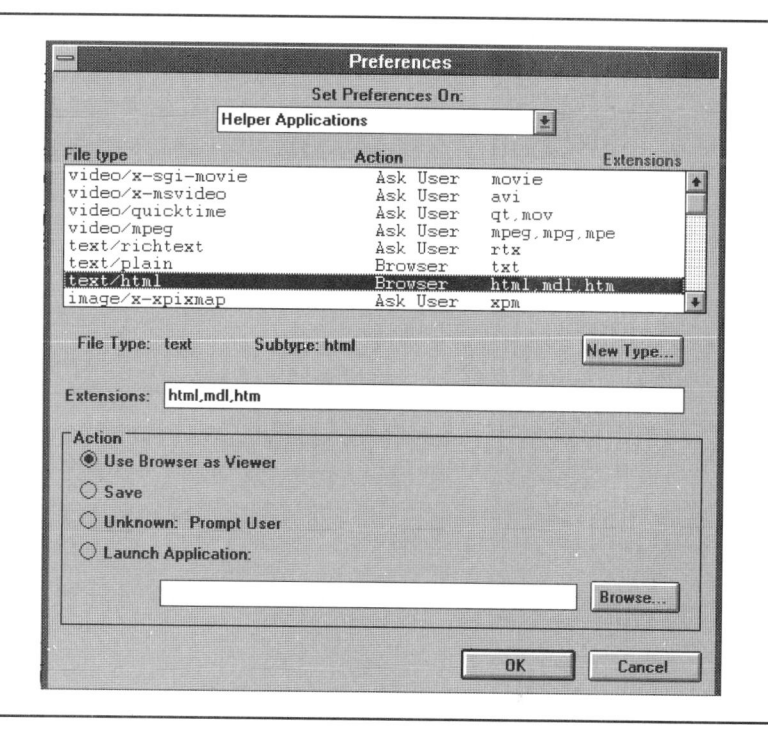

> **Other forms of Mosaic use a Hotlist instead of a Bookmark list.**

See Also   Bookmark; Document Title; Document View Window; Editing Bookmarks; Hotlist; URL

ADD CURRENT TO HOTLIST, ADD DOCUMENT TO HOTLIST

You can add the document currently displayed in the document view window to a Hotlist so you can locate it again quickly and easily. To better help you recognize the document, its title will be added to the Hotlist. Mosaic will also save the URL so it knows the document's location.

> **Netscape uses a Bookmark list instead of a Hotlist.**

See Also   Bookmarks; Browser Window; Changing a Hotlist; Document Title; Document View Window; File Cabinet; Hotlist; Hypertext Link; URL

Add Current to Hotlist: NCSA and Spyglass Mosaic

To add a document to a Hotlist with NCSA or Spyglass Mosaic:

1. Choose Add Current To Hotlist from the Navigate menu.

You can also add the current document to the Hotlist in NCSA Mosaic by clicking the Add to Hotlist button in the toolbar.

> **Tip**
>
> Since you can have several Hotlists in NCSA Mosaic, you may want to change the current Hotlist before you add the current document in order to have the document appear on a specific Hotlist. Since Spyglass Mosaic provides only one Hotlist, you do not have to change it before you add an item.

Add Document to Hotlist: Air Mosaic

To add a document to a Hotlist with Air Mosaic:

- Choose Add Document To Hotlist from the Navigate menu.

You can also add the current document to the Hotlist by clicking the Add button in the toolbar.

Add Document to Hotlist: Quarterdeck Mosaic

Quarterdeck Mosaic lets you drag and drop documents to add them to your Hotlist.

1. Place the mouse cursor on the document icon in the browser window.
2. Drag the document to the Hotlist tab in the Archives and release the mouse button to drop the document. You'll see the document icon as you drag it.

Adding a URL to a Hotlist: Quarterdeck Mosaic

Quarterdeck Mosaic also lets you add a document named within the current document to your Hotlist, even though it is not displayed. In other words, if the document you're looking at (document A) is already linked to other documents (B, C, D, etc.), besides adding A to your Hotlist you can also add all the ones A is linked to. When you see a hypertext link to a document you want to add:

1. Right-click on the hypertext link for the document in the browser window.

2. Choose Hypertext Link from the pop-up menu.

3. Choose Save to Hotlist from the cascading menu.

The document is added to the current Hotlist.

```
Annotation
Browser Configuration
Current Document      ▸
Change Font...
Hypertext Link        ▸
```

Adding from the History to the Hotlist: Quarterdeck Mosaic

Quarterdeck Mosaic also lets you add a document that's in your history list to your Hotlist—even if the document is no longer displayed in the browser window.

1. Place the cursor on the document icon to the left of the document title in the history list (see Figure A.2).

2. Drag the document to the Hotlist and release the mouse button to drop the document on it. You'll see the document icon as you drag it.

ADDING TO A MENU

In Air, NCSA, and Spyglass Mosaic, you can add items to special user-configurable menus.

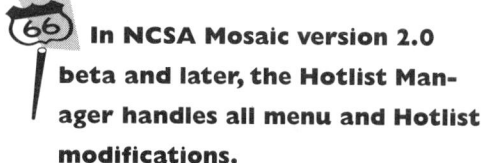

> **In NCSA Mosaic version 2.0 beta and later, the Hotlist Manager handles all menu and Hotlist modifications.**

Figure A.2

Drag the document icon to the Hotlist to add it to your Hotlist.

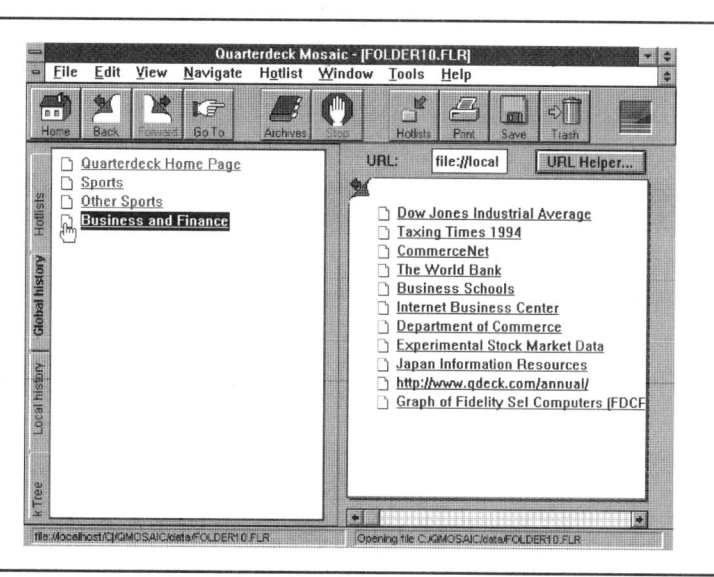

See Hotlist Manager; User Configurable Menus

Adding to a Menu: NCSA Mosaic

In NCSA Mosaic, the Menu Editor lets you create and add items to menus. You can add an item to an existing menu with these steps:

1. Choose Menu Editor from the Navigate menu. The Personal Menus dialog box opens (see Figure A.3).
2. In the Menus list box, click the menu to which you want to add the item. The item will be added to the end of the menu.
3. To add the new item before other items already on the menu, click in the Items list box to indicate the location.
4. Click Insert. The Add Item dialog box opens.
5. Select the Document Item option.
6. Type the name of the new menu item in the Title text box.
7. Type the URL in the URL text box (see Figure A.4).
8. Click OK to close the Add Item dialog box.
9. Click OK to close the Personal Menus dialog box.

Adding to a Menu: Air Mosaic

In Air Mosaic, the Hotlists dialog box is where you add items to menus. You can add an item to an existing menu with these steps:

1. Choose Hotlists from the File menu. The Hotlists dialog box opens (see Figure A.5).

Figure A.3

The Personal Menus dialog box in NCSA Mosaic lets you manage menus and Hotlists.

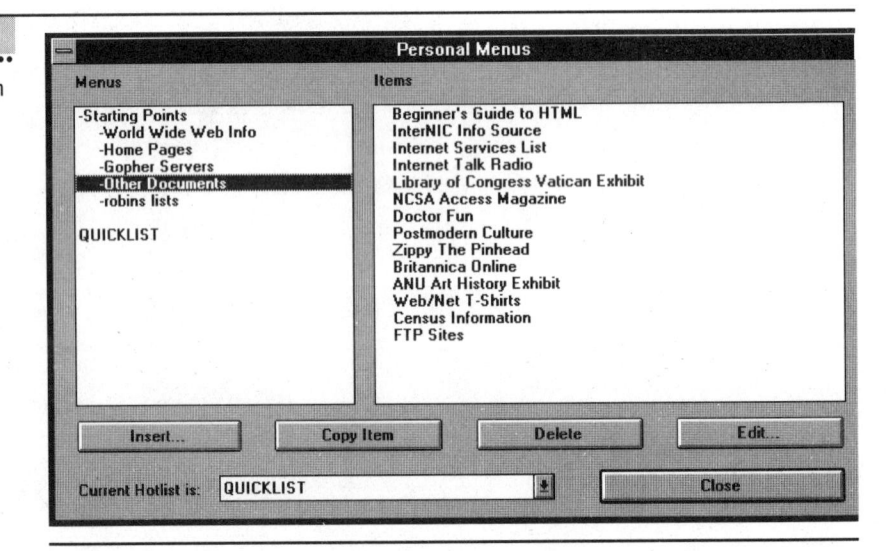

Figure A.4

You can add any document to the Menu with the Add Item dialog box.

Figure A.5

The Hotlists dialog box in Air Mosaic

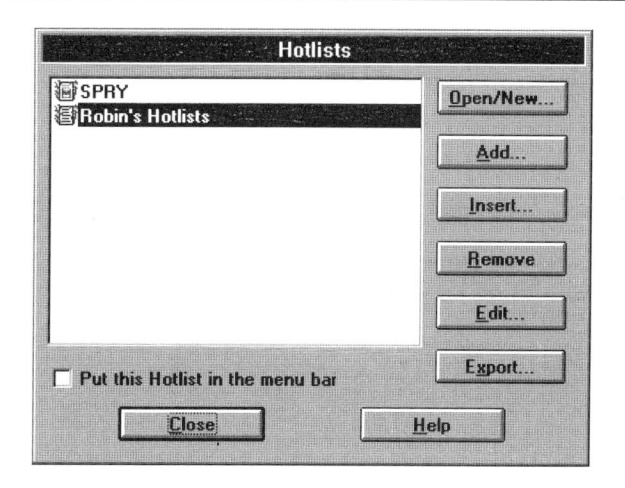

2. In the list box, click the menu to which you want to add the item. The item will be added to the end of the menu.

3. Click Add. The Add New dialog box opens.

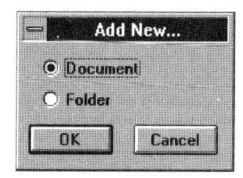

4. Select the Document option then click OK.

5. Type the Title of the new item in the Title text box.

6. Type the URL in the URL text box (see Figure A.6).

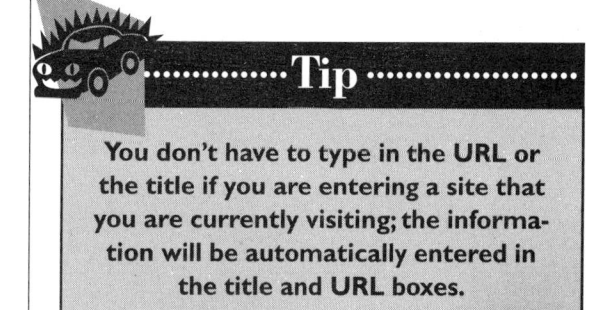

Tip

You don't have to type in the URL or the title if you are entering a site that you are currently visiting; the information will be automatically entered in the title and URL boxes.

Figure A.6

The Add Document dialog box in Air Mosaic

7. Click OK to close the Add Document dialog box.
8. Click Close to close the Hotlists dialog box.

> **Tip**
>
> If the Hotlist to which you want to add the new item is the Hotlist you're currently working with, choosing Add Current to Hotlist or Add Document to Hotlist will add the item to both the Hotlist *and* its corresponding menu—in one step. You won't have to fill in any dialog boxes at all.

See Also Creating a Menu; Menu Editor; Revising a Menu; URL

Adding an Item to the Starting Points Menu: NCSA Mosaic

You can also add an item to the NCSA Starting Points menu by first making it the current Hotlist and then adding the item to it.

1. Choose Open URL from the File menu.
2. Choose Starting Points from the Current Hotlist drop-down list.
3. Click Cancel. This will change the current Hotlist without opening a new document.
4. Choose Add Current To Hotlist from the Navigate menu to add the current document to the Starting Points Hotlist. It will also show up at the bottom of the Starting Points menu.

See Also Add Current To Hotlist; Hotlist Manager; Open URL; Starting Points

Adding an Item to the SPRY Menu: Air Mosaic

When you first install Air Mosaic, the Spry Hotlist is the current Hotlist, and adding a document to it automatically adds the document to the SPRY menu.

To add a document to the SPRY menu when you haven't created any new Hotlists:

✪ Choose Add Document To Hotlist from the Navigate menu.

See Also Creating a Menu; Deleting Items from a Menu; Menu Editor

ADDING TO A QUICKLIST: NCSA MOSAIC

In NCSA Mosaic, you can add the document currently displayed in the document view window to the Quicklist so you can locate it again quickly and easily. To better help you recognize the document, its title will be added to the Quicklist. Mosaic will also save the URL so it knows the document's location.

In order to add a document to a Quicklist, you must first make sure the Quicklist is the current Hotlist.

1. Choose Open URL from the File menu.
2. Choose Quicklist from the Current Hotlist drop-down list (Figure A.7).
3. Click Cancel. This will change the current Hotlist without opening a new document.
4. Choose Add Current To Hotlist from the Navigate menu to add the document to the Quicklist.

> **The Quicklist is only available in NCSA Mosaic.**

See Also Document Title; Document View Window; Hotlist; Quicklist; URL

Figure A.7
Choose Quicklist from the Current Hotlist drop-down list to easily add documents to it.

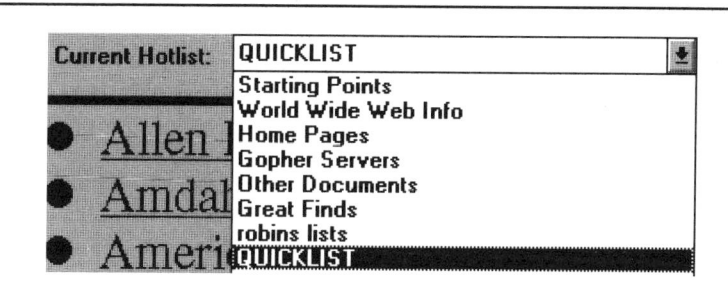

ANCHORS: NCSA MOSAIC

An anchor is the part of a link you see in a document and click on—it can be either text or a graphic. In NCSA Mosaic, you can change the appearance of the anchor and some related items with options on the Anchors tab of the Preferences dialog box.

Table A.1 shows the options that are available.

See Also **Change Cursor Over Anchor; Hypertext Links; Links; Preferences; Underline Anchors**

ANIMATE LOGO: AIR MOSAIC

In Air Mosaic, you can disable the feature which causes the product logo to move while a document is being retrieved.

While the movement provides a visual cue to confirm that downloading is in progress, on slower connections or older systems, the animation actually can slow down the process. If you think this is happening, try turning off the animation to see if it improves the performance of Air Mosaic on your computer. Here's how:

1. Choose Configuration from the Options menu.

Table A.1
Options Available on the Anchors Tab of the Preferences Dialog Box

Option	What It Does
Change Cursor Over Anchor	Toggles the cursor display between an arrow and a hand icon whenever you place it over a hyperlinked item.
Underlined	Underlines all anchors.
Show URL in Status Bar	When the cursor is over an anchor, displays its URL in the status bar.
Visually Age Visited Anchor	Changes the color of anchors after you select them.
Expire Visited Anchors	Displays anchors in the designated unvisited color after the number of days you specify.
Current Anchor Highlighting	Modifies the appearance of the anchor. Framed places a box with a solid line around the anchor. Button makes the anchor appear to be a three-dimensional button. Hatched places a box with a broken line around the anchor. None leaves the anchor as highlighted text only.
Current Anchor Highlighting Color	Numbers represent the current RGB value for the anchor highlighting color. Use Change to select another highlighting color.
Unvisited, Visited, Cached Anchor Color	Numbers represent the current RGB value for the anchor text color. Use Change to select another text color.
Change	Opens the Color dialog box where you can select another anchor color for any of the items in this dialog box.

2. Click the Animate logo option to remove the check.

3. Choose OK.

See Also **Configuration**

ANNOTATE MENU: NCSA MOSAIC

The Annotate menu contains the items that let you add notes about a document. Only NCSA Mosaic includes an Annotate menu. In Quarterdeck Mosaic, select Annotations from the Edit menu.

See Also **Annotating Documents**

ANNOTATING DOCUMENTS

In NCSA and Quarterdeck Mosaic, you can *annotate* (add your own notes to) any document you find on the Web. These notes are kept on your hard disk and linked (but *only on your system*) to the document; your annotations will not affect the document everyone else views.

Annotate: NCSA Mosaic

To annotate a document in NCSA Mosaic:

1. Choose Annotate from the Annotate menu. The Annotate Window displays with the Author and Title information already filled in (this is based on what's in your MOSAIC.INI file).

2. Type your annotation in the window under Enter the Annotation Text.

3. When you are finished, choose Commit.

4. To see the annotation at the bottom of the document, choose Reload from the Navigate window.

Additional options are available in the Annotation Window.

- **Author** by default is your name and e-mail address as it is entered in the "E-mail=" field of your MOSAIC.INI file. You can edit this text field.

- **Title** by default is "Personal Annotation by Mosaic User." The title is placed at the end of the document as a hypertext link. You can also edit this text field.

- **Clean Slate** deletes the content of the annotation, which is all the text currently in the text window.

- **Include File** opens the Windows Open File dialog box where you can select a file to include in the annotation.

- **Delete** removes the existing annotation shown in this window.

- **Commit** creates the annotation shown in this window.

- **Dismiss** cancels the creation of the annotation shown in this window. Use this if you change your mind.

Annotation: Quarterdeck Mosaic

To annotate a document in Quarterdeck Mosaic:

1. Choose Annotation from the Edit menu. The Edit Annotation window displays.
2. Type your annotation in the text area of the window.
3. When you are finished, choose OK.

You'll see a small box within an A in the upper left corner of the browser window. The note can be dragged around the page and placed wherever you want.

Viewing an Annotation: NCSA Mosaic

In NCSA Mosaic, the title of your annotation is placed at the end of the document and looks like a hypertext link. To view the contents, click the link.

Viewing an Annotation: Quarterdeck Mosaic

In Quarterdeck Mosaic, choose Annotation from the Edit menu to open the Edit Annotation window and view the contents of the annotation.

Or, double-click on the "A" note.

Editing an Annotation: NCSA Mosaic

In NCSA Mosaic, you can edit an existing annotation to add or change the information in it, or its author or title.

1. Click the link for the annotation.
2. Choose Edit this Annotation from the Annotate menu. The Annotate Window displays with the contents of the annotation.
3. Make any changes or additions to the information in the window.
4. When you are finished, choose Commit.

Editing an Annotation: Quarterdeck Mosaic

In Quarterdeck Mosaic, you can edit any existing annotation.

1. Choose Annotation from the Edit menu to open the Edit Annotation window or double-click the "A" note for the annotation.
2. Make any changes in the text portion of the window.
3. When you are finished, choose OK.

Deleting an Annotation: NCSA Mosaic

To delete an annotation in NCSA Mosaic:

1. Click the link for the annotation.
2. Choose Delete this Annotation from the Annotate menu.

Deleting an Annotation: Quarterdeck Mosaic

To delete an annotation in Quarterdeck Mosaic:

1. Choose Annotation from the Edit menu to open the Edit Annotation window or double-click the "A" note for the annotation.
2. Choose Delete.

Editing the Annotations Items in the NCSA MOSAIC.INI File

The MOSAIC.INI file in the Windows directory contains several lines which are used when you create annotations. (They're found in the [Annotations] section of the MOSAIC.INI file.) You can edit these items to change the defaults for annotations.

- **Directory=c:\ncsa\annotate** can be changed to *any* directory, including a network directory, where you'd like Mosaic to store the annotations. The annotations are stored as files.

- **Default Title="Personal Annotation by Mosaic User"** can be changed to the title you'd like to use each time you create a new annotation.

- **Group Annotation=no** can be changed to Yes if you are working on a network and you want others with whom you work to have access to your annotations.

See Also MOSAIC.INI File

ANONYMOUS FTP

Anonymous FTP is a method of accessing FTP servers when you don't have a specific account or password, so you can download files that are available to the general public. To log in as an anonymous user on a server, type anonymous when asked for the User name; when asked for your password, type your user name and Internet address. For example, rsmerrin@callamer.com.

> If you downloaded NCSA Mosaic as described in Part 1, you used anonymous FTP.

See Also FTP; FTP Sites

APPLICATIONS AND DIRECTORIES: NETSCAPE

The Applications and Directories section in the Netscape Preferences dialog box lets you enter directories for file storage and associated applications.

See **Bookmark File; Telnet Applications; Temporary Directory; TN3270 Application: View Source**

ARCHIE

Archie is the name of an Internet search service which searches through a database of documents found on anonymous FTP servers. With Archie, you can search for particular information or a document or program you need. However, the results are limited to the information entered in the database, and do not always yield perfect results. You can use the Archie Request Form found on the Starting Points menu or Telnet to initiate an Archie search.

See Also **Archie Request Form; Anonymous FTP; Starting Points; Telnet**

ARCHIE REQUEST FORM: NCSA MOSAIC

The Archie Request Form appears on the NCSA Mosaic Starting Points menu. It lets you do an Archie search by filling in the blanks on the displayed form. Archie searches are particularly handy when you are looking for a file or specific information and you do not know the location. Archie results are best, however, when you know the exact filename.

1. Choose Archie Request Form from the Starting Points menu. The Archie Request Form is displayed in the document view window, as shown in Figure A.8.

2. Each item and option requires an entry.

◘ **What would you like to search for?** is where you enter the filename you want to find. If you are unsure of the exact name, enter a partial filename and use wildcards for the rest. You can use the * and ? characters as wildcards and then choose the **Regular expressions** option below.

◘ **There are several types of search:** lets you choose the type of search from the following:

Exact finds only exact matches to the filename you enter.

Case-insensitive substring finds filenames which contain the partial filename you entered, and ignores the capitalization.

Case-sensitive substring finds filenames which contain the partial filename you entered when the capitalization also matches.

Regular expressions finds filenames which match the filename you specify when you use the * and ? wildcard characters. For example, if you want to find out where the mosaic files are, you might type in mos*.*.

By Host and **By Date** are both sorting options; just click the one that best suits your needs. Host names are sorted alphabetically. When sorting by

Figure A.8

Use the Archie Request Form to search for a file or information.

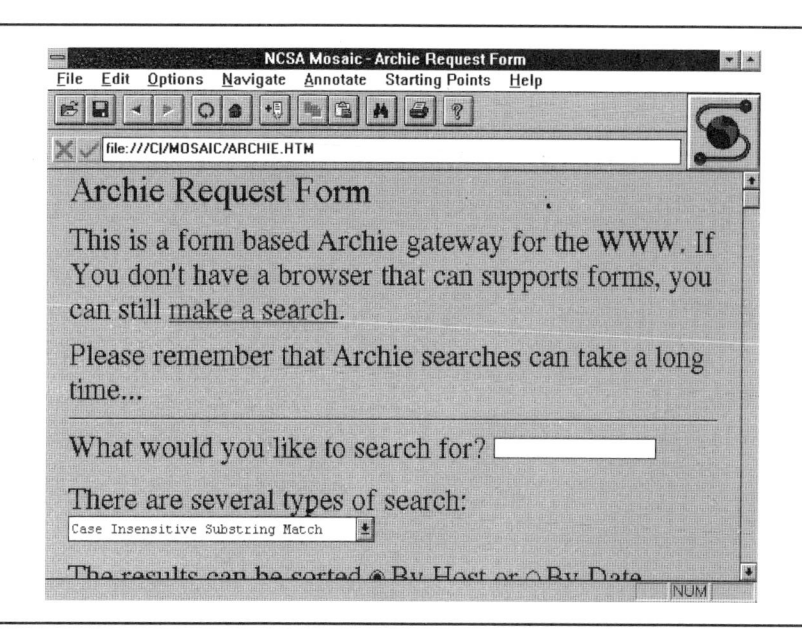

[Screenshot: NCSA Mosaic - Archie Request Form window showing the Archie Request Form page with search options]

date, recent files are listed first, based on the date you last modified them.

The impact on other users can be specifies the priority for your search. Five options are available: **Extremely nice** results in your search being handled with the lowest priority, **Not Nice At All** with the highest priority.

Several Archie Servers can be used is where you select the Archie server to use for the search. If you select a server that is close to you, the search may be quicker.

You can restrict the number of results returned if you do not want to see more than 95 possible results, so enter a number to indicate the maximum you want displayed.

3. When you have filled in the form, click the Submit button. The results are displayed in the document view window.

You can click any link in the window to view or download the file you were searching for.

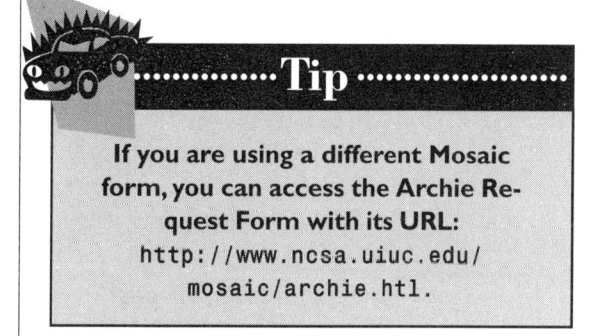

> **Tip**
>
> If you are using a different Mosaic form, you can access the Archie Request Form with its URL:
> `http://www.ncsa.uiuc.edu/mosaic/archie.htl`

See Also **Archie; Forms; FTP; Starting Points; URL**

ARCHIVES: QUARTERDECK MOSAIC

In Quarterdeck Mosaic, Hotlists are treated as folders, which are then saved and organized on a tab, which you can see on the screen in the Archives notebook on the left.

Tip: The Quarterdeck Archives can contain both folders and individual URLs as well as Hotlists and a Link Tree.

To display the contents of the Archives:

- Click on the Archives icon in the toolbar.

The notebook opens with the existing folders (see Figure A.9). The Hotlists folders are predefined by Quarterdeck to help you get started, and they already contain the URLs for some interesting documents. You can also change the way the contents are displayed, by using the "As" commands on the View menu.

To close the Archives:

- Click on the Archives icon again.

See Also As Icons; Icon List; Text List or Tree; Folders; Global History; Hotlists; Link Tree; Local History

Figure A.9
The Archives in Quarterdeck Mosaic

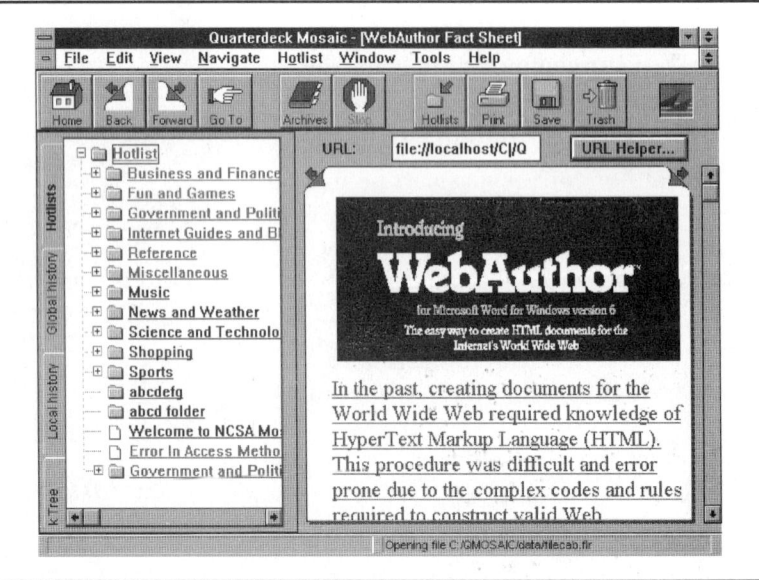

AS ICONS, ICON LIST, TEXT LIST, OR TREE: QUARTERDECK MOSAIC

In Quarterdeck Mosaic, you can change the way documents and folders appear in each Hotlist window by choosing one of four commands on the View menu:

- As Icons
- As Icon List
- As Text List
- As Tree

The names are self-explanatory; try them all to see which you like best.

AUDIO

NCSA Mosaic's Preferences dialog box includes an Audio tab which lets you associate WAV files with specific program actions, so that your computer plays a sound whenever you take an action; for example, every time you load a document, your computer can chime a bell.

To associate a sound with a program event:

1. Choose Preferences from the Edit menu. The Preferences dialog box is displayed.
2. Click the Audio tab to bring it forward.
3. In the Events list box, click the first program action to which you want to assign a sound.
4. In the WAV Files list box, click the sound you want to assign to the event.
5. Repeat steps 3 and 4 for each event to which you want to assign a sound.
6. Click the Enable Sounds check box to place a check in it.
7. Click OK to close the dialog box.

> **Tip**
>
> You can associate any **WAV** sound you have in any directory. If you don't know where to find **WAV** sounds, check your **WINDOWS** directory.

See Also Preferences

AUTO LOAD IMAGES, AUTOLOAD INLINE IMAGES

In each form of Mosaic, you can choose to display all images included in documents or turn off the automatic display of graphics. The Documents will be retrieved and displayed faster when their included graphics are not displayed and you can always display individual graphics when you want to. A graphic does not have to be displayed for its link to function properly.

To see an image that is displayed as an icon, place the mouse over the image's icon and click the *right* mouse button.

To retrieve the document associated with a link, place the mouse over the image's icon and click.

> This feature is available in NCSA Mosaic and Quarterdeck Mosaic as Display Inline Images. In Spyglass Mosaic it is Load Images Automatically.

See   Display Inline Images; Load Images Automatically; Preferences

Autoload Inline Images: Air Mosaic

In Air Mosaic, choose Autoload Inline Images from the Options menu to toggle the display of graphics.

Auto Load Images: Netscape

In Netscape, choose Auto Load Images from the Options menu to toggle the display of graphics.

To see the images in the current document, choose Load Images from the View menu. To retrieve the document associated with a link, place the mouse over the image's icon and click the *left* mouse button.

AUTOLOAD HOME PAGE: NCSA MOSAIC

The Autoload Home Page option lets you specify whether a home page is automatically loaded each time you start NCSA Mosaic. The option is found on the General tab in the Preferences dialog box. When you first install Mosaic, the option is turned on.

To turn it off:

1. Choose Preferences from the Options menu.
2. Click on the General tab to bring it forward.
3. Click Autoload Home Page to remove the check and change the status of this option.
4. Choose OK.

Now when you load Mosaic, the document view window will be blank. Follow the steps above whenever you want to turn the option back on.

············Tip············

The Home Page Text box below the Autoload Home Page option is where you enter the URL of the home page you want to load when this option is turned on.

> In Air Mosaic, this option is called **Load Automatically at Startup.** In Quarterdeck Mosaic, it is **Load Home Page.** In Netscape, it is found as **Start With: Home Page.**

See Also Home Page; Load Automatically at Startup; Load Home Page; Preferences; Start With; URL

B

BACK

The Back command lets you display documents you've previously displayed during the current session. It is available as soon as you display more than one document and always takes you to the previous document. You can choose Back more than once—to go back through all the documents you've viewed, in reverse order. A Back button is included on the toolbar in all Web browsers.

Tip

Use Forward to view the documents in the order you retrieved them.

Back: Air Mosaic, NCSA Mosaic, Spyglass Mosaic

In Air, NCSA, and Spyglass Mosaic, Back is found on the Navigate menu.

The Air Mosaic Back button

The NCSA Mosaic Back button

The Spyglass Mosaic Back button

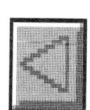

Back: Netscape

In Netscape, Back is on the Go menu and toolbar.

Back: Quarterdeck Mosaic

In Quarterdeck Mosaic, choose Go Back from the Navigate menu or the toolbar, or click the page turner in the upper-left corner of the window.

See Also   Forward; Go Menu; History; Show Page Turners

BACKGROUND COLOR: QUARTERDECK MOSAIC

In Quarterdeck Mosaic, you can change the background color of all documents in the Browser window with an option in the Preferences dialog box. To change the background color:

1. Choose Preferences from the Tools menu. The Preferences dialog box is displayed.
2. Click the Browser tab to bring it forward.
3. Select another color from the background color drop-down list.
4. Click OK.

See Also   Browser window; Color; Preferences

BOOKMARK FILE: NETSCAPE

The Bookmark File text box is where you enter the name of the file in which Netscape will store your bookmarks. This text box is found in the Applications and Directories area of the Preferences dialog box.

To enter the directory:

1. Choose Preferences from the Options menu.
2. Select Applications and Directories from the drop-down list at the top of the dialog box.
3. In the Bookmark File text box, type the name of the file where you want Netscape to store your bookmarks. You can also use the Browse button to locate and select a file.
4. Click OK.

See Also   Bookmarks; Preferences

BOOKMARKS: NETSCAPE

In Netscape, Bookmarks are used instead of Hotlists so you can locate a document again quickly and easily. When you add the current document to a list of Bookmarks, Netscape adds the document title to the Bookmark menu and saves the URL so it knows the document's location.

See Also Add Bookmark; Document Title; Hotlist; Modifying Bookmarks; URL; View Bookmarks

BROWSE: NETSCAPE AND QUARTERDECK MOSAIC

The Browse button found in the Preferences dialog boxes in Web browsers opens the Windows Browse File dialog box, where you can select a path and filename to insert in the text box above or to the right.

See Also Preferences

BROWSER: QUARTERDECK MOSAIC

The Browser tab in the Quarterdeck Mosaic Preferences dialog box specifies settings for the annotations and the appearance of the document page.

See Background Color; Show Annotations; Show Browser Margins; Show Page Turners; Show URL Field; Show URL Helper; Wipe Interval in Milliseconds

BROWSER WINDOW: QUARTERDECK MOSAIC

In Quarterdeck Mosaic, the window that displays the selected document is called a browser window.

See Document View Window

BROWSERS

An Internet viewer that lets you display hypertext documents on the World Wide Web and retrieve linked documents. Mosaic is a browser.

BUG LIST: NCSA MOSAIC

Since NCSA Mosaic is a work in progress, you may experience problems at times. You can see a list of bugs by choosing Bug List from the Help menu. This will help you find out if the problem you are experiencing is a result of some known Mosaic bug.

BULLET STYLE: QUARTERDECK MOSAIC

The Bullet Style drop-down list is where you select the appearance of bullets Quarterdeck Mosaic uses when it displays documents. This list is found on the HTML Viewer tab of the Preferences dialog box.

To select a bullet style:

1. Choose Preferences from the Tools menu.
2. Click on the HTML Viewer tab to bring it forward.
3. In the Bullet Style drop-down list, select the bullet type from those displayed.

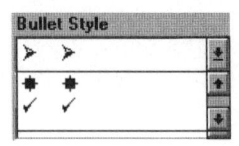

4. Choose OK.

See Also **Fonts; Styles**

C

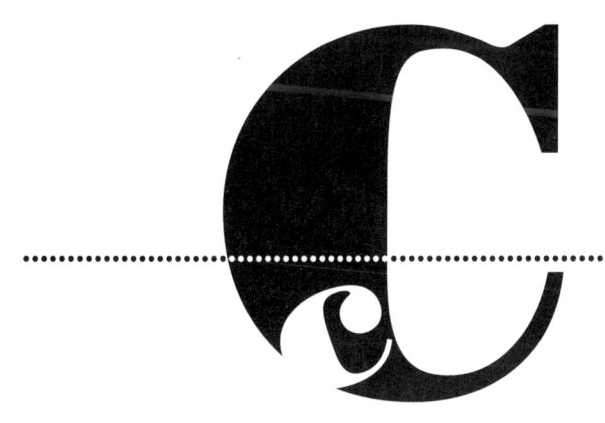

CACHE: NCSA MOSAIC

NCSA Mosaic's Preferences dialog box includes a Cache tab which lets you control how RAM and hard disk space are used to display and temporarily hold displayed documents in memory.

See **Document Caching**

CACHE ENABLED: QUARTERDECK MOSAIC

See **Document Caching**

CACHE TIMEOUT: QUARTERDECK MOSAIC

See **Document Caching**

CACHED DOCUMENTS: AIR MOSAIC

See **Document Caching**

CANCELING

In all forms of Mosaic, you can stop retrieving a document when you find it is taking too long, or if you change your mind about wanting to see it.

To cancel, just click the graphical icon to the right of the URL bar, or click the Stop button.

See Also **Stop**

Cancel Current Task: Air Mosaic

In Air Mosaic, choose Cancel Current Task from the Navigate menu.

CASCADE: QUARTERDECK MOSAIC, SPYGLASS MOSAIC

You can arrange open document view windows or browser windows with the Cascade command when multiple windows are open. Cascade overlaps the windows so each title bar is visible, but the window's contents are not. Cascade is available in Quarterdeck Mosaic and Spyglass Mosaic, which allow you to view more than one document at a time.

See Also   Browser Window; Document View Window; Tile

CERN

CERN is the abbreviation for the European Center for Nuclear Research, where the World Wide Web was developed. In NCSA Mosaic, you can view the CERN Home Page by selecting Home Pages from the Starting Points menu and then selecting CERN Home Page from the cascading menu.

See Also   Home Pages; Starting Points; World Wide Web

CHANGE CURSOR OVER ANCHORS

You can toggle the option that changes the cursor to a hand icon whenever you place it over a hyperlinked item.

Change Cursor Over Anchors: NCSA Mosaic

In NCSA Mosaic versions 1.0 and 2.0 alpha, choose Change Cursor Over Anchors from the Options menu to turn the display of this hand cursor on and off. In version 2.0 beta and later, choose Change Cursor Over Anchors from the Anchors tab in the Preferences dialog box.

See Also   Anchors; Preferences

Change Cursor Over Anchors: Quarterdeck Mosaic

In Quarterdeck Mosaic, this option can be found in the Preferences dialog box.

1. Choose Preferences from the Tools menu.
2. Click on the HTML Viewer tab to bring it forward.
3. Click Change Cursor Over Anchors to change the status of this option.
4. Choose OK.

CHANGE FIXED OR PROPORTIONAL FONT: NETSCAPE

You can change the font that Netscape uses when documents are displayed, so you can read them more easily. If you wish, you can change the typeface and size associated with both fixed and proportional fonts.

1. Choose Preferences from the Options menu.
2. Select Fonts and Colors from the drop-down list at the top of the dialog box.
3. Click the Choose Font button to the right of Use the Proportional Font.
4. In the Font dialog box, select a Font and Size from those displayed in the respective list boxes.
5. Click OK to confirm your selections.
6. Click the Choose Font button to the right of Use the Fixed Font.

> **The fonts displayed are those available on your computer. You may only have one non-proportional font installed, either Courier or Courier New. If so, you can only change the size of the text, not the font which is used.**

7. In the Font dialog box, select a Font and Size from those displayed in the respective list boxes.
8. Click OK to confirm your selections.
9. Choose OK to close the Preferences dialog box.

Netscape redisplays the current document and the change you made is applied immediately.

> **Air, NCSA, and Quarterdeck Mosaics have Font buttons and dialog boxes that let you modify the font. Spyglass Mosaic uses Style Sheets to change the fonts.**

See Choose Font; Font; HTML Tag; Styles; Style Sheets

CHANGING A HOTLIST

In NCSA and AIR Mosaic, you can have multiple Hotlists. You can change the current Hotlist before you add documents to that Hotlist with the Add Current To Hotlist or Add Document to Hotlist command.

> **Quarterdeck Mosaic uses folders instead of Hotlists; Netscape uses Bookmarks.**

See Add Current To Hotlist; Bookmarks; Folders; Hotlist Manager; Open URL; Set As Current

Changing a Hotlist: NCSA Mosaic

In NCSA Mosaic version 1.0 and 2.0 alpha, the Current Hotlist drop-down list is found in the Menu Editor dialog box and the Open URL dialog box.

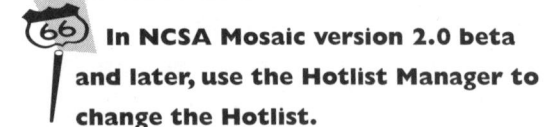

> In NCSA Mosaic version 2.0 beta and later, use the Hotlist Manager to change the Hotlist.

1. Choose Menu Editor from the Navigate menu. The Personal Menus dialog box opens.
2. Select another Hotlist from the Current Hotlist is drop-down list.
3. Click Close to close the Personal Menus dialog box.

Or, you can:

1. Choose Open URL from the File menu.
2. Choose another Hotlist from the Current Hotlist drop-down list.
3. Click Cancel. Clicking Cancel will change the current Hotlist without opening a new document.

Changing a Hotlist: AIR Mosaic

In AIR Mosaic, the Hotlists dialog box is where you change the current Hotlist:

1. Choose Hotlists from the File menu. The Hotlists dialog box opens as shown in Figure C.1.
2. In the list box, click the Hotlist to make it current.
3. Click Close to close the Hotlists dialog box.

CHOOSE FONT: NCSA MOSAIC

You can change the font that NCSA Mosaic uses when documents are displayed; this may help you read them more easily. If you wish, you can change the typeface, style and size associated with each HTML tag within a document. To change the font in version 1.0 and 2.0 alpha:

1. Select Choose Font from the Options menu. A cascading menu opens with all the HTML tags found in documents.

```
Normal
Header 1
Header 2
Header 3
Header 4
Header 5
Header 6
Header 7
Menu
Directory
Address
Block Quote
Example
Preformatted
Listing
```

Figure C.1

The Hotlists dialog box in Air Mosaic

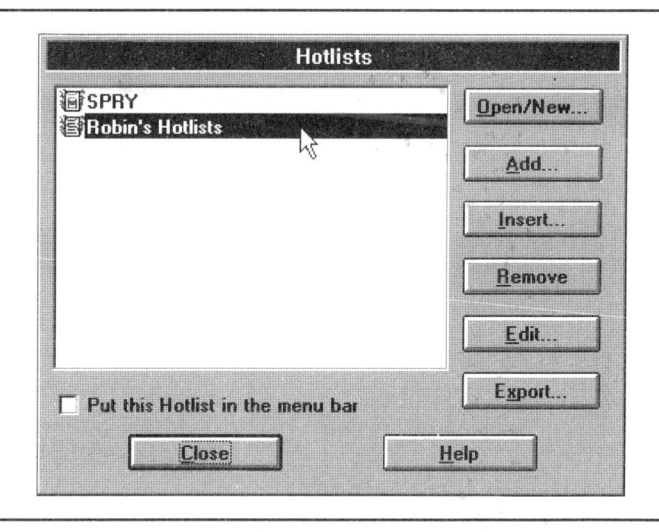

2. Choose any item on this menu. Normal changes most of the text within a document.

3. In the Font dialog box as shown in Figure C.2, select a Font, Font Style and Size from those displayed in the respective list boxes.

4. Click OK to confirm your selections.

Mosaic redisplays the current document and the change you made is applied immediately. Repeat the steps as many times as you like for each element (style) in the document.

Figure C.2

Use the Font dialog box in NCSA Mosaic to change the fonts used for displaying documents.

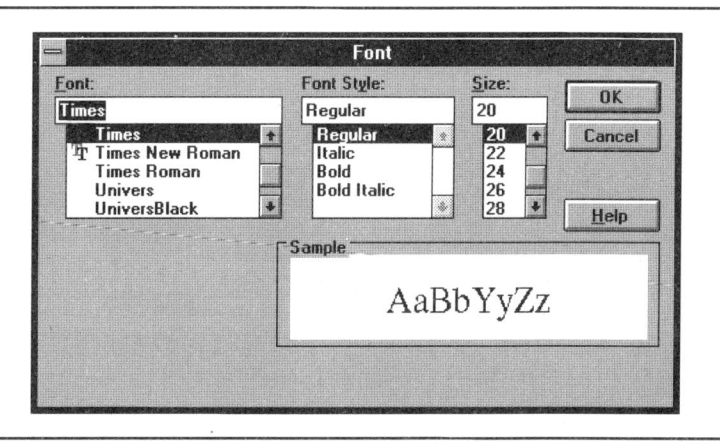

To change the font in version 2.0 beta and later:

1. Choose Preferences from the Options menu.
2. Click the Fonts tab to bring it forward.
3. Double-click on the Default folder in the Mosaic Font Group list box.
4. Click on any item in the list.
5. Click on the Change button.
6. In the Font dialog box select a Font, Font Style and Size from those displayed in the respective list boxes.
7. Click OK to confirm your selections.
8. Choose OK to close the Preferences dialog box.

Air Mosaic, Netscape and Quarterdeck Mosaic have Font buttons and dialog boxes that let you modify the font. Spyglass Mosaic uses Style Sheets to change the fonts.

See Change Fixed or Proportional Font; Font; HTML Tag; Styles; Style Sheets

CLEAR: SPYGLASS MOSAIC

In Spyglass Mosaic, the Clear command on the Edit menu deletes the selected text without placing it on the clipboard.

See Also Cut; Delete

CLOSE: QUARTERDECK MOSAIC, SPYGLASS MOSAIC

Both Quarterdeck Mosaic and Spyglass Mosaic allow you to open more than one document window at a time. The Close command on the File menu closes the current document view window or browser window. You can also close all the open document view windows with Close All. Close All is available in Spyglass Mosaic.

To close a document window, you can also double-click the Close box in the upper left corner of the window.

You can also open more than one document view window with Netscape, which does not have a Close command.

See Browser Window; Document View Window

COLOR: NETSCAPE

In Netscape, Color options are available in the Preferences dialog box. You can change the color of the background, text, and links within documents as well as followed (previously selected) links. To change the default colors:

1. Choose Preferences from the Option menu. The Preferences dialog box is displayed.

2. Select Fonts and Color from the Set Preferences drop-down list at the top.
3. Check any boxes whose colors you want to modify. Unchecked items display in the default colors.
4. Modify any color options (described in Table C.1).
5. Choose OK.

See Also **Anchors; Background Color; Links**

CONFIGURATION: AIR MOSAIC

In Air Mosaic, preferences for the application window (console) display items, viewers, the home page, servers and your e-mail address are specified in the Configuration dialog box (Figure C.3).

To open the Configuration dialog box in order to see or change the current settings:

1. Choose Configuration from the Options menu.

Table C.1
Color Modification Options

Option	What It Does
Colors	**Always Use Mine** overrides a document's background with the background you specify in this section.
	Let Document Override uses a document's background when you download and display it.
Links	Changes the color used to display links within documents.
Followed Links	Changes the color used to display links after you select them.
Text	Changes the color used to display text within documents.
Background	Changes the background displayed behind documents.
	Default applies a gray background.
	Custom applies the color you select with the Choose Color button.
	Image File applies the filename you enter in the text box as the background.
	Browse is used to select and insert the Image File filename.
Choose Color	Opens the Color dialog box where you can select another color for Links, Followed Links, Text, and Background.

Figure C.3

The Air Mosaic Configuration dialog box

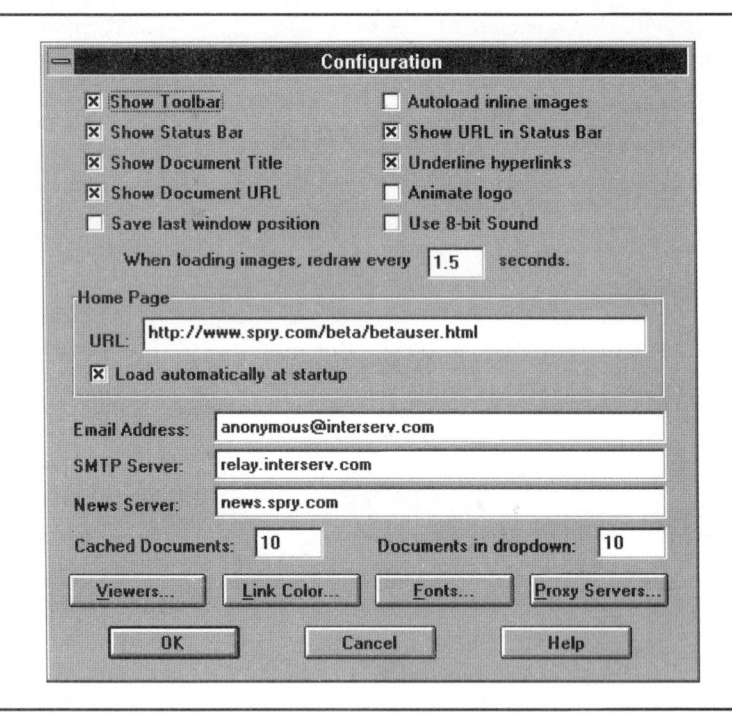

2. Change any option or setting. Options are described under their individual listing.
3. Choose OK.

In NCSA Mosaic and Netscape, choose Preferences from the Options menu to change the configuration and options. In Quarterdeck Mosaic, choose Preferences from the Tools menu. In Spyglass Mosaic, choose Preferences from the Edit menu.

See Also **Animate Logo; Autoload Inline Images; Cached Documents; Documents in Drop Down; E-mail Address; Fonts; Home Page; Link Color; Load Automatically at Startup; News Server; Preferences; Proxy Servers; Save Last Window Position; Show Document Title; Show Document URL; Show Status Bar; Show Toolbar; Show URL in Status Bar; SMTP Server; Underline Hyperlinks; URL; Use 8-Bit Sound; Viewers; When Loading Images, Redraw Every**

CONSOLE: AIR MOSAIC

The Air Mosaic application window is called the Air Mosaic console.

COPY

The Copy command on the Edit menu places the selected text on the clipboard without deleting it from its current location. Once text is on the clipboard, it can be inserted in another location or pasted to another document with a text editor which has a Paste command. Copy is available in Air, NCSA, Quarterdeck, and Spyglass Mosaics, and Netscape. In each form, text can be copied from different sources once it is selected from the URL text box, the Document Source window, and/or text boxes within some windows and dialog boxes.

You can also copy selected text in NCSA Mosaic by clicking the Copy button in the toolbar.

See Also   Cut; Paste; Selecting Text

CREATING A HOTLIST

You can create a new Hotlist in both Air and NCSA Mosaic.

Creating a Hotlist: AIR Mosaic

In AIR Mosaic, the Hotlists dialog box is where you create new Hotlists.

1. Choose Hotlists from the File menu. The Hotlists dialog box opens as shown in Figure C.4.
2. Click Add. The Add New dialog box opens.
3. Select the Folder option then click OK.
4. Type the Title of the new folder in the Title text box (see Figure C.5).
5. Click Close to close the Add Folder dialog box. The new Hotlist will also be the current Hotlist, unless you click on another Hotlist in the list box.
6. If you want the new Hotlist to be added as a new menu, check the option which reads Put the Hotlist in the menu bar.
7. Click OK to close the Hotlists dialog box.

Creating a Hotlist: NCSA Mosaic

To create a new Hotlist in NCSA Mosaic, create either a new menu or a new submenu.

See   Creating a Menu; Folders

Figure C.4

The Hotlists dialog box in AIR Mosaic

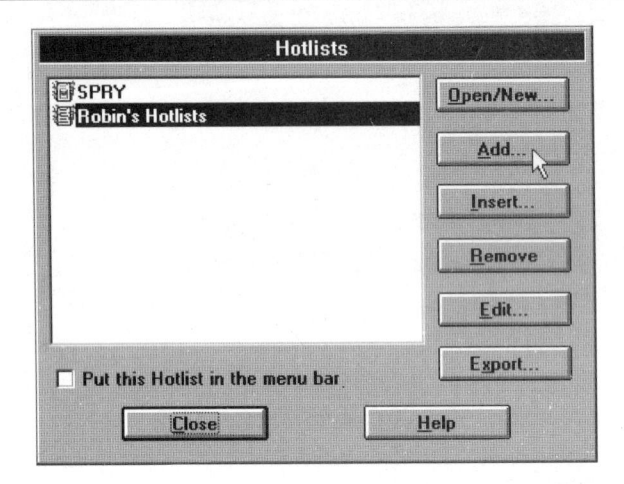

Figure C.5

Air Mosaic's Add Folder dialog box

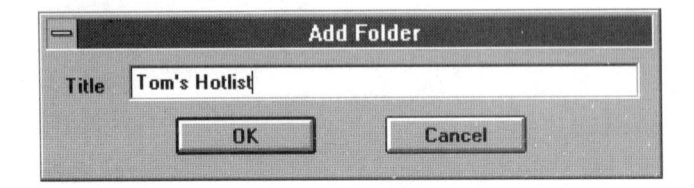

CREATING LISTS OF URLS

You can create a list of URLs in a text editor in order to share it with friends and colleagues. You can then give the text file to others. URLs can be added to the MOSIAC.INI file so they appear on Hotlists and menus. Since URLs are tedious to type, you might want to use the Copy command to copy them to the Windows clipboard, and then paste them into another text editor, for example Windows Write.

To copy a URL to a text file:

1. Select the URL in the URL text box.

2. Choose Copy from the Edit menu. The URL is copied to the clipboard.

3. Double-click the Write program icon in the Program Manager window or any Windows text editor.

4. Choose Paste from the Edit menu in Write. The URL is pasted to the current document.

5. Repeat steps 1, 2, and 4 for each URL you want to copy.

CREATING A MENU

6. Choose Save from the File menu in Write, and enter a filename for the document. Then choose OK.

> **Tip**
>
> You can also copy URLs from your **MOSAIC.INI** file to another text file in order to give the list of URLs to others. You can use **Write** or any text editor that can save files in ASCII format for this.

See Also   Copy; MOSAIC.INI File; URL

CREATING A MENU

You can create a new menu in both Air and NCSA Mosaic.

> **In NCSA Mosaic version 2.0 beta and later, these modifications are made with the Hotlist Manager, not the Menu Editor described in this section.**

See   Adding to a Menu; Creating a Hotlist; Hotlist Manager; Hotlists; Menu Editor; Revising a Menu

Creating a Menu: NCSA Mosaic

In NCSA Mosaic, you can create a new menu with the Menu Editor. When you create a new menu, you are also creating a new Hotlist.

1. Choose Menu Editor from the Navigate menu. The Personal Menus dialog box (Figure C.6) opens.
2. In the Menus list box, click the blank line above Quicklist.
3. Click Insert. The Add Item dialog box (see Figure C.7) opens and the Menu option is selected.
4. Type the name of the new menu and Hotlist in the Title text box.
5. Click OK to close the Add Item dialog box.
6. If you want to begin adding items to this menu and Hotlist immediately, select the new menu title from the Current Hotlist is drop-down list.
7. Click Close to close the Personal Menus dialog box.

The new menu will appear to the left of the Help menu in the menu bar.

Creating a Menu: Air Mosaic

To create a new menu in Air Mosaic, create a new Hotlist and check the option which

Figure C.6

The Personal Menus dialog box in NCSA Mosaic

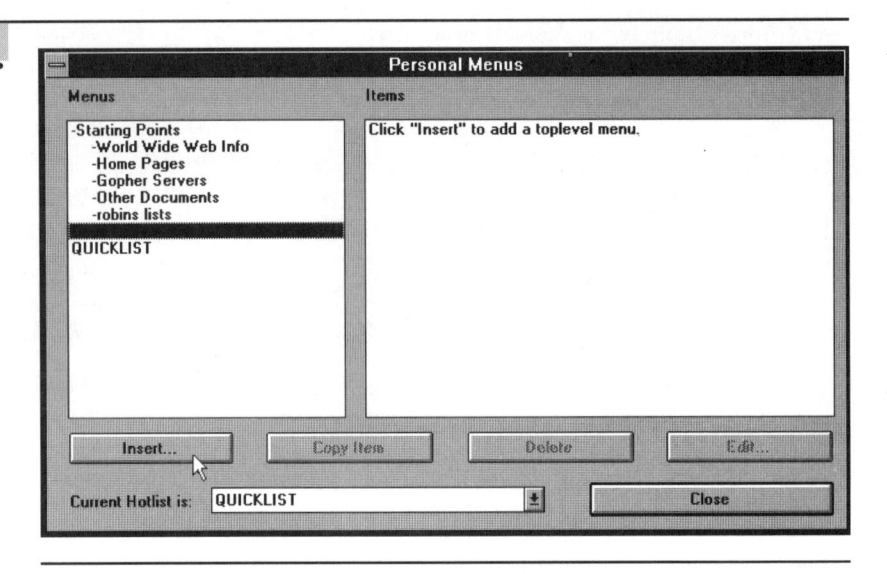

Figure C.7

NCSA Mosaic's Add Item dialog box

reads Put the Hotlist in the menu bar, in the Hotlists dialog box (see Figure C.8).

See **Creating a Hotlist**

Adding a Cascading Menu

In Air and NCSA Mosaic, you can also add a submenu or cascading menu to an existing menu. When you create a new submenu, you are also creating a new Hotlist.

Adding a Cascading Menu: NCSA Mosaic

To add a cascading menu in NCSA Mosaic:

1. Choose Menu Editor from the Navigate menu. The Personal Menus dialog box opens.
2. In the Menus list box, click on the menu to which you want to add the additional cascading menu.
3. Click Insert. The Add Item dialog box opens.

Figure C.8

In Air Mosaic, a check box option turns a Hotlist into a menu.

> ☒ Put this Hotlist in the menu bar

4. Select the Menu option.
5. Type the name of the new menu and Hotlist in the Title text box.
6. Click OK to close the Add Item dialog box.
7. If you want to begin adding items to this submenu and Hotlist immediately, select the Hotlist title from the Current Hotlist is drop-down list.
8. Click Close to close the Personal Menus dialog box.

The header for the new submenu will appear at the bottom of the selected menu.

Adding a Cascading Menu: Air Mosaic

To add a menu in Air Mosaic:

1. Choose Hotlists from the File menu. The Hotlists dialog box opens.
2. Click on the existing menu where you want to add the new cascading menu.
3. Click Add. The Add New dialog box opens.
4. Select the Folder option then click OK.
5. Type the Title of the new folder in the Title text box.

6. Click OK to close the Add Folder dialog box. The new menu will also be the current Hotlist, unless you click on another Hotlist in the list box.
7. Check the option which reads Put the Hotlist in the menu bar.
8. Click Close to close the Hotlists dialog box.

CUSTOMIZING THE MOSAIC WINDOW

You can turn some view options on and off to customize the Mosaic window. Turning options off increases the document viewing area.

See Also Configuration; Directory Buttons; Document Source; Kiosk Mode Location Bar; Notebook; Options; Presentation Mode; Status Bar; Title Bar; Toolbar; URL Bar

Customizing the Window: Air Mosaic

In Air Mosaic, you can turn off the toolbar, Title bar, URL bar, and status bar.

> **Tip**
> Kiosk Mode lets you maximize your viewing area for documents.

Customizing the Window: NCSA Mosaic

In NCSA Mosaic, select Options from the Menu bar to toggle the toolbar, URL bar, and status bar.

> Presentation Mode lets you maximize your viewing area for documents.

Customizing the Window: Netscape

In Netscape, you can turn off the Location bar and Directory buttons.

Customizing the Window: Quarterdeck Mosaic

In Quarterdeck Mosaic, you can turn off the toolbar, archives, and status bar.

Customizing the Window: Spyglass Mosaic

In Spyglass Mosaic, you can turn off the toolbar display.

CUT: NETSCAPE, QUARTERDECK AND SPYGLASS MOSAIC

Cut is available in Netscape, Spyglass Mosaic, and Quarterdeck Mosaic. The Cut command on the Edit menu places the selected text on the clipboard and also deletes it from its current location. Once text is on the clipboard, it can be inserted in another location with the Paste command.

See Also   Copy; Paste; Selecting Text

CYBERSPACE

Cyberspace is computer jargon for where you are when you are connected to the Internet. Although you can download documents from computers all over the world, as of this writing the Internet doesn't include computers on any other planets besides earth, and you are probably still in your home or office while you are in Cyberspace. Cyberspace is also a state of mind.

D

DATA ENGINE: QUARTERDECK MOSAIC

The Data Engine tab in the Quarterdeck Mosaic Preferences dialog box lets you select multimedia viewers for displaying audio and video files.

See **Extensions; MIME; Preferences; Viewers**

DELETE: QUARTERDECK MOSAIC

In Quarterdeck Mosaic, the Delete command on the Edit menu deletes the selected text without placing it on the clipboard.

See Also **Clear; Cut**

DELETE THIS ANNOTATION: NCSA MOSAIC

You can remove an existing annotation at any time.

See **Annotation**

DELETING A HOTLIST

You can delete any Hotlist you've created in Air or NCSA Mosaic.

If you are working with NCSA Mosaic version 2.0 beta or later, use the Hotlist Manager to delete a Hotlist.

See Also Deleting a Menu; Hotlist; Hotlist Manager; Menu Editor; Modifying Hotlists; Modifying Menus

Deleting a Hotlist: NCSA Mosaic

In NCSA Mosaic, the Menu Editor lets you delete a Hotlist. Remember: when you delete a Hotlist, you are also deleting the corresponding menu.

1. Choose Menu Editor from the Navigate menu. The Personal Menus dialog box opens. All the menus are shown in the Menus list box on the left.
2. In the Menus list box, click the Hotlist which you want to delete. When you delete a Hotlist, you also delete all the items on that Hotlist.
3. Click Delete.
4. Click Close to close the Personal Menus dialog box.

You cannot delete the NCSA Mosaic Quicklist.

Deleting a Hotlist: Air Mosaic

In Air Mosaic, the Hotlist dialog box is where you delete a Hotlist. When you delete a Hotlist, you are also deleting the corresponding menu.

1. Choose Hotlists from the File menu. The Hotlists dialog box opens.
2. In the list box, click on the menu you want to delete. When you delete a menu, you also delete all the items on that menu.
3. Click Remove. A confirmation dialog box opens.
4. Select Yes.
5. Click Close to close the Hotlists dialog box.

DELETING A MENU

You can delete an entire menu you've created, and all the items on it, in Air or NCSA Mosaic.

If you are working with NCSA Mosaic version 2.0 beta or later, use the Hotlist Manager to delete a menu.

See Also Deleting a Hotlist; Hotlist; Hotlist Manager; Menu Editor; Modifying Menus

Deleting a Menu: NCSA Mosaic

In NCSA Mosaic, the Menu Editor lets you delete a user-configurable menu, which includes the Starting Points menu or any menu you've created. When you delete a menu, you are also deleting the corresponding Hotlist.

1. Choose Menu Editor from the Navigate menu. The Personal Menus dialog box opens. All the menus which can be deleted are shown in the Menus list box to the left.

2. In the Menus list box, click the one which you want to delete. When you delete a menu, you also delete all the items on that menu.

3. Click Delete.

4. Click Close to close the Personal Menus dialog box.

Deleting a Menu: Air Mosaic

In Air Mosaic, the Hotlist dialog box is where you delete a menu. You can delete the SPRY menu or any menu you have created. When you delete a menu, you are also deleting the corresponding Hotlist.

1. Choose Hotlists from the File menu. The Hotlists dialog box opens.

2. In the list box, click on the menu you want to delete. When you delete a menu, you also delete all the items on that menu.

3. Click Remove. A confirmation dialog box opens.

4. Select Yes.

5. Click Close to close the Hotlists dialog box. The menu is no longer displayed.

Removing a Menu from the Menu Bar: Air Mosaic

In Air Mosaic, you can remove a menu you have added to the menu bar without deleting the entire Hotlist.

1. Choose Hotlists from the File menu. The Hotlists dialog box opens.

2. In the list box, click on the menu you want to remove.

3. Click on Put the Hotlist in the menu bar to remove the check (see Figure D.1).

4. Click Close to close the Hotlists dialog box. The menu is no longer displayed.

DELETING ITEMS FROM A HOTLIST

You can remove one or more items you've added to a Hotlist.

Figure D.1
In Air Mosaic, a check box option turns a Hotlist into a menu.

☐ Put this Hotlist in the menu bar

> **If you are working with NCSA Mosaic version 2.0 beta or later, use the Hotlist Manager to delete items from a Hotlist.**

See Also Deleting Items from a Menu; Hotlist; Hotlist Manager; Menu Editor; Modifying Hotlists; Modifying Menus

Deleting Items from a Hotlist: NCSA Mosaic

In NCSA Mosaic, the Menu Editor lets you delete items from a Hotlist. Remember: when you delete an item from a menu, you are also deleting it from its corresponding Hotlist.

1. Choose Menu Editor from the Navigate menu. The Personal Menus dialog box opens. All the menus which can be modified are shown in the Menus list box to the left.
2. In the Menus list box, click the menu from which you want to delete the item. All the items on that menu are shown in the Items list box to the right.
3. Click the Item you'd like to remove.
4. Click Delete.
5. Click Close to close the Personal Menus dialog box.

Deleting Items from a Hotlist: Air Mosaic

In Air Mosaic, the Hotlist dialog box is where you delete items from a Hotlist. When you delete an item from a Hotlist, you are also deleting it from its corresponding menu.

1. Choose Hotlists from the File menu. The Hotlists dialog box opens.
2. In the list box, click on the item you want to delete from the menu.
3. Click Remove. A confirmation dialog box opens.
4. Select Yes.
5. Click Close to close the Hotlists dialog box.

DELETING ITEMS FROM A MENU

You can delete one or more items from a menu in NCSA or Air Mosaic.

> **If you are working with NCSA Mosaic version 2.0 beta or later, use the Hotlist Manager to delete items from a menu.**

See Deleting Items from a Hotlist; Hotlist; Hotlist Manager; Menu Editor; Modifying Menus

Deleting Items from a Menu: NCSA Mosaic

In NCSA Mosaic, the Menu Editor lets you delete items from menus. You can delete an item from any user-configurable menu with these steps:

1. Choose Menu Editor from the Navigate menu. The Personal Menus dialog box opens. All the menus which can be modified are shown in the Menus list box to the left.
2. In the Menus list box, click the menu from which you want to delete the item. All the items on that menu are shown in the Items list box to the right.
3. Click the Item you'd like to remove.
4. Click Delete.
5. Click Close to close the Personal Menus dialog box.

When you delete an item from a menu, you are also deleting it from its corresponding Hotlist.

Deleting Items from a Menu: Air Mosaic

In Air Mosaic, the Hotlists dialog box is where you delete items from a menu.

See **Deleting Items from a Hotlist**

DELETING ITEMS FROM A QUICKLIST: NCSA MOSAIC

In NCSA Mosaic, the Menu Editor lets you delete items from the Quicklist, even though the Quicklist does not appear as a menu.

If you are working with NCSA Mosaic version 2.0 beta or later, use the Hotlist Manager to delete items from a Quicklist.

1. Choose Menu Editor from the Navigate menu. The Personal Menus dialog box opens. All the Hotlists which can be modified are shown in the Menus list box on the left.
2. In the Menus list box, click Quicklist. All the items in the Quicklist are shown in the Items list box on the right.
3. Click the Item you'd like to remove.
4. Click Delete.
5. Click Close to close the Personal Menus dialog box.

See Also **Hotlist Manager; Menu Editor; Quicklist**

DEMO DOCUMENT

Each form of Mosaic has its own way of demonstrating the different categories of documents you can retrieve.

Demo Document: NCSA Mosaic

The NCSA Demo Document, found on the Starting Points menu, is a good place to start browsing the Internet. It offers an interactive hypermedia tour of Mosaic's capabilities. You can also access it with its URL: http://www.ncsa.uiuc.edu/demowed.demo.htl.

Demo Document: Air Mosaic

On the Spry Home Page, click on Spry City (Figure D.2).

> **Tip**
>
> You can also retrieve it by choosing it from the Spry folder in the Hotlist drop-down menu.

Demo Document: Quarterdeck Mosaic

On the Quarterdeck Home Page, click on Internet Navigation System or any document in any folder in the archives.

Figure D.2
Spry City is found on the Spry Home Page in Air Mosaic.

Demo Document: Netscape

On the Welcome to Netscape page, click Internet Directory. Or click the Net Directory button.

Net Directory

Demo Document: Spyglass Mosaic

On the Welcome to Enhanced NCSA from Spyglass page, click on Cyberspace Sampler.

See Also Part 1: Browsing the Internet; Starting Points; Net Directory; URL

DIRECTORY AND FILE LOCATIONS: NETSCAPE

The Directory and File Locations options are found in the Applications and Directories section of the Netscape Preferences dialog box.

See Bookmark File; Supporting Applications; Temporary Directory

DISK CACHE: NETSCAPE

See Document Caching

DISK CACHE DIRECTORY: NETSCAPE

See Document Caching

DISPLAY INLINE IMAGES

You can choose to display all images included in documents or you can turn off the automatic display of graphics. The documents will be retrieved and displayed faster when their included graphics are not displayed. If you choose this option, you can still display individual graphics whenever you want to. A graphic does *not* have to be displayed in order for its link to function properly.

> **This feature is available in Netscape as Auto Load Images and in Air Mosaic as Autoload Inline Images. In Spyglass Mosaic, it is Load Images Automatically.**

See Also Auto Load Images; Load Images Automatically; Preferences

Display Inline Images: NCSA Mosaic

In NCSA Mosaic, choose Preferences from the Options menu, then check or uncheck Display Inline Images to toggle the display of graphics.

To retrieve the document associated with a link, place the mouse over the image's icon and click the *left* mouse button.

To see an image:

1. Place the mouse over the image's icon and click the *right* mouse button. A pop-up menu displays.
2. Click on Load Images. You will see the image after it has been retrieved from its source.

Display Inline Images: Quarterdeck Mosaic

In Quarterdeck Mosaic, choose Preferences from the Tools menu, then click the HTML Viewer tab and check or uncheck Display Inline Images to toggle the display of graphics.

To retrieve the document associated with a link, place the mouse over the image's icon and click the *left* mouse button.

DOCUMENT CACHING

In order for Mosaic to display a document, it first downloads the document from the server. When you move on to the next document, Mosaic keeps the contents of the previous document in memory in case you want to see it again. This process is called *document caching*—holding a document in memory. If a document is in memory, it can be redisplayed much more quickly than if it has to be downloaded again from the server.

Document Caching: NCSA Mosaic

In NCSA Mosaic, Memory Cache and Disk Cache options are available in the Preferences dialog box. To specify cache options:

1. Choose Preferences from the Edit menu. The Preferences dialog box is displayed.
2. Click the Cache tab to bring it forward.
3. In the Memory Cache section, enter the number of documents to be kept in memory in the text box.

> You can only use your system's available memory for document caching, so you may have to use trial and error in order to discover the best number for your work style and computer's resources.

4. Enter the name of the directory to be used for document caching in the Location text box. This is the directory where the temporary disk cache file will be stored.
5. Enter the amount of hard disk space to be allocated to document caching in the Size (KB) text box.
6. Choose OK.

The additional options available on the Cache tab are shown in Table D.1.

Document Caching: Air Mosaic

In Air Mosaic, document caching is controlled in the Configuration dialog box.

1. Choose Configuration from the Options menu. The Configuration dialog box (Figure D.3) is displayed.
2. Enter the number of documents to be cached in the Cached Documents text box.
3. Choose OK.

Document Caching: Netscape

In Netscape, Memory Cache and Document Cache options are available in the Preferences dialog box.

1. Choose Preferences from the Option menu. The Preferences dialog box is displayed.
2. Select Cache and Network from the drop-down list at the top as shown in Figure D.4.

DOCUMENT CACHING 93

Table D.1
Additional Options Available on the Cache Tab

Option	What It Does
Enabled	Toggles the disk cache status (on and off).
Fast Image Caching	Increases the display speed of inline images held in the cache by converting the images to bitmap format.
Never Purge Home Page	Causes your home page to always be kept in the cache.
Clear Cache on Exiting Mosaic	Removes the documents currently in the cache so other applications can access the memory.
Check Modification Date From Server	Confirms that you are viewing the most recent version of a document or image when a document has been held in your cache. If a more recent version is available, that version is retrieved instead of the version held in the disk cache. You can check the server only once per session or each time you choose the document.
Advanced Cache Manager	Lets you view the contents of your cache and manage how each MIME type is cached.

Figure D.3
The Air Mosaic Configuration dialog box lets you change the number of cached documents.

Figure D.4
The Netscape Preferences dialog box

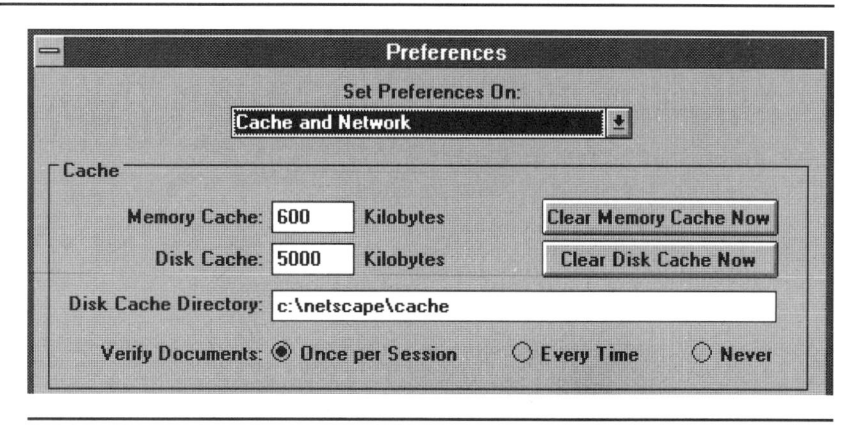

3. Enter the amount of system memory to be allocated to document caching in the Memory Cache text box.

4. Enter the amount of hard disk space to be allocated to document caching in the Disk Cache text box.

5. Enter the name of the directory to be used for document caching in the Disk Cache Directory text box. This is the directory where the temporary disk cache file will be stored.

6. Choose OK.

> You can also choose the Clear Memory Cache Now button or the Clear Disk Cache Now button to remove all documents currently being cached.

Document Caching: Quarterdeck Mosaic

In Quarterdeck Mosaic, document caching is accomplished with options in the Preferences dialog box.

1. Choose Preferences from the Tools menu. The Preferences dialog box is displayed.

2. Click the Network tab to bring it to the front.

3. Check the Cache Enabled check box to turn the disk caching option on.

4. Enter the amount of system memory to be allocated to document caching in the Max Cache Size (in K) text box.

5. Choose OK.

DOCUMENT DISPLAY AREA

See Browser Windows; Document View Window

DOCUMENT INFO: NETSCAPE

With Netscape, you can open a Document Information dialog box that contains some general information about the current document. Choose Document Info from the File menu. The dialog box (see Figure D.5) shows the title, location (URL), date the document was last modified, and security in place for the document.

DOCUMENT SOURCE

If you want to see what a document looks like with its HTML tags, use the Document Source command. When you choose Document Source, a new window opens with the contents of the current document (see Figure D.6). While this window is open, you can save the displayed document or copy selected text from it to the clipboard.

Figure D.5

The Document Information dialog box

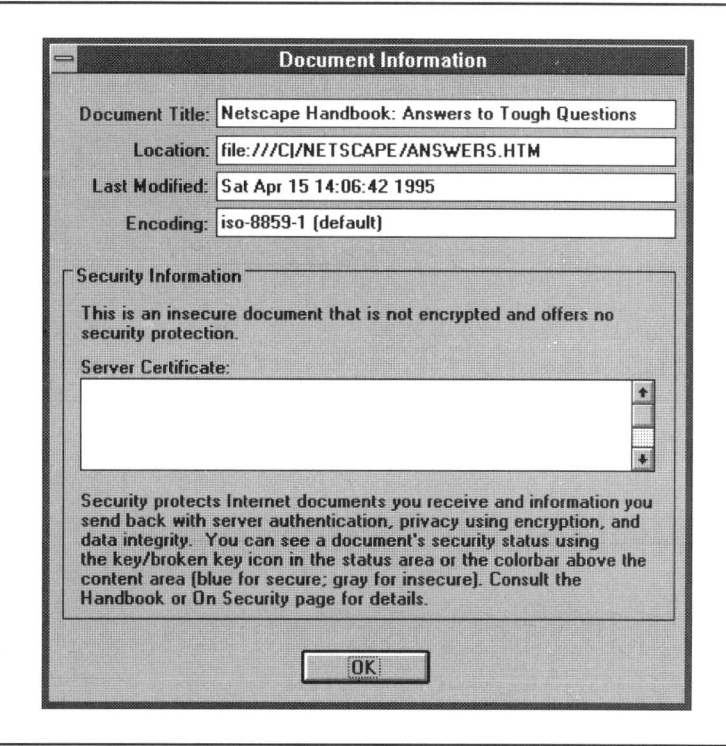

Figure D.6

The Document Source window in NCSA Mosaic

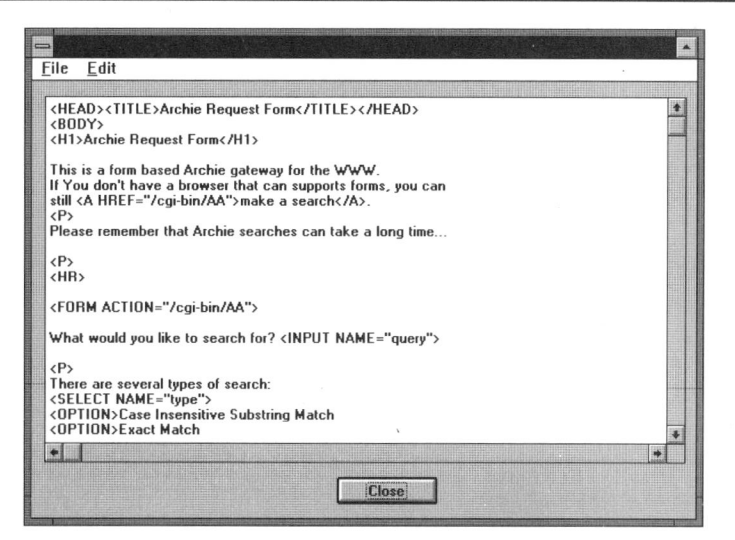

Document Source: Air and NCSA Mosaic

In Air and NCSA Mosaic, choose Document Source from the File menu to open the Document Source window.

Document Source: Quarterdeck Mosaic

In Quarterdeck Mosaic, choose Document Source from the View menu to open the Document Source window.

Document Source: Netscape

In Netscape, choose Source from the View menu to open the View Source window.

Document Source: Spyglass Mosaic

In Spyglass Mosaic, choose View Source from the Edit menu to open the View Source window. You can save a document displayed in this window by choosing the Save button.

DOCUMENT TITLE

The document title is shown in the title bar of the Mosaic window, or in the document window when more than one document is open. It is also frequently included as the first line in a document. The document title is often the text that was used as the link to the document (what you clicked on to get to the document).

Document Title Bar: Air Mosaic

The exception to this is Air Mosaic, which displays the title in a Document Title bar, displayed above the URL bar as shown in Figure D.7.

DOCUMENT VIEW WINDOW

The window which displays the selected document is known as the Document View window.

Figure D.7
The Air Mosaic Document Title bar

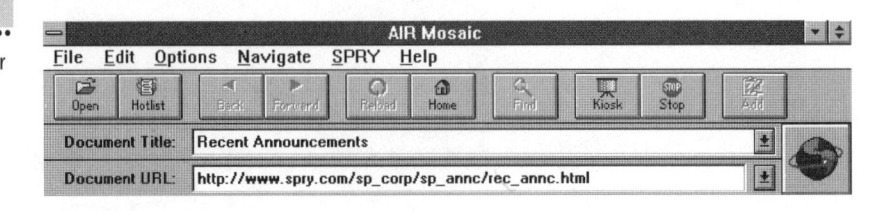

> **In Quarterdeck Mosaic, this window is called the Browser window.**

See Also Browser Window

DOCUMENTS IN DROP DOWN: AIR MOSAIC

In Air Mosaic, you can control how many documents are displayed in the Document Title and Document URL drop down lists. Drop down list entries are controlled in the Configuration dialog box (see Figure D.8).

1. Choose Configuration from the Options menu.
2. Enter the number of documents to be shown in the Documents in Drop Down text box.
3. Choose OK.

See Also Document Title; URL

DOORKEY ICON: NETSCAPE

In Netscape, when a doorkey icon on a blue background is displayed next to the status message, the document is secure.

When a broken doorkey icon on a gray background is displayed next to the status message, the document is not secure.

A blue color bar at the top of the document view window also marks a secure document, while a gray color bar marks an insecure one.

See Also Secure/Insecure Documents; Security

DUPLICATE: QUARTERDECK MOSAIC

In Quarterdeck Mosaic, you can use the Duplicate command on the Window menu to create another window identical to the current window.

Figure D.8
Air Mosaic's Configuration dialog box lets you specify the number of documents to hold in the drop down text box.

Documents in dropdown: 10

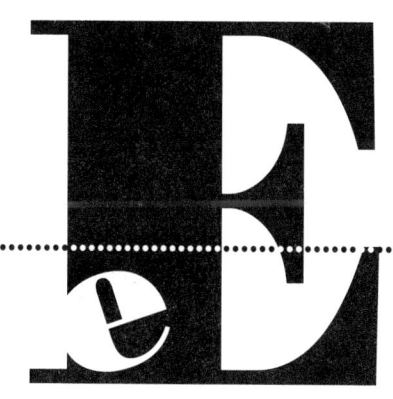

EDIT MENU

The Edit menu contains the items that let you select, cut, copy, paste, and find text within a document. All Web browsers include an Edit menu, each with a slightly different group of commands.

See Also   Annotating; Copy; Cut; Delete; Find; Paste; Preferences; Selecting Text; Undo; View Source

EDIT THIS ANNOTATION: NCSA MOSAIC

See   Annotating Documents

ELECTRONIC MAIL (E-MAIL)

The most popular and well-known feature of the Internet is its electronic mail capability. If you have an Internet address, you can send electronic mail to anyone else who also has one. However, the Web browsers described in this book are *not* electronic mail programs; they were developed for an entirely different purpose.

Quarterdeck Mosaic is the only Web browser we cover in this book which currently includes comprehensive electronic mail functionality. Air Mosaic, NCSA Mosaic, and Netscape each have very limited e-mail capabilities: they let you send, but not receive e-mail.

Electronic Mail: NCSA Mosaic

NCSA Mosaic lets you send e-mail to the NCSA Mosaic development team with its Mail Technical Support command on the Help menu. You can send e-mail to anyone else with the Send E-mail command on the File menu. NCSA Mosaic does not support receiving of electronic messages from other users on the Internet.

See Also E-mail Address; Send E-mail

Electronic Mail: Air Mosaic

Air Mosaic lets you send e-mail to Spry Corporation with its Send Mail to Spry command on the Help menu and send e-mail to others, but does not support the receiving of electronic messages from other users on the Internet.

See Also E-mail Address; Send Mail to Spry; Sending Mail

Electronic Mail: Quarterdeck Mosaic

Quarterdeck Mosaic supports the sending and receiving of electronic messages to other users on the Internet, through its combined Mail and News application, launched by choosing Mail/News from the Tools menu.

See Also Mail/News; Sending Mail

Electronic Mail: Netscape

With Netscape, you can send a document to an e-mail address with its Mail Document command on the File menu, but Netscape does not support the receiving of electronic messages from other users on the Internet.

See Also E-mail Address; Mail Document; Sending Mail

E-MAIL ADDRESS

In Air and NCSA Mosaic, and in Netscape, you can enter your e-mail address and this information will be automatically inserted in messages.

> **In Netscape, your name and e-mail address are entered in the Mail and News section of the Preferences dialog box.**

See Also Electronic Mail; Configuration; Mail; Mail and Proxies; Preferences

E-mail Address: NCSA Mosaic

NCSA Mosaic uses your e-mail address when you send messages to developers with the Mail Technical Support and Send E-mail commands. To enter your e-mail address in NCSA Mosaic:

1. Choose Preferences from the Options menu.
2. Click the Services tab to bring it forward.

3. Click in the E-mail Address text box and type your username and address. For example, `merrin@callamer.com`.

4. Choose OK.

E-mail Address: Air Mosaic

Air Mosaic uses your e-mail address when you send messages. To enter your e-mail address in Air Mosaic:

1. Choose Configuration from the Options menu.

2. Click in the E-mail Address text box and type your username and address. For example, `merrin@callamer.com`.

3. Choose OK.

ERROR MESSAGES

Web browsers display error messages when a document cannot be retrieved, a server cannot be reached, or a connection cannot be made. Sometimes you can resolve the problem, other times you can't. The most common messages you'll see are:

HTTP: File/Directory Does Not Exist You are trying to load a document that doesn't exist, or you've accidentally mistyped the URL. Check to make sure you've typed the URL—including the capitalization—in the text box correctly.

Failed DNS Lookup You are either trying to load from a site that doesn't exist (although it may have existed at one time) or the server from which you are trying to retrieve the document is so busy, you can't get a valid response. Try again to access that site at non-peak hours.

SOCKET: Connection has been refused, Host is down, Net has been reset and other similar messages indicate a temporary problem with your Internet connection. Reset your connection and try again. If this doesn't help, try again later.

See Also **Bug List; URLs**

EXIT

You can exit each program with either of these two standard Windows techniques:

○ Choose Exit from the File menu.

○ Double-click the Control box in the upper left corner.

> **·············· Tip ··············**
>
> After you exit, remember to close your connection if you are connected to the Internet via a **SLIP** or **PPP** account over a modem. Usually, you would choose the **Disconnect** command or the **Hangup** command.

See Also **Close**

EXPORTING A HOTLIST

When using Air or Spyglass Mosaic, you have the ability to export Hotlists you've created. Exporting a Hotlist creates an HTML document with a list of URLs that can be used by another person who is using any Web browser.

> **With NCSA Mosaic, you can create a list of the URLs in a Hotlist by copying them from the mosaic.ini file. Like all other .ini files, mosaic.ini is a text file and can be edited with any word processor or text editor. Just open C:\WINDOWS\MOSAIC.INI and, starting at the third or fourth line, you will see a list of URLs you can copy and paste to other locations.**

See Also Creating Lists of URLs; Home Page; Hotlist; Hotlist Manager; Mosaic.ini File

Exporting a Hotlist: Air Mosaic

When you export a Hotlist in Air Mosaic, an HTML file is created with the URLs for the pages in that Hotlist. To export a Hotlist:

1. Choose Hotlists from the File menu. The Hotlists dialog box opens.
2. In the list box, click the menu which you want to export.
3. Click Export. The Export Hotlist to HTML File dialog box opens, as shown in Figure E.1.
4. Type the name of the file in the File Name text box.
5. Click OK to close the Export Hotlist to HTML File dialog box.

Figure E.1
Air Mosaic's Export Hotlist to HTML dialog box

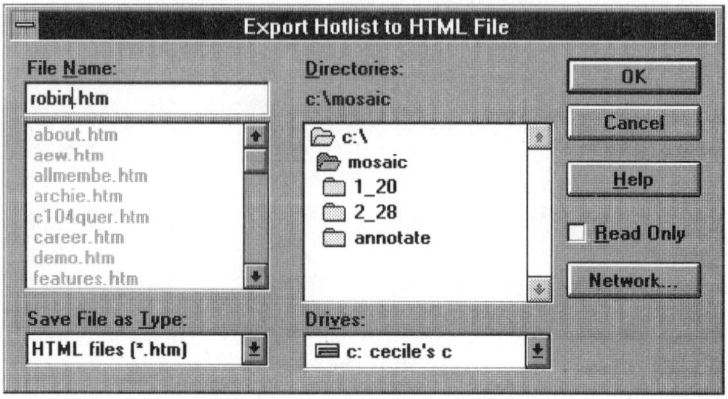

6. Click Close to close the Hotlists dialog box.

You can now display this page with the Open Local File command, or share it with others.

See Also **Hotlist; Open Local File**

Exporting a Hotlist: Spyglass Mosaic

When you export the Hotlist in Spyglass Mosaic, an HTML file is created with the URLs for the pages in that Hotlist, and the page is given the title "Hotlist Page." To create an HTML document from your Hotlist:

1. Choose Hotlist from the Navigate menu. The Hotlist dialog box opens.

2. Click Export. The Export Hotlist dialog box opens.

3. Type the name of the file in the File Name text box.

4. Click OK to close the Export Hotlist File dialog box. The file is saved on your local hard disk.

5. Click Close to close the Hotlist dialog box.

The page you just created is displayed and will look similar to the page in Figure E.2. You can give this file to others, who can display it with the Open Local command.

See Also **Hotlist; Open Local**

Figure E.2

The Hotlist Page created in Spyglass Mosaic

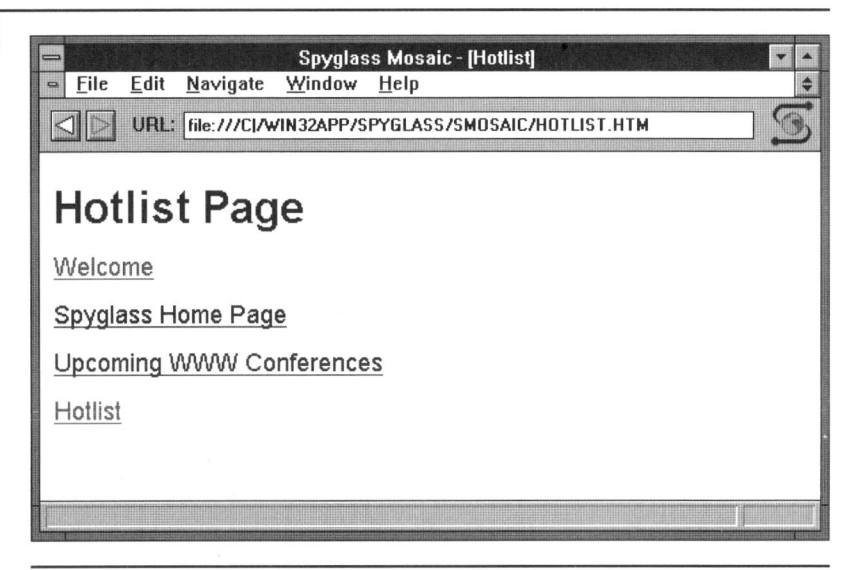

EXTENDED NEWS LISTING: AIR MOSAIC

When Air Mosaic displays a list of newsgroups, it also displays descriptions of each newsgroup if the Extended News Listing option is checked. This option also causes related articles to be grouped together. To change the status of this option:

- Choose Extended News Listing from the Options menu.

See Also   News

EXTENSIONS

The Extensions text box is included in Air Mosaic, Quarterdeck Mosaic and Netscape so you can change the file extensions associated with specific file types. You can add, modify and delete extensions.

Extensions: Air Mosaic

In Air Mosaic, the Extensions text box is found in the External Viewers Configuration dialog box, as shown in Figure E.3, which opens when you choose Viewers in the Configuration dialog box. Use the text box to change or add an extension to the MIME type selected in the Type box.

See Also   Configuration; MIME; MIME Types; Viewers

Extensions: Quarterdeck Mosaic

In Quarterdeck Mosaic, the Extensions option lets you associate file types with multimedia applications. File types are referenced by their extensions; the text box to

Figure E.3

Air Mosaic's External Viewer Configuration dialog box lets you change and add extensions.

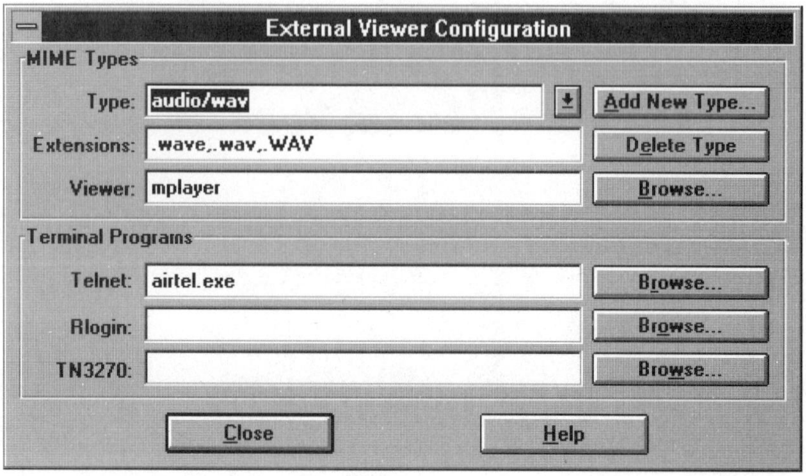

the right of the extension shows the file type.

To add an extension to a MIME type, or to modify an existing extension:

1. Choose Preferences from the Tools menu.
2. Click on the Data Engine tab to bring it forward.
3. Select the file type in the list box.
4. Edit an existing extension or type the extension to add and choose OK.

See Also MIME; MIME Type; Preferences; Viewers

Extensions: Netscape

In Netscape, the Extensions text box is found in the Helper Applications section of the Preferences dialog box. Use the text box to change or add an extension to the MIME type selected in the list box above.

See Also Helper Applications; MIME; MIME Type; Preferences

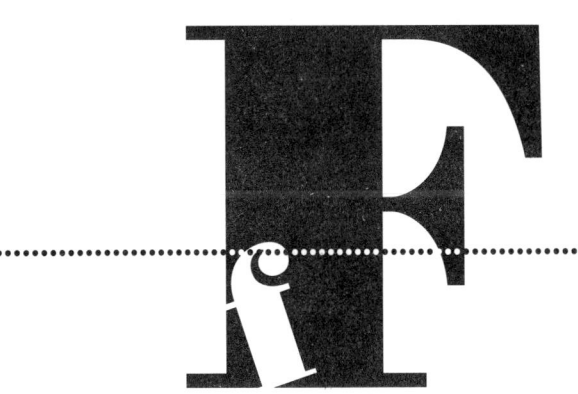

FAQ PAGE, FREQUENTLY ASKED QUESTIONS: NCSA MOSAIC, NETSCAPE

In NCSA Mosaic and Netscape you can retrieve a document that lists the most commonly asked questions along with the answers to these questions. This document is usually called an *FAQ* or Frequently Asked Questions page.

FAQ Page: NCSA Mosaic

In NCSA Mosaic, commonly asked questions and their answers can be displayed by choosing FAQ Page from the Help menu. The page titled NCSA for Windows Frequently Asked Questions displays, with links to additional related pages. The FAQ List link displays the most common questions. The URL for the FAQ page is http://www.ncsa.uiuc.edu/SDG/Software/WinMosaic/FAQ.html.

Frequently Asked Questions: Netscape

In Netscape, commonly asked questions and their answers can be displayed by choosing Frequently Asked Questions from the Help menu.

A Netscape-specific Frequently Asked Questions page displays, with links to additional related pages. The URL for the FAQ page is http://home.netscape.com/home/faq.html.

FEATURE PAGE: NCSA MOSAIC

As each version of NCSA Mosaic is released, information about the changes included in the new version can be displayed by choosing Feature Page from the Help menu. This page, which displays Mosaic's Features, Enhancements and Bug Fix List, can help you determine whether you want to download the newest version. Or, if you have recently downloaded the newest version, the Features page can help you understand the changes made since the last release. The URL for the Features page is `http://www.ncsa.uiuc.edu/SDG/Software/WinMosaic/Features.html`.

FILE MENU

The File menu contains the standard Windows items which let you open, save and print a document, and exit the application. All Web browsers include a File menu, each with a slightly different group of commands. For example, the commands to close document windows, look at a document's source or information, and manage Hotlists may also be found on this menu.

See Also Close, Close All; Document Info; Document Source; Exit; Hotlists; Mail Document; New Window; Open; Open File; Open Location; Open URL; Page Setup; Print; Print Margins; Print Preview; Print Setup; Reload; Save, Save As

FIND

In all the Web browsers covered in this book, you can search for a text string (characters, a word or a phrase) in the current document with the Find command.

See Also Searching Indexes

Find: NCSA and Quarterdeck Mosaic

To find a text string in NCSA and Quarterdeck Mosaic:

1. Open the document you want to search through. You can only search through one document at a time.
2. Choose Find from the Edit menu. The Find dialog box (see Figure F.1) opens.
3. Enter the letters, word or phrase you want to find.
4. If you want to search only for a text string in the identical case you entered, check the Match Case check box. If

Figure F.1
The NCSA Mosaic Find dialog box lets you search for a text string in a document.

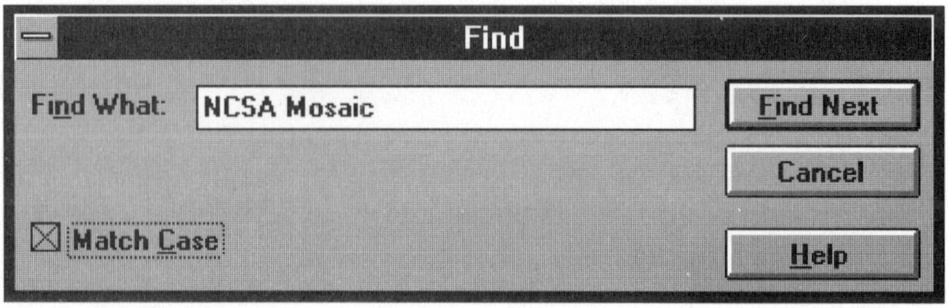

you don't want to perform a case-sensitive search, make sure this box is *not* checked.

5. Click on Find Next to find the first occurrence of the text string.

6. Continue clicking on Find Next to locate each occurrence of the text you are searching for.

7. When you are finished, click on Cancel to close the dialog box.

In Quarterdeck Mosaic, you can choose Find Again from the Edit menu to search for the text after the dialog box is closed.

Find: Netscape

To find a text string in Netscape:

1. Open the document you want to search through. Netscape can only search through one document at a time.

2. Choose Find from the Edit menu. The Find dialog box opens.

3. Enter the letters, word or phrase you want to find.

4. If you want to search only for a text string in the identical case you entered, check the Match Case check box. If you don't want to perform a case-sensitive search, make sure this box is *not* checked.

5. Netscape searches down through the document from the current cursor position. If you're at the bottom of the document and want to search up instead, click on the Up option under Direction.

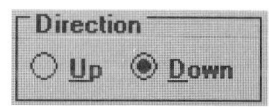

6. Click on Find Next to find the first occurrence of the text string. If the text is found, it is highlighted in the document. If not, the message "Search String Not Found" is displayed.

7. Continue clicking on Find Next to move the cursor to each occurrence of the text you are searching for.

8. When you are finished, click on Cancel to close the dialog box.

Find: Air Mosaic

To find a text string in Air Mosaic:

1. Open the document you want to search through. Air Mosaic can only search through one document at a time.

2. Click the Find button in the toolbar.

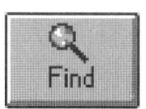

The Find dialog box opens.

3. Enter the letters, word, or phrase you want to search for.

4. If you're searching for a text string only in the identical case you entered, check the Match Case check box. If you don't want to perform a case-sensitive search, make sure this box is *not* checked.

5. Click on Find Next to find the first occurrence of the text string. If the text is found, the document is scrolled down so the text is at the top of the window.

6. Continue clicking on Find Next to locate each occurrence of the text.

7. When you are finished, click on Cancel to close the dialog box.

Find: Spyglass Mosaic

To find a text string in Spyglass Mosaic:

1. Open the document you want to search through. Air Mosaic can only search through one document at a time.

2. Choose Find from the Edit menu or click the Find button in the toolbar.

The Find dialog box opens.

3. Enter the letters, word, or phrase you want to search for.

4. If you want to search for a text string only in the identical case you entered, check the Match Case check box. If you don't want to perform a case-sensitive search, make sure this box is *not* checked.

5. Click on Find Next to find the first occurrence of the text string. If the text is found, the document is scrolled down and the text is highlighted.

6. To locate the next occurrence of the text you are searching for, choose Find Again from the Edit menu or click on Find Again in the toolbar.

7. Continue clicking on Find Again in the toolbar to locate each occurrence of the text.

FINGER

Finger is an Internet command that lets you look for a user at a particular site. The search yields information about the user, which may include:

- The user's real name
- The user's location and phone number
- The last time the user used his or her account
- Whether he or she has any unread mail
- Additional information the user may have made available.

Typically, you'd use Finger to find someone's e-mail address if you thought they were at a particular site. For example, you'd enter what you thought was his or her username and see if the resulting information confirmed that you had located the right person.

> **Tip**
> NCSA Mosaic offers a Finger Gateway command on the Starting Points menu to help you use Finger.

See Also Finger Gateway

FINGER GATEWAY: NCSA MOSAIC

NCSA Mosaic includes a Finger Gateway item on its Starting Points menu, which enables you to use the Finger command on the Web. The item opens the page titled The WWW to Finger Gateway (shown in Figure F.2); the URL for this page is `http://cs.indiana.edu/finger/gateway`. This page tells you more about Finger and how to use it on the Web.

> **Tip**
> If you are using another Web browser, you can use the Open or Open URL command to retrieve this page.

Figure F.2
The WWW to Finger Gateway

```
NCSA Mosaic - WWW-Finger Gateway with Faces
File  Edit  Options  Navigate  Annotate  Starting Points  toms list  Help

http://www.cs.indiana.edu/finger/gateway
```

The WWW to Finger Gateway

with support for [face icon] faces

To try the gateway, simply enter as a keyword an address of the form user@hostname. The gateway can also be used non-interactively by anchoring to a URL of the form:

`http://www.cs.indiana.edu/finger/hostname/username/w`

The last two components are optional; the /w provides more verbose output as per RFC 1288, but exactly what

Search Index: merrin@callamer.com

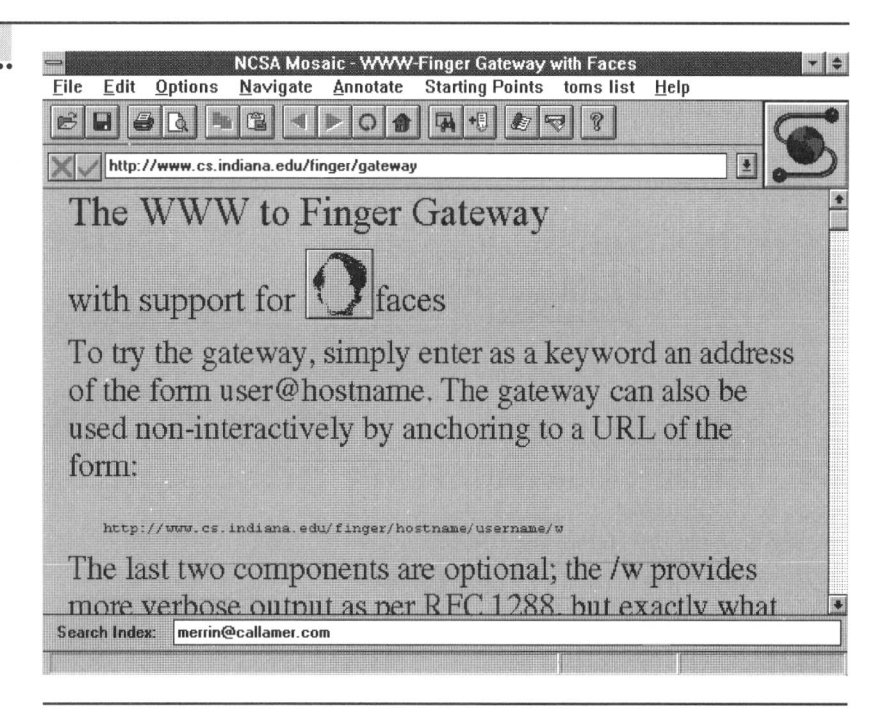

112 FIREWALL

> 🛣️ This Finger Gateway page is used quite a bit and is tough to get through to. You'll probably have to try these steps more than once before you succeed.

To locate a user at a particular site, follow these steps:

1. Choose Finger Gateway from the Starting Points menu to open the Finger Gateway page.
2. In the Search Index at the bottom of the page, type the username and host of the person you are trying to locate; for example, merrin@callamer.com. If the username exists at that location, you'll see whatever personal information is available.

See Also Finger; Open; Open URL

FIREWALL

If you are accessing the Internet from a computer network at work or at school, your network administrator may have set up a *firewall* for security purposes. Firewall is the term used to describe the software running on another computer which is used to regulate incoming and outgoing network traffic by intercepting network requests before processing them.

See Also Proxy

FOLDERS: QUARTERDECK MOSAIC

In Quarterdeck Mosaic, folders serve to organize your Hotlists. You use folders to save groups of URLs so you can locate and open certain documents easily whenever you need them.

📁 Business and Finance

These folders are organized into a Hotlist tab, the contents of which are displayed in the Archives window, shown in Figure F.3.

You can open a window for each folder in the Hotlist tab by clicking on the folder name or icon.

You can also change the way the contents are displayed, by using the "As" commands on the View menu.

> 🚗 **Tip**
> Folders are easily managed with the Properties command and the pop up menus.

See Also Add Current to Hotlist; Archives; As Icons, Icon List, Text List or Tree; Hotlists; Pop up Menus; Properties

Figure F.3

The Archives in Quarterdeck Mosaic

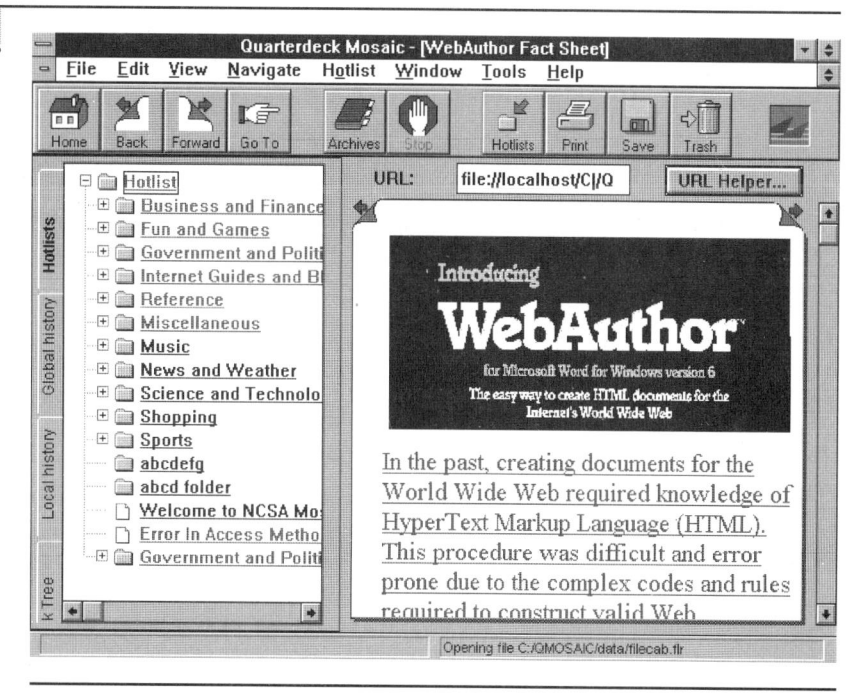

Add a Document to Folder: Quarterdeck Mosaic

Quarterdeck Mosaic lets you drag and drop documents to add them to a folder.

1. Click on the Archives icon in the toolbar then click the Hotlists tab.
2. Place the mouse cursor within the gray border of a document in the browser window.
3. Drag the document to the Hotlists tab and release the mouse button to drop the document. You'll see the document icon (which looks like a document with a corner turned down) as you drag.

Adding a URL to a Folder: Quarterdeck Mosaic

Quarterdeck Mosaic also lets you add a document referenced within the current document to a folder, even though the referenced document is not displayed. When you see a hypertext link to a document you want to add to a folder:

1. Click on the Archives icon in the toolbar then click the Hotlists tab.
2. Click the right mouse button on the hypertext link then choose Hypertext Link.
3. Click on Save to Hotlist, and the URL will be added to the folder.

Adding from the History to a Folder: Quarterdeck Mosaic

Quarterdeck Mosaic also lets you add a document that's in your history list to a folder, even though the document is no longer displayed in the browser window.

1. Click on the Archives icon in the toolbar so the Archives are visible.
2. Click on a folder in the Hotlists tab to open the folder window.
3. Click the Local or Global History tab.
4. Place the mouse cursor on the document icon to the left of the document title in the history list.
5. Drag the document to an empty area in the folder window and release the mouse button to drop the document. You'll see the document icon as you drag.

Creating New Folders: Quarterdeck Mosaic

You can create a new folder in an existing folder in order to organize URLs in folders within folders. To create a new folder in the file cabinet or a folder:

1. Right-click in a blank area of the folder window. The pop up menu opens.
2. Select Current Document ➤ New ➤ Folder from the cascading menus.

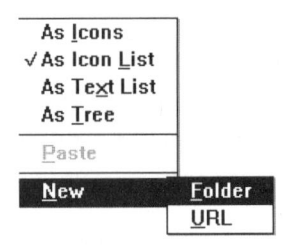

```
As Icons
√ As Icon List
As Text List
As Tree

Paste

New          Folder
             URL
```

The folder is added to the bottom (or end, depending on your current view) of the list and is named Folder. If you create a second new folder, it will be named Folder: 1, the next will be named Folder: 2, and so forth. You can give the folder a more useful name by simply renaming it.

Deleting Folders: Quarterdeck Mosaic

You can delete a folder which was included when you installed Quarterdeck Mosaic or a folder you created. When you delete a folder, all the folders and URLs within it are also deleted. To delete a folder:

1. Right-click on a folder name. The pop up menu opens.
2. Select Folder Object ➤ Delete from the cascading menu.
3. Choose Yes when you see the prompt.

The folder is removed from the file cabinet.

Renaming Folders: Quarterdeck Mosaic

You can rename folders you create, as well as folders that were included when you installed Quarterdeck Mosaic. To rename a folder:

1. Press Alt and click on the folder's name. The folder name becomes an editable text field, with the cursor after the last letter.

📁 | Music |

2. Edit the name by using Delete or Backspace to delete the existing folder name, and typing in the new name.
3. Press f when you are finished.

FOLLOWED LINKS EXPIRE: NETSCAPE

In Netscape, when you click on a link to retrieve a document, the appearance of that link changes. These *followed links* change in color from links you have not yet clicked on (unfollowed links).

This reminds you that you've already used the link to look at the referenced document. Followed links do not have to stay changed forever; you can specify how long you want links to stay changed in the Preferences dialog box.

To change the default setting for followed links:

1. Choose Preferences from the Options menu.
2. Choose Styles from the drop-down list to open the Styles section.
3. Choose one of three options:

   Never Expire   Followed links maintain a changed appearance until you select another option.

   Expire After *n* Days   Followed links are reset after the number of days you specify in the text box.

   Expire Now   Followed links are reset immediately.

4. Click OK to close the Preferences dialog box.

See Also   **Link Color; Preferences**

FONT STYLES: QUARTERDECK MOSAIC

In Quarterdeck Mosaic, the Font Styles determine how each HTML tag in a document looks on the screen. Each style or tag has a name; for example, Heading 1, Heading 2, and List. The Font Style option lets you change the font attributes for each style within each font scheme. If you wish, you can change the typeface, style and size associated with each HTML tag within a scheme.

1. Choose Preferences from the Tools menu to open the Preferences dialog box.
2. Click on the Fonts tab to display the available options.
3. Select any style in the Font Styles list box.
4. Click the Change Style Font button.
5. In the Choose Font dialog box, as shown in Figure F.4, select a Font, Font Style and Size from those displayed in the respective list boxes. Check either of the effects you want to apply, and select another color from the Color drop-down list.
6. Click OK to confirm your selections.
7. Repeat Steps 3 through 6 as many times as you like for each style in the document, then choose OK to close the Preferences dialog box.

Quarterdeck Mosaic redisplays the current document and the changes you made are applied immediately.

See Also **Fonts; Fonts: Scheme; HTML Tags**

Figure F.4
Use the Font dialog box in Quarterdeck Mosaic to change the fonts and font attributes used for displaying documents.

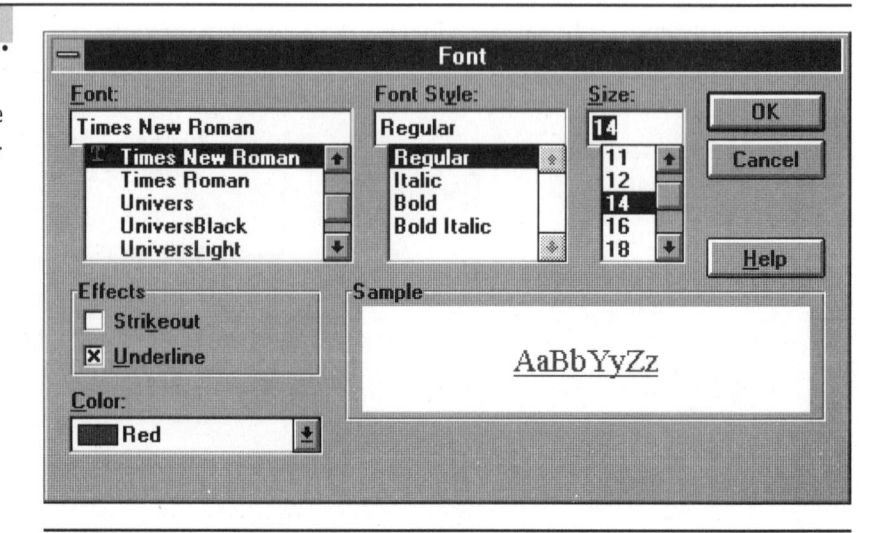

FONTS

You can change the font that each browser uses when documents are displayed, so you can read them more easily. If you wish, you can change the typeface and size associated with each HTML tag. In Air Mosaic, fonts are changed with the Fonts button in the Configuration dialog box. In NCSA Mosaic and Quarterdeck Mosaic, fonts are changed from the Preferences dialog box.

> **Netscape has two Choose Font buttons in the Fonts and colors section of the Preferences dialog box that let you modify the font. NCSA Mosaic includes a Fonts tab in the Preferences dialog box. Spyglass Mosaic uses Style Sheets to change the fonts.**

See Also Change Fixed Font; Change Proportional Font; Choose Font; Configuration; Font Styles; Fonts: Scheme; HTML Tags; Preferences; Styles; Style Sheet

Fonts: Air Mosaic

Air Mosaic's font options are accessed with the Fonts button in the Configuration dialog box. To customize the fonts used for one or more HTML tags:

1. Choose Configuration from the Options menu to open the Configuration dialog box.
2. Click on the Fonts button to open the Fonts dialog box.
3. Select any style in the Style drop-down list.
4. Click on the Change Font button.
5. In the Font dialog box select a Font, Font Style and Size from those displayed in the respective list boxes.
6. Click OK to confirm your selections and to close the Font dialog box.
7. Repeat steps 3 through 6 as many times as you like for each style in the document, then choose OK to close the Fonts dialog box.
8. Choose OK to close the Configuration dialog box.

Air Mosaic redisplays the current document and the changes you made are applied immediately.

> **Tip**
>
> You can use the Enlarge All or Reduce All buttons in the Fonts dialog box to quickly modify the size of all fonts used when displaying HTML documents, if you don't want to customize the fonts.

Fonts: NCSA Mosaic

In NCSA Mosaic version 2.0 beta and later, default fonts are modified with the Fonts tab in the Preferences dialog box.

> **In version 1.0 or 2.0 alpha of NCSA Mosaic, fonts are changed with the Choose Font command.**

See Also   Choose Fonts; Preferences

Fonts: Quarterdeck Mosaic

Quarterdeck Mosaic's fonts options are controlled with the options on the Fonts tab in the Preferences dialog box. These options fall into two categories, Scheme and Style.

See Also   Fonts: Scheme; Font Styles

FONTS: SCHEME: QUARTERDECK MOSAIC

A Font Scheme is similar to a style sheet in a word processing program in that it is a collection of styles that are applied to an HTML document as a whole. Quarterdeck Mosaic supplies a default Scheme which is used initially when displaying a document. You can:

- Create a new Scheme and modify the styles within it.
- Select a different Scheme to apply to the current and future documents you retrieve.
- Delete any scheme but the default scheme.

See Also   Fonts; Font Styles

Creating a Font Scheme

Once you create a new font Scheme, you can use it to customize the way HTML documents are displayed, while saving the default scheme to be used again whenever you want. To create a new Scheme:

1. Choose Preferences from the Tools menu to open the Preferences dialog box.
2. Click on the Fonts tab to display the available options.

3. Click on the Add New Scheme button below the Scheme text box. The Add a New Font Scheme dialog box opens.

4. Type a name for the Scheme in the text box.

5. Choose OK to close the dialog box. The new Scheme name you entered is shown in the drop-down list. You can now change the Styles in that Scheme with the Fonts button below.

6. When you are finished remember to choose OK to close the Preferences dialog box.

Choosing a Different Scheme

You can quickly change the appearance of a document by choosing a different Scheme to apply to it. To apply a different Scheme to documents Quarterdeck Mosaic displays in the browser window:

1. Choose Preferences from the Tools menu to open the Preferences dialog box.

2. Click on the Fonts tab to display the available options.

3. Select any scheme in the Scheme drop-down list.

4. Choose OK to close the Preferences dialog box.

The new scheme is applied to the HTML document in the current browser window, and to all new documents you display.

Removing a Font Scheme

At times you'll want to remove one or more Schemes from the list of those you've created, especially if you make a mistake and want to start over, or find you've created too many and just don't use them all.

To remove a Scheme from the drop-down list:

1. Choose Preferences from the Tools menu to open the Preferences dialog box.

2. Click on the Fonts tab to display the available options.

3. Select any scheme in the Scheme drop-down list.

4. Click on the Delete Scheme button and select Yes to confirm.

5. Choose OK to close the Preferences dialog box.

FORMS

The Web supports the use of online forms, which look very similar to paper-based forms. Forms are simply HTML documents which let you enter information within text boxes and send them to the recipient immediately. The form shown in Figure F.5 lets you register for a service by filling in an application form online.

You'll often see forms if you:

○ Use a search service such as Archie or Veronica. You'll fill out a form which guides the search for a file.

Figure F.5

An online fill-in form lets you immediately submit a request or application.

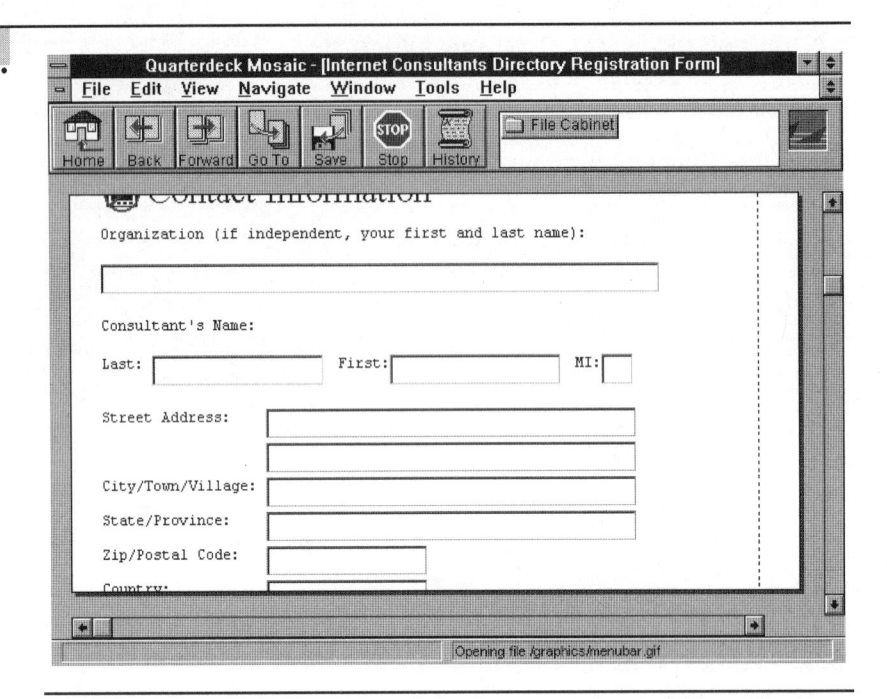

- Download a beta version of a Web browser. You'll be asked to provide feedback on a form supplied by the manufacturer.
- Shop online. You can order products from online catalogs by filling in a form.
- Register yourself or your company for a service or to be included in a database.

To use a form, you simply have to click in each field to place the cursor and type the necessary text. You can click on the buttons and check boxes within the form to select them, as you do in a window or dialog box. When you complete the form, submit it by choosing the Send, Submit (or similar) button.

Forms are created using a specific HTML tag, but as with all HTML documents, you do not need to understand how forms are created in order to use them.

See Also **HTML Tags**

FORWARD

The Forward command lets you display documents you've previously displayed during the current session. It is available as soon as you display more than one document and then display a previous document. You can choose Forward to look through all the documents you've viewed in order, after you have used the Back command or button. A Forward button is included on the toolbar in all forms except in Spyglass Mosaic, where it is displayed in the URL bar.

Tip

Use Back to view the documents in reverse order; use Home to start at the beginning; click Forward to see them all in order again.

See Also Back; Go; History; Home; Home Page

Forward: Air Mosaic, NCSA Mosaic, Spyglass Mosaic

In Air, NCSA, and Spyglass Mosaic, Forward is found on the Navigate menu.

Here's what they look like:

Air Mosaic

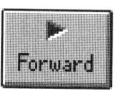

NCSA Mosaic

Spyglass Mosaic

Forward: Netscape

In Netscape, Forward is found on the Go menu and toolbar.

Forward: Quarterdeck Mosaic

In Quarterdeck Mosaic, choose Go Forward from the Navigate menu or the toolbar.

FTP

FTP is a file transfer program which lets you download files (which are not Web documents) from FTP servers on the Internet. FTP servers do not have the graphic capabilities that Web servers have, or provide the capability to jump between documents.

Chameleon Sampler includes an FTP program for downloading files, and the Web browsers also let you download files with FTP, without learning additional FTP commands.

> If you downloaded NCSA Mosaic with the steps in Part 1, you used NetManage's FTP program.

········· **Tip** ·········

You can search for a file that resides somewhere on an **FTP** server by using Archie. Archie lets you search for files when you do not know their location, but do know the filename or part of the filename.

See Also Part 1: Downloading NCSA Mosaic with Windows FTP; Archie; FTP Sites

Downloading Files with FTP

You can download files with FTP by connecting to the FTP site in much the same way as you retrieve a document. Use the Open or Open URL command and enter the URL for the FTP site. You'll see a page with directory and filenames, represented by folders and documents. You can click on each folder to see its contents, which are in turn displayed as folder and document icons. When you see the name of the file you want to download, click on it to begin copying the file to your hard disk.

See Also Open; Open URL

FTP PROXY: NETSCAPE

See Proxy

FTP SITES: NCSA MOSAIC

NCSA Mosaic includes a menu item to help you work your way through the maze of FTP servers, in order to reach the server which has the file you want to download. If you know the name of the file, you'll be able to find it and load it by clicking on it, as you do to retrieve Web documents.

FTP SITES: NCSA MOSAIC   123

> **Tip**
>
> Starting with the **FTP Sites** item is not an efficient method for retrieving files; it is much more efficient to use the **Open URL** command and enter the server location directly in the text box. However, if you don't know the server location, this technique will help you locate it.

To see how this works, use this menu item to access an FTP server and download a document from a college or university, or from a government site in your state.

1. Choose Other Documents from the Starting Points menu, then drag your cursor down to the item FTP Sites on the cascading menu. The FTP Interface document, shown in Figure F.6, is displayed.

> **Tip**
>
> You can open this document with another Web browser by using its URL: `http://hoohoo.ncsa.uiuc.edu:80/ftp-interface.html`

Figure F.6

The FTP Interface page displays when you choose FTP Sites in NCSA Mosaic.

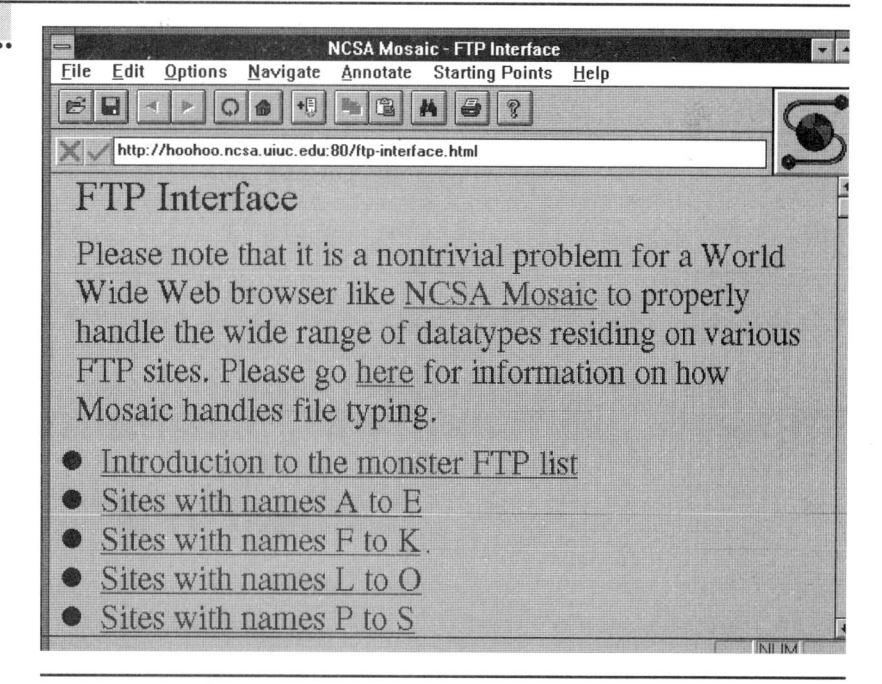

```
NCSA Mosaic - FTP Interface
File  Edit  Options  Navigate  Annotate  Starting Points  Help

http://hoohoo.ncsa.uiuc.edu:80/ftp-interface.html

FTP Interface

Please note that it is a nontrivial problem for a World
Wide Web browser like NCSA Mosaic to properly
handle the wide range of datatypes residing on various
FTP sites. Please go here for information on how
Mosaic handles file typing.

 • Introduction to the monster FTP list
 • Sites with names A to E
 • Sites with names F to K
 • Sites with names L to O
 • Sites with names P to S
```

2. You may want to click on the link *Introduction to the monster FTP* list before you proceed. Read the information, then click on the Back button.

3. Click on the *Sites with Names* that represent the location you want to go to. You'll see the names of the FTP servers you can access. These will include the colleges, universities and other institutions from which you can download certain documents.

4. Click on the name of the college you want to access. You'll see a menu of the available documents; usually this first menu includes folders and documents.

5. Continue selecting folders by clicking on the link, until you display the documents available on the server, then click on the first document which interests you.

6. When you are finished downloading the document, use the Back button to display the previous page, then choose another document if you wish.

See Also   FTP

G

GATEWAY

A gateway is a computer which enables other computers on the Internet to communicate with each other. There are many different types of computers, operating systems and applications on the Internet which must translate the information in order to share it. A gateway connects two computer networks which are not the same and lets them send and receive information. Gateways are also used to connect two applications. For example, an application which lets you send and receive Internet mail may be used at your office along with an application which lets you send and receive local e-mail. A gateway converts the information between the two so you can use your local e-mail application to send and receive mail on the Internet.

GENERAL: NCSA MOSAIC

The General tab in the NCSA Mosaic Preferences dialog box lets you specify many display items as well as your home page. Table G.1 lists the options that are available.

See Also Autoload Home Page; Home Page; Initial Window Placement; Inline Images; Preferences; Toolbars at Startup; Use Internal Sound

GENERAL: QUARTERDECK MOSAIC

The General tab in the Quarterdeck Mosaic Preferences dialog box lets you specify the URL for the home page, whether to load the home page at startup, and how to show the toolbar.

Table G.1

Options Available in the General tab of the NCSA Mosaic Preferences Dialog Box

Option	Description
Toolbars at Startup	**Show Toolbar** toggles the display of the toolbar when you start NCSA Mosaic.
	Show Location Bar toggles the display of the location (URL) bar.
	Show Status Bar toggles the display of the status bar.
Inline Images	**Display Inline Images** toggles the loading and display of inline images when you retrieve a document.
	3D Borders optionally displays the images with a three-dimensional border.
Miscellaneous	**3D Rules** toggles two styles of horizontal line drawing in a document; 3D Rules slows performance but gives horizontal lines a three-dimensional appearance.
	Round List Bullets toggles round and plain dash bullets in a document; round bullets slow performance.
	Use Internal 8-bit Sound uses your NCSA Mosaic's built-in sound driver to play audio files.
Background Color	Opens the Color dialog box where you can select another color for the document window background.
Home Page	**Autoload** lets you specify whether a home page is automatically loaded each time you start NCSA Mosaic. The Home Page text box below is where you enter the URL of the home page you want to load when this option is turned on.
Initial Window Placement	Lets you specify the starting size and position for the application window.
Display	**Display Text While Loading** lets you display text either while a document is being retrieved or after the entire document has been retrieved.
	Display Images While Loading lets you display images after each image is retrieved or after all the images in a document have been retrieved.
	Disable Display While Loading causes NCSA Mosaic to display the document one section at a time so you can begin reading it or download the entire document first and then display it.

See Also Home Page; Initial; Load Home Page; Toolbar Icon Settings

GIF IMAGES

GIF images are graphics files, specifically Graphic Interchange Format (GIF) files in a format developed by CompuServe. GIF files are internally compressed files which take up less disk space than most other graphic file formats and so they are commonly distributed on the Internet. They can be recognized by the extension .GIF.

See Also GIF Viewer; Images; JPEG Images; XBM Images

GIF VIEWER: QUARTERDECK MOSAIC

The GIF Viewer tab in Quarterdeck Mosaic's Preferences dialog box is where you can specify the Interlace method used when a GIF file is displayed.

See Also GIF Images; Interlace Method; Preferences

GLOBAL HISTORY: QUARTERDECK MOSAIC

All browsers keep track of the pages you display during a session; this is called the history. Quarterdeck Mosaic has a more sophisticated history feature than other Web browsers, in that it can maintain a history list for any period of time, not just for the current session. This ongoing history list is called the Global history. The time limits for this list are modified on the Global History tab in the Preferences dialog box.

> **Tip**
> The History for an individual browser window is called the Local History.

> NCSA also lets you maintain a global history by defining anchor colors for URLs you have accessed.

See Also Anchors; Archives; History; Local History

Displaying the Global History: Quarterdeck Mosaic

To display the Global History when the Archives are displayed, click the Global History tab.

To display the Global History when the Archives are *not* displayed:

1. Choose Global History from the Window menu. The History pane is displayed to the left of the Browser window in the Archives and the Global

History tab is initially selected, as shown in Figure G.1.

2. To retrieve any document shown in the list, click on it.

Changing the Global History Options

You can change the number of days each type of document remains in the list. To modify the global history options:

1. Choose Preferences from the Tools menu to open the Preferences dialog box.

2. Click on the Global History tab to display the available options.

3. Use the Entries Expire After text box to change the number of days that the class of items will remain on the history list. The default for all types is seven days. If you don't want them removed, check Never.

4. Change the Entries to Keep to create a smaller or larger Global history.

5. Change the Max # of Links in the Link Tree to allow fewer or more anchors kept within the Global history.

6. Choose OK to close the dialog box and apply the new time limit.

See Also **Anchors; Link Tree; Preferences**

Figure G.1

The Global History is displayed to the left of Quarterdeck Mosaic's browser window in the Archives.

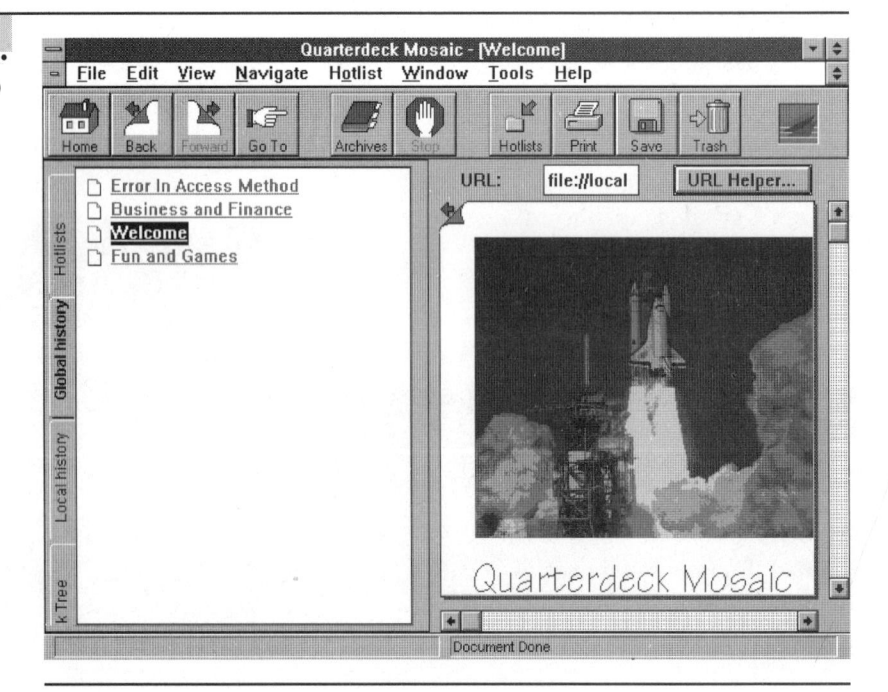

GO: NETSCAPE

The Go menu in Netscape contains the items that let you navigate through documents.

> **Unlike other Web browsers, Netscape does not include a Navigate menu; the Go menu is used instead.**

See Also Back; Forward; Home; Navigate; Stop Loading; View History

GO TO: QUARTERDECK MOSAIC

In Quarterdeck Mosaic, you can retrieve a document by using the Go To tool and entering the document's URL. The Go To tool and the Open command are similar in function. Both open the requested document in the current window, if you check Open in New Window.

1. Choose Go To from the Navigate menu or the toolbar.

The Go To URL dialog box is displayed as shown in Figure G.2.

2. In the URL text box, type the URL for the document. You can also use the URL Helper button to make this easier.

3. Click OK. The page you requested is retrieved and then displayed in the current window (or in a new window if you checked this option).

> **A Go To button is found in the History windows in Spyglass Mosaic and Netscape.**

See Also History; Open; URLs; URL Helper

GO TO NEWSGROUPS: NETSCAPE

In Netscape, the Go To Newsgroups command and the Newsgroups button let you read newsgroup articles.

See Also Reading News; Subscribing to News

Figure G.2

In Quarterdeck Mosaic, you can type the URL in the text box found in the Go To URL dialog box.

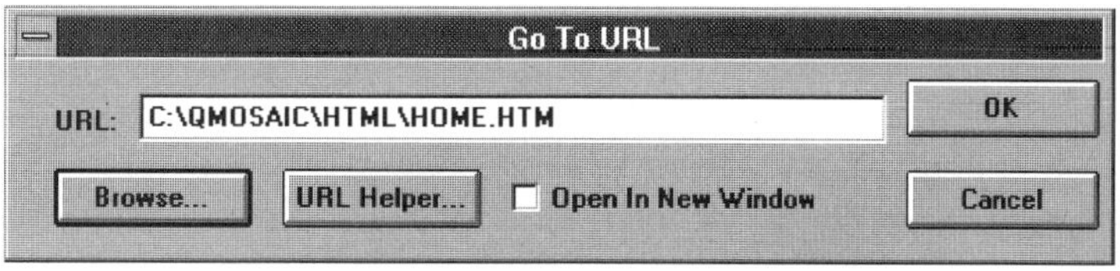

GOPHER

Gopher is a menu-based file transfer program which lets you download files (which are not Web documents) from Gopher servers on the Internet. Gopher servers do not have the graphic capabilities that Web servers have, or provide the capability to jump between documents.

The Web browsers let you download files with Gopher, without learning additional Gopher commands. NCSA Mosaic helps you connect to a Gopher server with items on the Starting Points menu.

> **Tip**
>
> You can search for a file that resides somewhere on a Gopher server by using Veronica. Veronica lets you search for files when you do not know their location, but do know the filename or part of the filename.

See Also Gopher Servers; Gopher-Space; Overview; Starting Points; Veronica

Downloading Files with Gopher

You can download files with Gopher by connecting to a Gopher server in much the same way as you retrieve a document. Use the Open or Open URL command and enter the URL for the Gopher site. You'll see a page with directory and filenames, represented by folders and documents. You may also see image or sound files or other Internet services.

Gopher Menu:
- :The UofI Weather Machine
- :maintenance
- :programmer.job
- Canada
- Caribbean
- Case Studies

You can click on each folder to see its contents, which are in turn displayed as folder and document icons. When you see the name of the file you want to download, click on it to begin copying the file to your hard disk.

See Also Open; Open URL

GOPHER PROXY: NETSCAPE

See Proxies

GOPHER SERVERS: NCSA MOSAIC

The Starting Points menu includes a Gopher Servers item which helps you download data from Gopher servers, with the same point-and-click technique you use to download Web pages. When you choose Gopher Servers, a cascading menu opens with the names of additional Gopher sites.

To use this menu to perform a Gopher search, try this example, which will let you search for the weather in your community.

1. Choose Gopher Servers from the Starting Points menu, then drag your cursor down to the item *UUIC Weather Machine* on the cascading menu.

```
Gopherspace Overview
Veronica Search
NCSA Gopher
PSC Gopher
SDSC Gopher
Original (UMN) Gopher
UIUC Gopher
UIUC Weather Machine
SDSU Sounds
```

Tip

You can open this document with another Web browser by using its URL: gopher://wx.atmos.uuic.edu:70/1

The page that displays is a Gopher menu with document and folder icons. If you click on an item with a folder icon, you'll see another Gopher menu. If you click on an item with a document icon, you'll retrieve that document. You can use this menu to search for information about the weather in your area.

2. Click on *States* and then click on the state in which you live. You'll see a list of documents which contains various types of weather-related information for your state.

3. Click on the Metro Area Extended Fcsts (Forecast) for your community. The National Weather Service forecast page is displayed.

See Also Gopher; GopherSpace; Veronica

GOPHERSPACE OVERVIEW: NCSA MOSAIC

The GopherSpace Overview item on the Gopher Servers cascading menu provides easy access to Gopher servers. It does not, as the name implies, provide you with an overview of GopherSpace, but it can help you locate Gopher servers all over the world. On the Gopher Menu which displays when you choose GopherSpace Overview, you'll have access to servers organized geographically.

To see how this works, use this menu item to access a Gopher server and download a document from a college, university or government institution in your state.

1. Choose Gopher Servers from the Starting Points menu, then drag your cursor down to the item GopherSpace Overview on the cascading menu.

> **Tip**
>
> You can open this document with another Web browser by using its URL:
> `gopher://gopher.micro.umn.edu:70/11/Other%20Gopher%20and%20Information%20Servers`

2. Click on North America, on the next page click on USA, and finally click on your state. You'll see the names of the Gopher servers you can access in your state. These will include the institutions from which you can download certain documents.

3. Click on the name of the server you want to access. You'll see a menu of the available documents; usually this first menu includes folders and documents.

4. Continue selecting folders by clicking on them, until you see a document which interests you.

5. Click on a document to copy it to your hard disk.

6. When you are finished reading the document, use the Back button to display the previous page, then choose another document if you wish.

See Also **Gopher; Gopher Servers; Veronica**

H

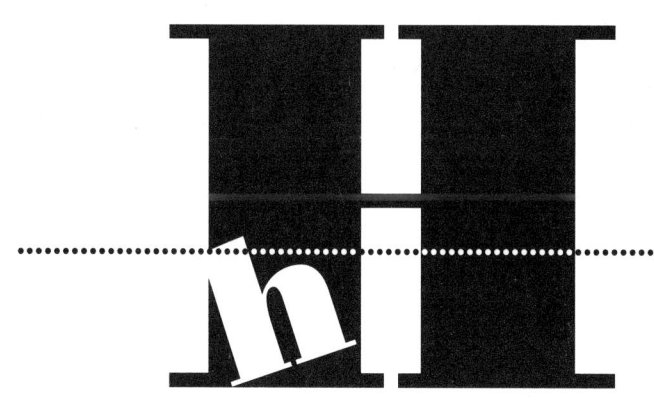

HANDBOOK: NETSCAPE

Netscape ships with an online user guide called Netscape Handbook, which includes a tutorial and reference. To download this document, choose Handbook from the Help menu. You can also:

- Read the document online.
- Use its links to locate information.
- Save the document to your hard disk for later reference.
- Print the document.

> **(66)** NCSA Mosaic includes a similar feature called Online Documentation on the Help menu. In Spyglass Mosaic, online documentation is available by choosing Mosaic Help Page from the Help menu.

See Also Mosaic Help Page; Online Documentation; Print; Save

HELP MENU

The Help menu contains the items that let you access either online Windows-style help or online documentation in the form of a user guide. You can also contact the software developers or manufacturers with items on some of the Help menus. All Web browsers include a Help menu, although each has a slightly different group of commands.

See Also About; FAQ Page; Feature Page; Frequently Asked Questions; Mail to Developers; Mosaic Help Page; Online Documentation; Send Mail to Spry

HELPER APPLICATIONS: NETSCAPE

In Netscape, the Helper Applications section of the Preferences dialog box lets you select multimedia viewers for displaying audio and video files as well as additional viewers for text files.

See Action; Extensions; MIME; MIME Type; Preferences; Viewers

HELPERS: SPYGLASS MOSAIC

In Spyglass, the Helpers command lets you select multimedia viewers for displaying audio and video files, and additional viewers for text files that are not supported.

HTML and plain text files, as well as JPEG and GIF image files, are supported and do not have to be configured for helper applications. To configure a helper application:

1. Choose Helpers from the Edit menu. The Helpers dialog box displays (see Figure H.1).
2. Select the file type you want to associate with an application and click the Edit button. The Configure File Type dialog box opens.
3. Type the full path and name of the application you want to associate in the Helper Application text box or use the Browse button to select and insert the path and filename.
4. Choose OK to close the Configure File Type dialog box.

Figure H.1

The Helpers dialog box in Spyglass Mosaic lets you associate viewers with specific file types.

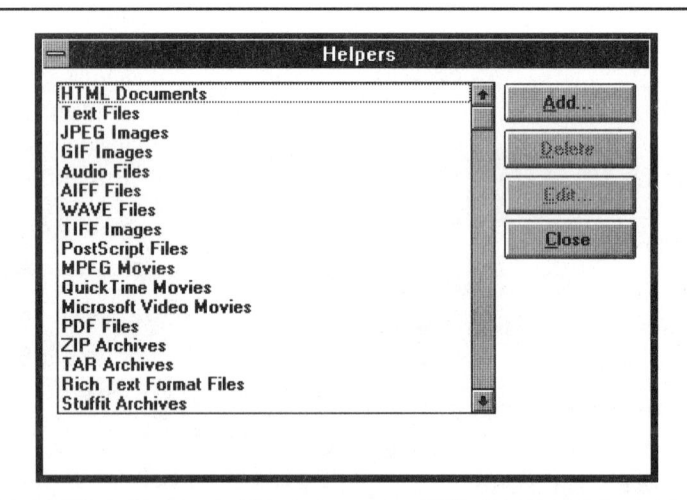

HISTORY   135

> If the application you enter is compatible with the Mosaic Software Development Interface, you can enter its DDE Service name in the Service Name text box below. If you leave this field blank, the application is launched with the command line specified in the Helper Application text box.

5. Choose Close to close the Helpers dialog box.

> **Tip**
> The Viewers section provides information about applications that can launch different file types and where to obtain those viewers.

See Also Extensions; GIF Images; Helper Application; HTML Documents; JPEG Images; MIME; MIME Types; Viewers

HISTORY

All browsers keep track of the pages you display during a session; this is called the history. You can display this list at any time and choose a page from it, thus enabling you to quickly return to a page you've already viewed. You don't have to remember the URL for the page, but you will have to recognize it in order to find it in the list.

> **Tip**
> You can leave the History window open throughout a session and use it—instead of the Back and Forward buttons—to return to a previously viewed page.

> Quarterdeck Mosaic has both a Global history, which tracks URLs from session to session, and a Local history for the current session.

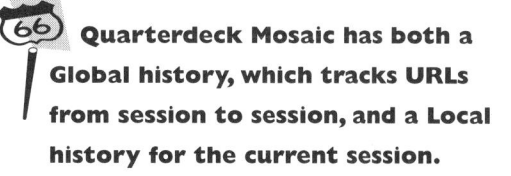

See Also Back; Forward; Global History; Local History; URL

Using the History Window: Air Mosaic, NCSA Mosaic

To select a page from the history in Air Mosaic or NCSA Mosaic:

1. Choose History from the Navigate menu. The History window opens with a list of all the pages you've displayed since you started your current session. Figure H.2 shows the NCSA Mosaic History window, which is similar to the Air Mosaic History window.

2. Click on any URL then click the Load button or double-click on any URL in the list. The page associated with that URL is displayed.

3. When you are finished, click Close, Cancel, or Dismiss in the History window.

Using the History Window: Spyglass Mosaic

To select a page from the history in Spyglass Mosaic:

1. Choose History from the Navigate menu. The History window opens with a list of the titles of all the pages you've displayed in the last 60 days (Figure H.3).

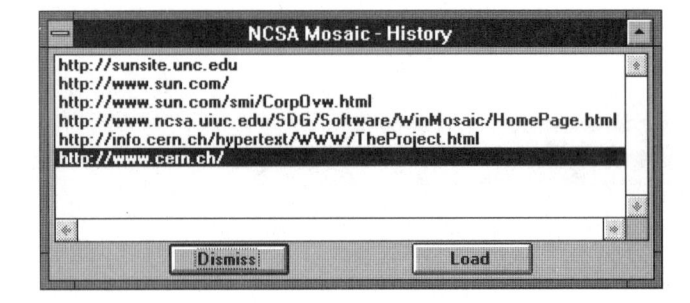

Figure H.2

The NCSA Mosiac History window shows the URLs for every page you've looked at thus far in the current session.

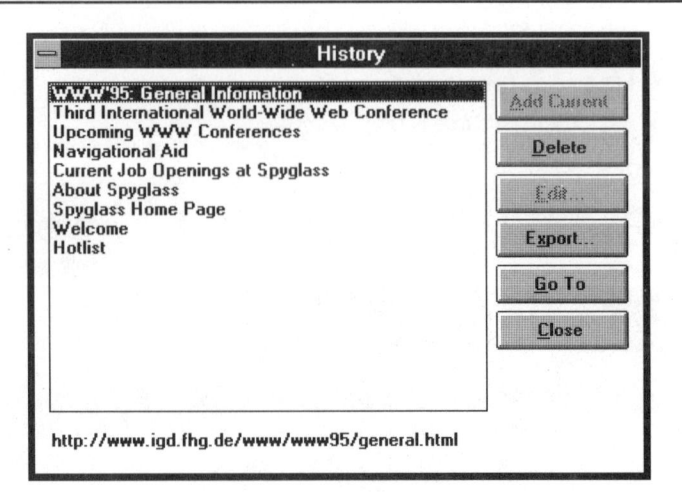

Figure H.3

The Spyglass Mosaic History window

2. Click on any title then click the Go To button or double-click on any title in the list. (Notice that as you click on a title, its URL displays at the bottom of the dialog box.) The page associated with the selected title is displayed.

3. When you are finished, click Close in the History window.

Using the History Window: Netscape

To select a page from the history in Netscape:

1. Choose View History from the Go menu. The History window opens with a list of all the pages you've displayed since you started this Netscape session (see Figure H.4).

2. Click on any URL/title then click the Go To button or double-click on any URL/title in the list. The page associated with that item is displayed.

3. When you are finished, click Close in the History window.

> **Tip**
>
> The Go menu also has a mini-history, with the titles of the most recently opened documents displayed at the bottom.

HOME

The Home command lets you display the document you've selected as your Home Page at any time during a session. All versions include a Home command and a Home button on the toolbar.

See Also **Home Page**

Figure H.4

The Netscape History window shows the titles and URLs of every page you've looked at thus far in the current session.

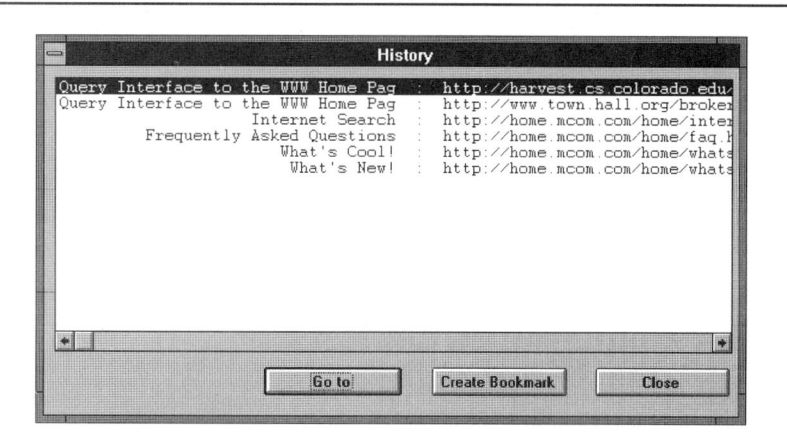

Home: Air Mosaic, NCSA Mosaic, Spyglass Mosaic

In Air, NCSA, Quarterdeck, and Spyglass Mosaic, the Home command is found on the Navigate menu; Home is also on the toolbar:

Air Mosaic

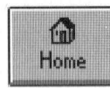

NCSA Mosaic

Quarterdeck Mosaic

Spyglass Mosaic

Home: Netscape

In Netscape, the Home command is found on the Go menu and toolbar. The Netscape Home button:

HOME PAGE

Home pages help organize the whole process of searching the Web by giving you a convenient and logical starting point. A home page is the first document that is displayed when you start your Web browser and when you connect to a remote site.

Each Web browser ships with its own customized home page which you see the first time you start it, and each subsequent time you start it until you choose not to see it. These home pages are designed specifically to help you browse the World Wide Web (and usually to learn more about each company's products).

> **Tip**
> You can retrieve any of the home pages displayed by the other Web browsers by entering the URL for that home page. You'll find the URL on the chart at the back of this book.

Any company or individual can create a home page—you can even create your own, by creating an HTML document. You can also start your Web browser and not display a home page, in order to save time, or you can change your home page. Each Web browser includes options that let you define your home page, and all but Spyglass Mosaic let you specify whether it should display automatically.

You might want to create your own personal home page to display whenever you start your Web browser. Your home page could include the titles of and links to all the pages you retrieve on a regular basis, and a description of those pages. Once you create your home page, you can also share it with anyone else, since unlike Hotlists and bookmarks, home pages, which are really HTML documents, work with every Web browser. To share your home page, just pass along a copy of the HTML document file.

To cancel the automatic display of *any* home page, use one of the following options:

Air Mosaic Options ➤ Configuration ➤ Load Automatically at Startup

NCSA Mosaic Options ➤ Preferences ➤ General ➤ Autoload

The Netscape Bookmark List Becomes a Home Page

If you are using Netscape, you can turn your Bookmark list into a home page that links you to all your favorite places, and you can do it in just a few mouse clicks. This is possible because Netscape actually stores your bookmarks in an HTML file that can be viewed and navigated like any other Web home page. With Netscape running, follow these steps:

1. From the menu bar, select Bookmarks ➤ View Bookmarks. The Bookmarks List window will appear.

2. Click on the Edit button. The window will expand. Click on the Export Bookmarks button. The Save As dialog box will appear.

3. In the Save As dialog box, type a filename—something like `myhome.htm`, or whatever you like that will remind you that this is your own personal Bookmark List page filled with your favorite pages. (Use the usual DOS filenaming conventions, and then end it in `.htm` because it's an HTML file.) Click on the OK button to save the file. The Bookmark List window will reappear. Click on the Close button to close this window, and you'll see the Netscape window.

Now you can open up MYHOME.HTM (or whatever you called it) just as you would any other HTML file you've saved to your local machine. You'll have created a home page version of your Bookmark list, which you can use as your own home page or pass on to friends and colleagues for their use. All the headings and organization you've included in your Bookmark list will be in the page. And any descriptions you've provided for individual items (in the Bookmark window's Description box) will appear as text describing the links. ...Yes, links. Because, of course, all the items you've bookmarked appear in this page as clickable links to those resources you found so appealing or useful that you just had to bookmark them.

Quarterdeck Mosaic Tools ➤ Preferences ➤ General ➤ Load Home Page

Netscape Options ➤ Preferences ➤ Styles ➤ Start With

To change your home page, use one of the following options:

Air Mosaic Options ➤ Configuration ➤ Home Page

NCSA Mosaic Options ➤ Preferences ➤ General ➤ Home Page

Quarterdeck Mosaic Tools ➤ Preferences ➤ General ➤ Initial

Spyglass Mosaic Edit ➤ Preferences ➤ Home Page

Netscape Options ➤ Preferences ➤ Styles ➤ Home Page Location

See Also Autoload Home Page; Home Page Location; HTML Documents; Load Automatically at Startup; Load Home Page; Start With

Home Page: Air Mosaic

The Home Page option in Air Mosaic lets you enter the URL for the document you want to use as your home page. Any document on a remote or local server, or on your hard disk, can be used as a home page. This document will be displayed each time you start Air Mosaic if you've checked the Load Automatically at Startup option.

The Home Page option is found in the Configuration dialog box. To change your default home page:

1. Choose Configuration from the Options menu.
2. Click in the Home Page text box, then use the Delete and Backspace keys to delete the current URL and type in the URL for the document you want to use as your home page.
3. Choose OK.

Home Page: NCSA Mosaic

The Home Page option in NCSA Mosaic lets you enter the URL for the document you want to use as your home page. The Home Page option is found on the General tab of the Preferences dialog box. To change your default home page:

1. Choose Preferences from the Options menu.
2. Click in the Home Page text box (see Figure H.5), then use the Delete and Backspace keys to delete the current URL and type in the URL for the document you want to use as your home page.
3. Choose OK.

Home Page: Spyglass Mosaic

The Home Page option in Spyglass Mosaic lets you enter the URL for the document

Figure H.5

Options in the NCSA Mosaic Preferences dialog box let you change your home page.

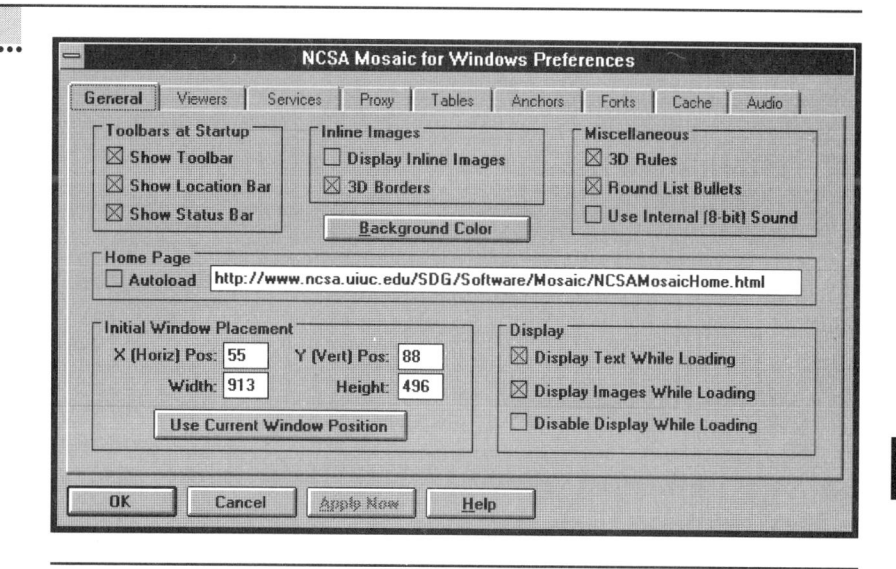

you want to use as your home page. The Home Page option is found in the Preferences dialog box. To change your home page:

1. Choose Preferences from the Edit menu.
2. Click in the Home Page text box, then use the Delete and Backspace keys to delete the current URL and type in the URL for the document you want to use as your home page.
3. Choose OK.

Home Page: Quarterdeck Mosaic

The Home Page option lets you enter the URL for the document you want to use as your home page. Any document on a remote or local server, or on your hard disk, can be used as a home page. This document will be displayed each time you start Quarterdeck Mosaic, if Load Home Page is checked. The Home Page option is found on the General tab of the Preferences dialog box. To change your home page:

1. Choose Preferences from the Tools menu.
2. Click on the General tab to bring it forward.
3. Click in the Home Page text box, then use the Delete and Backspace keys to delete the current URL and type in the URL for the document you want to use as your home page.

4. Choose OK.

HOME PAGE LOCATION: NETSCAPE

The Home Page Location option in Netscape lets you enter the URL for the document you want to use as your home page. Any document on a remote or local server, or on your hard disk, can be used as a home page. This document will be displayed each time you start Netscape if you've selected the Start With: Home Page Location option. The Home Page option is found in the Preferences dialog box, Styles section. To change your home page:

1. Choose Preferences from the Options menu, then select Styles from the drop-down list.
2. Click in the Home Page Location text box (which is not labeled), then use the Delete and Backspace keys to delete the current URL and type in the URL for the document you want to use as your home page.
3. Choose OK.

See Also **Home Page; Preferences; Start With**

HOTLIST

A Hotlist is a personalized list of documents and Web sites and their URLs, stored on your hard disk. Each Web browser presents Hotlists in different ways—some only allow you to have one, while others let you have as many as you like.

However, the basic idea behind all of them is the same—you can save the URLs for any documents you retrieve or Internet sites you visit, without ever typing in the URL. Once you've saved the URL you'll be able to select it at any time in the future.

> **Quarterdeck Mosaic organizes Hotlists within folders and places them within the Archives. Netscape calls Hotlists Bookmarks and places them on the Bookmark menu.**

See Also **Archives; Bookmarks; Folders**

Using the Hotlist: Air Mosaic

Air Mosaic lets you create multiple Hotlists and choose documents from them at any time. To select a URL from the Hotlist in Air Mosaic:

1. Choose Hotlists from the File menu or click the Hotlists button in the toolbar.

The Hotlist window (see Figure H.6) opens with a list of all the pages you've added to your personal Hotlist.

2. Double-click on any URL in the list. The page associated with that URL is displayed.

Figure H.6

The Air Mosaic Hotlist window shows the URLS for every page you've added to your personal Hotlist.

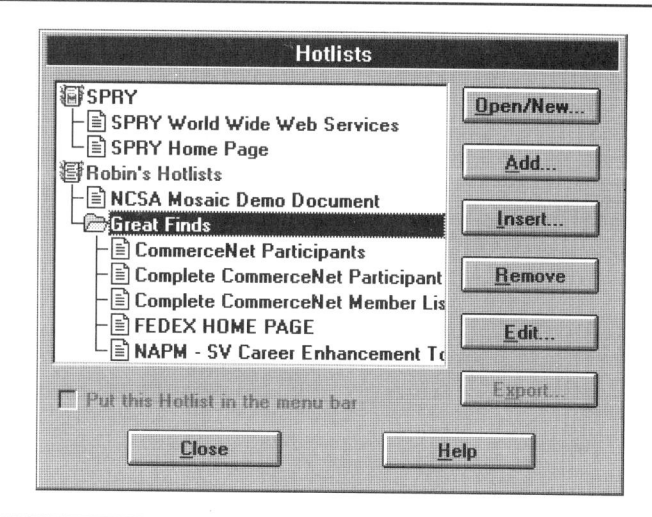

> **Tip**
>
> You can also display all the items on a Hotlist in Air Mosaic on a menu that you create, and choose items from the menu in even fewer steps than it takes to open the Hotlist window. This is explained under Creating a Menu.

See Also Add Document to Hotlist; Changing a Hotlist; Creating a Menu; Exporting a Hotlist

Using the Hotlist: NCSA Mosaic

NCSA Mosaic lets you create multiple Hotlists, create a menu for each Hotlist, and name the menus. The Hotlists can be on menus, and you can change your Hotlist with the Open URL command. To select an item from a Hotlist in version 1.0 or 2.0 Alpha:

1. Choose Open URL from the File menu.
2. Select the Hotlist you want from the Current Hotlist drop-down list as shown in Figure H.7.
3. Select the URL you want from the Hotlist.
4. Click on OK.

To select an item from a Hotlist in version 2.0 Beta and later:

1. Choose Hotlist Manager from the Navigate menu.
2. Double-click on any Hotlist in the window.
3. Double-click on any item in the window.
4. Choose Close from the Hotlist Manager File Menu to close the window.

Figure H.7

You can select an item from a Hotlist with NCSA Mosaic's Open URL dialog box.

> **Tip**
>
> The Starting Points menu is actually a Hotlist that is provided to get you started moving around the Web. You can modify this Hotlist to suit your needs.

See Also **Add Current To Hotlist; Changing a Hotlist; Creating a Hotlist; Starting Points**

Using the Hotlist: Spyglass Mosaic

Spyglass Mosaic only lets you create one Hotlist. To select a URL from the Hotlist in Spyglass Mosaic:

1. Choose Hotlists from the Navigate menu. The Hotlist window opens (see Figure H.8) with a list of all the pages you've added to your personal Hotlist.

2. Click on any URL in the list then click on Go To or double-click on any URL in the list. The page associated with that URL is displayed.

Figure H.8

The Spyglass Mosaic Hotlist window shows the URLs for every page you've added to the Hotlist.

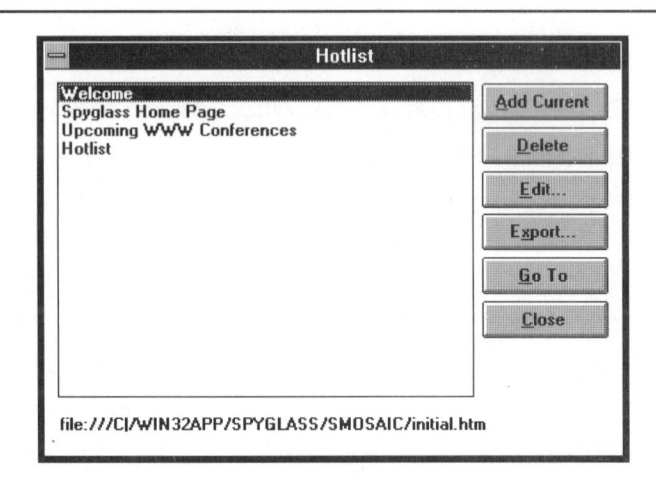

See Also **Add Current To Hotlist; Exporting a Hotlist; Hotlist Manager**

HOTLIST MANAGER: NCSA MOSAIC

NCSA Mosaic's Hotlist Manager, available in version 2.0 Beta and above, lets you modify and manage Hotlists and menus in several ways. You can:

- Create new Hotlists
- Delete Hotlists
- Add items to Hotlists
- Change the current Hotlist
- Remove items from Hotlists
- Place Hotlists on menus
- Import Hotlists

Choosing Hotlist Manager from the Navigate menu opens the Hotlist Manager window (see Figure H.9).

> In NCSA Mosaic version 1.0 and 2.0 Alpha, the Menu Editor provides the capabilities listed above.

> **Tip**
> You can reorganize your Hotlists and items within Hotlists by dragging and dropping items within the Hotlist Manager's window. For example, you can move items from one Hotlist to another and create cascading menus.

See Also **Hotlist; Menu Editor**

Figure H.9
The NCSA Mosaic Hotlist Manager window lets you manage menus and Hotlists.

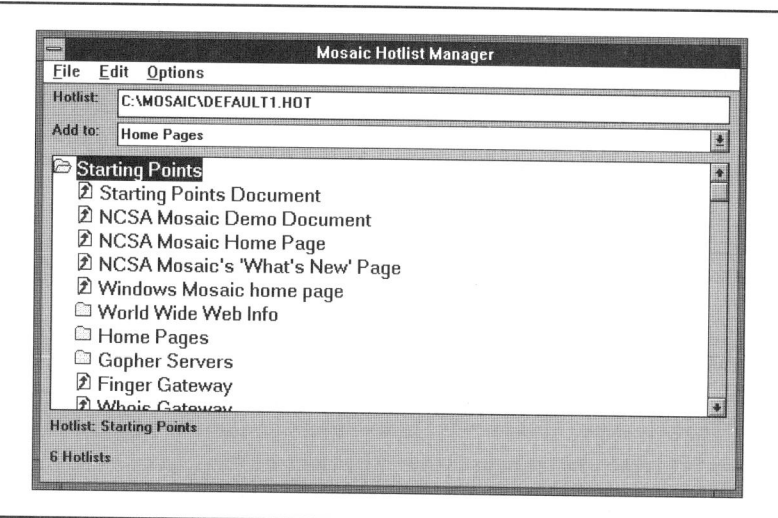

Creating a Hotlist

To create a new Hotlist in NCSA Mosaic:

1. Choose Hotlist Manager from the Navigate menu. The Hotlist Manager window opens.
2. In the Hotlist Manager window, click on the item currently at the location where you want to add the new Hotlist. The Hotlist will be added at that location and the highlighted item will be moved down.
3. Select Insert New Hotlist from the Edit menu in Hotlist Manager. The Edit Item dialog box opens.
4. Type the name of the new Hotlist in the Title text box.
5. Click OK to close the Edit Item dialog box.
6. If you want to begin adding items to this Hotlist immediately, make it the current Hotlist.
7. Choose Close from the Hotlist Manager's File menu to close the window.

Each Hotlist you create is stored in a file which has a .HOT extension. The file includes a list of document titles and their related URLs or other types of links, such as links to ftp sites or gopher sites.

Deleting a Hotlist or Menu

You can delete any Hotlist you've created in NCSA Mosaic. When you delete a Hotlist, you are also deleting the corresponding menu.

1. Choose Hotlist Manager from the Navigate menu. The Hotlist Manager window opens.
2. In the Hotlist Manager window, click the Hotlist which you want to delete. When you delete a Hotlist, you also delete all the items on that Hotlist.
3. Select Delete from the Edit menu in Hotlist Manager. You will see a confirmation dialog box before the Hotlist is deleted.
4. Click Yes.
5. Choose Close from the Hotlist Manager's File menu to close the window.

Adding to a Hotlist or Menu

The Hotlist Manager lets you add items which are not currently displayed to Hotlists and menus. You can add an item to a Hotlist or menu with these steps:

1. Choose Hotlist Manager from the Navigate menu. The Hotlist Manager window opens.
2. In the Hotlist Manager window, click on the item at the location that you want to add the new item. The item will be added at that location and the highlighted item will be moved down.
3. Select Insert New Item from the Edit menu in Hotlist Manager. The Edit Item dialog box opens.

4. Type the name of the new item in the Title text box.

5. Type the URL in the URL text box.

6. Click OK to close the Edit Item dialog box.

7. Choose Close from the Hotlist Manager's File menu to close the window.

Adding an Item To the Current Hotlist: NCSA Mosaic

To add the currently displayed document to a Hotlist with NCSA Mosaic:

- Choose Add Current To Hotlist from the Navigate menu.

You can also add the current document to the Hotlist in NCSA Mosaic by clicking the Add to Hotlist button in the toolbar.

Tip

You may want to change the current Hotlist before you add the current document in order to have the document appear on a specific Hotlist. This is explained in the Changing the Current Hotlist section.

Changing the Current Hotlist

In NCSA Mosaic, you can have multiple Hotlists. You can change the current Hotlist before you add documents to that Hotlist with the Add Current To Hotlist command. Use Hotlist Manager to change the current Hotlist:

1. Choose Hotlist Manager from the Navigate menu. The Hotlist Manager window opens.

2. Select the Hotlist to open in the Add to drop-down list. The Hotlist you open becomes the current Hotlist.

3. Choose Close from the Hotlist Manager's File menu to close the window.

Removing Items from a Hotlist or Menu

In order to keep your Hotlists and menus a manageable size, you'll want to remove items you no longer need. When you remove an item from a Hotlist, you are also deleting it from its corresponding menu.

1. Choose Hotlist Manager from the Navigate menu. The Hotlist Manager window opens.

2. In the Hotlist Manager window, double-click the Hotlist from which you want to delete the item. All the items on that Hotlist are shown below.

3. Click the Item you'd like to remove to select it.

4. Choose Delete from the Hotlist Manager's Edit menu.

5. Choose Close from the Hotlist Manager's File menu to close the window.

Placing Hotlists on the Menu Bar

You can create menus out of Hotlists and add those menus to the menu bar. If you find yourself opening the Hotlist Manager window frequently to select items from one or more Hotlists, you may prefer to have those items displayed on menus for the convenience menus offer. To place a Hotlist on the menu bar:

1. Choose Hotlist Manager from the Navigate menu. The Hotlist Manager window opens.

2. In the Hotlist Manager window, click the Hotlist you want to add as a menu.

3. Choose On Menu Bar from the Hotlist Manager's Options menu and also make sure that the One Root option on this menu is not checked. When choosing On Menu Bar with One Root option not checked, *all* the Hotlists are added to the menu, not just the highlighted one.

4. Choose Close from the Hotlist Manager's File menu to close the window.

To place all your Hotlists in the menu bar on a single Hotlists menu:

1. Choose Hotlist Manager from the Navigate menu. The Hotlist Manager window opens.

2. Choose On Menu Bar from the Hotlist Manager's Options menu if it is not currently checked.

3. Choose One Root from the Hotlist Manager's Options menu. A Hotlist menu is added to the menu bar and each of your Hotlists is added to the Hotlist menu.

4. Choose Close from the Hotlist Manager's File menu to close the window.

Importing a Hotlist

You can turn the links in any HTML document into a Hotlist by importing the Hotlist with Hotlist Manager. Here's how:

1. Display the HTML document you want to import in the document window.

2. Choose Hotlist Manager from the Navigate menu. The Hotlist Manager window opens.

3. Choose Import from the Hotlist Manager's File menu. The current document is imported as a Hotlist and its title is the same as the document's title. Each link in the document becomes an item on the Hotlist.

4. Choose Save from the Hotlist Manager's File menu to save the Hotlist.

5. Choose Close from the Hotlist Manager's File menu to close the window.

HTML COMMANDS

HTML stands for Hypertext Markup Language, the language used to create the documents with links that you find on the Web. HTML commands are used to control the appearance of a document as well as the embedded links to other documents. Because HTML commands are used to create all the documents available on the Web, documents are standardized and can be viewed with any Web browser.

> **HTML commands are also sometimes referred to as HTML tags, and more recently, as HTML styles.**

See Also   HTML Documents; HTML Tags; Hypertext Link

HTML DOCUMENTS

The documents found on the Web are ASCII text files with embedded tags, called HTML (Hypertext Markup Language) documents. HTML documents have two special capabilities:

- They contain links to other documents, which can be included in either text or graphic form.

- Their physical display characteristics can be controlled by you, the user, by specifying your preferences. (However, the document's creator creates several suggested defaults when encoding the document with HTML tags.)

For example, the document's creator decides what part of the document should be a heading, what should be plain body text, what should be displayed as a list, and so on. You can decide whether you'd like headings displayed in 14-point or 20-point type, whether the font should be Helvetica or Times Roman, and which special character you'd like to use for bullets. Once you've made your choices, all your documents will be displayed in the format you prefer, regardless of who created them.

HTML documents also are reformatted onscreen to fit the window in which they are displayed. This means they can be viewed by any Web browser.

See Also   Change Fixed Font; Change Proportional Font; Choose Font; Font; HTML Commands; HTML Tags; Hypertext Link

HTML TAGS

HTML tags are the codes used to turn an ASCII text file into a Web document with hypertext links and built-in formatting for display purposes. HTML tags work similarly to styles found in many Windows desktop publishing and word processing applications: You apply a tag (or style) to a block of text in order to define how it should look or what it should do in the final document. Once the tags are read by your Web browser, the document is converted into the useable form you see onscreen.

You cannot create HTML tags on your own; these are predefined as part of the Hypertext Markup Language which is standardized and interpreted by all Web browsers. In addition, you can't specify how each tag will look when you create it, except by viewing documents by changing your individual preferences or configuration.

> **Tip**
>
> Creating HTML documents is outside the scope of the book, however there are both books and applications dedicated to making this process easy. See the sidebar called "Quarterdeck's WebAuthor" for a basic description of this powerful HTML authoring tool.

See Also   **HTML Command; HTML Documents**

HTML VIEWER: QUARTERDECK MOSAIC

The HTML Viewer tab in Quarterdeck Mosaic's Preferences dialog box is where you can specify the display characteristics for HTML documents when they are displayed on your system. Select Preferences from the Tools menu then click the HTML tab to see the HTML Viewer settings.

Quarterdeck's WebAuthor

As part of its line of Internet products, Quarterdeck recently released WebAuthor, an application you can use in conjunction with Microsoft Word for Windows 6.0 to create HTML documents. If you are a current Word for Windows user, you won't have to learn a new product to create HTML documents.

WebAuthor is designed so you don't have to learn the HTML commands—you can select them as though you were applying styles, and the codes are embedded in the text file. You'll also be able to view the converted form of the document as you are working, so there isn't any guesswork about whether you've chosen the right HTML tag or how the document will look when you've finished.

Other features of WebAuthor include a spelling checker (with HTML codes already in the dictionary so you can easily check your document), easy forms creation, and a Windows online Help system.

See Also Bullet Style; Change Cursor Over Anchors; Display Inline Images; Fonts: Scheme; Font Style; HTML Documents; Hypertext Link Style; Indent Width; Numbered Lists Style; Paragraph; Show Anchor URLs; Wait for Images

HTTP

HTTP is the abbreviation for HyperText Transport Protocol, the communication protocol that is used when a Web document is retrieved on the Internet.

··············· **Tip** ·······················

If the first part of a document's URL is `http://`**, you know it's a Web document.**

See Also URL

HTTP/0.9: Air Mosaic

Occasionally when you are running Air Mosaic, a hyperlink to a document will display a message telling you that the document requires HTTP version 0.9 (an older version of the HTTP protocol), in order to be downloaded. If you see this message, choose the HTTP/0.9 command from the Options menu.

HTTP PROXY: NETSCAPE

See Proxy

HYPERMEDIA

Hypermedia is a term used to describe the combination of hypertext and multimedia. Hypermedia embodies the concept of placing links between different media and file types (text, sound, graphics and video) that work in the same manner as hypertext links—they allow you to jump from document to document.

See Also Hypertext; Multimedia

HYPERTEXT

Text that enables you to jump to other text is considered hypertext. Hypertext is the primary system on the Web (in addition to hypermedia) that enables you to move through documents that are connected only by references. This lets you quickly and easily search for and access information you need.

See Also Hypertext Link

HYPERTEXT LINK

Hypertext links are the links (connections) between two documents or between two parts of the same document which enable you to display the referenced information immediately. Hypertext links are used in Windows help systems and in Web documents to enable you to select a document (or a specific section of a document) to retrieve and display.

The text of hypertext links is displayed on your screen underlined or in a contrasting color. As you move the cursor over a hypertext link, the cursor changes to a hand. When you see the hand, clicking the text under it will take you to the referenced document.

World-Wide Web.

In addition to linking text to text, you can create hypertext links to other Internet services such as Gopher, FTP and Telnet, as well as sound, graphic, and animation files.

See Also Anchors; Hypertext; Hypertext Link Style

HYPERTEXT LINK STYLE: QUARTERDECK MOSAIC

The Hypertext Link Style drop-down list is where you select the appearance of links Quarterdeck Mosaic uses when it displays documents. This list is found on the HTML Viewer tab of the Preferences dialog box. To select a hypertext link style:

1. Choose Preferences from the Tools menu.
2. Click on the HTML Viewer tab to bring it forward.
3. In the Hypertext Link Style drop-down list, select the link style from those displayed.
4. Choose OK.

> In Air and Spyglass Mosaic, a similar option is called Link Color. In Netscape, it's called Link Styles. In NCSA Mosaic, several similar options are included on the Anchors tab of the Preferences dialog box.

See Also Anchors; Hypertext Link; Link Color; Link Style; Preferences; Styles

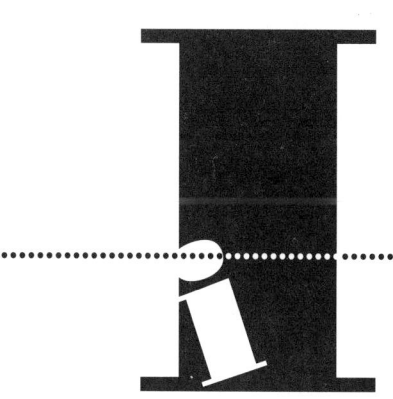

IMAGES

Images are incorporated into Web documents in one of two ways:

- They can be included as inline images (see Figure I.1), which are displayed as part of the document.
- They can be linked to a document but not displayed with it, and subsequently displayed in another application called a *viewer* (see Figure I.2).

Images: Netscape

In Netscape you can turn off the automatic display of images in order to speed the display of a document, with the Auto Load Images option.

You can click the Images button in the toolbar to display the inline images in the current document only when they are not being automatically loaded.

See Also Autoload Inline Images; GIF Images; Inline Images; JPEG Images; Viewers

IMAGES: COLORS: NETSCAPE

In Netscape, you can display inline images with or without *dithering*. Dithering is the process of arranging adjacent pixels to paint an image on the screen. For example, if you needed to display an image which had green in it, and your computer did not have the color green, it would alternate between blue and yellow pixels, creating the illusion of green. Dithering is used when

Figure I.1

An inline image displayed as part of a document

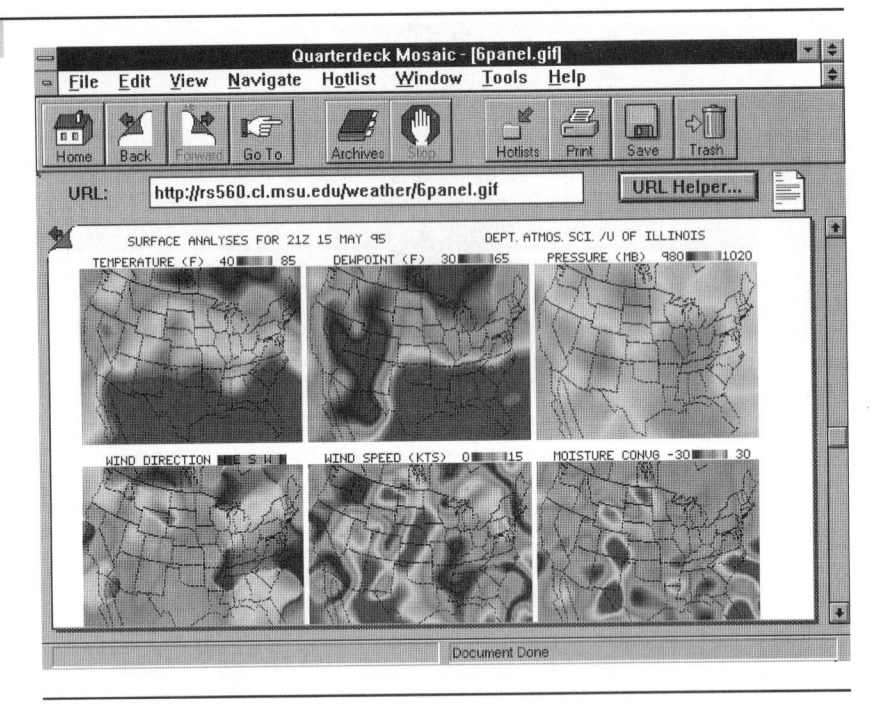

Figure I.2

An image displayed in a separate window with an external viewer

the colors available on a computer do not exactly match the colors that are in the image. It is one solution to the problem—the alternative is the substitution of a color with a similar color. For example, if an image had in it hot pink, and the nearest color on your computer was shocking pink, shocking pink would be substituted everywhere in the image for hot pink.

You can specify how you'd like images displayed in the Preferences dialog box (Figure I.3).

> **JPEG images are always dithered.**

To specify how you'd like inline images displayed:

1. Choose Preferences from the Options menu.
2. Choose Images and Security from the drop-down list to display these Images options.
3. Choose one of two options:

- **Dither to Color Cube** The colors available on your computer are arranged, pixel by pixel, in an attempt to reproduce (or closely match) the colors in the original image.

Figure I.3

Netscape's Images options affect the speed and display quality of inline images.

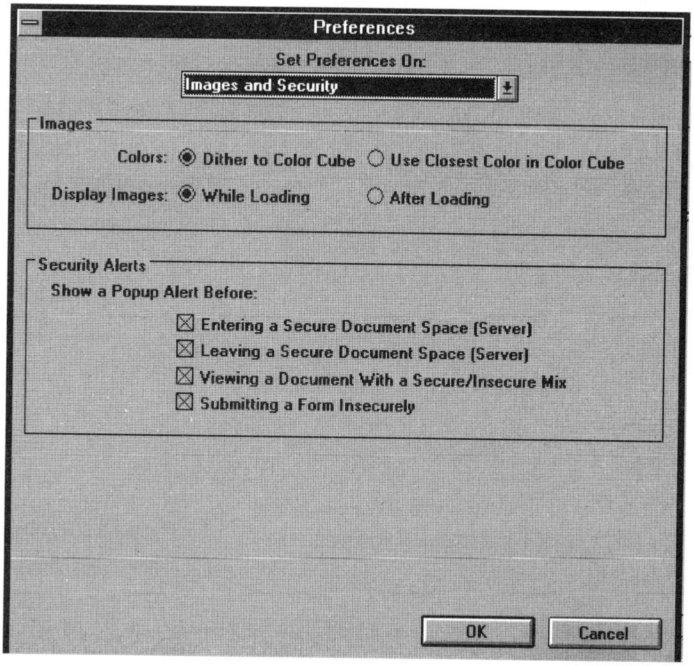

- **Use Closest Color in Color Cube** The closest matching color on your computer is substituted for each unavailable color in the image.

4. Click OK to close the Preferences dialog box.

> **Tip**
>
> Use Closest Color in Color Cube is usually the faster of the two options.

See Also   Inline Images; Preferences

IMAGES: DISPLAY IMAGES: NETSCAPE

In Netscape, you can display inline images gradually as you retrieve a document, or you can display them in their entirety after they have been downloaded to your computer. You can make your choice in the Preferences dialog box (see Figure I.3). To specify how you'd like inline images displayed:

1. Choose Preferences from the Options menu.
2. Choose Images and Security from the drop-down list to display these Images options.

3. Choose one of two options:

- **While Loading** Lets you watch the progress of the image as it is downloaded.
- **After Loading** Does not let you see the progress, but on a fast network may cause the complete image to be downloaded more quickly.

4. Click OK to close the Preferences dialog box.

See Also   Inline Images; Preferences

IMPORT NCSA MENU AS HOTLIST: AIR MOSAIC

If you use NCSA Mosaic and create one or more personalized Hotlists, and then move to Air Mosaic, you'll probably want to bring your Hotlists with you. Air Mosaic's Import NCSA Menu as Hotlist feature lets you do just that. Here's how:

1. Choose Import NCSA Menu as Hotlist from the Options menu. The Import NCSA Menu as Hotlist dialog box displays (see Figure I.4).
2. In the text box called "INI file containing menu," enter the full path for your MOSAIC.INI file. For example, C:\WINDOWS\MOSAIC.INI. You can use the Browse button to open the Browse dialog box and select the file with its path.

Figure I.4

Air Mosaic's Import NCSA Menu as Hotlist dialog box lets you convert any menu from NCSA Mosaic to an Air Mosaic Hotlist.

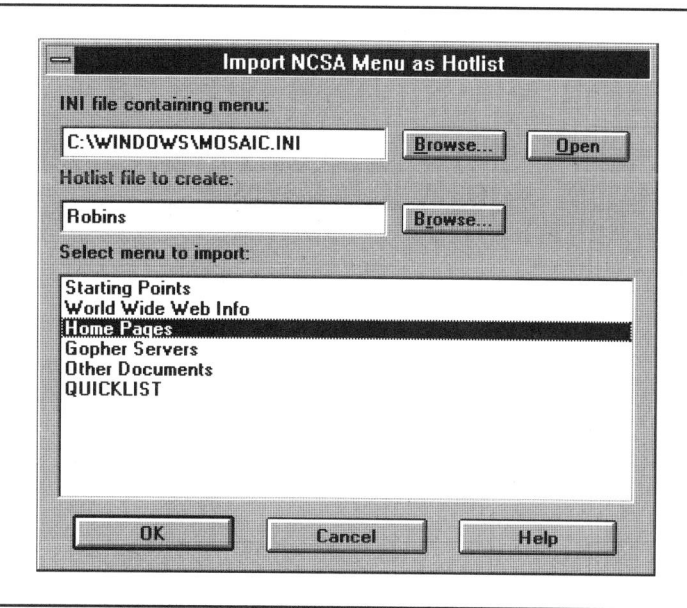

3. Click on the Open button. The available Hotlists are displayed in the list box.

4. In the text box called "Hotlist file to create," enter a name for the Hotlist file; for example, `mylist.hot`. If you enter the name of an existing file, it will be overwritten, not appended and you *won't* be prompted.

5. In the list box called "Select menu to import," click on the menu/Hotlist you want to import. You can import a Hotlist you created, or any Hotlist that you downloaded with NCSA Mosaic.

6. Click on OK to import the Hotlist. The Name this Hotlist dialog box is displayed, with the name of the current NCSA Hotlist you are importing.

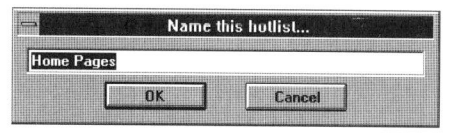

7. You can edit this name if you wish, then click on OK. The dialog box closes and the Hotlist is imported.

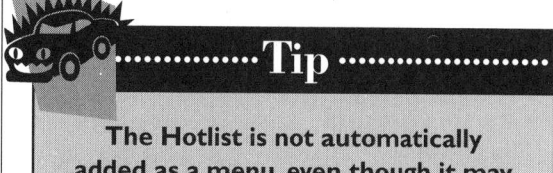

> ············· **Tip** ·····················
>
> The Hotlist is not automatically added as a menu, even though it may have been a menu in NCSA Mosaic. You'll need to check the Put the Hotlist in the menu bar option, in the Hotlists dialog box.

See Also **Creating a Menu; Exporting a Hotlist**

INDENT WIDTH: QUARTERDECK MOSAIC

In Quarterdeck Mosaic, you can change the space before indented lines in documents with the Indent Width option. This option is found on the HTML Viewer tab of the Preferences dialog box. To change spacing, in pixels:

1. Chose Preferences from the Tools menu.
2. Click on the HTML Viewer tab to bring it forward.
3. In the Paragraph text box delete the current number (which represents the amount in pixels) and type a new number. A higher number increases the space, a lower number decreases it.
4. Choose OK.

INITIAL WINDOW PLACEMENT: NCSA MOSAIC

In NCSA Mosaic, not only can you move and resize the application window (as in any Windows program) but you can specify the starting size and position for the application window. The Initial Window Placement options in the Preferences dialog box provide this feature.

Here's a quick way to specify the size and position of the application window:

1. Use the mouse cursor to resize and move the window to a position you are satisfied with.
2. Choose Preferences from the Options menu. The Preferences dialog box opens and the General tab is displayed.
3. Click on Use Current Window Position to set the current size and position as the default.

| Use Current Window Position |

4. Click on OK to close the dialog box and save the settings you have entered.

You can also use the Initial Window Placement options to size and position the window with precision.

Initial Window Placement			
X (Horiz) Pos:	55	Y (Vert) Pos:	88
Width:	913	Height:	496

To position the window precisely, enter the values for the upper left corner of the window in the X (Horizontal) Position and Y (Vertical) Position text boxes. To size the window precisely, enter the values in the Width and Height text boxes. These numbers are screen values, measured in pixels.

See Also **General; Preferences**

INLINE IMAGES

Inline images are graphics (photos, illustrations, Windows bitmaps and icons) which are included within a document, and by default, displayed when you download a document. Inline images must be GIF or XBM files. Figure I.5 shows a document with several inline images.

> **Tip**
>
> You can choose to display inline images or turn off their automatic display. This feature is available in **NCSA Mosaic** as Display Inline Images, in **Netscape** as Auto Load Images, and in **Air Mosaic** as Autoload Inline Images. In **Spyglass Mosaic**, it is Load Images Automatically. In **Quarterdeck Mosaic**, it is Display Inline Images.

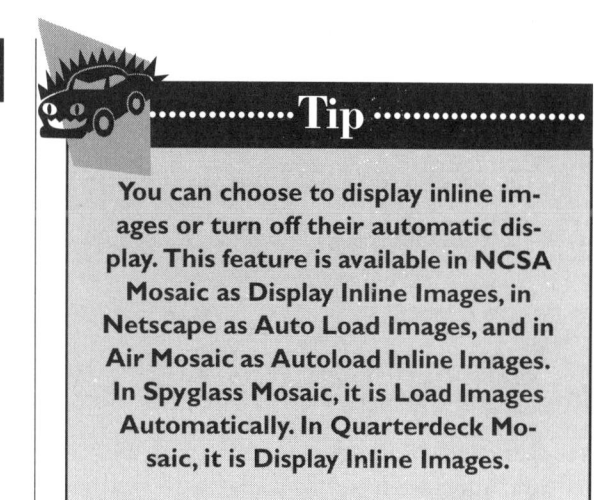

Figure I.5

All Web browsers can display pages with multiple inline images.

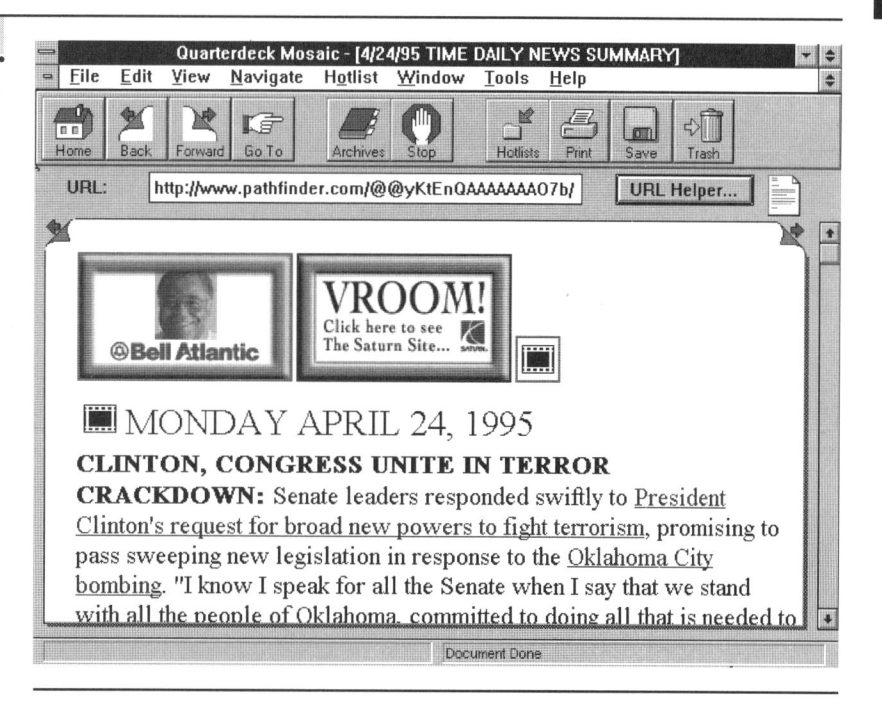

See Also Auto Load Images; Autoload Inline Images; Display Inline Images; GIF Images; Images; JPEG Images; Load Images Automatically; XBM Images

INTERLACE METHOD: QUARTERDECK MOSAIC

The Interlace Method option lets you specify how interlaced GIF files are displayed by Quarterdeck Mosaic. This option is found on the GIF Viewer tab of the Preferences dialog box. You'll need to try each method to find the best one for your video card and monitor. To change the status of this option:

1. Choose Preferences from the Tools menu.
2. Click on the GIF Viewer tab to bring it forward.
3. Click on one of the three options to change the Interlace method.

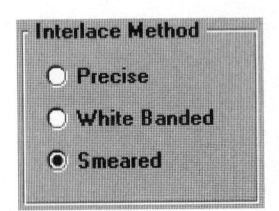

```
Interlace Method
○ Precise
○ White Banded
◉ Smeared
```

4. Choose OK.

See Also GIF Images

INTERNET ADDRESS

Your personal Internet address is your e-mail address. This is your username and the name of the computer on which you have your Internet account; for example, merrin@callamer.com.

Every computer also has an Internet address. The address can be its name in text form; for example, callamer.com is the name of the computer where I have my account. When computers communicate with each other, the name in text form, called the domain name, is converted to a series of numbers, called the IP address. An IP address would look like this: 555.123.45.6.

See Also E-mail Address

INTERNET (USENET) NEWSGROUPS

Newsgroups found on the Internet are called Usenet newsgroups. Contrary to what it might sound like, Usenet news does *not* resemble news summaries available from a wire service. News on Usenet is actually a message of some type, and by convention, it is called an *article*. Articles can be newspaper articles, but they can also be scholarly papers, general information, a message to the group, or someone's response to a previously posted article.

A newsgroup is a collection of articles on a specific topic which are labeled explicitly for that newsgroup when they are posted (sent). Some examples of newsgroups are:

- `news.announce.newusers` includes articles that describe different aspects of Usenet. (You might want to subscribe to this newsgroup first if you are a new user.)
- `alt.culture.usenet` includes articles that provide insight into Usenet culture.
- `bit.listserv.c+health` offers articles on how computers may affect your health.
- `rec.arts.sf.reviews` has reviews of science fiction books, magazines, and videos.

Quarterdeck Message Center

. . . .

The most sophisticated news reading and subscription capabilities of any Web browser are included with Quarterdeck Mosaic as part of the Quarterdeck Message Center. This application, launched from Quarterdeck Mosaic by choosing Mail/News from the Tools menu, lets you read Usenet news as easily as you would read a message sent directly to you. If you are already familiar with any Windows mail application, for example, Lotus' cc:Mail Mobile, you'll appreciate the ease with which you can subscribe to newsgroups, download and read news articles, and post articles of your own.

There are currently more than 10,000 newsgroups and new ones are created almost daily. By subscribing to newsgroups of your choosing, you will be able to access information that *may* be of interest. Table I.1 describes the categories of newsgroups distributed globally to all sites. Table I.2 describes the alternative newsgroups categories distributed locally by agreement between sites.

See Also Expanded News Listing; Go To Newsgroup; Mail/News; News Server; Newsgroups; Open URL; Reading News; Subscribing to Newsgroups

INTERNET RELAY CHAT (IRC)

Internet Relay Chat (IRC) is a service that is not currently included with any of the Web browsers described in this book. It is, however, very popular on the Internet. IRC lets multiple people have an online group discussion. Discussions are classified by subject (called *channels*) and are ongoing. You can join and leave a discussion at any time.

Table I.1
Global Usenet Newsgroups

Category	Description
comp	Newsgroups dealing with computer-related topics including hardware, software, commercial applications, and distribution of public domain and shareware programs.
misc	Newsgroups that cut across categories or that address themes not easily classified under any of the other groups.
news	Discussions related to Net News distribution and software.
rec	Groups discussing recreational activities, the arts and other enjoyable things.
sci	Discussions related to topics in the sciences.
soc	Discussion groups for social issues.
talk	Groups providing an opportunity for open-ended debate.

Table I.2
Categories for Alternative Newsgroups

Category	Description
alt	A collection of "alternative" newsgroups distributed voluntarily by a collection of sites. Many Usenet sites do not receive these groups.
bionet	Newsgroups for topics of interest to biologists, originating from net.bio.net.
bit	Newsgroups redistributing discussions from popular BitNet LISTSERV mailing lists.
biz	Newsgroups concerned with business products, particularly computer products and services. Postings include product reviews and announcements of product releases, bug fixes, and enhancements.
clarinet	Newsgroups publishing material from commercial news services and other sources. Sites carrying the ClariNet groups pay a licensing fee for the groups.
gnu	Newsgroups connected with Internet mailing lists of the GNU Project of the Free Software Foundation.
hepnet	Discussions dealing with High Energy Physics and Nuclear Physics. These groups, too, are connected to mailing lists and automatically archived.
ieee	Newsgroups related to the Institute of Electrical and Electronics Engineers (IEEE).
Inet/DDN	Discussions, many affiliated with Internet mailing lists. Groups in this category do not have a unique category name.
Info	A diverse collection of mailing lists (many technical, some cultural and social) connected into news at the University of Illinois.

Table I.2
Categories for Alternative Newsgroups (continued)

Category	Description
k12	Conferences concerned with K-12 education: curriculum, language exchanges, and classroom-to-classroom projects.
relcom	A hierarchy of Russian-language newsgroups distributed mostly on the territory of the former Soviet Union (non-CIS countries included). These groups are available in Europe and Northern America; because of the 8-bit encoding (KOI-8) of Cyrillic letters, minor software modifications may be required.
u3b	Groups dealing with AT&T 3B series computers.
vmsnet	Topics for VAX/VMS users. Maintenance of these groups is a project of the VMSnet work group of the VAX SIG of the US Chapter of DECUS (the Digital Equipment Computer User's Society).

JK

JPEG IMAGES

Joint Photographic Experts Group (JPEG) images are graphics files that use a different compression method than GIF files. JPEG files can be compressed to about one-twentieth of their original size and, therefore, are commonly distributed on the Internet. However, the quality of JPEG files is usually not as good as with GIF files. JPEG images files can be recognized by the extension .JPEG (more likely to show up in your directory as .JPG since PC extensions are three characters).

See Also **GIF Images; Images**

KIOSK MODE: AIR MOSAIC

Air Mosaic's Kiosk Mode feature lets you maximize your document display area by temporarily turning off all the other items on the screen, as shown in Figure K.1. This is a handy feature if you are giving a presentation.

When you choose Kiosk mode from the Options menu or click the Kiosk Mode button in the toolbar, you'll see a reminder of how to return to a normal view.

Figure K.1

When Air Mosaic is in Kiosk Mode, you'll have a larger area for displaying documents.

```
Archives of previous months' NEW pages.

Wed Mar 1 19:41:37 EST 1995:
 ○ AHguitargirl.gif, Guitar Girl... (Hargreaves,
   Alan )
 ○ AHguitargirl.jpg, Guitar Girl... (Hargreaves,
   Alan )
 ○ AHstonehenge.gif, Stonehenge... (Hargreaves,
   Alan )
 ○ AHstonehenge.jpg, Stonehenge... (Hargreaves,
   Alan )
 ○ Dumas.jpg, Dumas?... (Volk, Oleg Bernard )
 ○ PearlsJade.jpg, Pearls&Jade</b>... (Volk,
   Oleg Bernard )
For Help, press F1                                    NUM
```

The message: **To exit Kiosk mode, press Ctrl-K or the Escape key** displays. After you choose OK, you'll switch to Kiosk mode.

·········· Tip ··········

You can retrieve several documents, then select Kiosk mode, and use the shortcut keys for Back (B) and Forward (F) to display several documents in Kiosk mode during a presentation.

NCSA Mosaic's Presentation Mode offers similar capabilities.

See Also   Back; Forward; Presentation Mode

L

LAUNCH APPLICATION: NETSCAPE

See **Action**

LINK

Links are the highlighted text or graphics within a document that let you download and display other documents by clicking on them. Each Web browser displays links slightly differently, and each offers some options that let you control the appearance of links. Basically, though, all links function in the same way—just point and click. Links are also called Anchors.

See Also **Anchors; Hypertext Link**

LINK COLOR

Both Air and Spyglass Mosaic let you change the color for links displayed in documents. You'd want to do this to improve the contrast of links onscreen, in order to see them more easily, or just for the fun of it.

See Also **Anchor Color; Configuration; Hypertext Link; Preferences**

Link Color: Air Mosaic

To change the color for links displayed in documents in Air Mosaic:

1. Choose Configuration from the Options menu to display the Configuration dialog box.
2. Click on the Link Color button to open the Link Color dialog box.

   [Link Color...]

3. Click on any color square in the Link Color dialog box (see Figure L.1).

168 LINK COLOR

Figure L.1

The Air Mosaic Color dialog box lets you change the color of links.

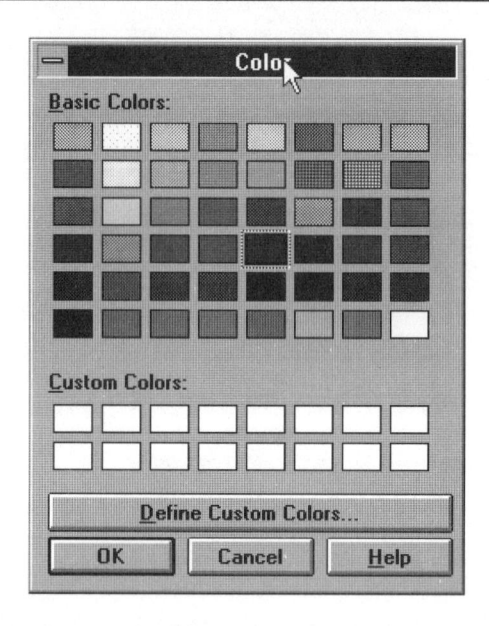

---

4. Click on OK to close the Link Color dialog box and apply the change.

5. Click on OK to close the Configuration dialog box and apply the change.

> **Tip**
>
> You can also create custom colors for your links by choosing the Define Custom Colors button.

Link Color: Spyglass Mosaic

To change the color for links displayed in documents in Spyglass Mosaic:

1. Choose Preferences from the Edit menu to display the Preferences dialog box.
2. Click on the Link Color button to open the Link Color dialog box.
3. Click on any color square in the dialog box.
4. Click on OK to close the Link Color dialog box and apply the change.
5. Click on OK to close the Preferences dialog box.

LINK STYLES: NETSCAPE

In the Styles section of the Preferences dialog box, Netscape offers two Link Style options that let you control how links are displayed:

- Links are: Underlined
- Followed Links Never Expire or Expire After__Days

   See **Followed Links Expire**

LINK TREE: QUARTERDECK MOSAIC

Quarterdeck Mosaic includes a Link Tree tab within the Archives that shows every link within the current document as an item on the tree (see Figure L.2).

You can use the Link Tree to quickly scan all the links in a document, and then choose a link without scrolling through the document. In large documents, this is a real time saver. To display the Link Tree

Figure L.2

Quarterdeck Mosaic's Link Tree shows you all the links in the current document.

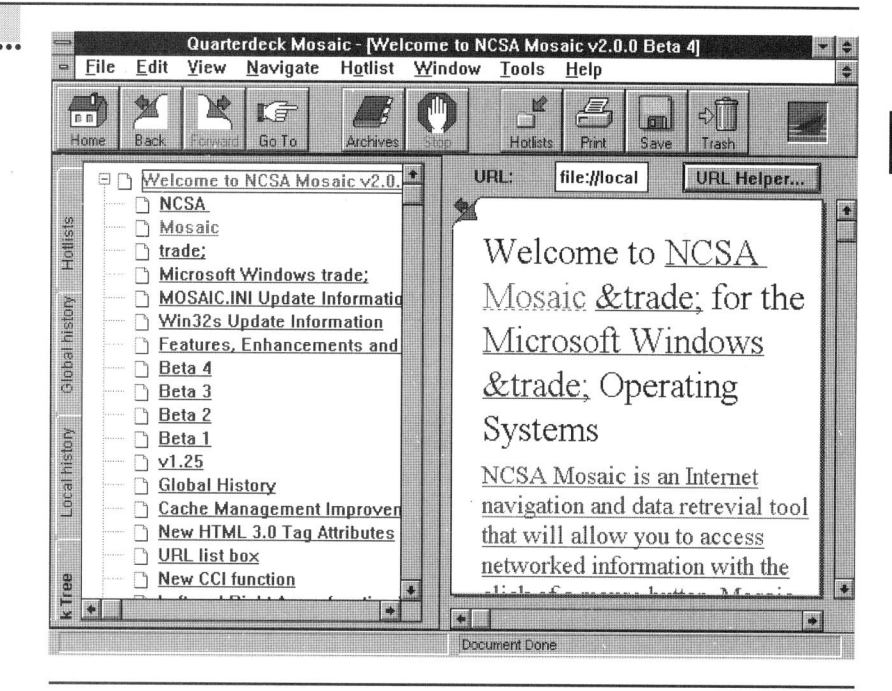

when the Archives are not displayed:

- Click Link Tree from the Window menu.

To display the Link Tree when the Archives are displayed:

- Choose the Link Tree tab to bring it forward.

To choose a link from the Link Tree:

- Click on it. The document you chose displays in the browser window.

See Also   Archives; Links

LOAD HOME PAGE: QUARTERDECK MOSAIC

The Load Home Page option lets you turn off the automatic display of your home page each time you start Quarterdeck Mosaic. This option is found on the General tab of the Preferences dialog box. To change the status of this option:

1. Choose Preferences from the Tools menu.
2. Click on the General tab to bring it forward.
3. Click on Load Home Page on Startup to remove the check from (or place one in) the box.
4. Choose OK.

In Air Mosaic, this option is called **Load Automatically at Startup**. In NCSA Mosaic, it is called **Autoload Home Page**. In Netscape, it is **Start With: Home Page**.

······Tip······

If you turn off the automatic home page display, you can still view your default home page at any time by clicking on the Home button.

See Also   Autoload Home Page; Home Page; Load Automatically at Startup; Start With

LOAD IMAGES: NETSCAPE

In Netscape, when you are not loading in-line images automatically, you can click the Images button or choose Load Images from the View menu to see the images in the current document.

LOAD MISSING IMAGES: SPYGLASS MOSAIC

> **Tip**
>
> To retrieve the document associated with a link, you can also place the mouse over the image's icon and click the left mouse button.

See Also Auto Load Images; Images

LOAD IMAGES AUTOMATICALLY: SPYGLASS MOSAIC

In Spyglass Mosaic, you can choose to display all images included in documents you're retrieving, or you can turn off the automatic display of graphics with the Load Images Automatically option. Documents are retrieved and displayed faster when their included graphics are not displayed, and you can always display individual graphics when you want to. A graphic does not have to be displayed in order for its link to function properly.

To change the status of the Load Images Automatically option:

1. Choose Preferences from the Edit menu to display the Preferences dialog box.
2. Click on the Load Images Automatically check box to change its status.

☒ Load Images Automatically

3. Click on OK to close the dialog box and apply the change.

To see an image that is displayed as an icon, place the mouse over the image's icon and click the *right* mouse button.

To retrieve the document associated with a link, place the mouse over the image's icon and click.

> This feature is available in NCSA Mosaic and Quarterdeck Mosaic as Display Inline Images. In Air Mosaic, it is Autoload Inline Images. In Netscape, it is Auto Load Images.

See Also Auto Load Images; Autoload Inline Images; Display Inline Images; Load Missing Images

LOAD MISSING IMAGES: SPYGLASS MOSAIC

In Spyglass Mosaic, when you are not loading inline images automatically, you can choose Load Missing Images from the Navigate menu or the toolbar to see the images in the current document.

172   LOAD TO DISK: AIR MOSAIC, NCSA MOSAIC

> **Tip**
>
> To retrieve the document associated with a link, place the mouse over the image's icon and click the *left* mouse button.

See Also   Load Images Automatically

LOAD TO DISK: AIR MOSAIC, NCSA MOSAIC

In both Air and NCSA Mosaic, when you click on a link, you can save a copy of the selected document as a file on your hard disk, instead of displaying it. In NCSA Mosaic version 1.0 and 2.0 alpha, this feature is controlled by the Load to Disk command; in Air Mosaic, it is controlled by the Load to Disk Mode command. Both are found on the options menu, and when in effect, are checked on the menu.

When you turn on the Load to Disk feature, you won't see a selected document displayed. Instead, each time you click on a line, the Save As dialog box will be displayed. To save a document, enter a filename, or accept the default shown in the File Name text box, and click OK.

Since documents are downloaded from many computers running varying operating systems, the filenames of documents do not always conform to the limitations of MS-DOS (eight characters plus a three character extension). If you try to save a document with an invalid name, it will be automatically truncated to the 11 character limit.

If you occasionally want to save a document to disk, but don't want to turn this mode on and save *all* selected documents, use the shortcut available in both products—press Shift and click on the link to save an individual document to disk. The Save As dialog box will be displayed and you'll be able to name and save the document.

See Also   Save

LOCAL FILES

Local files are files that exist on your hard disk. They may be either files you downloaded from a server anywhere on the Internet and saved to your hard disk, or files you created yourself. To view local files in each Web browser, use one of the following commands:

- **Air Mosaic** File ➤ Open Local File
- **NCSA Mosaic** File ➤ Open Local File
- **Quarterdeck Mosaic** File ➤ Open (URL)
- **Spyglass Mosaic** File ➤ Open Local
- **Netscape** File ➤ Open File

See Also Open; Open Local File; Open File; Open URL

LOCAL HISTORY

All browsers keep track of the pages you display during a session; this is called the history. Quarterdeck Mosaic has a more sophisticated history feature than other Web browsers, in that it can maintain a separate history list for each browser window you open during the current session. This window-specific history list is called the Local History.

> **Tip**
> In Quarterdeck Mosaic, the ongoing history for all browser windows combined is called the Global History.

See Also Archives; History; Global History

Displaying the Local History: Quarterdeck Mosaic

To display the Local History:

1. Choose Local History from the Window menu. The History pane is displayed to the left of the Browser window and the Local History tab is initially selected (see Figure L.3).
2. To retrieve any document shown in the list, double-click on it.

To display the Local History pane any time the Archives are displayed, you can also click the Local History tab.

LOCATION: NETSCAPE

In Netscape, if you are displaying the Location box in the application window, you can enter a URL to quickly retrieve a document.

1. Delete the URL currently shown in the Location box and type the URL for the page you want to retrieve. You can highlight the entry and press Delete or click in the box and press Backspace to delete part of the entry.
2.
   Location: http://harvest.cs.colorado.edu/

   Press f to retrieve the document.

The page is displayed on your screen.

LOCATION: NETSCAPE

Figure L.3

The Local History is displayed to the left of Quarterdeck Mosaic's browser window.

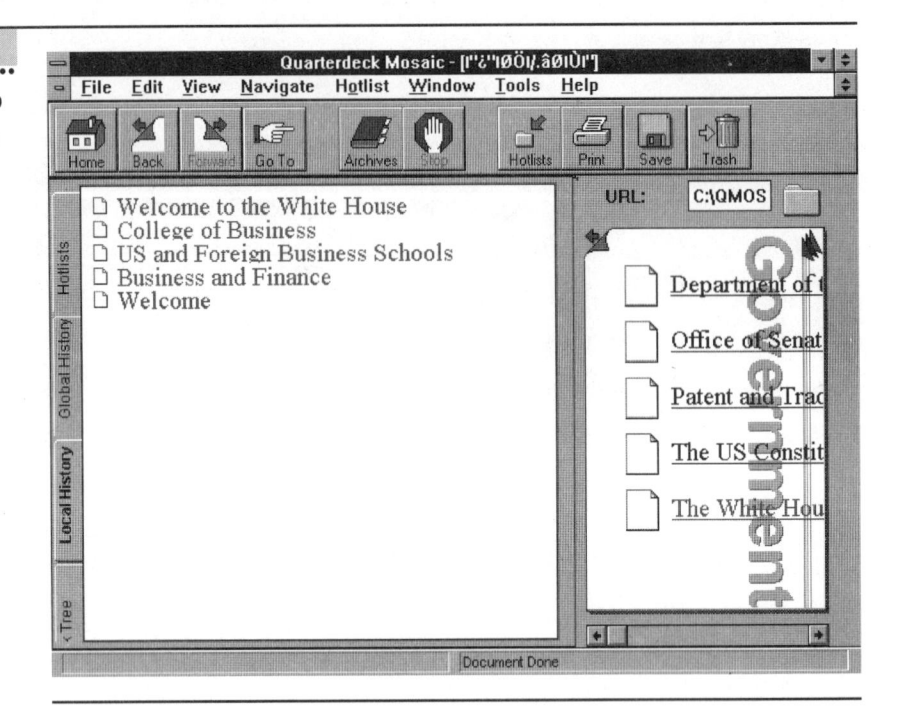

> **In Air Mosaic, this is called the Document URL box; in Spyglass Mosaic, it is the URL box; and in NCSA, it is an untitled text box.**

See Also Document URL; URL Box; URLs

M

MAIL AND NEWS: NETSCAPE

In Netscape, the Mail and News section of the Preferences dialog box lets you enter the name of your mail server, and your own name and e-mail address.

See Also   Mail Server; Your E-mail; Your Name

MAIL DOCUMENT: NETSCAPE

Netscape lets you send the text of a document (but not the inline images or any multimedia files included with the text of the document) to any e-mail address including your own. You can send the page as the text of the message, or as an attachment to a message.

> **Netscape can only include a document with a maximum of 30,000 characters.**

To send a document, first open the document, then follow these steps:

1. Choose Mail Document from the File menu. The Send Mail/Post News dialog box (see Figure M.1) is displayed.
2. Type the e-mail address of the recipient in the Mail To text box.
3. Type the subject of the document in the Subject text box.
4. Click on the Quote Document button to include the text of the document within the body of the message. Text is included in Internet quotation style, which means it is preceded by a right angle bracket (>).

176 MAIL DOCUMENT: NETSCAPE

Figure M.1

Netscape's Send Mail/Post News dialog box helps you send the text of an HTML document.

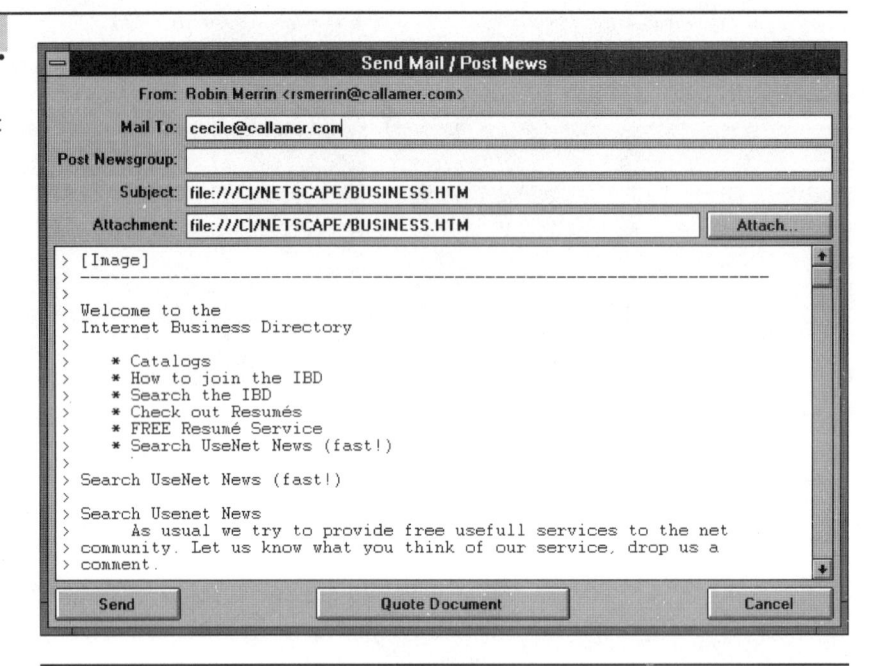

5. Click on the Send button to send the message.

You can send the document as an attachment instead of as the text of the message by clicking Attach and choosing one of these two options from the Mail/News Attachments dialog box:

Document Text Sends only the text of the message, but not the HTML codes which format the text onscreen. The text is not sent with quotation brackets.

Document Source Sends the text with its HTML codes so that the document remains an HTML document and can be used as such on another computer by its recipient.

Tip

Use the Text option to mail the text of a document to yourself if you want to be able to open it in a word processing program without its HTML tags.

You can also select the file option in the Mail/News Attachments dialog box to attach any other file to a message. Click Attach again to attach the selected document or file and close this dialog box.

See Also   E-mail Address; HTML Codes; HTML Document; HTML Tags

MAIL/NEWS: QUARTERDECK MOSAIC

Quarterdeck Mosaic's Mail/News command on the Tools menu launches a separate application, called the Quarterdeck Message Center (Figure M.2), which lets you:

- Compose, send and receive e-mail.
- Maintain a customized personal Internet address book.
- Automate the process of checking for new Internet mail while you are connected.
- Organize messages you receive by placing them in customized folders.
- Subscribe to newsgroups.
- Update newsgroups on a regular, scheduled basis.
- Post to newsgroups.
- Organize news articles you download by placing them in customized folders.

> **The steps for using Quarterdeck Message Center to read and send mail, and to subscribe to and read news, are included in the applicable sections of this book.**

Figure M.2

Quarterdeck Message Center is a full-featured mail and news management application.

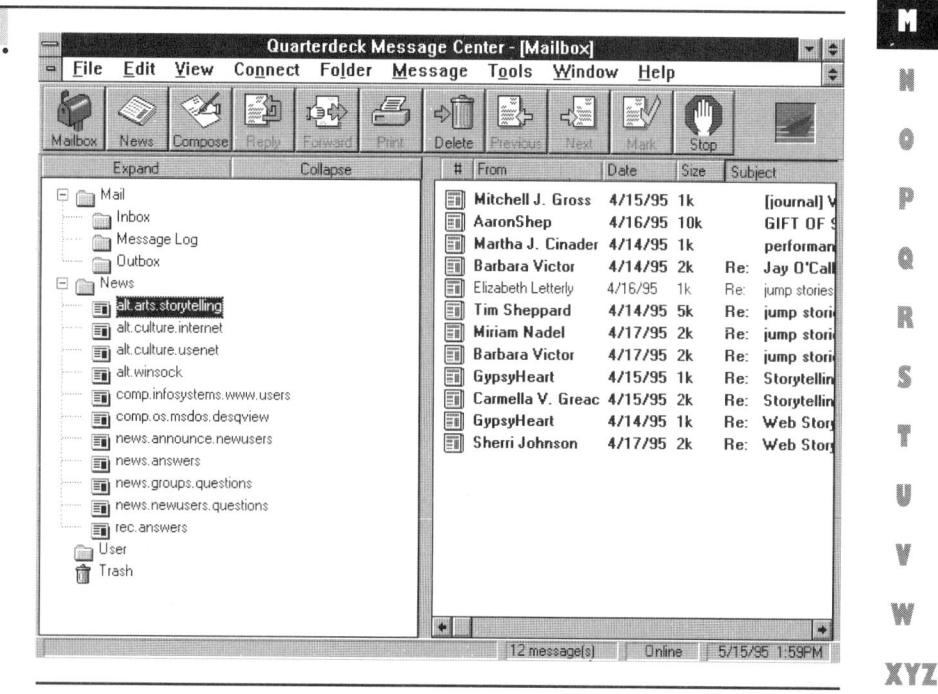

See Also Electronic Mail (E-mail); Internet Newsgroups; Reading Mail; Reading News; Sending Mail; Subscribing to Newsgroups

MAIL SERVER: NETSCAPE

Netscape's Mail option in the Preferences dialog box is where you enter the name of the SMTP (Simple Mail Transport Protocol) server which handles your mail. You'll need to enter this before you can access a newsgroup or send e-mail.

To find out the name of this server, if you have a remote account, you'll need to ask your service provider. To enter the name of your SMTP server:

1. Choose Preferences from the Options menu. The Preferences dialog box is displayed.
2. Choose Mail and News from the drop-down list.
3. Enter the name of your mail server in the Mail Server text box.

Mail (SMTP) Server: mail.callamer.com

4. Click on OK to close the dialog box.

> In Air, NCSA and Quarterdeck Mosaic, this information is entered in the SMTP Server text box.

See Also E-mail Address; Go To Newsgroup; Mail Document; Reading Mail; Send Mail; Sending Mail; SMTP Server

MAIL TECHNICAL SUPPORT: NCSA MOSAIC

If you are having difficulty with NCSA Mosaic, and cannot find the solution to your problem in this book, or in NCSA's own documentation, you can send a request for technical support to the developers of NCSA Mosaic. Choose Mail Technical Support from the Help menu, and fill out the form shown in Figure M.3, then click on the Send button.

> **NCSA's Tech Support is not user support**—they do not have a staff paid and trained to help users get started on their product. So be sure you are sending a true technical support question, and be patient when waiting for a response.

·············· Tip ··············

Make sure to also check the **FAQ** Page to see if an answer to your question has already been posted.

Figure M.3

NCSA Mosaic's Tech Support form lets you send a request for technical assistance.

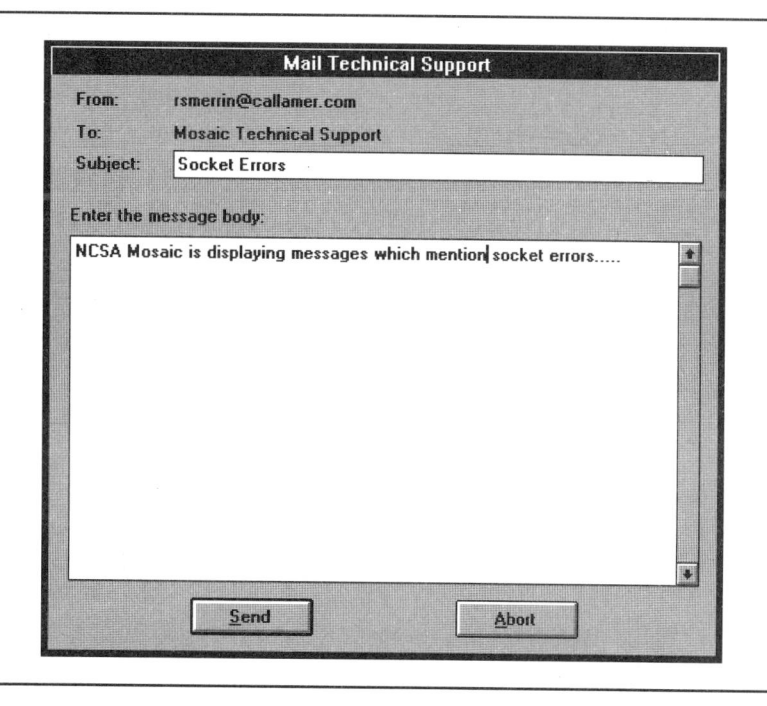

See Also FAQ Page; Forms; Online Documentation

MAX CACHE SIZE: QUARTERDECK MOSAIC

See Document Caching

MEMORY CACHE: NETSCAPE

See Document Caching

MENU EDITOR: NCSA MOSAIC

In NCSA Mosaic versions 1.0 and 2.0 alpha, the Menu Editor lets you create and add items to menus and Hotlists, reorganize your menus and menu items, and remove menus and menu items. Choosing Menu Editor from the Navigate menu opens the Personal Menus dialog box (see Figure M.4).

> In NCSA Mosaic version 2.0 beta and later, the Hotlist Manager provides all menu editing capabilities.

Figure M.4

The NCSA Mosaic Personal Menus dialog box lets you manage menus and Hotlists.

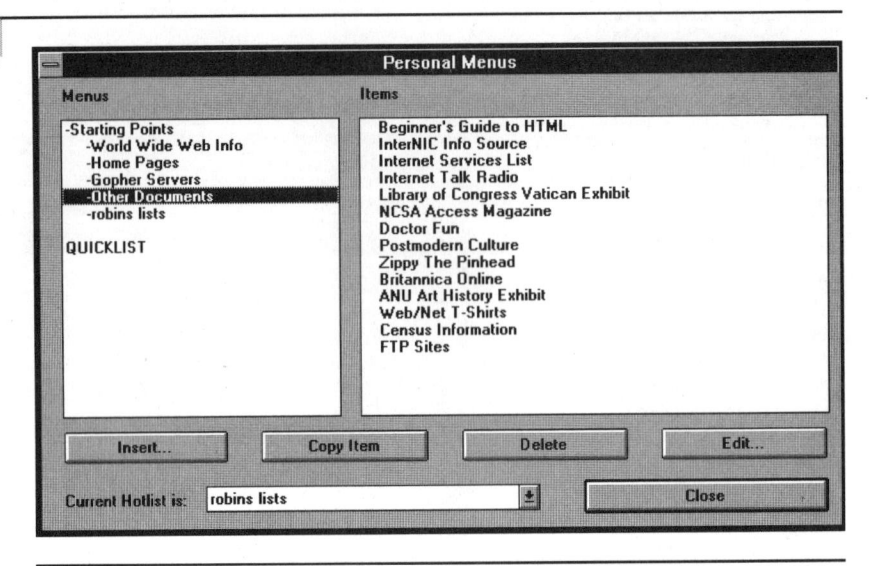

See Also Adding to a Menu; Creating a Menu; Deleting a Menu; Deleting Items from a Menu

MIME

MIME is the abbreviation for Multipurpose Internet Mail Extensions. A file's MIME type is simply its type (HTML, JPEG, plain text, image) which is often indicated by its extension (.HTML, .JPEG, .TXT, .IMG). Web browsers use a file's extension to determine how to handle the file and the application that should be used to retrieve or open the file for viewing.

See Also Extensions; MIME Type; Viewers

MIME TYPE: NETSCAPE

When you retrieve a file, Netscape usually can retrieve the file's MIME type from the server. If not, Netscape uses the file's extension to look up the file type in the MIME type list box and to determine how to display or open the file. Once Netscape knows a file's type, it can determine whether to display it in the document window or with a helper application.

In Netscape, the MIME type list box shows the file types associated with various applications. To add an extension to a MIME type, or to modify an existing extension:

1. Choose Preferences from the Options menu.
2. Select Helper Applications from the drop-down list box.

3. Select the MIME type in the list box at the top of this dialog box by clicking on it.
4. Edit the existing extension in the Extensions text box or choose New Type to add a new extension.
5. Select Launch Application under the Action heading.
6. Click the Browse button.
7. In the File Name text box, select the application in which this type of file can be opened.
8. Choose OK.

> **Tip**
>
> The Viewers section provides information about applications that can launch different **MIME** types and where to obtain those viewers.

> A similar list box is found on Quarterdeck Mosaic's Data Engine tab in the Preferences dialog box.

See Also Extensions; Helper Application; MIME; Preferences; Viewers

MODIFYING BOOKMARKS: NETSCAPE

In Netscape, Bookmarks help you locate a document again quickly and easily. When you add the current document to a list of Bookmarks, Netscape adds the document title to the Bookmark menu and saves the URL with the document's location. You can also:

- Display your personal bookmarks on the Bookmarks menu.
- Remove items you've added.
- Rename items.
- Reorder items.
- Import and export bookmarks.

All these modifications can be made in the Bookmark List dialog box (Figure M.5), which you open by choosing View Bookmarks on the Bookmarks menu.

> Other forms of Mosaic described in this book use a Hotlist instead of a Bookmark list.

See Also Add Bookmark; Bookmark; Hotlist; Modifying Hotlists; URL

Figure M.5

Netscape's Bookmark List dialog box

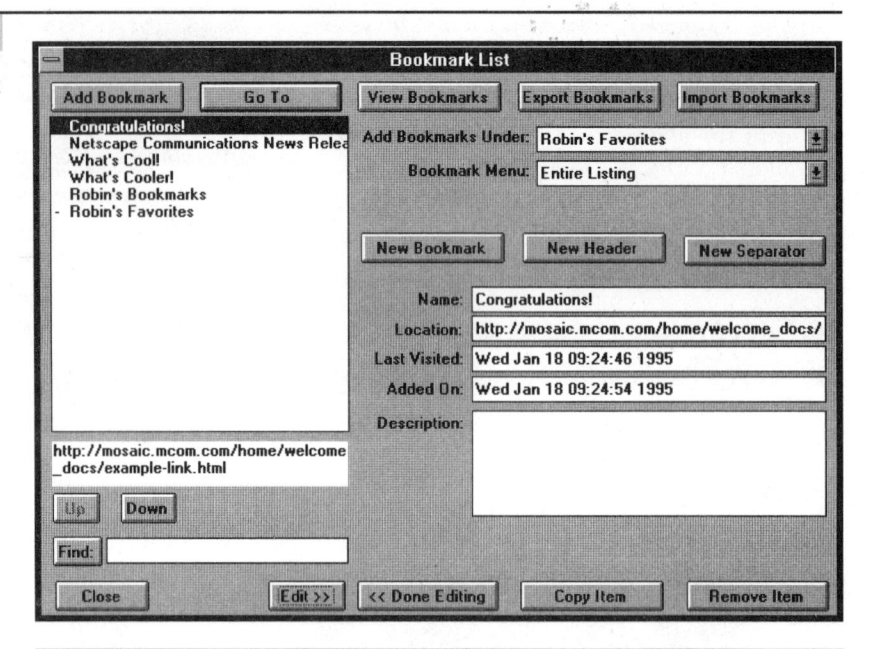

Displaying Bookmarks: Netscape

You can decide whether or not the bookmarks you add are displayed as part of the Bookmarks menu. To display the bookmarks (if they aren't currently displayed), use the Bookmark List dialog box.

1. Choose View Bookmarks from the Bookmarks menu.
2. Click on Edit to display all the options.

   Edit >>

3. Choose Entire Listing from the Bookmark Menu drop-down list.
4. Choose Close.

Removing Items from Bookmarks: Netscape

Bookmarks can quickly become cluttered after you've used Netscape for awhile. At first, you may be tempted to add every interesting page you find so you can easily find it again. Later on, you'll realize you've saved a number of pages you don't really need. When this happens, remove the items that no longer interest you.

1. Choose View Bookmarks from the Bookmarks menu.
2. Click on Edit to display all the options.
3. In the list box on the left, choose the item you want to remove.

4. Click the Remove Item button.

[Remove Item]

5. Repeat Steps 3 and 4 for any additional items you want to remove from the list.

6. When you are finished, choose Close.

Renaming Bookmark Items: Netscape

When you add a page to a bookmark, the title of that page is automatically added to the Bookmarks list. Unfortunately, that title may not be particularly helpful if you go looking for the page a few days or weeks later. You can change the title to whatever you want in order to recognize it more easily.

1. Choose View Bookmarks from the Bookmarks menu.

2. Click on Edit to display all the options.

3. In the list box on the left, click on the item you want to rename. The item's title displays in the Name text box to the right.

4. Edit the title of the page in the Name text box. You can enter any title you'd like, since it will appear only in your personal Bookmark list.

5. Repeat Steps 3 and 4 for any additional items you want to rename.

6. When you are finished, choose Close.

Reordering Bookmarks: Netscape

As you add new items to Bookmarks, they are always placed at the bottom of the list. You can use the Up and Down buttons to move items so that they are organized in a manner you find more efficient.

[Up] [Down]

These buttons let you reorganize and indent bookmark items. Indented items are not displayed on the Bookmark menu, although they are in your Bookmark list.

The Up button does any and all of the following:

- If the selected item and the one above are both individual items and neither is indented, Up moves the selected item above the one above it.

- If the selected item is a header, Up moves the header and all the items beneath it.

- If the selected item is not indented and the one above is indented, Up indents the selected item.

The Down button does any and all of the following:

- If the selected item and the one below are both individual items and neither is indented, Down moves the item below the one below it.

- If the selected item is a header, Down moves the header and all the items beneath it down.

To reorder Bookmark items:

1. Choose View Bookmarks from the Bookmarks menu.
2. Click on Edit to display all the options.
3. In the list box on the left, click on the first item you want to move.
4. Click the Up or Down button to move the item. Click as many times as necessary to move the item to the correct position.
5. Repeat Steps 3 and 4 for any additional items you want to move.
6. When you are finished, choose Close.

Importing Bookmarks: Netscape

Netscape's Import Bookmark feature lets you import any HTML file which contains hypertext links, or someone else's Netscape bookmark files. When you import the file, Netscape converts those links to new items on your bookmark.

1. Choose View Bookmarks from the Bookmarks menu.
2. Click on Edit to display all the options.
3. Click on the Import Bookmark button to open the Import File as Bookmarks dialog box (Figure M.6). The available files are displayed in the list box. You may have to change the drive or directory to display the HTML files (which have .HTM extensions).
4. In the Files list box, click on the HTML file you want to import.
5. Click on OK to import the HTML file as a bookmark. The hypertext link items in the HTML file are added to your master list of bookmarks in the Bookmark List dialog box.

Tip

You can also import a Hotlist that was created in Air or Spyglass Mosaic and then exported as an HTML file.

Figure M.6

Netscape's Import File as Bookmarks dialog box lets you convert a list of URLs to a Netscape Bookmarks list.

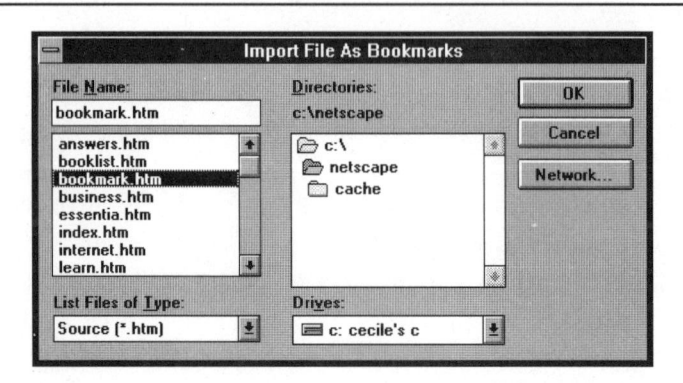

Exporting Bookmarks: Netscape

Netscape's Export Bookmark feature lets you export any bookmark file to an HTML file that contains hypertext links. When you export the file, it can be opened as an HTML document in any Web browser.

1. Choose View Bookmarks from the Bookmarks menu.
2. Click on Edit to display all the options.
3. Click on the Export Bookmark button to open the Export Bookmark dialog box.
4. In the Files list box, type the name of the HTML file you want to export.
5. Click on OK to export the bookmark as an HTML file. The hypertext link items in your bookmarks are saved in the HTML file.

MODIFYING HOTLISTS

In Air, NCSA, or Spyglass Mosaic, you have the ability to modify Hotlists you've created.

> You can also modify Quarterdeck Mosaic's Hotlists by modifying folders, and Netscape's Hotlists by modifying bookmarks.

See Also Folders; Modifying Bookmarks

Modifying Hotlists: Air Mosaic

Air Mosaic's Hotlists are modified in the Hotlist dialog box, shown in Figure M.7. You cannot move items but you can edit them and insert new folders or documents anywhere within existing Hotlists. To insert a new item in Air Mosaic:

1. Choose Hotlists from the File menu. The Hotlists dialog box opens.
2. Click on an existing menu or item. The new item will be added above the item on which you click.
3. Click Insert. The Insert New dialog box opens.

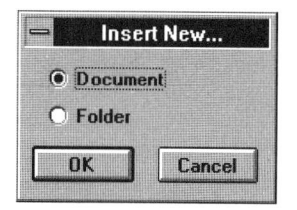

4. Select the Document or Folder option, then click OK.
5. Type the Title of the new document or folder in the Title text box.
6. If this is a document, also type the URL for the document.
7. Click OK to close the Insert dialog box.
8. Click Close to close the Hotlists dialog box.

Figure M.7

Air Mosaic's Hotlist dialog box lets you add and insert new folders and dialog boxes.

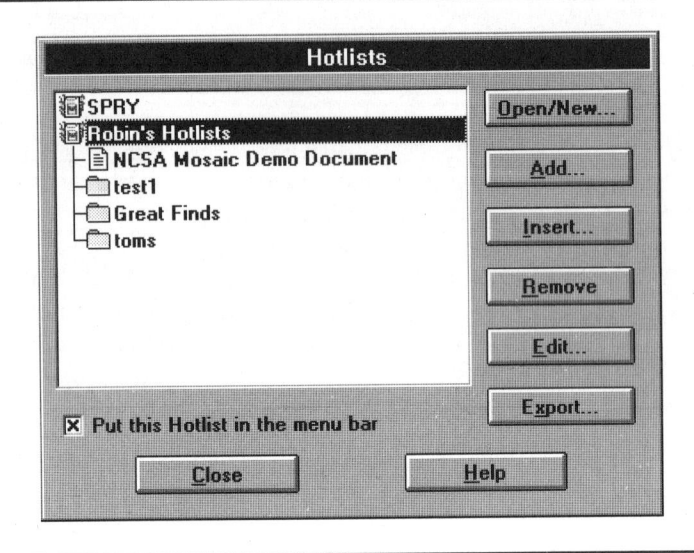

The new folder or document is added within the existing Hotlist, at the cursor location.

> **Tip**
>
> To add an item to the bottom of the Hotlist, use the Add button instead of opening the Hotlist dialog box.

You may find that you'd like to change the titles of some menus or documents after you've added them. Or you might want to change the URL for a particular document. You can edit titles and URLs with the editing feature. To modify the title or URL of a document or folder:

1. Choose Hotlists from the File menu. The Hotlists dialog box opens.
2. Click on the folder or document you want to modify.
3. Click Edit. The Edit List Title dialog box opens (Figure M.8).
4. Type a new title for the new document or folder in the Title text box.
5. If this is a document, you can also type a different URL for it.
6. Click OK to close the Edit Item or Edit List Title dialog box.
7. Click Close to close the Hotlists dialog box.

Figure M.8

Air Mosaic's Edit List Title dialog box lets you change a title or URL.

See Also **Add Current To Hotlist; Add Document to Hotlist; Adding to a Menu; Changing a Hotlist; Creating a Menu; Deleting a Hotlist; Deleting a Menu; Deleting Items from a Menu; Exporting a Hotlist; Hotlist**

Modifying Hotlists: NCSA Mosaic

NCSA Mosaic's Hotlist Manager, available in version 2.0 beta and above and found in the Navigate drop-down menu, lets you modify Hotlists in several ways. You can:

- Add new Hotlists
- Remove Hotlists
- Edit Hotlists
- Add items to Hotlists
- Remove items from Hotlists
- Edit items on Hotlists
- Place Hotlists on menus
- Import Hotlists

NCSA Mosaic's Menu Editor, available in version 1.0 and in version 2.0 alpha, found in the Navigate drop-down menu, also lets you modify Hotlists. You can:

- Add new Hotlists
- Remove Hotlists
- Edit Hotlists
- Add items to Hotlists
- Remove items from Hotlists
- Edit items on Hotlists
- Place Hotlists on menus
- Copy items from one Hotlist to another
- Change the current Hotlist

See **Hotlist Manager; Menu Editor**

Modifying Hotlists: Spyglass Mosaic

Spyglass Mosaic's Hotlist is modified in the Hotlist dialog box. You can change the titles and URLs of documents with the editing feature and you can remove documents you no longer need. To modify the title or

URL of a document in the Hotlist:

1. Choose Hotlists from the Navigate menu. The Hotlists dialog box opens (Figure M.9).
2. Click on the document you want to modify then click Edit.
3. The Edit Hotlist Entry dialog box opens (Figure M.10).
4. Edit the title of the document in the Title text box.
5. Type a different URL for it in the URL text box.
6. Click OK to close the Edit Hotlist Entry dialog box.
7. Click Close to close the Hotlists dialog box.

To remove a document from the Hotlist:

1. Choose Hotlists from the Navigate menu to open the Hotlists dialog box.
2. Click on the document you want to remove, then click Delete.
3. Click Close to close the Hotlists dialog box.

Figure M.9

Spyglass Mosaic's Hotlist dialog box lets you modify titles and URLs and remove items.

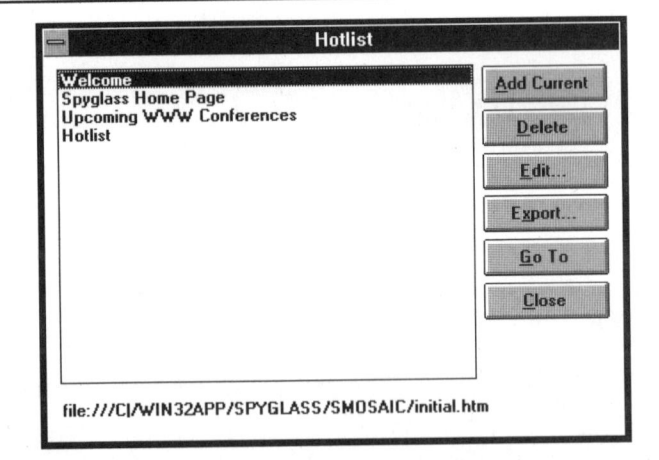

Figure M.10

Spyglass Mosaic's Edit Title-URL dialog box

See Add Current To Hotlist; Deleting Items from a Hotlist; Exporting a Hotlist; Hotlist

MODIFYING MENUS

When using Air or NCSA Mosaic, you can modify menus you've created based on your Hotlists.

> **You can also modify Netscape's Bookmark menu by modifying bookmarks.**

See Hotlists; Modifying Bookmarks; Modifying Hotlists

Modifying Menus: Air Mosaic

Air Mosaic's menus are Hotlists that are added to the menu bar. These can be modified in the Hotlist dialog box.

See Adding to a Menu; Creating a Menu; Deleting a Menu; Deleting Items from a Menu; Modifying Hotlists

Modifying Menus: NCSA Mosaic

NCSA Mosaic's Hotlist Manager, available in version 2.0 beta and above, lets you modify menus in several ways. NCSA Mosaic's Menu Editor, available in version 1.0 and in version 2.0 alpha, also lets you modify menus you create. Both of these commands are found in the Navigate drop-down menu.

See Also Adding to a Menu; Creating a Menu; Deleting a Menu; Deleting Items from a Menu; Hotlist Manager; Menu Editor; Modifying Hotlists

MOSAIC HELP PAGE

Spyglass Mosaic is documented in an online user guide, titled Mosaic Help Page, which includes a tutorial and reference. To download this document, choose it from the Help menu. You can read the document online, use its links to locate information, save the document to your hard disk for later reference, or print it.

> **NCSA Mosaic includes a similar feature called Online Documentation on the Help menu. In Netscape, online documentation is available by choosing Handbook from the Help menu.**

See Also Handbook; Online Documentation; Print; Save

MOSAIC WINDOW

Each Web browser includes most of the same elements in its main application window:

- Title bar
- Menu bar
- Toolbar
- URL bar or box
- Program icon
- Document view window or browser window
- Status bar

Air Mosaic's application window is shown in Figure M.11.

See **Browser window; Document View Window; Menu Bar; Part 1: Looking at Mosaic: A Guided Tour; Program Icon; Status Bar; Title Bar; Toolbar; URL Box**

MOSAIC.INI FILE: NCSA MOSAIC

The MOSAIC.INI file is an ASCII, or text file used by Windows which holds information about how you run NCSA Mosaic and the options you select. In NCSA Mosaic

Figure M.11

Air Mosaic's application window.

versions 1.0 and 2.0 alpha, you had to edit the MOSAIC.INI file to modify your configuration and preferences, as well as to enter your Internet address. This is no longer the case with NCSA Mosaic versions 2.0 beta and later. Instead, you now must use the Preferences command on the Edit menu, which will in turn modify your MOSAIC.INI file.

See Also **Internet Address; Preferences**

MOVIES

Videos that are shared on the Internet are often referred to as movies. Movie files are most often found in MPEG format. All the currently recognized movie formats are listed below with their file extensions. You'll need a viewer to play movies.

File type	Extensions
MPEG	mpg, mpeg, mpe
QuickTime	mov, qt
X-msmovie	avi
X-sgi-movie	movie

See Also **MPEG Movies; QuickTime Movies; Viewers**

MOVING BACKWARD AND FORWARD

Each Web browser lets you move backward and forward through documents with the Back and Forward commands and buttons.

See Also **Back; Forward; Part 1: Going Back and Forth**

MOVING BETWEEN DOCUMENTS USING LINKS

Each Web browser lets you move from one document to another by selecting a link or anchor.

See Also **Anchors; Hypermedia; Hypertext; Links; Part 1: Browsing With Hypertext Link**

MOVING BETWEEN DOCUMENTS USING URLS

Each Web browser lets you display another document by entering its URL in the URL text box.

See Also **Open URL; Part 1: Using Uniform Resource Locators; URL Box; URL Helper; URLs**

MPEG MOVIES

MPEG movies are videos that are shared on the Internet. Although movie files in MPEG format are the most common, you may also come across video files in other formats. You'll need a viewer to play MPEG movies and can download the

MPEGPLAY viewer with anonymous ftp from the same server where NCSA Mosaic is stored: `ftp::://web/mosaic/windows/viewers`. You can also find MPEGPLAY at `ftp://gatekeeper.dec.com/pub/micro/msdos/win3/desktop`. The file name to look for is MPEGW32H.ZIP, the zip version of MPEGPLAY.EXE.

> **Tip**
>
> Once you download this viewer, use the **Extensions** or **MIME** type option to associate it with **MPEG** files.

See Also   Extensions; MIME Type; Movies; QuickTime Movies; Viewers

MULTIMEDIA FILES

Web browsers can view multimedia files—files or documents with text, images, audio, and/or video content. Some files can be handled by the browser itself, while others must be viewed with a viewer installed on your computer.

See Also   GIF Images; Hypermedia; Images; JPEG Images; Movies; MPEG Movies; QuickTime Movies; Viewers

N

NAVIGATE MENU

The Navigate menu contains items that let you select, load, and move between documents. All forms of Mosaic (except Netscape) include a Navigate menu, each with a slightly different group of commands.

In Netscape, similar items are found on the Go menu.

See Also   Back; Cancel; Forward; Go; History; Home; Hotlist; Load Missing Images; Reload; Stop Current Read

NAVIGATING THE WEB

Whenever you use one of the Web browsers described in this book to open a document, you are *navigating the Web*. Remember, the Web is not the entire Internet—just the graphical portion of it.

Tip

For an overview of how to navigate the Web, see Part 1.

See Also   Part 1: Browsing the Internet; World Wide Web

NCSA

NCSA is the abbreviation for the National Center for Supercomputing Applications, developers of the first Mosaic, NCSA Mosaic version 1.0, and the more recent version 2.0, described in this book.

NETWORK: QUARTERDECK MOSAIC

The Network tab in Quarterdeck Mosaic's Preferences dialog box is where you can specify the name of a proxy server (a computer established for network security), specify your mail and news servers, and manage the document caching process.

> Netscape's Network options in the Preferences dialog box also manage the document caching process.

See Also Document Caching; Mail Server; NNTP Server; Proxy; User Name

NEWS: NCSA MOSAIC AND NETSCAPE

In NCSA Mosaic and Netscape, you'll need to enter some information in the News section of the Preferences dialog box before you can subscribe to newsgroups or read news. In NCSA Mosaic, News options are found on the Services tab. In Netscape, News options are found in the Mail and News section.

See News RC File; NNTP Server; Preferences; Reading News; Services; Subscribing to Newsgroups; Subscriptions

NEWS PROXY

See Proxies

NEWS RC FILE: NETSCAPE

Netscape uses a file, called the News RC File, to maintain a list of the newsgroups to which you subscribe. You can see that list by choosing the Go to Newsgroups command or the Newsgroups button. To enter a name for News RC File:

1. Choose Preferences from the Options menu.
2. Choose Mail and News from the drop-down list at the top of the dialog box.
3. Enter the path and file name in the News RC File text box; for example, C:\NETSCAPE\NEWSRC.

News RC Directory: c:\netscape\news

4. Choose OK to close the Preferences dialog box.

See Also Go To Newsgroups; Internet Newsgroups; Reading News; Subscribing to Newsgroups

NEWS SERVER

See NNTP Server

NEWSGROUPS

See Internet (Usenet) Newsgroups; Subscriptions

NNTP SERVER

The NNTP server is the Network News Transfer Protocol-supported server, the news server you use to subscribe to Internet newsgroups. Ask your network administrator or Internet service provider for the name of the NNTP server that lets you access newsgroups and news. Then enter the NNTP server name in the appropriate text box. A server name might look something like: news.abcdef.com.

See Also Internet Newsgroups; Preferences

NNTP Server: NCSA Mosaic

To enter the NNTP server name in NCSA Mosaic:

1. Choose Preferences from the Options menu.
2. Click the Services tab to bring it forward.
3. Enter the NNTP server name in the NNTP Server text box.
4. Choose OK to close the Preferences dialog box.

NNTP Server: Quarterdeck Mosaic

To enter the NNTP server name in Quarterdeck Mosaic:

1. Choose Configure Network from the Tools menu.
2. Enter the NNTP server name in the NNTP Server text box.
3. Choose OK to close the dialog box.

News (NNTP) Server: Air Mosaic

To enter the NNTP server name in Quarterdeck Mosaic:

1. Choose Configuration from the Options menu.
2. Enter the NNTP server name in the News Server text box.
3. Choose OK to close the Configuration dialog box.

News (NNTP) Server: Netscape

To enter the NNTP server name in Netscape:

1. Choose Preferences from the Options menu.
2. Choose Mail and News from the drop-down list at the top of the dialog box.
3. Enter the NNTP server name in the News (NNTP) Server text box.

4. Choose OK to close the Preferences dialog box.

NO PROXY ON

See **Proxies**

NUMBERED LISTS STYLE: QUARTERDECK MOSAIC

In Quarterdeck Mosaic, you can change the appearance of numbered lists in documents by selecting an alternative from the Numbered Lists Style drop-down list. This option is found on the HTML Viewer tab of the Preferences dialog box. To select a different numbered list style:

1. Choose Preferences from the Tools menu.
2. Click on the HTML Viewer tab to bring it forward.
3. In the Numbered Lists Style drop-down list, select the numbering style from those displayed.

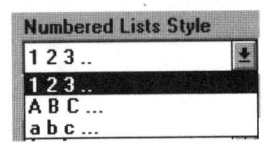

4. Choose OK.

See Also **Styles**

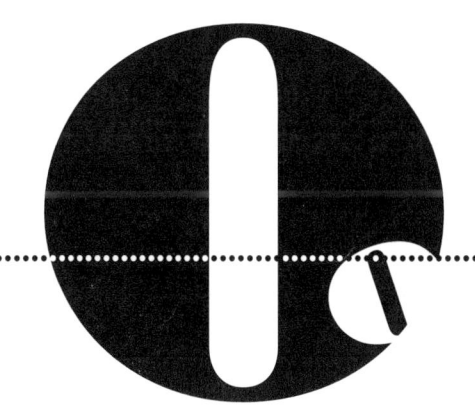

ONLINE DOCUMENTATION

NCSA Mosaic is documented in an online user guide, appropriately titled Online Documentation, which includes a tutorial and reference. To download this document, choose Online Documentation from the Help menu. You can also:

- Read the document online.
- Use its links to locate information.
- Save the document to your hard disk for later reference.
- Print the document.

> **Netscape includes a similar feature called Netscape Handbook on the Help menu. In Spyglass Mosaic, online documentation is available by choosing Mosaic Help Page from the Help menu.**

See Also Mosaic Help Page; Online Documentation; Print; Save

OPEN: QUARTERDECK MOSAIC

In Quarterdeck Mosaic, you can retrieve a document by entering its URL in the Open URL dialog box.

1. Choose Open from the File menu. The Open URL dialog box is displayed as shown in Figure O.1.
2. In the URL text box, type the exact URL for the document, making sure you use the correct case. You can open a file on your hard disk or retrieve a file from the Internet.

Tip

You can also click the **URL Helper** button to open the **URL** dialog box and enter the **URL** more easily.

Figure O.1

The Quarterdeck Mosaic Open URL dialog box

3. Click OK. The document whose URL is entered is displayed in a new window.

You can also retrieve a document by entering its URL in the URL bar below the toolbar, if it is displayed.

> **Tip**
>
> If you want to retrieve a document and open it in the current window, use Go To on the Navigate menu instead.

In Air Mosaic, NCSA Mosaic, and Spyglass Mosaic, choose **Open URL** or **Open Local File**. In Netscape, choose **Open File** or **Open Location**.

See Also Go To; Open File, Open Location; Open Local File, Open URL; URL; URL Box

OPEN FILE, OPEN LOCATION: NETSCAPE

In Netscape, you can retrieve a document by entering its URL in the Open File or Open Location dialog box. You can also retrieve a document by entering its URL in the URL box below the toolbar, if it is displayed.

Open File

In Netscape, you can open a file you've previously saved on your hard disk with the Open File command.

1. Choose Open File from the File menu to open a file saved on your hard disk. The File Open dialog box is displayed.

2. In the File Name list box, select the name of the file to display.

3. Click OK. The document is displayed in the document window.

Open Location

In Netscape, you can retrieve a file from the Internet with the Open command or the Open button in the toolbar.

1. Choose Open Location from the File menu to retrieve a file from the Internet. The Open Location dialog box is displayed. You can also click on the Open button to display the Open Location dialog box.

2. In the Location text box, type the URL for the document exactly, making sure you use the correct case.

3. Click OK. The document whose URL is entered is displayed in the document window.

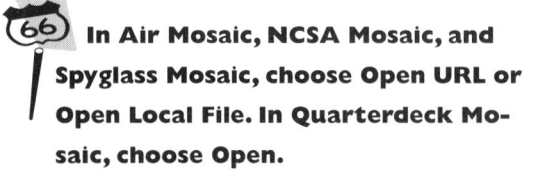

> **In Air Mosaic, NCSA Mosaic, and Spyglass Mosaic, choose Open URL or Open Local File. In Quarterdeck Mosaic, choose Open.**

See Also Open; Open Local File, Open URL; URL; URL Box

OPEN LOCAL FILE, OPEN URL: AIR, NCSA, AND SPYGLASS MOSAIC

In Air, NCSA and Spyglass Mosaic, you can retrieve a document by entering its URL in the Open Local File or Open URL dialog box. You can also retrieve a document by entering its URL in the URL box, if it is displayed.

Open Local File

In Air, NCSA, and Spyglass Mosaic, you can open a file you've previously saved on your hard disk with the Open Local File command.

1. Choose Open Local File from the File menu to open a file saved on your hard disk. (If you're in Spyglass Mosaic, you can check on the Open Local File button.) The Open (or Open Local or Open Local File) dialog box is displayed.

2. In the File Name list box, select the name of the file to display.

3. Click OK. The document you selected is displayed in the document window.

Open URL

In Air, NCSA and Spyglass Mosaic, you can retrieve a file from the Internet with the Open URL command or the Open button in the toolbar.

1. Choose Open URL from the File menu to retrieve a file from the Internet. The Open URL dialog box is displayed. You can also click on the Open URL button in NCSA Mosaic or the Open button in Air Mosaic to display the Open URL dialog box.

   NCSA Mosaic Open URL button

   Air Mosaic Open button

   Spyglass Mosaic Open button

2. In the URL text box, type the URL for the document exactly, making sure you use the correct case.

3. Click OK. The document whose URL is entered is displayed in the document window.

> **In Quarterdeck Mosaic, choose Open to enter a document's URL. In Netscape, choose Open File or Open Location.**

See Also   Open; Open File, Open Location; URL; URL Box

OPTIONS MENU: NCSA AND AIR MOSAIC, AND NETSCAPE

The Options menu contains items that let you control which elements display on your screen and access all the programs' preferences and configuration settings. NCSA and Air Mosaic and Netscape include an Options menu, each with a slightly different group of commands.

> **Similar items are found on Quarterdeck Mosaic's View and Tools menus.**

See Also   Preferences; View Menu; Tools Menu

P

PAGE SETUP: SPYGLASS MOSAIC

Spyglass Mosaic's Page Setup command lets you change the margins on your documents as well as include page headers and footers with page numbers. When you choose Page Setup from the File menu, the Page Setup dialog box (Figure P.1) is displayed. Each of the Header and Footer text boxes contains a default value to insert text when the document prints.

To change the margins, edit the numbers in the Left, Right, Top and Bottom text boxes.

To add a header or footer, type the text for it in the appropriate text box. To include a page number in the header or footer use the &p option described in Figure P.1.

> You can change margins in Air Mosaic with the Print Margins command.

See Also Print; Print Margins; Print Setup

PARAGRAPH SPACING

In Quarterdeck Mosaic, you can change the space between paragraphs in documents with the Paragraph Spacing option. This option is found on the HTML Viewer tab of the Preferences dialog box. To change paragraph spacing:

1. Choose Preferences from the Tools menu.
2. Click on the HTML Viewer tab to bring it forward.
3. In the Paragraph Spacing text box, delete the current number (the default is 8) and type a new number. A higher number increases the space, a lower number decreases the space.
4. Choose OK.

Figure P.1

Spyglass Mosaic's Page Setup dialog box lets you change the margins and add headers and footers.

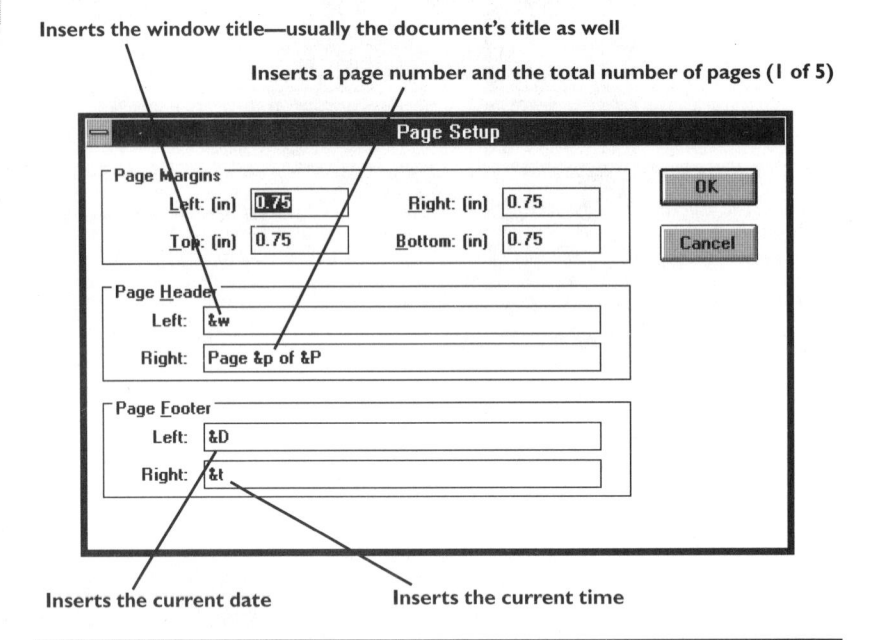

- Inserts the window title—usually the document's title as well
- Inserts a page number and the total number of pages (1 of 5)
- Inserts the current date
- Inserts the current time

PASTE: NCSA, QUARTERDECK AND SPYGLASS MOSAIC, AND NETSCAPE

The Paste command on the Edit menu places the text on the clipboard into the current text box at the location of the cursor. Text must first be placed on the clipboard with either the Copy or Cut command. Paste is available in NCSA, Quarterdeck, and Spyglass Mosaic, and Netscape. Each Mosaic form lets you paste text into the URL bar or text box. You can also paste text within some dialog boxes and document windows.

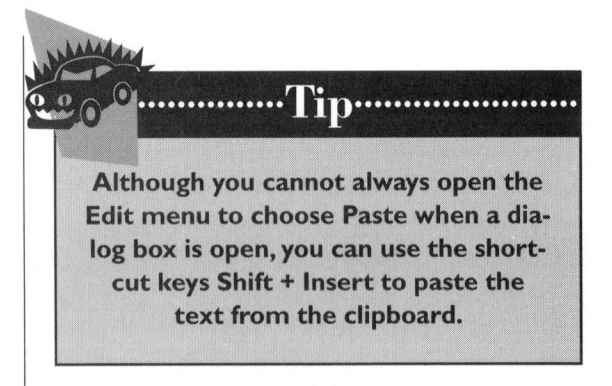

Tip

Although you cannot always open the Edit menu to choose Paste when a dialog box is open, you can use the shortcut keys Shift + Insert to paste the text from the clipboard.

See Also Copy; Cut

POP-UP MENUS: NCSA MOSAIC, Q MOSAIC, NETSCAPE

NCSA and Quarterdeck Mosaic, and Netscape include pop-up menus that help you quickly access a number of product features. To choose an item from a pop-up menu, just click on it.

To display the pop-up menu in NCSA Mosaic, right-click on any link (anchor), image or any blank area in the document window. Different options display when you click on each item.

To display the pop-up menu in Quarterdeck Mosaic, right-click on any text or image in the browser window or on any item in the archives. As in NCSA Mosaic, different options display when you click on each item.

Netscape includes one pop-up menu. To display it, right-click on any link.

See Also Anchors; Archives; Browser Window; Document Window; Inline Image; Link

PREFERENCES

In NCSA, Quarterdeck, and Spyglass Mosaic and in Netscape, configuration items and customization options are specified in the many tabs and sections found in each product's Preference dialog box.

In Air Mosaic, preferences are specified in the Configuration dialog box.

See Also Configuration

Preferences: NCSA Mosaic

To open the NCSA Mosaic Preferences dialog box to see or change the current configuration and options settings:

1. Choose Preferences from the Options menu. The Preferences dialog box opens with the General tab already in front.
2. Change any option or setting on the tab. Use standard windows techniques to select options and edit text boxes.

Options for NCSA Mosaic version 2.0, which were changing shortly before this book was completed, are generally described under the listing for the tab on which they appear. Some are also described under separate headings.

3. In NCSA Mosaic, choose the Apply Now button to apply your changes immediately and keep the dialog box open.

[Apply Now]

4. Click on any tab to display additional options and make any other changes.

5. When you have completed your changes, choose OK. OK saves your changes to the MOSAIC.INI file and also closes the Preferences dialog box.

See Also   Anchors; Caching; Font Styles; General; MOSAIC.INI File; Proxy; Services; Tables; Viewers

Preferences: Quarterdeck Mosaic

To open the Quarterdeck Mosaic Preferences dialog box to see or change the current configuration and options settings:

1. Choose Preferences from the Tools menu. The preferences dialog box opens with the Network tab already in front.

> **If you've already opened the Preferences dialog box during this session, the last tab you used will be in front.**

2. Change any options or settings on the tab. Use standard windows techniques to select options and edit text boxes.

> **Quarterdeck Mosaic options are described under their individual listings in this book.**

3. Click on any tab to display additional options and make any other changes you wish.

4. When you have completed your changes, choose OK. OK saves your changes to the QMOSAIC.INI file and also closes the Preferences dialog box.

Preferences: Spyglass Mosaic

To open the Preferences dialog box to see or change the current configuration and options settings:

1. Choose Preferences from the Edit menu. The Spyglass Mosaic Preferences dialog box opens (Figure P.2).

2. Change any options or settings. Use standard windows techniques to select options and edit text boxes.

> **Spyglass Mosaic options are described under their individual listings in this book.**

3. Choose OK to save the information to your SMOSAIC.INI file.

Preferences: Netscape

To open the Preferences dialog box to see or change the current configuration and

Figure P.2

The Preferences dialog box in Spyglass Mosaic lets you customize your copy of Spyglass Mosaic.

options settings:

1. Choose Preferences from the Options menu. The Preferences dialog box opens and the section you last used displays.
2. Change any options or settings in this section. Use standard windows techniques to select options and edit text boxes.

Netscape options are described under their individual listings in this book.

---

3. Open the drop-down list at the top of the dialog box to display additional options and then make any other changes.
4. When you have completed your changes, choose OK to save the information to your NETSCAPE.INI file.

PRESENTATION MODE

NCSA Mosaic's Presentation Mode feature lets you maximize your document display area by temporarily turning off almost all the other items on the screen. In Figure P.3, for example, only the scroll bars are visible.

To return to a normal view at any time, press Alt + P or Escape.

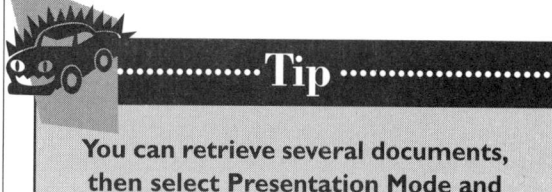

...............Tip........................

You can retrieve several documents, then select Presentation Mode and use the shortcut keys for Back and Forward (B and F) to display each document during a presentation.

Figure P.3

NCSA Mosaic's Presentation Mode gives you a larger area for displaying documents.

> Welcome to NCSA Mosaic™ for the Microsoft Windows ™ Operating Systems
>
> NCSA Mosaic is an Internet navigation and data retrevial tool that will allow you to access networked information with the click of a mouse button. Mosaic is capable of accessing data from the World Wide Web servers (HTTP), Gopher servers, FTP servers and News servers (NNTP). Mosaic can access other data services through gateway servers. These services provide you search capabilities in database environments such as PH, Archie, WAIS, and Veronica. NCSA Mosaic was designed to provide its user transparent access to these information sources and services. NCSA Mosaic software is copyrighted by The Board of Trustees of the University of Illinois

Air Mosaic's Kiosk Mode offers similar capabilities.

See Also   Back; Forward; Kiosk Mode

PRINT

You can print the current document in every form of Mosaic by choosing the Print command from the File menu or one of the following Print tools from the appropriate toolbar.

Spyglass Mosaic

NCSA Mosaic

Netscape

Quarterdeck Mosaic

The Windows Print dialog box (Figure P.4) opens. You can change selections and access the Print Setup dialog box if necessary, then click OK to print.

See Also   Page Setup; Print Margins; Print Preview; Print Setup

Figure P.4
The Print dialog box is available from every form of Mosaic and in Netscape.

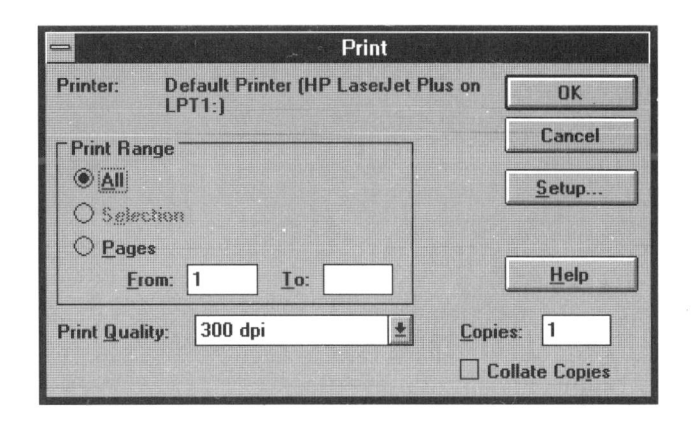

PRINT MARGINS: AIR MOSAIC

Air Mosaic's Print Margins command lets you change the margins on documents you print. When you choose Print Margins from the File menu, the Print Margins dialog box (Figure P.5) displays and you can enter a number (in inches) to change the default margins for the current document. Choose OK when you are finished, then choose Print to print the document.

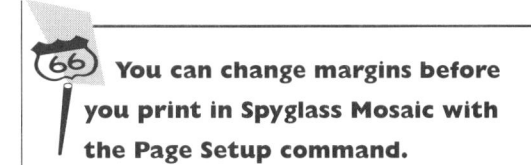

You can change margins before you print in Spyglass Mosaic with the Page Setup command.

See Also   Print; Print Preview; Print Setup

Figure P.5
The Air Mosaic Print Margins dialog box lets you change the margins for a document before you print it.

PRINT PREVIEW: NCSA, AIR AND QUARTERDECK MOSAIC, NETSCAPE

You can preview the current document in NCSA, Air, and Quarterdeck Mosaics and in Netscape before you print it. The Print Preview window (Figure P.6) shows you how the current options and styles will look in the printed document. Choose the Print Preview command from the File menu to open the Print Preview window.

The Print Preview window includes these button options:

Print Prints the current document.

Next Page Displays the next page of the document.

Prev Page Displays the previous page of the document.

Two Page Displays the document in a side-by-side two page layout.

Zoom In Increases the magnification to enlarge the document, but you no longer see the document in full page view. You can choose Zoom In twice.

Zoom Out Available only after you've used Zoom In, decreases the magnification to reduce the document until the document is in full page view again.

Close Closes the Print Preview window.

Figure P.6

The NCSA Mosaic Print Preview window lets you see how a document will look when printed.

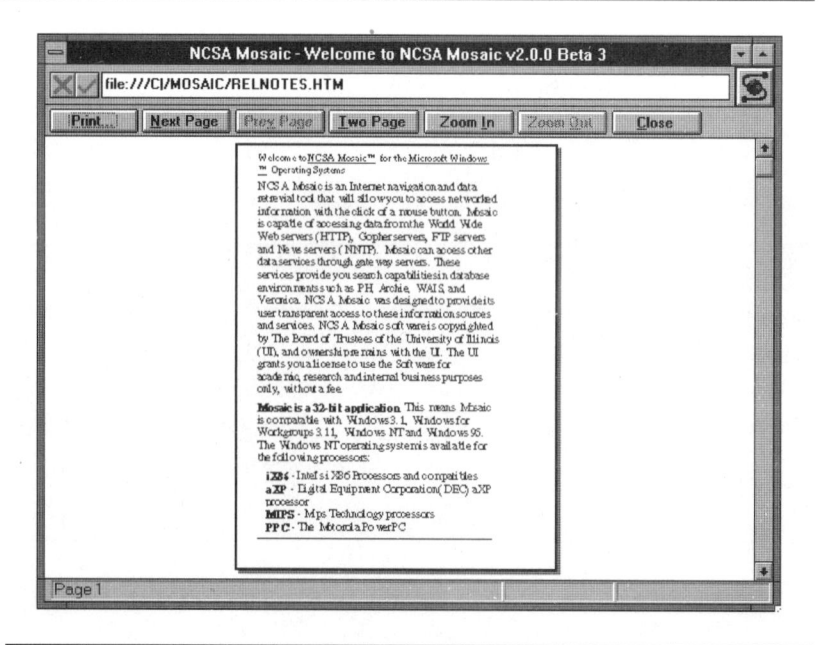

PROGRAM ICON   209

> **Tip**
>
> You can also increase the magnification by clicking on the document with the magnifying glass cursor (shown below). To see the magnifying glass cursor, place the mouse cursor anywhere on the page.

> **Tip**
>
> In NCSA and Quarterdeck Mosaic, you can also choose the Print Setup command from the File menu. In Spyglass Mosaic, choose Printer Setup from the File menu.

See Also Page Setup; Print; Print Margins; Print Setup; Styles

The Windows Print Setup dialog box (Figure P.7) opens and you can select another printer and change the paper orientation, size, and source. Click OK to save your selections, then print the document.

See Also Page Setup; Print; Print Margins; Print Preview

PRINT SETUP, PRINTER SETUP

You can change the currently selected printer in your Web browser by choosing the Setup button in the Print dialog box.

PROGRAM ICON

In all Web browsers, the program icon to the right of the URL bar is animated

Figure P.7

The Print Setup dialog box is accessible from each Web browser.

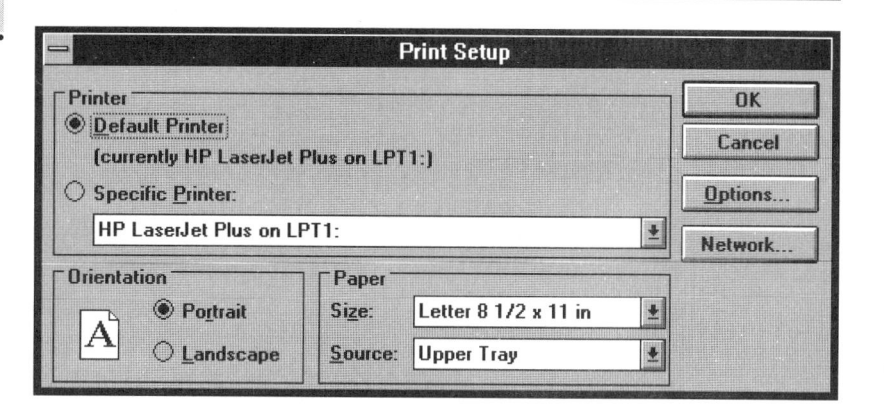

whenever a server is being accessed (for example, whenever you try to retrieve a document). In NCSA version 1.0 you can click the program icon to stop retrieving a document if you find it is taking too long, or if you change your mind about wanting to see it. Here are the program icons for each browser:

- Air Mosaic
- NCSA Mosaic
- Quarterdeck Mosaic
- Spyglass Mosaic
- Netscape

See Also **Cancel; Stop**

PROPERTIES: QUARTERDECK MOSAIC

Quarterdeck Mosaic's Properties command displays information about the current document or a selected URL. Use the Properties dialog box, shown in Figure P.8, to change the icon associated with a document. The dialog box displays:

- The document's URL
- The document's title
- The date and time you last accessed the document
- The MIME type associated with the document

To display a document's properties, choose Properties from the File menu. To change a document's associated icon:

1. Choose Properties from the File menu.
2. Click the Change Icon button to open the Change Icon dialog box (Figure P.9).

Figure P.8
Quarterdeck Mosaic's File Properties dialog box summarizes a URL and lets you change its icon.

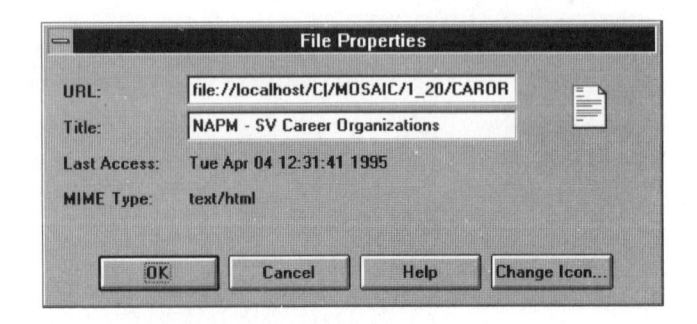

Figure P.9

Quarterdeck Mosaic's Change Icon dialog box lets you change a document's icon.

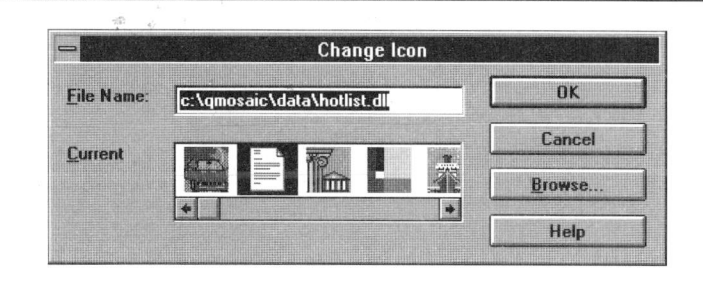

---

3. Scroll through the icons in the Current Icon box until you find one you like, then click on it.
4. Choose OK to apply your selection and close the Change Icon dialog box.
5. Choose OK to close the File Properties dialog box.

> **While the Change Icon dialog box is open, click on the Browse button. Then, open another file that contains icons to select an icon from another source.**

See Also   Document Title; MIME Type; URL

PROXIES: NETSCAPE

In Netscape, you can enter the name and port of any proxy servers in use on your network in the Proxies section of the Preferences dialog box. You can enter a proxy and port for FTP, Gopher, HTTP, News, and WAIS protocols.

> **You will have to ask your network administrator for the names and port numbers of the proxy servers.**

To enter proxy information:

1. Choose Preferences from the Options menu.
2. Select Proxies from the drop-down list box to display the Proxies section (Figure P.10).
3. Click and type the name in the appropriate text box.
4. Click and type the port number in the text box to the right.
5. Repeat Steps 3 and 4 for each proxy you need to enter, then choose OK to close the Preferences dialog box.

See Also   Proxy

Figure P.10

The Proxies section of the Netscape Preferences dialog box

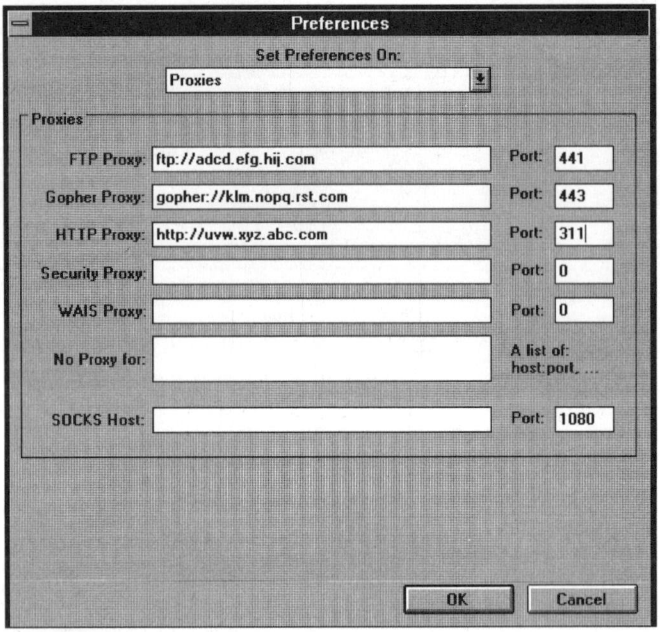

Preferences

Set Preferences On: Proxies

Proxies:
- FTP Proxy: ftp://adcd.efg.hij.com Port: 441
- Gopher Proxy: gopher://klm.nopq.rst.com Port: 443
- HTTP Proxy: http://uvw.xyz.abc.com Port: 311
- Security Proxy: Port: 0
- WAIS Proxy: Port: 0
- No Proxy for: A list of: host:port, ...
- SOCKS Host: Port: 1080

OK Cancel

PROXY

If you are accessing the Internet from a computer network, at work or at school, your network administrator may have set up a firewall for security purposes. A proxy (also called a proxy server) is a computer that runs along with the firewall to process your request (for example the URL you enter to retrieve a document) and send it to a remote server outside the firewall. It also enables the response (the document you requested) to be sent back through the firewall.

Your network administrator will give you the name and port number of any proxy servers in use on your local area network. You'll need to enter them in the Preferences or Configuration dialog box of your Web browser. Table P.1 shows examples of a proxy name and port number for each protocol.

> **If you are running your Web browser through a SLIP or PPP account over a modem, you won't have to enter the name of a proxy server.**

See Also Firewall; Proxies; Proxy Server; Socks

Table P.1

Sample Proxy Names and Port Numbers

Protocol	Proxy name and port number
HTTP	http://abcd.efg.hij.com:448/
FTP	ftp://abcd.efg.hij.com:448/
GOPHER	gopher://abcd.efg.hij.com:448/
WAIS	wais://abcd.efg.hij.com:448/

Proxy: NCSA Mosaic

In NCSA Mosaic, you can enter the name of any proxy servers in use on your network on the Proxy tab (Figure P.11) of the Preferences dialog box. You can enter a proxy and port for HTTP, FTP, WAIS and Gopher protocols.

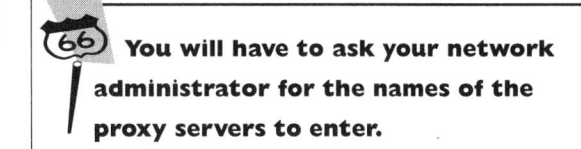

> You will have to ask your network administrator for the names of the proxy servers to enter.

To enter the proxy information:

1. Choose Preferences from the Options menu.

Figure P.11

The Proxy tab of the NCSA Mosaic Preferences dialog box

2. Click the Proxy tab to bring it forward.
3. Click and type the name of the proxy server in the appropriate text box.
4. Repeat Step 3 for each proxy you need to enter, then choose OK to close the Preferences dialog box.

The following additional options are available on the Proxy tab:

Machine/Domain List If you are behind a firewall, you can create a list of domains and specify whether they will be affected by the proxy server.

Add Lets you enter a domain name or IP address to add to the Machine/Domain list.

Remove Lets you remove the selected domain name from the Machine/Domain list.

Proxy Lets you specify that the selected domain name in the Machine/Domain list will use the proxy server.

No Proxy Lets you specify that the selected domain name in the Machine/Domain list will not use the proxy server.

Proxy: Quarterdeck Mosaic

In Quarterdeck Mosaic, you can enter the name of proxy servers in use on your network with the Configure Network command.

> **You will have to ask your network administrator for the name of the proxy server to enter.**

To enter the proxy information:
1. Choose Configure Network from the Tools menu.
2. Click and type the name in the Proxy Location text box.
3. Choose OK to close the dialog box.

PROXY SERVER: SPYGLASS MOSAIC

In Spyglass Mosaic, you can enter the name of a proxy server in use on your net-

> **You will have to ask your network administrator for the name of the proxy server to enter.**

work in the Preferences dialog box.

To enter the proxy information:
1. Choose Preferences from the Edit menu.
2. Click and type the name in the HTTP Proxy Server text box.
3. Choose OK to close the Preferences dialog box.

See Also Proxy

PROXY SERVERS: AIR MOSAIC

In Air Mosaic, you can enter the name of any proxy servers in use on your network in the Proxy Server dialog box. You can enter a proxy and port for FTP, HTTP, WAIS, or Gopher protocols.

> **You will have to ask your network administrator for the names of the proxy servers to enter.**

To enter the proxy information:

1. Choose Configuration from the Options menu.
2. Click the Proxy Servers button to open the dialog box.
3. Click and type the name in the appropriate text box.
4. Repeat Step 3 for each proxy server you need to enter, then choose OK to close the Proxy Servers dialog box.
5. Choose OK to close the Preferences dialog box.

See Also **Proxy**

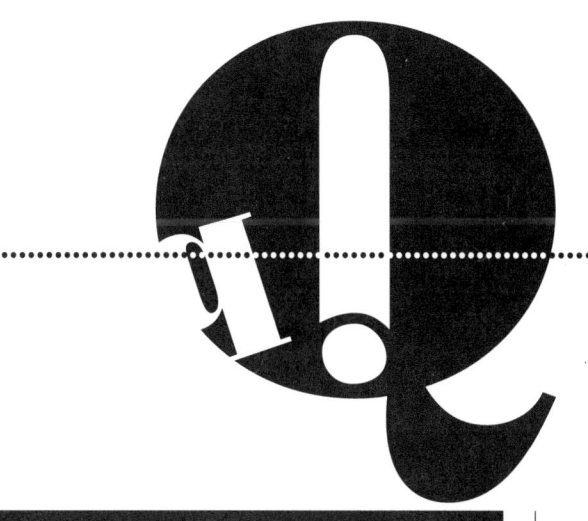

QUICKLIST: NCSA MOSAIC

The NCSA Quicklist is simply a Hotlist of documents, Web sites, and their URLs, provided for you in NCSA Mosaic to help you get started. NCSA Mosaic lets you create multiple Hotlists, but only one Quicklist, which you can include as a menu. You can make the Quicklist your current Hotlist with the Open URL command. You can also modify the Quicklist with the Hotlist Manager.

To select an item from the Quicklist when it is not a menu:

1. Choose Open URL from the File menu.
2. Select Quicklist from the Current Hotlist drop-down list.
3. Select the URL you want from the Quicklist.
4. Click on OK.

See Also Add Current To Hotlist; Adding to a Quicklist; Changing a Hotlist; Deleting Items from a Quicklist; Hotlist Manager

QUICKTIME MOVIES

QuickTime movies are videos that are shared on the Internet. You can recognize them by the extensions .mov, and .qt. Although movie files in MPEG format are the most common, you will also come across video files in QuickTime format.

You'll need a viewer to play QuickTime movies, and can download the QuickTime viewer with anonymous ftp from the same server where NCSA Mosaic is stored: `ftp:://web/mosaic/windows/viewers`. The file name to look for is QTW11.ZIP.

> **Tip**
> Once you download this viewer, use the Extension or MIME type option to associate it with QuickTime files.

See Also Extensions; Movies; MIME Type; MPEG Movies; Viewers

READING MAIL: QUARTERDECK MOSAIC

Of the Web browsers described in this book, only Quarterdeck Mosaic lets you receive and read e-mail. (With Air Mosaic, NCSA Mosaic, and Netscape, you can send—but not receive—e-mail.

Quarterdeck Mosaic includes the Quarterdeck Message Center (QMC), a full featured mail (and news) reader, which lets you create, send, receive, and read mail. To retrieve and read mail with Quarterdeck Mosaic:

1. Choose Mail/News from the Tools menu. The Quarterdeck Message Center opens.
2. Choose Check Mail from the Connect menu to check for and retrieve your mail. QMC displays a message box telling you how many new messages you have.
3. Click on OK. The list of new messages is added to the Inbox folder in the Message window (see Figure R.1). The messages currently in the Inbox display in the message list on the right.
4. To read any message, double click on the message line to open the Message window. The message opens in a new Message window (see Figure R.2).
5. Choose Next or Previous from the Message menu or the toolbar to read the next or previous message in the message list.

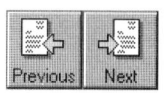

Tip

When you choose **Next** or **Previous**, the next or previous message in the message list displays in the active Message window; no new Message windows open. You can select and open more than one message at a time by double-clicking on another message while leaving current messages open.

Figure R.1

The Mailbox window in Quarterdeck Mosaic's Quarterdeck Message Center

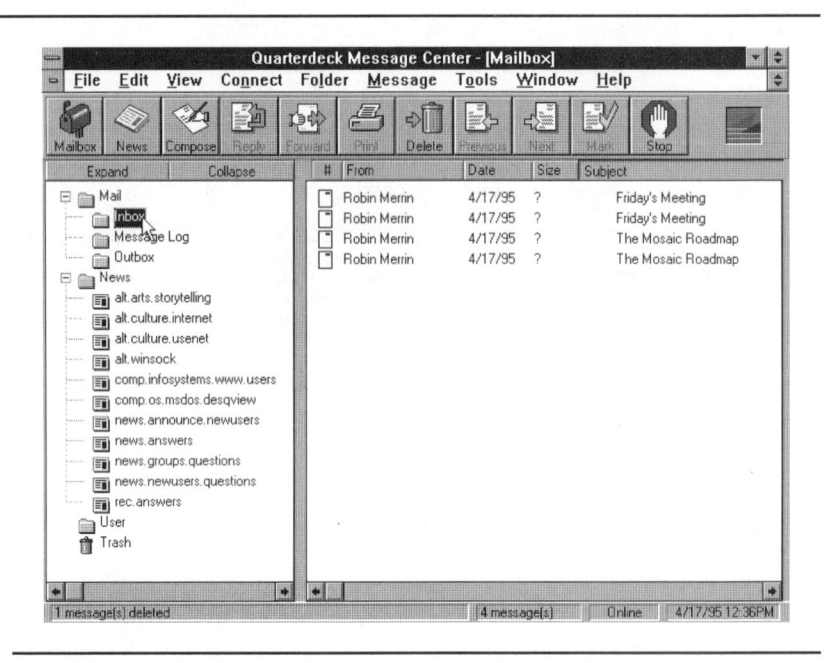

Figure R.2

The Message window in Quarterdeck Mosaic's Quarterdeck Message Center

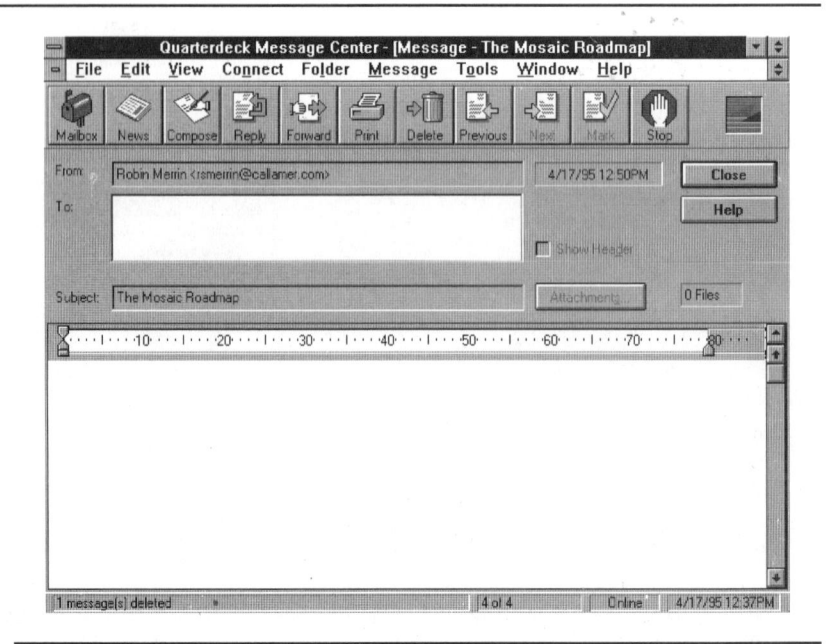

> **Tip**
>
> You can also reply to or forward messages as soon as you finish reading them, by clicking on the Reply or Forward button.

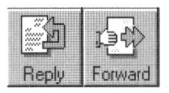

See Also Mail/News; Sending Mail

READING NEWS

Although Web browsers are not designed as news readers, you can read Usenet news with all of them.

Reading News: Air Mosaic

Air Mosaic lets you read news and post to newsgroups by accessing a news server with its Open URL command. If you know the name of the newsgroup you want to connect to, follow these steps.

1. Choose Open URL from the File menu. The Open URL dialog box is displayed.
2. In the URL text box, type the name in the form *news:newsgroup.name*; for example, news:news.announce.newusers.
3. Click OK. You'll see news articles listed as items with bullets. To read an article, click on its title.

> **Tip**
>
> You can enter news:* in the URL text box to display a list of all available newsgroups, and then select a newsgroup to connect to. You can also use the * wildcard to narrow down the search; for example, you could enter news:alt.* to display all the newsgroups that begin with alt. If you have the Expanded News Listing option checked, you'll also see a description of each newsgroup.

Reading News: NCSA Mosaic

NCSA Mosaic lets you subscribe to newsgroups and then read news from those newsgroups.

> **To read news with NCSA Mosaic, you'll first have to subscribe to newsgroups. See the section "Subscribing to Newsgroups" if you haven't subscribed to any newsgroups yet, then return to this section to learn how to read news.**

Once you've subscribed, follow these steps:

1. Choose Newsgroups from the File menu. The Subscribed Newsgroups page is displayed. This shows the list of newsgroups to which you have previously subscribed. Each of these newsgroups is displayed as a link.

2. Click on any Newsgroup in the list. The list of articles in that newsgroup (see Figure R.3) is displayed and buttons appear at the top and bottom of the screen to help you navigate through newsgroups and articles.

3. Click on any article in the list. The content of the article is displayed for you to read, print, or save.

4. When you are finished, click the Back button to redisplay the list of articles again, then click on another article to read it.

See Also Subscribing to Newsgroups

Reading News: Netscape

Netscape lets you subscribe to a newsgroup and then read news from those newsgroups.

Figure R.3

When you read news with NCSA Mosaic, the list of articles in each newsgroup is displayed.

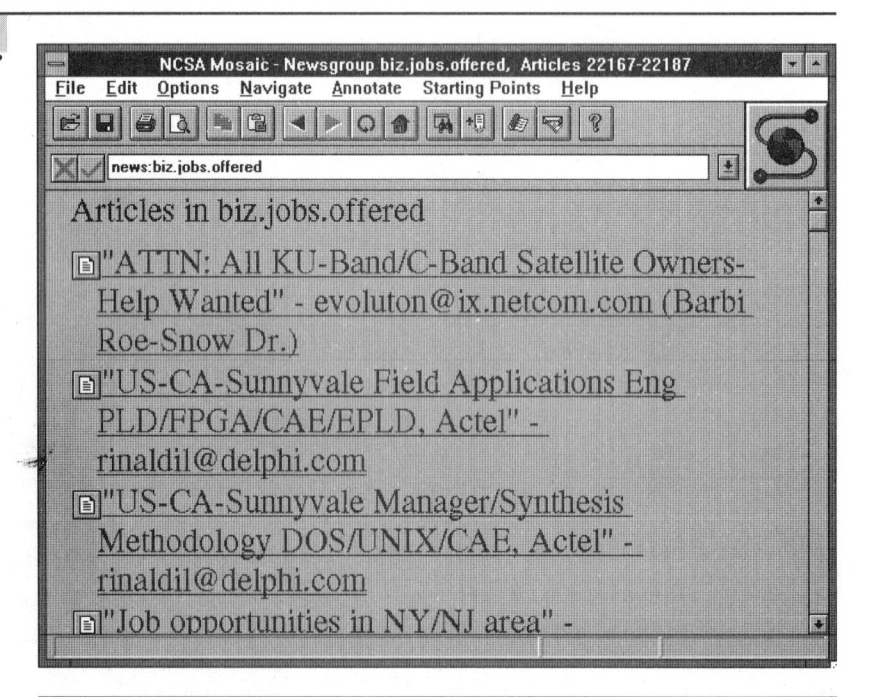

READING NEWS

> **To read news with Netscape, you'll first have to subscribe to newsgroups. See the section "Subscribing to Newsgroups" if you haven't subscribed to any newsgroups yet, then return to this section to learn how to read news.**

Once you subscribe, follow these steps:

1. Click the Newsgroups button or choose Go To Newsgroups from the Directory menu.

   [Newsgroups]

   The Server list page is displayed and the server names to which you have access are shown as links.

2. Click on a server on which you have subscribed newsgroups. The Subscribed Newsgroups page is displayed. This shows the list of newsgroups to which you have previously subscribed, each of which is displayed as a link.

3. Click on any Newsgroup in the list. The list of articles in that newsgroup (see Figure R.4) is displayed and buttons display at the top and bottom of the screen to help you navigate through newsgroups and articles.

4. Click on any article in the list. The article is displayed for you to read, print, or save.

Figure R.4

In Netscape, you can select newsgroup articles to read.

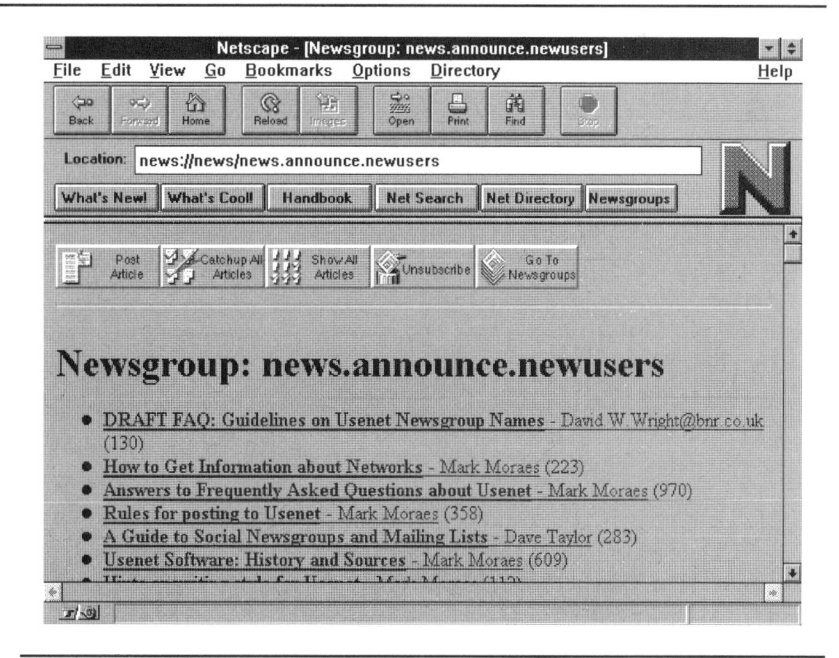

5. When you are finished, click the Back button or the This Newsgroup button at the top of the page to redisplay the list of articles again. To read another, just click on it.

See Also Subscribing to Newsgroups

Reading News: Quarterdeck Mosaic

Quarterdeck Mosaic includes the Quarterdeck Message Center (QMC), a full featured news (and mail) reader, that lets you create, send, receive, and read newsgroup articles.

After you subscribe to newsgroups with Quarterdeck Mosaic, you can read articles in those newsgroups. You can retrieve new articles with Quarterdeck Mosaic and then read them offline. To retrieve articles with Quarterdeck Mosaic:

1. Choose Mail/News from the Tools menu. The Quarterdeck Message Center opens.
2. Highlight a newsgroup in the folder tree and choose Check Selected News from the Connect menu to retrieve new articles in one newsgroup. Alternatively, you can choose Check All News from the Connect menu to download new articles from all the newsgroups to which you subscribe.

Once articles are retrieved, you can read them at any time. You do not have to be connected to a service provider to read articles. To read any article:

1. Click on the newsgroup in the folder tree on the left. The list of articles displays on the right (see Figure R.5).
2. Double click on the message line for that article to open the Message window or highlight the article and choose Open from the Message menu.
3. Choose Next or Previous from the Message menu or the toolbar to read the next or previous article in the list.

> Once you retrieve articles in Quarterdeck Mosaic, the procedures for reading, printing and deleting them are identical to those for e-mail messages.

See Also Mail/News

Reading News: Spyglass Mosaic

Spyglass Mosaic lets you read news by accessing a news server with its Open URL command. If you know the name of the newsgroup you want to connect to, follow these steps.

1. Choose Open URL from the File menu. The Open URL dialog box is displayed.
2. In the URL text box, type the name (*news:newsgroup.name*); for example, news:news.announce.newusers.

Figure R.5

In Quarterdeck Mosaic, newsgroups display in the folder tree on the left, and the highlighted newsgroup's articles display on the right.

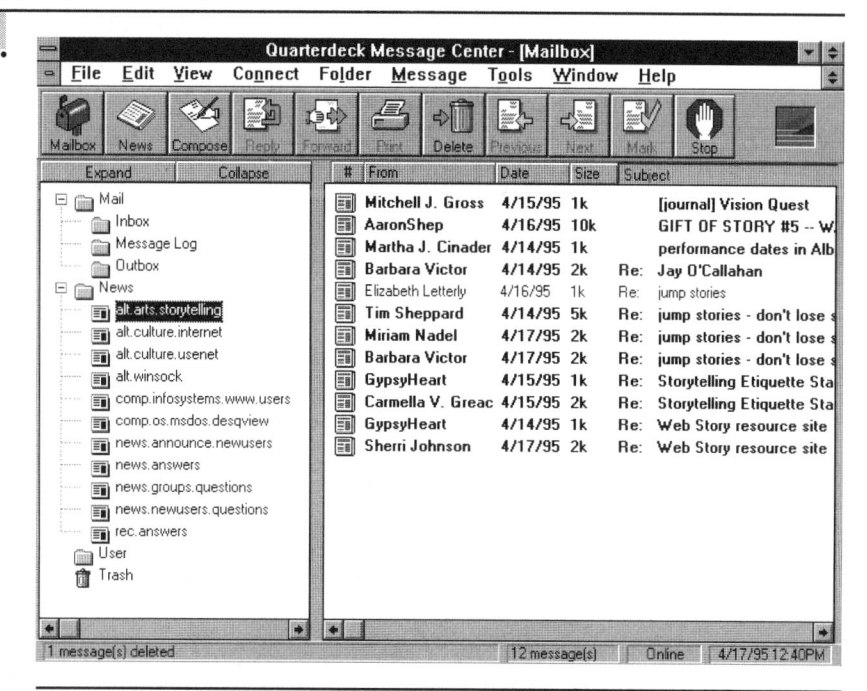

---

3. Click OK. You'll see the subject lines of the first twenty news articles listed. To read an article, click on it.

> **Tip**
>
> You can enter news:* in the URL text box to display a list of all available newsgroups, and then connect to a specific newsgroup by clicking on it. You can also use the * wildcard to narrow down the search; for example, you could enter news:alt.* to display all the newsgroups that begin with alt.

> **If you want to limit the number of articles you retrieve, specify the article number(s) when you enter the URL by entering two numbers with a hyphen between them. For example, you can enter** news:news.announce .newusers/18125-18145.

REFRESH: NETSCAPE

The Refresh command on the View menu redisplays the current Netscape page by replacing the page you originally loaded with

RELOAD

The Reload command redisplays the document in the document window, beginning at the top, by retrieving the document from the server again (if it has changed since you retrieved it) or from the document cache (if the document hasn't changed). All Web browsers include a Reload command and a Reload button on the toolbar (Table R.1 shows you where to find the Reload commands and buttons). You may want to reload a document if you the page held in local memory. Unlike the Reload command, the refreshed page does not display changes made to the source page from the time you originally loaded it.

You might want to refresh, for example, if you'd turned off the display of graphics prior to loading a document, then turned them on and wanted to display all the graphics in the current document in one step.

See Also   Document Caching; Document Window; Reload

Table R.1
Reload Commands

If you're using...	Choose Reload from the...	Or use this button
Air Mosaic	Navigate menu	Reload
NCSA Mosaic	Navigate menu	
Netscape	View menu	Reload
Quarterdeck Mosaic	File menu	Reload
Spyglass Mosaic	Navigate menu	

select the option that automatically loads all the graphics after you've loaded the document. Reloading will then cause all the graphics to be loaded with the document.

> **Tip**
>
> If you annotate a document in NCSA Mosaic, choose Reload to see your annotation at the bottom of the document.

See Also   Annotations; Document Caching; Document Window; Refresh

RETRIEVING A WAIS DOCUMENT

See   WAIS

ROUND LIST BULLETS: NCSA MOSAIC

See   General

S

SAVE

In Quarterdeck Mosaic and Spyglass Mosaic, the Save button on the toolbar is a shortcut for the Save As command.

> **Quarterdeck Mosaic and Netscape also offer a Save option within the Action options in the Preferences dialog box.**

See Action; Save As

SAVE AS

You can save the document currently displayed in the document window in every Web browser except Air Mosaic by choosing the Save As command from the File menu. NCSA Mosaic also includes a Save button on the toolbar. Quarterdeck Mosaic and Spyglass Mosaic include Save buttons that select the Save As command.

NCSA Mosaic Save As button

Quarterdeck Mosaic Save button

Spyglass Mosaic Save button

To save the document displayed in the document window:

1. Choose Save As from the File menu. The Save As dialog box (Figure S.1) opens and you can choose a drive and directory and specify the filename.
2. Choose a drive and directory and type a filename in the File Name text box, or accept the one shown.
3. Choose OK to save the file to your hard disk.

Figure S.1

The Save As dialog box is available in every form of Mosaic.

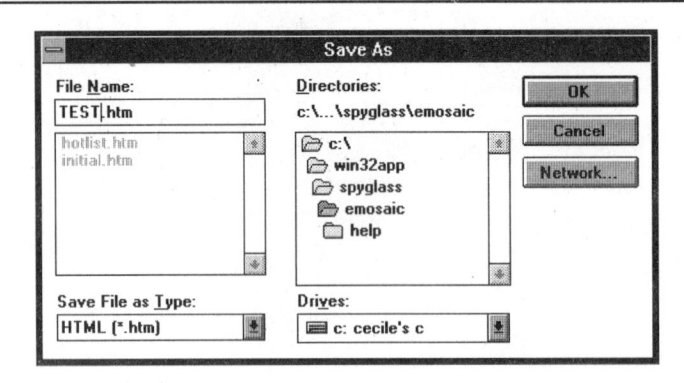

Tip

In both Air Mosaic and NCSA Mosaic (versions 1.0 and 2.0 alpha), use the Load to Disk command to automatically save documents to disk instead of displaying them.

In Air Mosaic, you can also save a document which isn't displayed by holding down the Shift key while you click on a hypertext link. To save the current document, select Load to Disk Mode from the Options menu, and then click the Reload button. You'll see the Save As dialog box described above. If you only want to save the current document, don't forget to select Load to Disk Mode again to turn it off.

See Also **Load to Disk; Save As Text**

SAVE AS TEXT: NCSA MOSAIC

In NCSA Mosaic, you can save the document currently displayed in the document window as a plain text (ASCII) file by using the Save As Text command. The file is saved without any HTML tags, so you can print it easily outside of NCSA Mosaic, and open it in any text editor or word processor. To save the document in the document window:

1. Choose Save As Text from the File menu. The Save As Text dialog box opens.
2. Choose a drive and directory and type a filename in the File Name text box, or accept the one shown. A .TXT extension is added to the filename when it is saved.
3. Choose OK to save the file as a text file to your hard disk.

See Also **HTML Tags; Save As**

SAVE LAST WINDOW POSITION: AIR MOSAIC

In Air Mosaic, you can specify the starting size and position for the application window with an option in the Configuration dialog box. Here's a quick way to specify the size and position of the application window:

1. Use the mouse cursor to adjust the window to a size and location you're satisfied with.
2. Choose Configuration from the Options menu. The Configuration dialog box opens.
3. Click on Save Last Window Position to check the option and save the current size and position when you exit.
4. Choose OK.

If you *don't* want to save the changes you make in window size and position when you exit make sure that the next time you run Air Mosaic you open the Configuration dialog box and remove the check.

> A similar option, Initial Window Placement, is available in NCSA Mosaic.

See Also Configuration; Initial Window Placement

SAVE OPTIONS: NETSCAPE

In Netscape, you can toggle the status of several options by checking or unchecking them on the Options menu, instead of changing them in the Preferences dialog box. The options you can change are:

- Show Toolbar
- Show Location
- Show Directory Buttons
- Autoload Images
- Show FTP File Information

When you make these changes on the Options menu only, they are not saved for the next session. If you want to save your changes, choose Save Options from the Options menu, and the changes you made will become your defaults.

See Also Autoload Images; Show Directory Buttons; Show FTP File Information; Show Location; Show Toolbar

SAVE TO CURRENT: QUARTERDECK MOSAIC

In Quarterdeck Mosaic, you can add documents to the current Hotlist folder with the Save To Current command on the Hotlists menu. You can also click on the Hotlist button in the toolbar to save the current document to the Hotlist.

See Also **Adding to a Hotlist; Folders; Hotlists; Set As Current**

SEARCHING INDEXES

Archie and Veronica are Internet search tools that search through a database of documents found on anonymous FTP and gopher servers.

See **Archie; Veronica**

SEARCHING FOR INFORMATION IN A DOCUMENT

In every Web browser you can search for a text string (characters, a word or a phrase) in the current document, with the Find command (found by clicking on Edit in the menu bar).

See **Find**

SECURE AND INSECURE DOCUMENTS

See **Security**

SECURITY: SPYGLASS MOSAIC, NETSCAPE

Both Spyglass Mosaic and Netscape support document and transaction security, thus enabling you to send and retrieve Web documents that no one else on the Internet will be able to access. Netscape was the first popular Web browser to incorporate security into its application, as recently as December of 1994. Its developers recognized the need in the marketplace for some system that protects documents and information from being misappropriated.

> **Because security is such an important feature to companies expecting to do business on the Internet—not to mention all their potential customers—you can expect Air Mosaic, NCSA Mosaic, and Quarterdeck Mosaic to include security features in upcoming releases of their products.**

Security: Netscape

Netscape uses a patented RSA public key cryptography technology and custom software to provide document security. This technology allows a Netscape server and the Netscape application to authenticate Internet servers so that only the true destination of the information you send can actually decrypt the encrypted data. Document security is indicated in several ways in Netscape.

- ✪ A popup dialog box indicates secure and insecure documents.
- ✪ The color bar changes from blue (a secure document) to gray (an insecure document).
- ✪ The doorkey icon changes from unbroken (a secure document) to broken (an insecure document).

The security technology used by Netscape is considered an *open technology* and is available to other vendors.

See Also **Doorkey Icon; Security Alerts; Show a Popup Alert Before**

Security: Spyglass Mosaic

Spyglass Mosaic provides an open framework for security that lets it accommodate multiple security technologies, instead of supporting only a single proprietary solution. When running Spyglass Mosaic, you can exchange information with servers running either of two pre-installed security modules and an electronic payment module:

- ✪ **Basic Authentication security** is a simple username/password authentication system that does not use encryption. It is defined by HTTP 1.0 and is compatible with existing CERN NCSA HTTP servers.
- ✪ **Digest Authentication security** uses an enhanced username/password system that employs the RSA Data Security, Inc. MD-5 Message-Digest Algorithm.
- ✪ **First Virtual Holding Company's Internet Payment System** serves as an electronic payment system.

Each of these three security features can be configured with the Security command on the Edit menu. You can also enter and replace passwords and Account ID information.

SECURITY ALERTS: NETSCAPE

Netscape can display a popup dialog box to provide a security alert, with the Show a Popup Alert Before option.

See **Show a Popup Alert Before**

SECURITY PROXY: NETSCAPE

In Netscape, you can enter the name of the Security Proxy at your site in the Proxies section of the Preferences dialog box.

See **Proxies; Security**

SELECT ALL: NCSA MOSAIC AND SPYGLASS MOSAIC

In NCSA Mosaic and Spyglass Mosaic, you can select all the text in a document with the Select All command on the Edit menu. Selected text can be copied to the Windows clipboard and subsequently pasted into another application.

See Also   Selecting Text

SELECTING TEXT

In each Web browser (except Air Mosaic), you can select text in a document window, copy it to the Windows clipboard, and subsequently paste it into another application. To select text, use the standard Windows method of clicking at the starting point and dragging the cursor to the ending point of the block of text you want. The selected text is highlighted (see Figure S.2).

When copying selected text, any links or graphics within the selection block are ignored when you subsequently paste the text.

See Also   Copy; Links; Select All

SEND MAIL: NCSA MOSAIC

The Send Mail command in NCSA Mosaic lets you send an electronic message. However, NCSA Mosaic does *not* allow you to receive electronic mail.

Figure S.2

Selected text in the document window in NCSA Mosaic

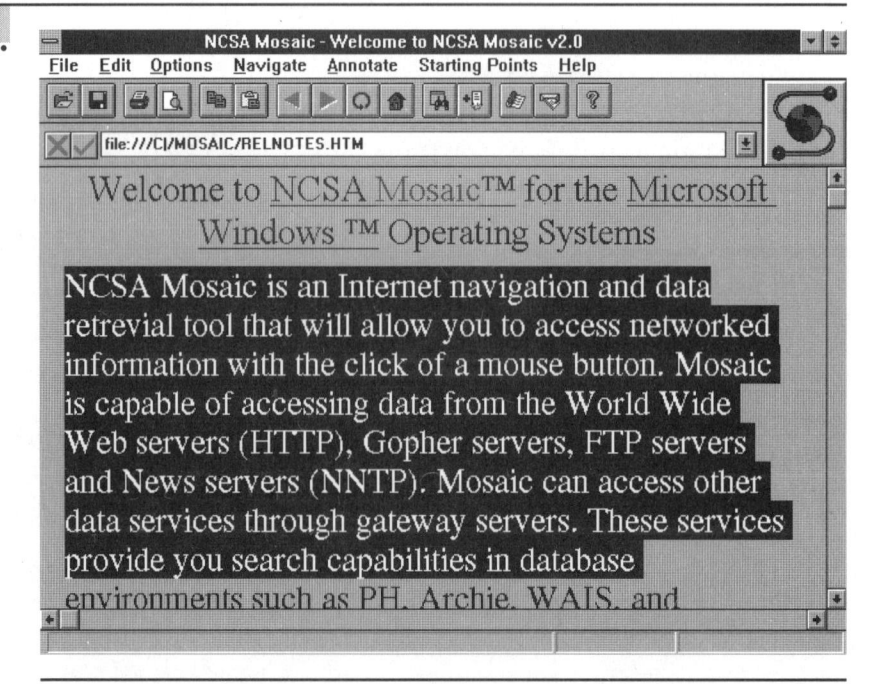

🛣️ **If you already have e-mail capabilities through another application, make sure your Internet address for e-mail is entered correctly in the E-mail Address text box in the Services tab of the Preferences dialog box. Mail you send through NCSA Mosaic will have this Internet address listed as your return address. Also enter your SMTP server name on this tab.**

To send a message:

1. Choose Send E-mail from the File menu or click the Send Internet E-mail button.

The NCSA Mail window appears (see Figure S.3) with your e-mail address already entered next to "From."

2. Type the recipient's Internet address in the To text box.

3. Type the subject of your message in the Subject text box.

Figure S.3

In NCSA Mosaic, you can send mail from the Mail window.

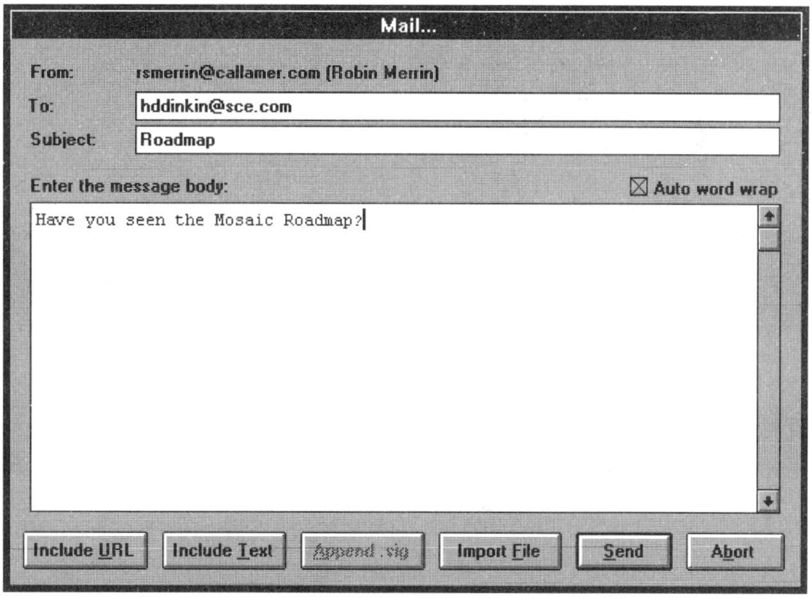

4. Type the content of your message in the editing area of the window.

> **Tip**
>
> You can drag a file from File Manager or a similar Windows application to the editing window in order to insert the file's contents into the body of your message. Currently, NCSA Mosaic only lets you insert ASCII text files into messages.

5. When your message is complete, Click on Send.

Table S.1 shows the additional options available in the Mail window.

See Also Sending Mail; Services

SENDING MAIL: AIR, QUARTERDECK MOSAIC

Of the Web browsers described in this book, only Quarterdeck Mosaic allows you to receive as well as send e-mail. Air Mosaic provides a method for you to send, but not receive e-mail. Spyglass Mosaic offers no e-mail capabilities.

Netscape's Mail Document command and NCSA's Send E-mail command let you send a message or post to a newsgroup.

See Also Mail Document; Mail/News; Send E-mail

Table S.1
Additional Options Available in the NCSA Mosaic Mail Window

Option	What it Does
Auto word wrap	Automatically wraps the text you enter at the end of each line, as a word processing program would.
Include URL	Inserts the URL of the document displayed in the document window into the body of the message.
Include Text	Inserts the text of the document displayed in the document window into the body of the message.
Append Sig	Adds your Internet signature, as entered in your Sig File (specified in the Services tab), to the end of the message.
Import File	Inserts the file you select into the body of the message as an ASCII text file.
Abort	Cancels the message you started creating and closes the dialog box.

Sending Mail: Air Mosaic

A *Send* or *Mail* command is not available in Air Mosaic. But you *can* send electronic messages using the steps outlined in this section. However, you still won't be able to *receive* electronic mail.

If you already have e-mail capabilities through another application, make sure your Internet address for e-mail is entered correctly in the E-mail Address text box in the Configuration dialog box. Mail you send through Air Mosaic will automatically list this Internet address as your return address. Do not change the SMTP server name provided by Air Mosaic and shown in the Configuration dialog box.

To send a message:

1. In the URL text box, type mailto: and press Enter. Or type mailto: and the recipient's Internet address; for example, mailto:merrin@callamer.com ƒ. The Air Mosaic Mail window appears (see Figure S.4), with the e-mail address already entered in the Recipient text box if you typed it in the URL box.

2. Type the recipient's Internet address in the Recipient text box (if you didn't type it before) and the Internet address of any additional recipients in the CC: text box.

3. Type the subject of your message in the Subject text box. The Content type will appear as text/plain.

4. Type the content of your message in the editing area of the window.

············ **Tip** ············

You can drag a file from File Manager or a similar Windows application to the editing window in order to insert the file's contents into the body of your message. Air Mosaic lets you insert ASCII text files and HTML files into messages.

5. When your message is complete, click on Send.

Sending Mail: Quarterdeck Mosaic

Quarterdeck Mosaic includes the Quarterdeck Message Center, a full featured mail (and news) reader, which lets you create, send, receive, and read mail. You can also send files by attaching them to messages, and detach files from messages you receive. To create and send mail with Quarterdeck Mosaic:

1. Choose Mail/News from the Tools menu. The Quarterdeck Message Center opens.

Figure S.4

Air Mosaic's Mail window lets you send e-mail.

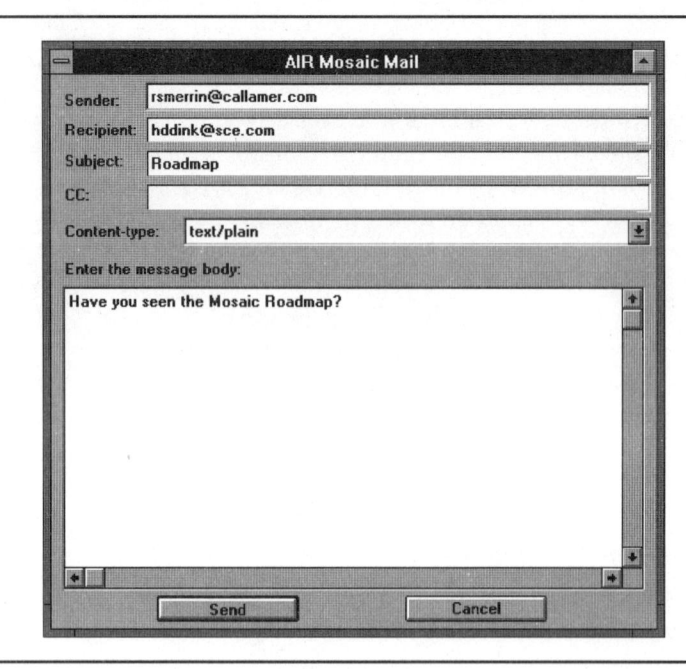

2. Click on the Compose button.

The New Message window opens (see Figure S.5) and the cursor is in the To text box.

3. Type the Internet address of the person to whom you are sending the message and click on the To button. You can also indicate recipients to receive a copy or blind copy of the message by typing the Internet address of each person and clicking on either the cc or Bcc button.

4. Click in the Subject text box then type the subject of your message.

5. Click below in the message area and type the text of your message.

6. When you finish typing the message, click on the Send button in the window or choose Send from the Message menu. The New Message window closes and the message is placed in the Outbox folder. If you are offline, the message will not be sent from the Outbox folder until you choose one of the Send commands from the Connect menu. If you are online, the message is sent immediately.

7. If you are not online, choose Send Messages from the Connect menu to send the message.

Figure S.5

The New Message window in Quarterdeck Mosaic's Message Center

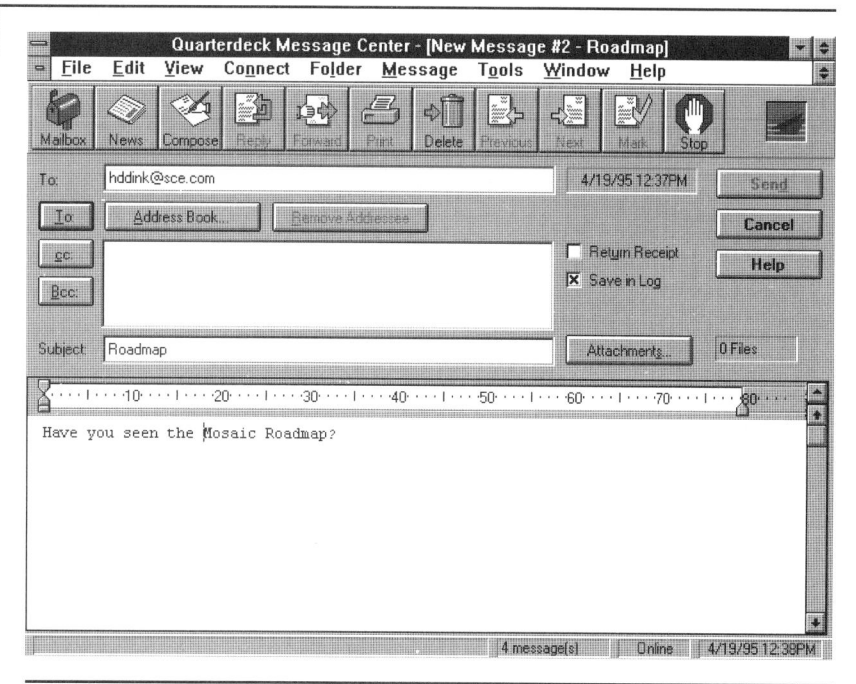

> **Tip**
>
> You can repeat Steps 2 through 6 for each message you want to create and then follow Step 7 once you have created all your messages.

The New Message window opens whenever you choose Compose, Reply or Forward from the Message menu or toolbar. Table S.2 shows all the functions and options associated with creating a message in this window.

See Also   Mail/News; Reading Mail

SERVICES

The Services tab in the NCSA Mosaic Preferences dialog box lets you specify options that allow you to send e-mail, read news, and use FTP and Telnet to retrieve files. Table S.3 shows the available options.

See Also   FTP; NNTP Server; Preferences; Show FTP File Information; SMTP Server; Subscribing to Newsgroups; Subscriptions; Telnet

Table S.2
Functions Available in the QMC New Message Window

Function	What it Does
To	Lets you type the name and Internet address of each recipient
Date and Time	Shows the date and time the message was created.
To, cc, Bcc	Designates the name and address currently entered in the To text box as a direct recipient (To), recipient of a carbon copy (cc) or recipient of a blind copy (Bcc) of your message.
Address Book	Opens your personal book of Internet addresses. You can select a name from the lists when composing and addressing a new message instead of typing names and Internet address in the To text box.
Remove Addressee	Deletes the currently selected recipient from the list box below.
Subject	Lets you type the subject of the message. If this is a reply to a message or a forwarded message, the subject of the original message is entered here.
Return Receipt	Requests that a confirmation message be sent to you when this message is received.
Save in Log	Saves a copy of the message in the Message Log folder of the Mail branch.
Attachments	Opens the Attachments dialog box where you can select one or more files to attach to the message.
Message area	Lets you type the text of the message. The original text may be shown in this area as a quote if this is a reply or forwarded message.
Send	Places a copy of this message in your Outbox folder. If you are currently online, the message is sent from the Outbox folder immediately. If you are currently offline, the message is sent when you choose one of the Send commands from the Connect menu.

Table S.3
Options Available in the Services Tab of NCSA Mosaic's Preferences Dialog Box

Option	What it Means/What it Does
Name	Your name. This information is included in a message when you send mail with the Send Mail command.
E-mail Address	Your E-mail address; for example, rmerrin@callamer.com. This information is also included in a message when you send mail with the Send Mail command.

Table S.3
Options Available in the Services Tab of NCSA Mosaic's Preferences Dialog Box (continued)

Option	What it Means/What it Does
SMTP Server	The Simple Mail Transfer Protocol-supported server, the mail server you use to send e-mail via the Internet.
Display Options	Controls how newsgroup messages are sorted when they are displayed in the document window.
	Thread View displays the top level messages without displaying replies to the message.
	Group View displays the top level messages and also displays the first level of replies.
	Tree View displays the top level messages and all replies in a tree structure (similar to Windows File Manager).
Number of Articles to Load	NCSA Mosaic downloads the specified number of articles from the news server at one time.
Number of Articles to Display	NCSA Mosaic displays the specified number of articles in the document window at one time.
NNTP Server	The Network News Transfer Protocol-supported server, the news server you use to subscribe to Internet newsgroups.
Sig File	The name of the file that contains your personal signature in ASCII format. This signature will be appended to every e-mail message or newsgroup posting you send.
Subscriptions	Lets you choose the newsgroups from which you want to download articles on a regular basis.
Use Extended FTP	Associates file type icons and file sizes for each file on the FTP server to which you are connected.
Display FTP Messages	Opens a dialog box that displays messages from the FTP server to which you are connected.
Telnet	The path and filename of your Telnet application. You can use the Browse button to locate and select this.
Host:port/Host port	Choose *Host:port* if your Telnet application uses a colon to distinguish a port number. Choose *Host port* if your Telnet application uses a space to distinguish a port number.

SET AS CURRENT: QUARTERDECK MOSAIC

In Quarterdeck Mosaic, you can have multiple Hotlists saved in folders. You can change the current Hotlist folder with the Set As Current command on the Hotlists menu before you add documents to it with the Save to Current command or Hotlist button.

> NCSA Mosaic and AIR Mosaic offer similar flexibility by letting you change the current Hotlist.

See Also   Adding to a Hotlist; Changing a Hotlist; Folders; Save To Current

SHOW A POPUP ALERT BEFORE: NETSCAPE

Netscape can alert you to a number of security issues by displaying a popup alert box when specific conditions occur. You can indicate the conditions you want to be alerted to by selecting them in the Image and Security section of the Preferences dialog box, under Security Alerts. These alerts can help you recognize when private information you are sending or receiving is protected by Netscape's security feature.

The following options are available (more than one can apply):

- Entering a Secure Document Space (Server)
- Leaving a Secure Document Space (Server)
- Viewing a Document with a Secure/Insecure Mix
- Submitting a Form Insecurely

See Also   Security

SHOW ANNOTATIONS: QUARTERDECK MOSAIC

In Quarterdeck Mosaic, you can display annotations you add to documents. Check Show Annotations on the Browser tab of the Preferences dialog box (see Figure S.6) to enable this feature.

See Also   Annotations; Preferences

SHOW BROWSER MARGINS: QUARTERDECK MOSAIC

In Quarterdeck Mosaic, you can give your documents a more realistic, three-dimensional look by displaying them with a gray border. Check Show Browser Margins on the Browser tab of the Preferences dialog box (see Figure S.6) to enable this feature.

See Also   Preferences

Figure S.6

Quarterdeck Mosaic's Browser tab in the Preferences dialog box includes several Show options

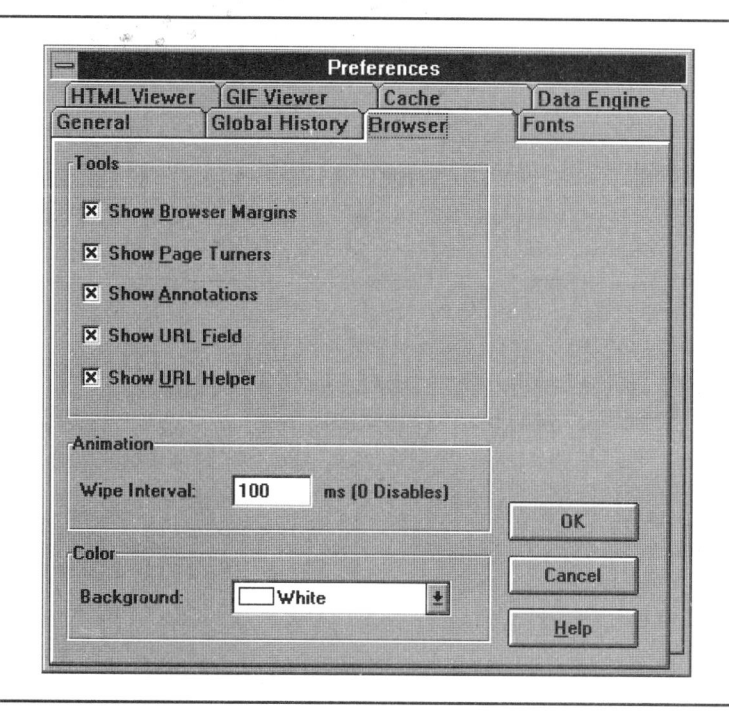

SHOW CURRENT URL: NCSA MOSAIC

In NCSA Mosaic, you can display a document's URL in the URL bar below the toolbar. Choose Show Current URL from the Options menu to toggle the display of the URL bar.

> Quarterdeck Mosaic uses the Show URL Field option to toggle the display of a document's URL. Netscape uses Show Location. Air Mosaic uses Show Document URL.

See Also Browser Window; Preferences; Show Document URL; Show Location; Show URL Field; URL; URL Bar

SHOW DIRECTORY BUTTONS: NETSCAPE

In Netscape, you can display additional buttons, called Directory buttons, which launch commands on the Directory menu.

When turned on, Directory buttons display below the Location bar. Choose Show Directory Buttons from the Options menu to toggle the display of the Directory buttons as shown in Figure S.7.

See Also Show Location; Show Toolbar

SHOW DOCUMENT TITLE: AIR MOSAIC

In Air Mosaic, you can display a document's title in the title bar below the toolbar. Check the Show Document Title checkbox in the Configuration dialog box (see Figure S.8) to enable the display of the title bar.

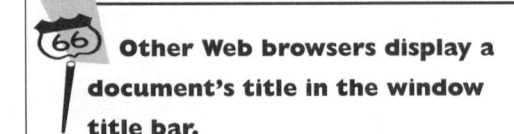

Other Web browsers display a document's title in the window title bar.

See Also Document Title

SHOW DOCUMENT URL: AIR MOSAIC

In Air Mosaic, you can display a document's URL in the URL bar below the toolbar and title bar. Check the Show Document URL checkbox in the Configuration dialog box (Figure S.8) to enable the display of the URL bar.

Figure S.7

Netscape's toolbar, location bar, and directory buttons can be turned on and off from the Options menu.

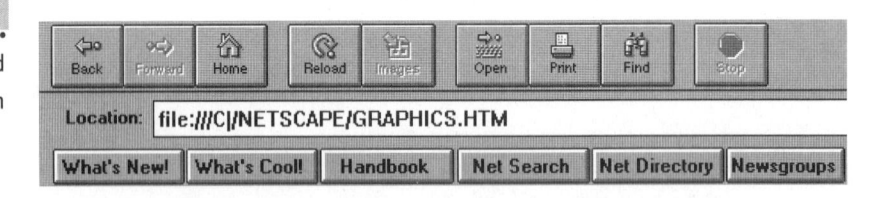

Figure S.8

Air Mosaic's Configuration dialog box contains several Show options.

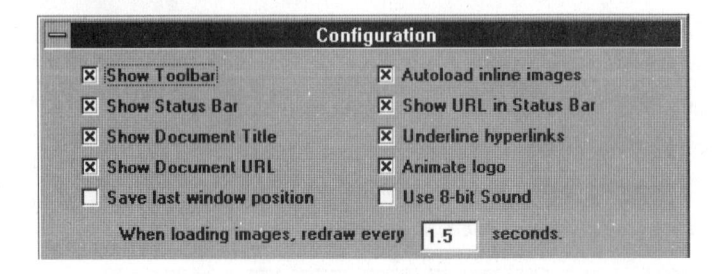

> **Quarterdeck Mosaic uses the Show URL Field option to toggle the display of a document's URL. Netscape uses Show Location. NCSA Mosaic uses Show Current URL.**

See Also   Show Current URL; Show Location; Show URL Field; URL; URL Bar

SHOW FTP FILE INFORMATION: NETSCAPE

In Netscape, you can display messages from the FTP server to which you are connected by checking Show FTP File Information on the options menu.

> **NCSA Mosaic's Display FTP Messages option in the Services tab of the Preferences dialog box provides a similar capability.**

See Also   FTP; Services

SHOW LINK URL(S): QUARTERDECK MOSAIC

In Quarterdeck Mosaic, you can display the URL of any anchor (link) in the status bar when you place the cursor on it. Check Show Link URL(s) on the HTML Viewer tab of the Preferences dialog box to enable this feature.

See Also   Anchors; Preferences; Status Bar; URL

SHOW LOCATION: NETSCAPE

In Netscape, you can display a document's URL in the URL bar below the toolbar. Choose Show Location from the Options menu to enable the display of the URL bar.

> **Quarterdeck Mosaic uses the Show URL Field option to toggle the display of a document's URL. NCSA Mosaic uses Show Current URL.**

See Also   Document Window; Preferences; Show Current URL; Show URL Field; URL; URL Bar

SHOW PAGE TURNERS: QUARTERDECK MOSAIC

In Quarterdeck Mosaic, you can display page turners in the upper-right and upper-left corners of a document window (see Figure S.9). Page turners let you move backward and forward among documents

Figure S.9

Quarterdeck Mosaic's page turners let you move backward and forward among documents

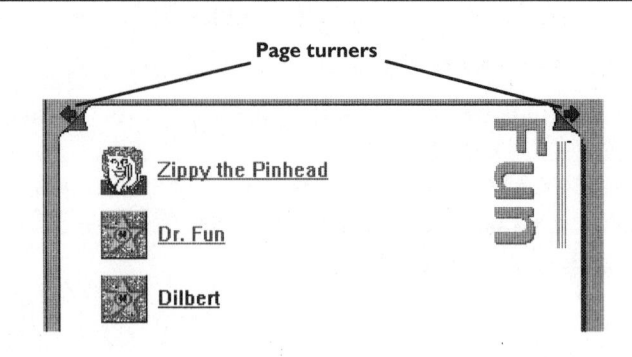

that have already been displayed (they work exactly like the Back and Forward commands).

Check Show Page Turners on the Browser tab of the Preferences dialog box to display these page turners. Once you display them, click on either to move back or forward.

See Also   Back; Browser Window; Forward; Preferences

SHOW STATUS BAR: AIR MOSAIC, NCSA MOSAIC

In Air and NCSA, you can toggle the display of the status bar at the bottom of the application window with the Show Status Bar command or option. In Air Mosaic, choose Configuration from the Options menu, then check Show Status Bar. In NCSA, choose Show Status Bar from the Options menu.

> **In Quarterdeck Mosaic, this option displays as Status Bar on the View menu.**

See Also   Configuration; Status Bar

SHOW TOOLBAR: AIR MOSAIC, NCSA MOSAIC, SPYGLASS MOSAIC, NETSCAPE

In Air Mosaic, NCSA Mosaic, and Spyglass Mosaic, and Netscape you can display the toolbar in the application window below the menu bar by using the Show Toolbar command or option (see Table S.4).

See Also   Configuration; Preferences; Toolbar

Table S.4
Show Toolbar Commands and Options

Product	To Display the Toolbar, Choose...
Air Mosaic	Configuration from the Options menu, then check Show Toolbar.
NCSA Mosaic	Show Toolbar from the Options menu.
Netscape	Show Toolbar from the Options menu.
Spyglass Mosaic	Preferences from the Edit menu, then check Show Toolbar.
Quarterdeck Mosaic	Toolbar from the View menu.

SHOW TOOLBAR AS: NETSCAPE

In Netscape, you can display the toolbar with Pictures, Text, or Pictures and Text, by choosing one of the Show Toolbar As alternatives in the Styles section of the Preferences dialog box, under Window Styles (see Figure S.10).

> The Toolbar Icon Settings option in Quarterdeck Mosaic provides similar capabilities.

See Also Toolbar; Toolbar Icon Settings

SHOW URL FIELD: QUARTERDECK MOSAIC

In Quarterdeck Mosaic, you can display a document's URL at the top of its browser window, in addition to its title. Check Show URL Field on the Browser tab of the Preferences dialog box to display the URL field.

Figure S.10
The Show Toolbar As options in Netscape

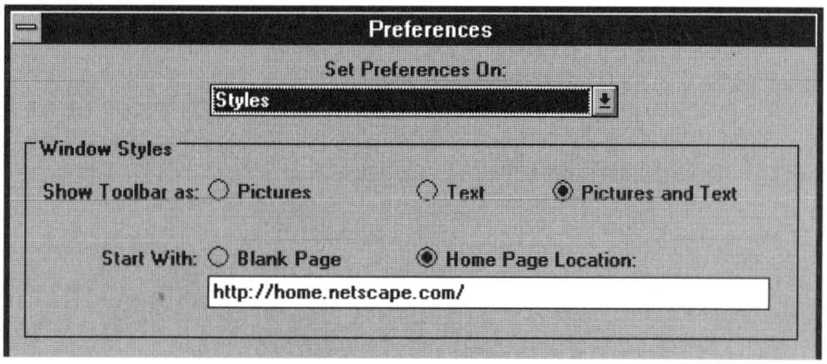

> **Other Web browsers use the URL bar to display a document's URL.**

See Also Browser Window; Preferences; Show Current URL; URL; URL Bar

SHOW URL HELPER: QUARTERDECK MOSAIC

In Quarterdeck Mosaic, you can display the URL Helper button at the top of each browser window.

| URL Helper... |

Check Show URL Helper on the Browser tab of the Preferences dialog box to display the URL Helper button.

See Also Browser Window; Preferences; URL; URL Helper

SHOW URL IN STATUS BAR: AIR MOSAIC, NCSA MOSAIC

In Air Mosaic and NCSA Mosaic, when the cursor is over a link's anchor in the document window its URL displays in the status bar.

In Air Mosaic you can toggle this feature on and off with the Show URL in Status Bar checkbox in the Configuration dialog box.

In NCSA Mosaic you can toggle this feature on and off with the Show URL in Status Bar checkbox on the Anchors tab of the Preferences dialog box.

See Also Anchors; Configuration; Link; Preferences; Status Bar; URL

SIGNATURE FILE: NETSCAPE

In Netscape you can indicate the name of the file that contains your personal signature in the Preferences dialog box. This signature will be appended to every e-mail message or newsgroup posting you send.

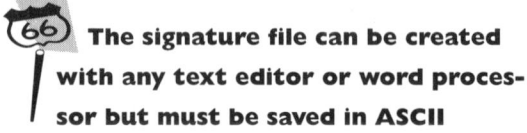

> **The signature file can be created with any text editor or word processor but must be saved in ASCII format.**

To enter the signature file name in Netscape:

1. Choose Preferences from the Options menu.
2. Choose Mail and News from the drop-down list at the top of the dialog box.
3. Click and type the signature path and filename in the Signature File text box. You can use the Browse button to open the Browse dialog box and select the signature path and filename to insert.

4. Choose OK to close the Preferences dialog box.

> **In NCSA Mosaic, enter the signature file name in the Sig text box on the Services tab of the Preferences dialog box.**

See Also   Preferences; Sending Mail; Services

SMTP SERVER

The SMTP server is the Simple Mail Transfer Protocol-supported server, the mail server you use to send e-mail via the Internet. Ask your network administrator or Internet service provider for the name of the SMTP server that lets you send mail, then enter the SMTP server name in the appropriate text box. A server name might look like: mail.abcdef.com.

See Also   Configuration; Preferences; Sending Mail

SMTP Server: Air Mosaic

To enter the SMTP server name in Air Mosaic:

1. Choose Configuration from the Options menu.

2. Click and type the SMTP server name in the SMTP Server text box.

3. Choose OK to close the Configuration dialog box.

SMTP Server: NCSA Mosaic

To enter the SMTP server name in NCSA Mosaic:

1. Choose Preferences from the Options menu.

2. Click the Services tab to bring it forward.

3. Click and type the SMTP server name in the SMTP Server text box.

4. Choose OK to close the Preferences dialog box.

SMTP Server: Netscape

To enter the SMTP server name in Netscape:

1. Choose Preferences from the Options menu.

2. Choose Mail and News from the drop-down list at the top of the dialog box.

3. Click and type the SMTP server name in the Mail (SMTP) Server text box.

4. Choose OK to close the Preferences dialog box.

SMTP Server: Quarterdeck Mosaic

To enter the SMTP server name in Quarterdeck Mosaic:

1. Choose Configure Network from the Tools menu.
2. Click and type the SMTP server name in the SMTP Server text box.
3. Choose OK to close the dialog box.

SOCKS

SOCKS is software that enables a computer inside a firewall to exchange files with the Internet. The SOCKS software is usually installed on a server either between you and the firewall or directly on the firewall itself. Computers inside the firewall access the server running SOCKS, which in turn lets them transmit their request outside the firewall to the Internet.

> **In Netscape, use the SOCKS Host text box in the Proxies section of the Preferences dialog box to enter the name and port number of a server running SOCKS.**

See Also   Firewall; Proxies; Proxy

SOURCE: NETSCAPE

See   Document Source

START WITH: NETSCAPE

You can start with a blank page or load a specific home page each time you start Netscape. Just choose either Start With option (Blank Page, Home Page) in the Styles section of the Preferences dialog box, under Window Styles (see Figure S.11).

> **Each Web browser includes options that let you define your home page, and/or specify whether or not to display it automatically. In Air Mosaic, the option to load your home page is Load Automatically at Startup. In NCSA Mosaic, it's Autoload Home Page. In Quarterdeck Mosaic, it's Load Home Page. In Spyglass Mosaic, you can specify your home page with the Home Page option, but you can't turn the display on and off.**

See Also   Autoload Home Page; Load Automatically at Startup; Load Home Page; Home Page; Preferences

Figure S.11

Netscape's Start With options

STARTING MOSAIC

See Part I: Looking at Mosaic: A Guided Tour

STARTING POINTS: NCSA MOSAIC

NCSA Mosaic includes a Starting Points menu (and Hotlist) as a convenience, displayed in the menu bar. Figure S.12 shows the titles of some of the available pages accessed by choosing them from this menu. Several cascading menus are also included.

Items on the Starting Points menu provide an overview of some of the Web pages available and help you start browsing around right away. You don't have to invest time researching the URLs of all these sites. The Starting Points offer you the opportunity to access a number of servers at different sites and display their home pages. Those home pages in turn offer a number of hypertext links to documents on a vast assortment of topics.

> **Tip**
>
> If you don't want to load the **NCSA Mosaic Home Page** each time you start **NCSA Mosaic**, you can use this menu as an alternate access method. It duplicates some of the items on the **NCSA Mosaic** home page and provides many more.

You can add to this menu as you do any other menu/Hotlist, with Add to Hotlist. In versions 1.0 and 2.0 alpha, use the Menu Editor to modify this menu. In versions 2.0 beta and later, use the Hotlist Manager.

Figure S.12

NCSA Mosaic's Starting Points menu

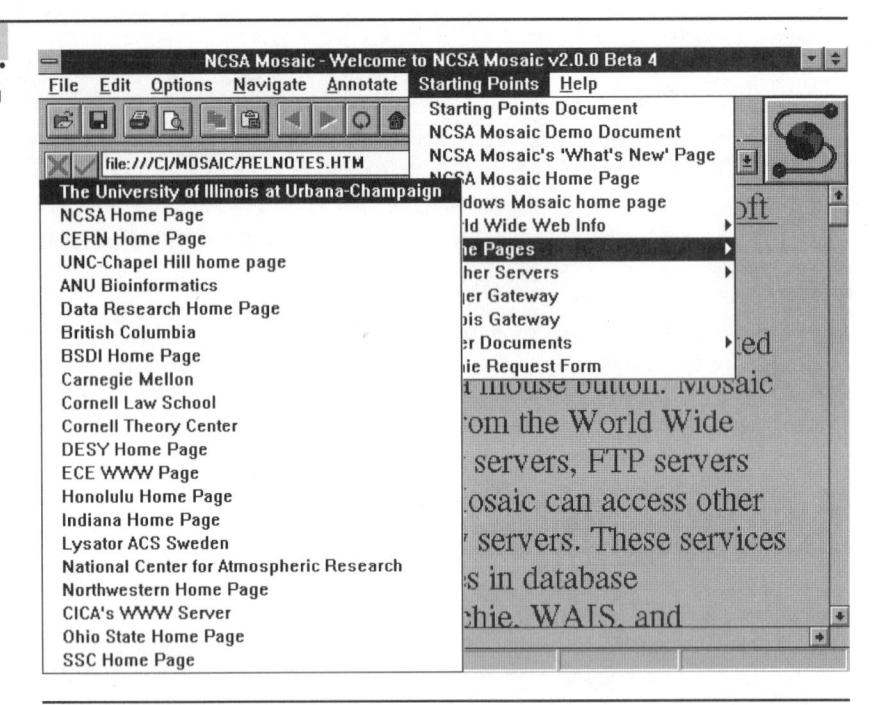

Tip

If you use NCSA Mosaic and then move to Air Mosaic, you'll probably want to bring the Starting Point menu/Hotlists with you. Air Mosaic's Import NCSA Menu as Hotlist feature lets you do just that.

See Also Adding to a Menu; Hotlist Manager; Import NCSA Menu as Hotlist; Menu Editor; Modifying a Menu

STATUS BAR: QUARTERDECK MOSAIC

In Quarterdeck Mosaic, you can toggle the display of the status bar at the bottom of the application window with the Status Bar command on the View menu.

In NCSA Mosaic, choose Show Status Bar from the Options menu to toggle the status bar display. In Air Mosaic, check Show Status Bar in the Configuration dialog box.

See Also Configuration; Show Status Bar

STOP

Each Web browser gives you more than one method to stop the retrieval process once you begin retrieving a document. Several include Stop commands and buttons. To stop retrieving in NCSA Mosaic you can just click the program icon to the right of the URL bar or press Escape. In Air Mosaic, choose Cancel Current Task from the Navigate menu.

See Also Cancel; Program Icon

Stop Current Read: Quarterdeck Mosaic

To stop retrieving a page or file in Quarterdeck Mosaic, choose Stop Current Read from the Navigate menu or click on the Stop button in the toolbar.

Stop Loading: Netscape

To stop retrieving a page or file in Netscape, choose Stop Loading from the Go menu or click on the Stop button in the toolbar or press Escape.

Interrupt Current Operation: Spyglass Mosaic

To stop retrieving a page or file in Spyglass Mosaic, click on the Interrupt Current Operation button in the toolbar or press Escape.

STYLE SHEET: SPYGLASS MOSAIC

Most Web browsers let you modify the fonts in a displayed document individually by letting you change the attribute of each HTML tag. Spyglass Mosaic does not offer this feature, but does let you change the appearance of a displayed document by letting you select from several predefined style sheets. Style sheets are collections of predefined fonts for each HTML tag.

You'll have to use trial and error to determine which style sheet you prefer and which is easiest to read on your monitor. To change style sheets:

1. Choose Preferences from the Edit menu. The Preferences dialog box displays.
2. Select a different style sheet from the Style Sheet drop-down list (Figure S.13).
3. Choose OK to close the Preferences dialog box.

The style sheet you selected is immediately applied to the displayed document.

Figure S.13

In Spyglass Mosaic, you can select a different style sheet in the Preferences dialog box.

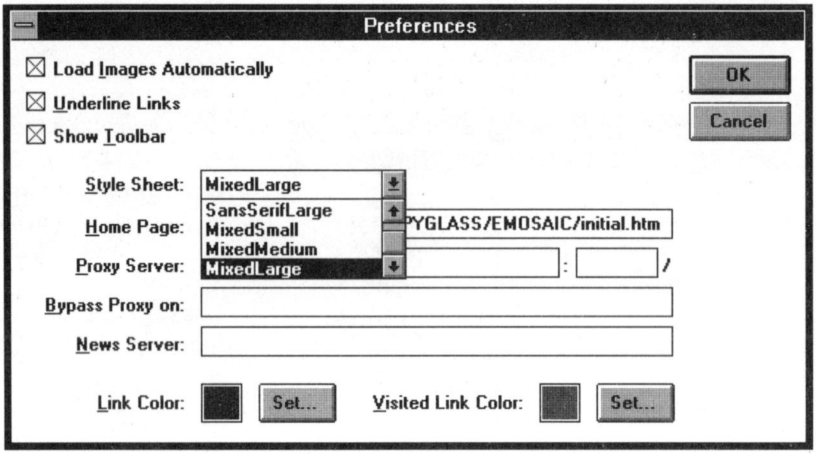

🚩 **There is no reason to change the style sheet unless you feel a different look would be more appealing to you.**

🚩 **In Air Mosaic, fonts are changed with the Fonts button in the Configuration dialog box. In Quarterdeck Mosaic, fonts are changed in the Preferences dialog box. Netscape has two Choose Font buttons that let you modify the font. NCSA Mosaic includes a Fonts tab in the Preferences dialog box.**

See Also Change Fixed and Proportional Font; Choose Font; Configuration; Fonts: Scheme; Font: Style; HTML Tags; Preferences

STYLES: NETSCAPE

The Styles section of Netscape's Preferences dialog box (see Figure S.14) lets you specify display options for the toolbar, home page and links.

See Also Followed Links Expire; Show Toolbar; Start With; Underline Links

Figure S.14

The Styles section of the Preferences dialog box in Netscape

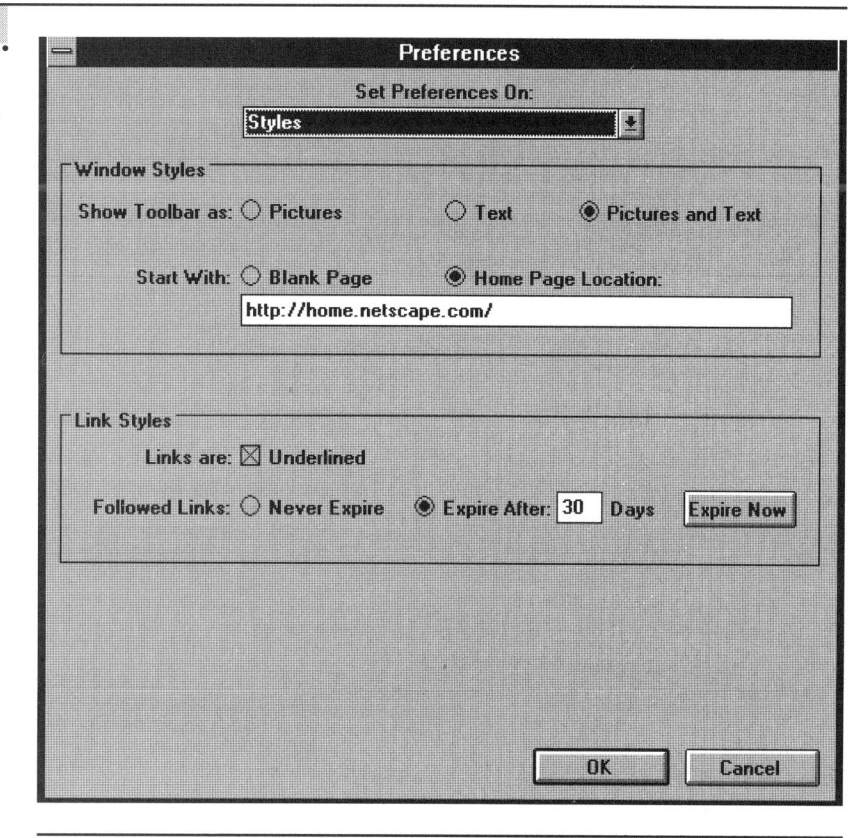

SUBSCRIBING TO NEWSGROUPS

There are currently more than 10,000 newsgroups, and new ones are added every day. You can subscribe to any number of newsgroups that interest you and then retrieve and read articles within that newsgroup. *Subscribing* simply means selecting them and placing them on a list of newsgroups that your Web browser will check for you on a regular basis.

> **Make sure you have already entered your NNTP (news) server before you try to subscribe to a newsgroup.**

See Also NNTP Server; Reading News

Subscribing to Newsgroups: NCSA Mosaic

NCSA Mosaic (version 2.0 beta and later) lets you subscribe to newsgroups and then read news. To subscribe, follow these steps:

1. Choose Preferences from the Options menu, then click the Services tab.
2. Click on the Subscriptions button to open the News Subscriptions dialog box.

   [Subscriptions]

3. If you've never subscribed before, first click on the Update button to display a list of the newsgroups available on your news server.

> There may be hundreds or even thousands of newsgroups on the news server, so don't be surprised if retrieving the list takes several minutes.

4. Click on any newsgroup in the top portion of the list, then click the Subscribe button. The newsgroup is added to your personal list of subscribed newsgroups in the bottom of the dialog box. Repeat this step to subscribe to additional newsgroups.
5. When you are finished, choose OK.

You can now read the articles in newsgroups to which you've subscribed.

Subscribing to Newsgroups: Netscape

Netscape lets you subscribe to a newsgroup and then read news from those newsgroups. To subscribe, follow these steps:

1. Click the Newsgroups button or choose Go To Newsgroups from the Directory menu.

   [Newsgroups]

   The Server list page is displayed and the server names to which you have access are shown as links.

2. Click on a server on which you have subscribed newsgroups. The Subscribed Newsgroups page is displayed (see Figure S.15). This shows the list of newsgroups to which you have previously subscribed and the newsgroups are displayed as links.

> If you haven't subscribed before, you will often have default newsgroup subscriptions provided by your network or service provider.

3. If you know the name of the newsgroup you want to subscribed to, enter it in the Subscribe to this Newsgroup text box.

Figure S.15

Netscape's Subscribed Newsgroups page

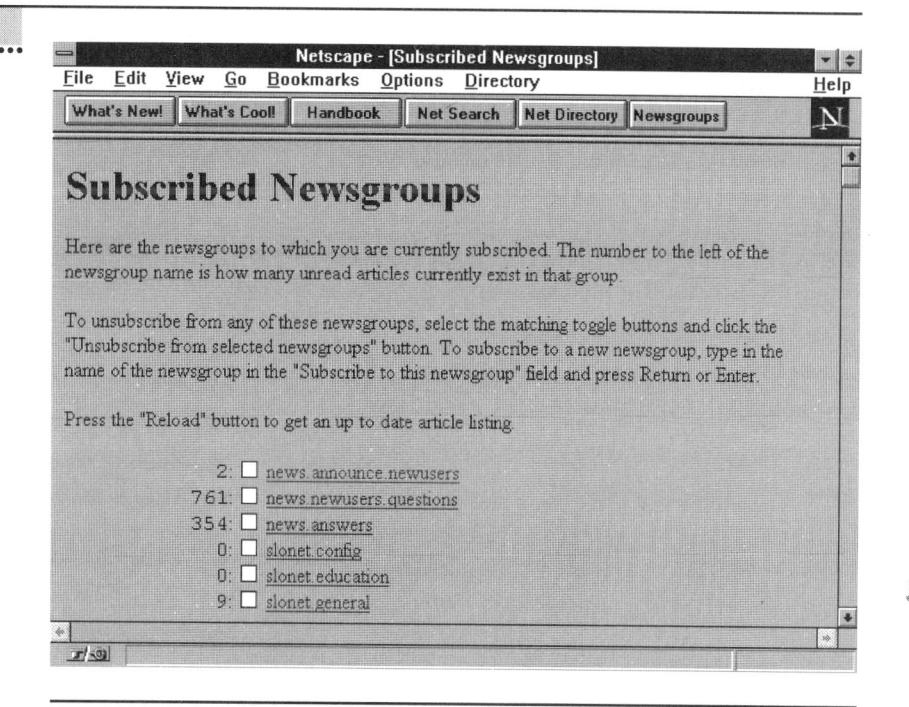

4. If you want to see the list of all available newsgroups on the server, Click the View All Newsgroups button and then choose OK when you see the confirmation prompt.

> **There may be hundreds or even thousands of newsgroups on the news server, so don't be surprised if retrieving the list takes several minutes.**

When the Newsgroups list finally displays it is organized by categories, so that you won't see all the newsgroups on this page—there are just too many.

5. Click on a newsgroup category. The newsgroups within the category display.

6. Click on the checkbox to the left of any Newsgroup in the list and then click on the Subscribe to selected newsgroups button.

Repeat Steps 4 through 6 until you have subscribed to all the newsgroups which interest you. You can also update your subscriptions at any time by following the preceding steps.

See Also **Go To Newsgroups; Reading News**

Subscribing to Newsgroups: Quarterdeck Mosaic

The Message Center included with Quarterdeck Mosaic lets you subscribe to newsgroups and download articles. You can organize your downloaded articles in separate folders, one for each newsgroup. To subscribe to a newsgroup:

1. Choose Mail/News from the Tools menu.
2. Click on the News folder.
3. Choose Newsgroups from the Folder menu. The Newsgroups dialog box (see Figure S.16) opens and you can select the newsgroup to add.
4. Select a server from the News Server drop down list.
5. If this is the first time you have subscribed to newsgroups on this server, click on Retrieve List to display the list of the server's newsgroups. If you have subscribed to newsgroups on this server before, skip this step.

There may be hundreds or even thousands of newsgroups on the news server, so don't be surprised it retrieving the list takes several minutes.

6. When the list is retrieved, click on a newsgroup in the Newsgroup list box then click on Subscribe. You can begin typing the name of any newsgroup to scroll the list to that name.

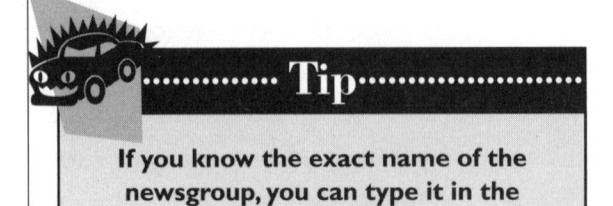

·········· **Tip** ······················

If you know the exact name of the newsgroup, you can type it in the Newsgroup text box.

Figure S.16

The Newsgroup dialog box in Quarterdeck Mosaic's Message Center

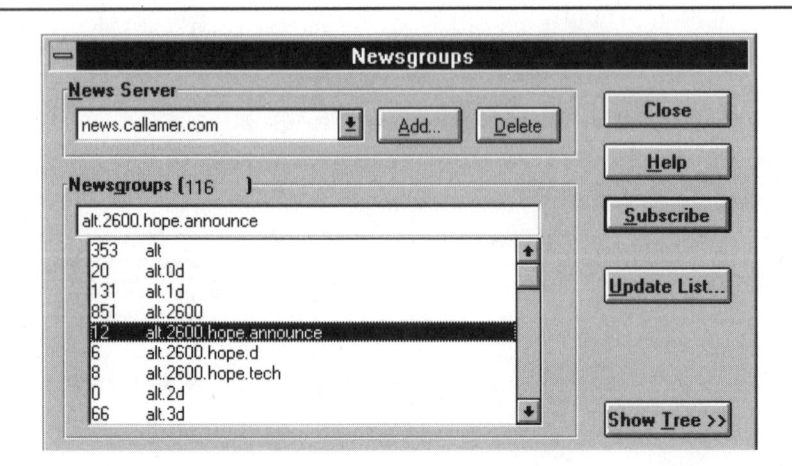

7. Repeat this step to subscribe to additional newsgroups.

8. Click on Close in the Subscribe to Newsgroup dialog box. The newsgroups you subscribed to will be added to the News branch in the selected folder.

The Newsgroups dialog box contains the options that let you subscribe to newsgroups and modify or delete those subscriptions (see Table S.5).

SUBSCRIPTIONS: NCSA MOSAIC

The Subscriptions button on the Services tab of the NCSA Preferences dialog box opens the Subscriptions dialog box where you can select newsgroups that interest you.

See **Reading News; Subscribing to Newsgroups**

SUPPORTING APPLICATIONS: NETSCAPE

In Netscape, you can use the Applications and Directories section of the Preferences dialog box to enter the path and filename of several supporting applications. Netscape uses supporting applications to establish connections and format pages (See Table S.6).

See Also **Document Source; Telnet**

Table S.5
Newsgroup Subscription Options in the Newsgroups Dialog Box in Quarterdeck Mosaic

Option	What it Does
News Server	Lists the available news servers.
Add	Opens the Add News Server dialog box where you can enter the name of the news server you want to add to your list.
Delete	Removes the selected news server from the list.
Newsgroups	Lists newsgroups you can subscribe to on the selected news server.
Subscribe	Adds the selected Newsgroup to the tree.
Retrieve List	Refreshes the list of newsgroups on the selected News Server.
Show Tree/Hide Tree	Shows or hides the News branch of the tree.
News Folder	The selected newsgroup is added to the highlighted folder. You can select any folder in the tree.
Unsubscribe	Removes the selected newsgroup from the folder tree.

Table S.6
Use the Browse Buttons to Locate and Select These Applications in Netscape's Preferences Dialog Box

Option	What it Is
Telnet Application	The path and filename of your Telnet application. Telnet uses standard Internet protocols to enable your computer to connect to and interact with another computer.
TN3270 Application	The path and filename of your TN3270 application. TN3270 establishes a Telnet connection to IBM mainframes.
View Source	The path and filename of your HTML Source Viewer application. The source viewer displays a page's text with its embedded HTML formatting commands.

T

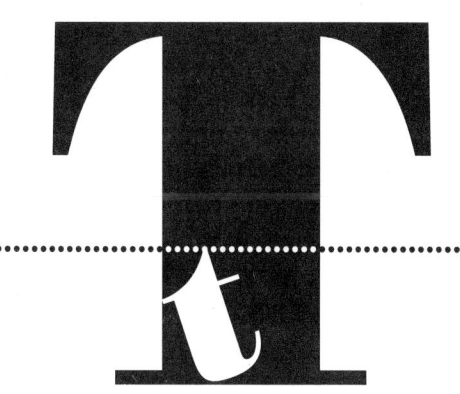

TABLES: NCSA MOSAIC

In NCSA Mosaic, you can modify the appearance of tables in documents displayed in the document window by changing options on the Tables tab of the Preferences dialog box. Table T.1 shows you the available options.

See Also **Preferences**

TELNET

Telnet is a command-line based program that lets you directly log into any servers on the Internet that permit direct logins or on which you have an account. For example, there are many library systems to which you can log in with Telnet. Telnet was one of the earliest methods available

Table T.1
Available Options in the Tables Tab in NCSA Mosaic

Option	What it Does
3D Tables	Makes tables appear to have a three-dimensional frame.
Recessed Tables	Makes tables appear to have an inverted three-dimensional frame.
Display Empty Cells	Leaves empty cells empty. When unchecked, empty cells are filled in with the color selected for the table frame.
Table Color Settings	Numbers represent the current RGB value for the table frame.
Change	Opens the Color dialog box where you can select another table frame color.

for retrieving files from other servers, developed long before the Web and Web browsers. It lets you connect to the remote computer (the computer you log in to) in order to browse through and work with the files housed there. Web browsers, on the other hand, merely retrieve and display files but do not connect you to the computer where the files actually reside.

Most servers on the Internet support Telnet, but you can't log in to most servers simply by running Telnet. You have to have a specific account on the sever—a different account from the one you have on your local network or with your dial up service provider.

Web browsers currently offer only limited support for Telnet—they do not let you use Telnet to log in to another computer—but they do let you use Telnet to retrieve files from computers by specifying the `telnet:\\` prefix in their URL.

> .... **Tip** ....
> The Chameleon Sampler application provided with this book includes a Windows-based interface for the Telnet application.

See Also   Services; Supporting Applications; Terminal Programs; URL

In Netscape, you can specify your Telnet application in the Supporting Directories section of the Preferences dialog box. In Air Mosaic, specify your Telnet application in the Terminal Programs section of the External Viewer Configuration dialog box. In NCSA Mosaic, specify your Telnet application on the Services tab of the Preferences dialog box.

TELNET APPLICATION: AIR MOSAIC, NETSCAPE, NCSA MOSAIC

See   Services; Supporting Applications; Terminal Programs

TEMPORARY DIRECTORY: NETSCAPE

In Netscape, you can use the Applications and Directories section of the Preferences dialog box to enter the path and filename of a Temporary Directory. Netscape stores a file in the temporary directory before launching it with an external viewer.

See Also   Preferences; Viewers

TERMINAL PROGRAM: AIR MOSAIC

In Air Mosaic, you can enter the name of supporting Telnet and remote terminal applications in the External Viewers Configuration dialog box (see Figure T.1).

To specify a terminal application in Air Mosaic:

1. Choose Configuration from the Options menu to open the Configuration dialog box.

2. Click the Viewers button to open the External Viewers Configuration dialog box.

3. Enter any supporting terminal programs you want Air Mosaic to launch, described in Table T.2. You can use the Browse buttons to locate and select the programs listed in the Table.

4. Click the Close button to close this dialog box.

5. Click OK to close the Configuration dialog box.

See Also Supporting Applications; Telnet

TILE: QUARTERDECK MOSAIC, SPYGLASS MOSAIC

You can arrange open document view windows or browser windows with the Tile command. Tile arranges the windows so their contents are visible. Tile is available in Quarterdeck Mosaic and Spyglass

Figure T.1

Air Mosaic's External Viewers Configuration dialog box lets you specify terminal programs.

Table T.2
Supporting Terminal Programs That Can Be Launched From Air Mosaic

Application	What to Enter and What It Does
Telnet Application	The path and filename of your Telnet application. Telnet uses standard Internet protocols to enable your computer to connect to and interact with another computer.
Rlogin	The path and filename of your rlogin application. The rlogin application was developed to enable you to log in from one UNIX host to another UNIX host.
TN3270 Application	The path and filename of your TN3270 application. TN3270 establishes a Telnet connection to IBM mainframes.

Mosaic, and allows you to view more than one document at a time.

See Also **Browser Window; Document View Window; Cascade**

TN3270 APPLICATION: AIR MOSAIC, NETSCAPE

See **Supporting Applications; Telnet; Terminal Applications**

TOOLBAR

Each Web browser includes a toolbar with buttons that execute the most frequently chosen commands. Most display buttons for the Open, Save, Back, Forward, Reload, Home Page, Add to Hotlist, Copy, Paste, Find, Print, and Stop commands. Each toolbar also includes a few unique buttons such as Kiosk Mode, Images, Find, Find Again. Quarterdeck Mosaic (see Figure T.2), Netscape (see Figure T.3) and Air Mosaic (see Figure T.4) let you display toolbars with text, to help you identify the buttons easily.

Figure T.2
Quarterdeck Mosaic's toolbar

Figure T.3
Netscape's toolbar

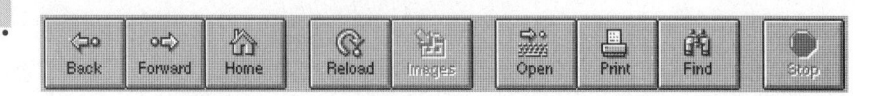

Figure T.4

Air Mosaic's toolbar

> **Tip**
>
> Quarterdeck Mosaic's toolbar offers additional shortcuts not matched in the other products. You can print or save a document by dragging and dropping it from the browser window to the Print or Save button, respectively. You can also drag a URL to either button to first retrieve the document and then print or save it. To add a document to the current Hotlist, drag and drop a document or a URL on the Hotlist button. To remove URLs from anywhere in the Archives, drag and drop them on the Trash button.

> **Tip**
>
> To see a brief description of each button's function in the status bar in Air Mosaic, hold down the button (use the mouse cursor), but don't release it. After you read the button's description, drag the mouse cursor off the button before releasing it. This way, you won't accidentally execute the command.

NCSA Mosaic (see Figure T.5) displays popup help for each button on the toolbar when you hold the mouse cursor over it.

When you hold the mouse cursor over a button in Spyglass Mosaic (see Figure T.6), the button's function displays in the status bar.

See Also Show Toolbar; Preferences

Moving the Toolbar: Quarterdeck Mosaic

Quarterdeck Mosaic is the only Web browser that lets you reshape and move the toolbar. Although it is initially displayed below the menu bar, you don't have to leave it there. You can also turn it into a floating toolbar and change its shape. To move the toolbar:

1. Place the mouse cursor in the blank area between the tools in the toolbar and the program icon. You'll see the hand cursor.

2. Drag the toolbar to the extreme bottom, left or right of the application window and release the mouse button. The toolbar will move to the new location.

Figure T.5

NCSA Mosaic's toolbar

Figure T.6

Spyglass Mosaic's toolbar

Or, drag the toolbar to any area within the application window *except* the extreme bottom, left, or right and release the mouse button. The toolbar will move to the new location and become a floating toolbar (see Figure F.7), which can be dragged around the screen.

To move the toolbar back to the top of your application window:

1. Place the mouse cursor in the blank area between the tools in the toolbar and the program icon. You'll see the hand cursor.

2. Drag the toolbar to the extreme top of the application window and release the mouse button.

See Also Archives; Show Toolbar As; Toolbar Icon Settings

TOOLBAR ICON SETTINGS: QUARTERDECK MOSAIC

In Quarterdeck Mosaic, you can display the toolbar with small icons, large icons, or small or large icons with text by choosing one of the Toolbar Icon Settings on the General tab of the Preferences dialog box. (The screen captures in this book were taken with the Large Icons with Text option selected.)

Toolbar Icon Settings

○ Titles Only

○ Small Icons Only

○ Small Icons and Titles

○ Large Icons Only

● Large Icons and Titles

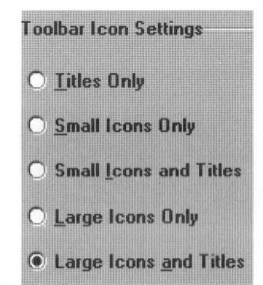

Figure T.7

Quarterdeck Mosaic's floating toolbar can be moved within the application window.

🛣️ 66 **The Show Toolbar As option in Netscape and Toolbar Style command in Air Mosaic provide similar capabilities.**

See Also Show Toolbar As; Toolbar; Toolbar Style

TOOLBAR STYLE: AIR MOSAIC

In Air Mosaic, you can display the toolbar with pictures, text, or pictures and text together by choosing one of the Toolbar Style alternatives in the Toolbar Style dialog box (see Figure T.8). The screen captures in this book were taken with the Both Text and Picture option selected.

To change the way the toolbar displays:

1. Choose Toolbar Style from the Options menu to display the Toolbar Style dialog box.
2. Select one of the three options.
3. Click OK.

See Also Show Toolbar As; Toolbar; Toolbar Icon Settings

TOOLBARS AT STARTUP: NCSA MOSAIC

The General tab in the Preferences dialog box lets you specify whether the toolbars are displayed when you launch NCSA Mosaic.

Show Toolbar toggles the display of the toolbar.

Show Location Bar toggles the display of the URL bar.

Show Status Bar toggles the display of the status bar.

See Also General; Preferences

Figure T.8

The Toolbar Style options in Air Mosaic

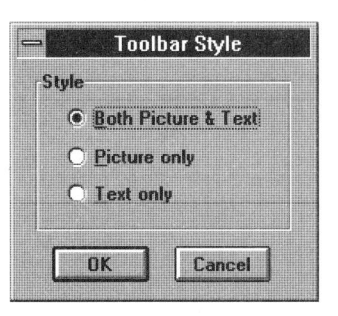

TRASH: QUARTERDECK MOSAIC

In Quarterdeck Mosaic, you can use the Trash button on the toolbar to delete unwanted URLs from the Archives. Either select an item and click the Trash button or drag and drop the item on the Trash button.

See Also   **Archives; Delete; Toolbar**

U

UNDERLINE LINKS

You can underline links in each Web browser. You may want to use underlining instead of, or in addition to, using a contrasting color to highlight links.

> *See Also* Anchors; Configuration; Hypertext Link Style; Links; Preferences

Underline: Quarterdeck Mosaic

To underline links in Quarterdeck Mosaic, select Underline from the Hypertext Links drop-down list on the HTML Viewer tab of the Preferences dialog box.

Underline Hyperlinks: Air Mosaic

To specify whether or not links are underlined in Air Mosaic, use the Underline Hyperlinks option in the Configuration dialog box.

Underline Links: Spyglass Mosaic

To specify whether or not links are underlined in Spyglass Mosaic, use the Underline Links option in the Preferences dialog box.

Underlined: NCSA Mosaic

To specify whether or not anchors (links) are underlined in NCSA Mosaic, use the Underlined option, found under Miscellaneous on the Anchors tab of the Preferences dialog box.

Underlined: Netscape

To specify whether or not links are underlined in Netscape, use the Links are: Underlined option in the Styles section of the Preferences dialog box.

UNDO: NETSCAPE

In Netscape, you can reverse the effects of the last editing action you performed with either Cut, Copy, or Paste by choosing the Undo command from the Edit menu. When you use Undo, the text on the clipboard is not removed, but the editing action within your document or text box is reversed.

See Also **Copy, Cut, Paste**

URL BAR

The URL bar in each Web browser includes a text box that displays the URL (Uniform Resource Locator) for the current document. You can also type the URL directly into the URL text box and press ƒ to retrieve a document. The URL bar is usually displayed below the toolbar.

In NCSA Mosaic (see Figure U.1), just click the check icon after you've entered the URL.

In NCSA Mosaic and Air Mosaic (see Figure U.2), you can select a URL from the drop-down list box. The list box holds URLs entered during the current session.

In Quarterdeck Mosaic (see Figure U.3), the URL bar displays on each individual browser window.

The Spyglass Mosaic URL bar (see Figure U.4) displays to the right of the Back and Forward buttons.

The Netscape URL bar (see Figure U.5) is labeled Location.

See Also **URL Helper; URLs**

URL HELPER: QUARTERDECK MOSAIC

In Quarterdeck Mosaic, a URL Helper button is included in the Go To URL and

Figure U.1
The NCSA Mosaic URL bar

Figure U.2
The Air Mosaic URL bar

Figure U.3
The Quarterdeck Mosaic URL bar

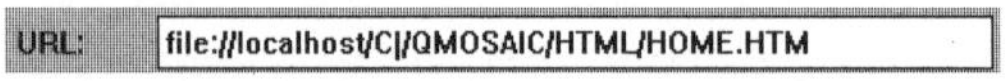

Figure U.4

The Spyglass Mosaic URL bar

URL: `file:///C|/WIN32APP/SPYGLASS/EMOSAIC/initial.htm`

Figure U.5

The Netscape URL bar

Location: `http://home.netscape.com/`

Open URL dialog boxes, and optionally on the Browser window. The URL Helper helps you enter a syntactically correct URL without having to type the entire URL in the URL box. To enter a URL using the URL Helper:

1. Click the URL button to open the URL Helper dialog box (see Figure U.6).

   URL Helper...

2. Select the correct prefix from the Scheme list box to insert the prefix and its correct punctuation into the URL field. Once a prefix is selected, the other fields in the dialog box change to provide the additional required information.

3. Enter the other text boxes in the dialog box. The text you enter is added to the URL field.

Figure U.6

Quarterdeck Mosaic's URL Helper dialog box helps you enter URLs correctly.

4. After entering all the necessary data, click OK.

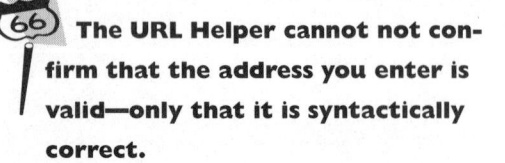

> The URL Helper cannot not confirm that the address you enter is valid—only that it is syntactically correct.

> **Tip**
>
> NCSA includes accelerator keys that help you enter URL prefixes correctly.

See Also Accelerator Keys; Go To; Open; URL

URLS

URL is an abbreviation for Uniform Resource Locator, which is the name of the file combined with its location; for example, the server it is located on and the directory path it can be found in. Web browsers use a page's URL to find the page and retrieve it. URLs consist of the following specific parts, *all* of which must be present in a valid URL:

1. **The protocol**, which is followed by a colon, For example `http:`.

2. **The server**, which is preceded by two forward slashes. For example, `//www.ncsa.uiuc.edu`.

3. **The item's pathname**, each segment of which is preceded by a single slash. For example, `/Mosaic/NCSAMosaicHome.html`.

See Also URL Bar; URL Helper

USE BROWSER AS VIEWER: NETSCAPE

The Use Browser as Viewer option is one of the Action options in the Helper Applications section in Netscape's Preferences dialog box.

See Also Action; Preferences; Viewers

USE CURRENT WINDOW POSITION: NCSA MOSAIC

See Initial Window Placement

USE EXTENDED FTP: NCSA MOSAIC

When you check the Use Extended FTP option in the Service tab of the Preferences dialog box, NCSA Mosaic associates file type icons and file sizes for each file on the FTP server to which you are connected.

It also shows you a little more (esoteric) info about files.

See Also **Services; Preferences**

USE INTERNAL (8-BIT) SOUND: NCSA MOSAIC, AIR MOSAIC

Air Mosaic and NCSA Mosaic provide internal support for recently manufactured, high-quality sound cards. If you have a low-quality, older or no sound card installed in your computer, and audio files do not seem to play properly, enable the Use Internal (8-bit) Sound or Use 8-bit Sound option. NCSA Mosaic and Air Mosaic will use their built-in sound drivers to play audio files when this option is turned on.

In NCSA Mosaic, the General tab in the Preferences dialog box contains the Use Internal 8-bit Sound option. In Air Mosaic, you'll find the Use 8-bit Sound option in the Configuration dialog box.

See Also **Configuration; General; Preferences**

USENET NEWSGROUPS

See **Internet Newsgroups**

USER CONFIGURABLE MENUS: AIR MOSAIC, NCSA MOSAIC, NETSCAPE

Air Mosaic and NCSA Mosaic let you create and modify menus based on your Hotlists. Netscape lets you modify your Bookmark menu to include your bookmarks.

See Also **Modifying Bookmarks; Modifying Hotlists; Modifying Menus**

USER NAME: QUARTERDECK MOSAIC

The User Name you enter in Quarterdeck Mosaic is used as your password when you attempt to connect to a remote system via anonymous ftp. Your e-mail address, not your real name, should be entered here. To enter your User Name in Quarterdeck Mosaic:

1. Choose Configure Network from the Tools menu.
2. Click in the User Name text box and type your user name and address. For example, merrin@callamer.com.
3. Choose OK.

See Also **Anonymous FTP; E-mail Address**

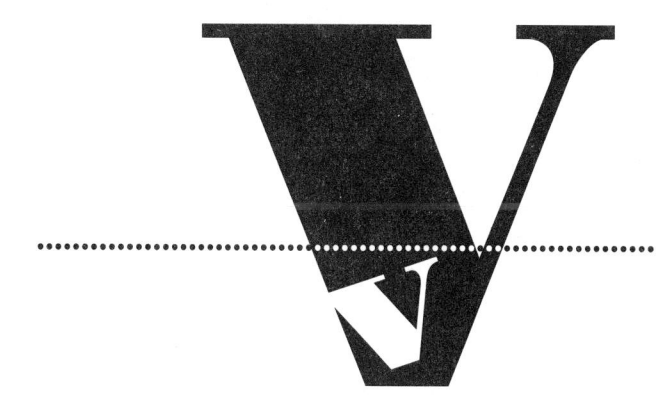

VERONICA

Veronica is the name of an Internet search service that searches through a database of documents found on gopher servers. With Veronica, you can search for a specific document or piece of information. However, the results are limited to the information currently in the database, and you will often have to search more than one server to find what you are looking for. You'll also experience frequent delays because of the heavy use of Veronica and the gopher servers you are searching.

Performing a Veronica Search

To search gopher servers with Veronica:

1. In the URL text box in your Web browser, enter the URL to retrieve the Gopher menu: gopher://veronica.scs.unr.edu:70/11/veronica and press ƒ. The Gopher Menu (see Figure V.1)

> **Tip**
>
> If you are using NCSA Mosaic, you can use the Veronica Search item on the Gopher Servers section of the Starting Points menu to begin a Veronica search, instead of entering the URL shown in Step 1.

that serves as the starting point for a Veronica search displays.

2. Choose one of the "Simplified" options, for your first search. Or use one of the options described below:

- Items that begin "Find Gopher Directories" will display only the directories that contain the item you are searching for on that server.

- Items that begin Search GopherSpace by Title Word(s) will display files and

Figure V.1

The Gopher Menu serves as the starting point for a Veronica search.

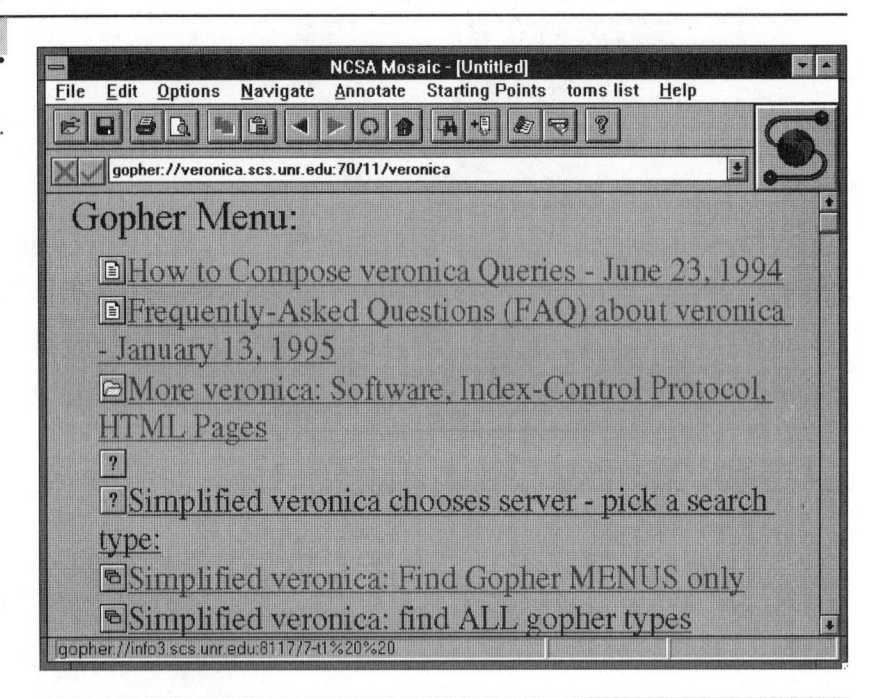

> **Gopher Menu:**
> - How to Compose veronica Queries - June 23, 1994
> - Frequently-Asked Questions (FAQ) about veronica - January 13, 1995
> - More veronica: Software, Index-Control Protocol, HTML Pages
> - Simplified veronica chooses server - pick a search type:
> - Simplified veronica: Find Gopher MENUS only
> - Simplified veronica: find ALL gopher types

> **Tip**
>
> Before you go any further, you may want to retrieve the first two items listed on the Gopher Menu page. "How to Compose Veronica Queries" and "Frequently Asked Questions About Veronica" provide a great overview and introduction to Veronica.

directories that contain the item you are searching for on that server.

3. Click in the Search Index text box at the bottom of the page (see Figure V.2)

and enter the text to search for. Searches are not case-sensitive.

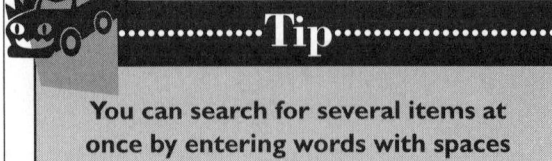

> **Tip**
>
> You can search for several items at once by entering words with spaces between them. For example, you can enter Mosaic Windows Macintosh to find files and directories which include Mosaic and both platforms in their title.

Table V.1 lists the most common options you can use in your search string.

Figure V.2

Enter the text string at the bottom of the Searchable Gopher Index page

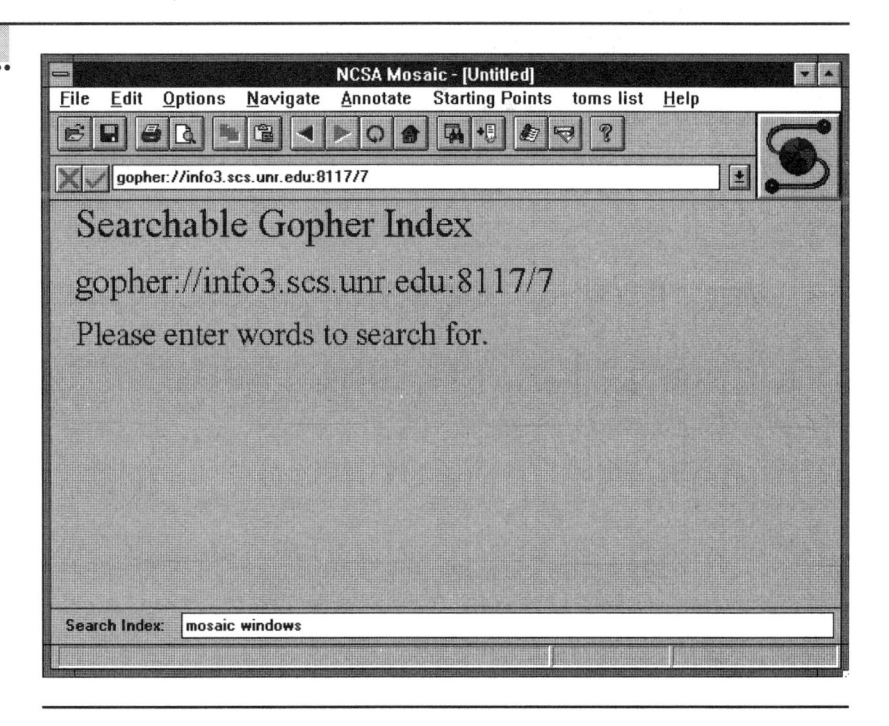

Table V.1

Search String Options Available with Veronica

Option	What It Does
and	Searches for text before and after the *and*. For example: `Mosaic and Windows` searches for files and directories containing *both* words.
or	Searches for text before or after the *or*. For example: `Mosaic or Windows` searches for files and directories containing *either* word.
not	Searches for the text before the *not* and then makes sure the text after the not isn't included. For example: `Mosaic not Windows` searches for files and directories with the word Mosaic but excludes files with the word Windows.
*	Searches for the specified text with any additional characters after it. For example: `Mos*` searches for files and directories with the words Mosaic, most, moss, etc.
( )	Searches for a string of text as a phrase; For example `(Mosaic Windows)` searches for files and directories with the words Mosaic Windows exactly. Phrases such as "Mosaic for Windows" or "Mosaic with Windows" would not be retrieved.

4. Press *f* to begin the search.

When the search is completed, you'll see a list of the items that match the text you specified.

> **Tip**
>
> By default, no more than 200 items are returned at any one time. To see more than 200, type -m at the end of your text entry in Step 3.

> Gopher servers are frequently busy, so don't be surprised if you have to retry your search several times.

See Also   Archie; Gopher

VIEW BOOKMARKS: NETSCAPE

In Netscape, all bookmark modifications are made by choosing View Bookmarks from the Bookmarks menu to open the Bookmark List dialog box.

See Also   Modifying Bookmarks

VIEW HISTORY: NETSCAPE

To select a page from the History in Netscape, choose View History from the Go menu, then double-click on any page in the list.

See Also   History

VIEW SOURCE: SPYGLASS MOSAIC

In Spyglass Mosaic, choosing View Source from the Edit menu displays the document source in the View Source window.

See Also   Document Source

VIEWERS

Your Web browser can display a file you want to retrieve only if it recognizes the type of file and can determine how to display or open it. Once the browser knows a file's type, it can determine whether to display it in the document window or with a helper application. If the file is an HTML or plain text file, or a GIF or JPEG image, all browsers described in this book will display it immediately. For other file types, to display the file, you'll have to obtain the additional viewers and then associate the viewer with the file type. You can download some viewers from sites on the Internet, and you can purchase others. See the Sidebar "Where To Find Viewers" for some recommendations for downloading viewers. Table V.2 lists the viewers to download or obtain elsewhere, to view the files most commonly found on the Web.

> **Remember that after you download a viewer in zip format, you'll have to unzip (extract) it and then install it before associating it with a file type. If you don't remember how to extract files, you'll find a good explanation in Part One.**

> **In Spyglass, you can associate viewers by choosing Helpers from the Edit menu. In Netscape, you can associate viewers in the Helper Application section of the Preferences dialog box.**

See Also Action; Configuration; Helper Applications; Helpers; MIME; MIME Types; Preferences; Viewers

Table V.2
Viewers Needed For Common File Types

File Extension	Viewer Name	File to Download
GIF, JPEG	Image View	lview31.zip
MPEG	MPEG Player	mpegw32h.zip
MOV	QuickTime viewer	qtw11.zip
AU, WAV	WHAM	wham131.zip
AVI	Video Player	avipro2.exe
PDF	Acrobat Reader	acroread.exe

Where To Find Viewers

Shareware versions of popular viewers are available from several Internet sites via ftp. Connect to any or all of the following sites to see which viewers are currently available:

```
ftp://ftp.ncsa.uiuc.edu/Mosaic/Windows/viewers
ftp://gatekeeper.dec.com/pub/micro/msdos/win3/desktop
ftp://gatekeeper.dec.com/pub/micro/msdos/win3/sounds
ftp://ftp.spry.com/ms-windows/viewers
```

Downloading Viewers

Viewers are files, not Web documents, so to download them from the Internet, you'll use ftp. If you've downloaded NCSA Mosaic with the Chameleon Sampler version of ftp on the disk included with this book, you know how to download viewers. You can also download the viewers by entering the URL for their site, and clicking on the link for the file. To download a viewer with your Web browser:

1. Choose the Open or Open URL command from the File menu.
2. Enter the URL for the ftp site in the text box and press f. For example, type `ftp://ftp.ncsa.uiuc.edu/Mosaic/Windows/viewers` and press f. You'll see a page with directory and filenames similar to the page shown in Figure V.3. The viewers available at each site display as links.
3. Click on the name of the file you want to download to begin copying the file to your hard disk.
4. When you are finished, you can download another file immediately by clicking on the name of the file.

Associating Viewers: Air Mosaic

In Air Mosaic, viewers are associated in the External Viewers Configuration dialog box (see Figure V.4) which opens when you choose Viewers in the Configuration dialog box.

To associate a viewer with an application in Air Mosaic:

1. Choose Configuration from the Options menu to open the Configuration dialog box.

Figure V.3

You can download ftp viewers by clicking on the links.

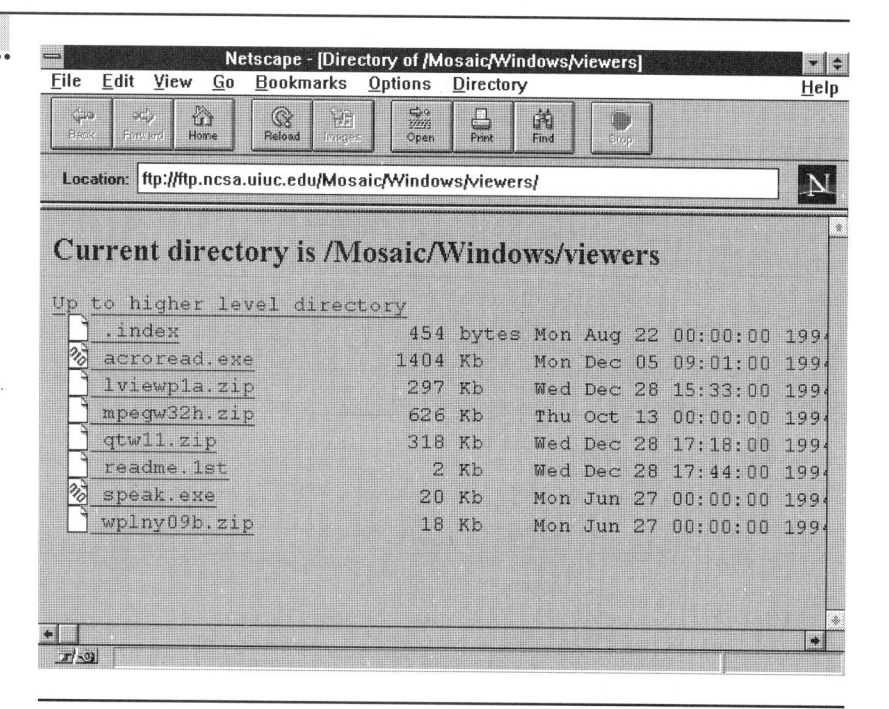

Figure V.4

Air Mosaic's External Viewers Configuration dialog box lets you associate files with viewers.

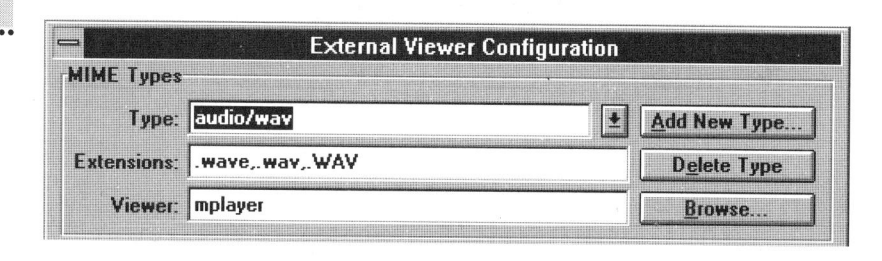

2. Click the Viewers button to open the External Viewers Configuration dialog box.

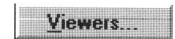

3. Select the file type you want to associate with a new viewer from the Type drop-down list box.

4. Edit the existing extension in the Extensions text box only if necessary. For most file types, the correct extensions display automatically.

5. Enter the path and filename in the Viewer text box You can click the Browse button to open the Browse dialog box where you can select the file to enter.

6. Click the Close button to close this dialog box.

7. Click OK to close the Configuration dialog box.

Associating Viewers: NCSA Mosaic

In NCSA Mosaic, viewers are associated on the Viewers tab of the Preferences dialog box (see Figure V.5).

To associate a viewer with an application in NCSA Mosaic:

1. Choose Preferences from the Options menu to open the Configuration dialog box.

2. Click the Viewers tab to display the MIME Type options.

3. Select the file type you want to associate with a new viewer from the Associate Mime Type of drop-down list.

4. Edit the existing extension in the With This Extensions text box only if necessary. For most file types, the correct extensions display automatically.

5. Enter the path and filename of the viewer in the To This Application text box. You can click the Browse button to open the Browse dialog box where you can select the file to enter.

6. Click the OK button to close the Preferences dialog box.

Figure V.5

NCSA Mosaic's Viewers tab lets you associate files with viewers.

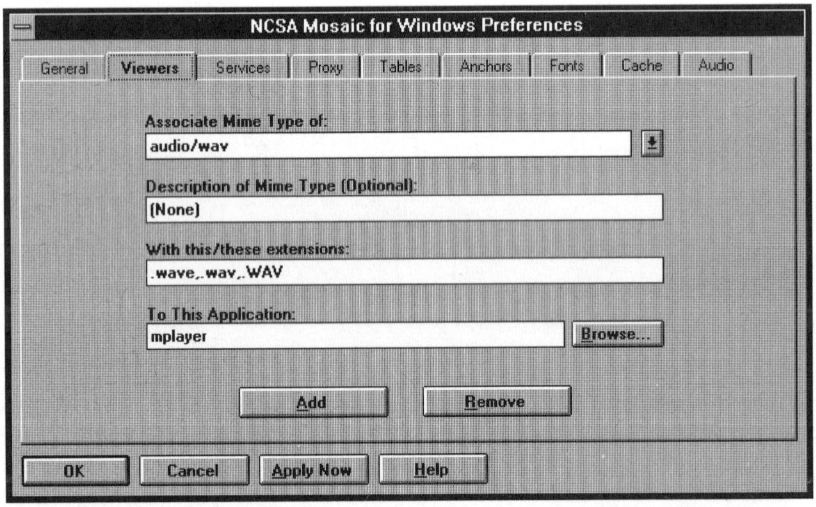

Associating Viewers: Quarterdeck Mosaic

In Quarterdeck Mosaic, viewers are associated on the Viewers tab of the Preferences dialog box (see Figure V.6).

To associate a viewer with an application in Quarterdeck Mosaic:

1. Choose Preferences from the Tools menu.
2. Click on the Data Engine tab to bring it forward.
3. Select the file type you want to associate with a new viewer from the list box.
4. Select the External Viewer Application option shown under Action.
5. Enter the path and filename of the viewer in the text box below. You can click the Browse button to open the Browse dialog box where you can select the file to enter.
6. Click the OK button to close the Preferences dialog box.

VISITED LINK COLOR: SPYGLASS MOSAIC

With Spyglass Mosaic's Visited Links option, you can change the color for links displayed in documents after you select them.

Figure V.6

Quarterdeck Mosaic's Data Engine tab lets you associate files with viewers.

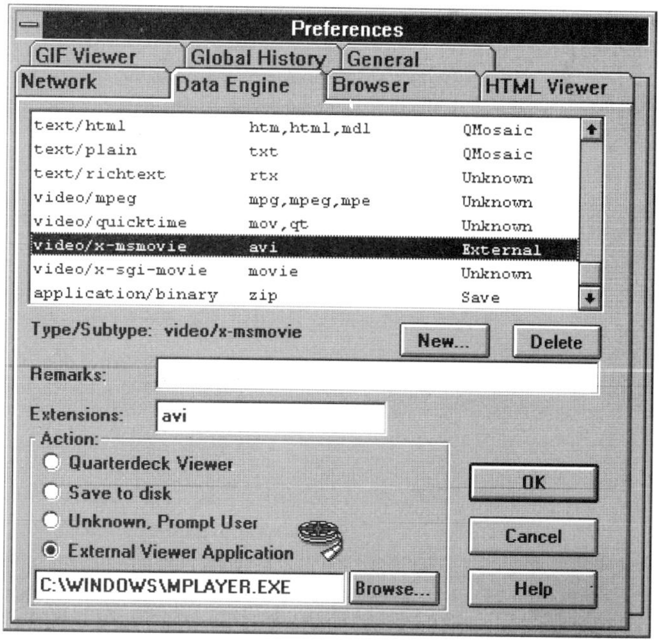

Changing the visited link color will help you keep track of which links you've clicked on already and which documents you've looked at. To change the color for visited links in documents in Spyglass Mosaic:

1. Choose Preferences from the Edit menu to display the Preferences dialog box.
2. Click on the Set button to the right of Visited Link Color to open the Visited Link Color dialog box (see Figure V.7).
3. Click on any color square in the dialog box.
4. Click on OK to close the Visited Link Color dialog box and apply the change.
5. Click on OK to close the Preferences dialog box.

To change the appearance of visited links in NCSA Mosaic, choose Visually Age Visited Anchor from the Anchors tab of the Preferences dialog box. In Quarterdeck Mosaic, choose Anchor Visited Color from the HTML Viewer tab of the Preferences dialog box. In Netscape, choose Followed Links from the Fonts and Color section of the Preferences dialog box.

See Also Anchor Color; Anchors; Color; Link Color

Figure V.7
Spyglass Mosaic's Visited Link Color dialog box

W

WAIS

WAIS is the abbreviation for Wide Area Information Server, a standardized technology that lets you access and search databases that are organized in a variety of ways at a variety of locations on the Internet. WAIS lets you specify information and receive a list of matching documents that you can browse through, and retrieve.

The Web browsers described in this book do not facilitate a WAIS search by filling out an online form, as they do an Archie or Veronica search. You can, however, connect to a WAIS server with this URL: `http://info.cern.ch/hypertext/Products/WAIS/Overview.html`. The WAIS overview page is shown in Figure W.1

On the WAIS overview page, clicking on the "gateway" link displays additional background information and a summary of some data available through the WAIS gateway.

> To learn more about WAIS, you can also subscribe to the newsgroup `comp.infosystems.wais`.

See Also Forms; Gopher; Subscribing to Newsgroups; Veronica

WAIS PROXY

See Proxies; Proxy; WAIS

WAIT FOR IMAGES: QUARTERDECK MOSAIC

Quarterdeck Mosaic's Wait for Images option, found on the HTML Viewer tab of the Preferences dialog box, lets you specify whether a document should be displayed

Figure W.1

Retrieve the WAIS overview page to find out more about WAIS.

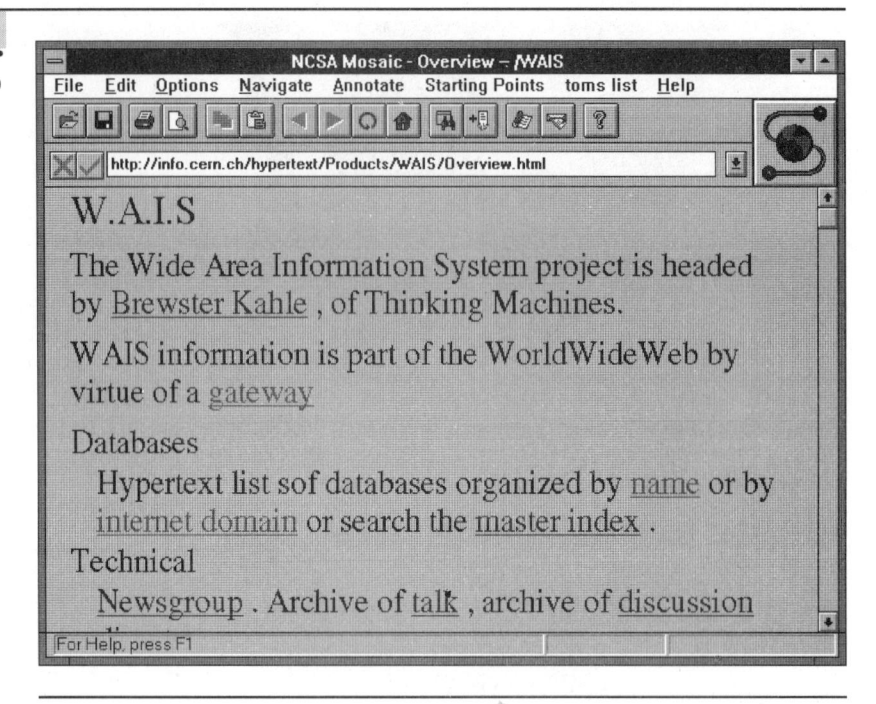

---

immediately or after the full size of the image is known. When Wait for Images is checked, Quarterdeck Mosaic does not start displaying images until it receives information about the size of that image. When not checked, an icon is displayed as a placeholder until the image is downloaded. Then, the document is reformatted around the image.

See Also HTML Viewer; Preferences

WHAT'S NEW PAGE

See Part One: What's New on the Internet?

WHEN LOADING IMAGES, REDRAW EVERY: AIR MOSAIC

In Air Mosaic, the When Loading Images, Redraw Every option lets you specify how often a document containing inline graphics is redisplayed while loading. Enter a higher number (start with 5) to load most or all of a document's images before the screen is redrawn—especially if you are using a dial up connection and images seem to load slowly. Enter a lower number (start with 1) to redraw the screen each time a new image is loaded. Try several different values, using the following steps, until you are satisfied with the way documents are loaded.

1. Choose Configuration from the Options menu to open the Configuration dialog box.
2. Change the number in the When Loading Images, Redraw Every text box.
3. Choose OK to close the dialog box and apply the change.

See Also   Configuration; Inline Images

WINDOW STYLES: NETSCAPE

The Window Styles options found in the Styles section of Netscape's Preferences dialog box let you display the toolbar with pictures, text, pictures and text together, and specify a home page and whether to load the home page at startup.

See Also   Home Page Location; Show Toolbar As; Start With

WIPE INTERVAL: QUARTERDECK MOSAIC

Quarterdeck Mosaic's Wipe Interval option, found on the Browser tab of the Preferences dialog box lets you control how quickly a document is erased from the browser window when you choose the Back button or page turner to display the previous document. You can disable this option by entering 0 (zero) in the text box. If you have a fast connection and system, you may like this visual effect for its state-of-the-art look. But if your connection or system are a little slower, this feature may slow down the redisplay of documents and you might prefer simply to turn it off.

See Also   Preferences

WORLD WIDE WEB

Table W.1 will give you a small sampling of interesting Web sites and pages.

See Also   Part One: What Is the World Wide Web (WWW)?

WWW

See   Part One: What Is the World Wide Web (WWW)?

Table W.1
Interesting Web Sites and Pages

Web Page or Site Name	Uniform Resource Locator (URL)
AskERIC Virtual Library	http://ericir.syr.edu
Cardiff Movie Database	http://www.cm.cf.ac.uk/Movies/
CBS Television Home Page	http://www.cbs.com
Cdnow! The Internet Music Store	http://cdnow.com
City Net Guide to World Communities	http://www.city.net
CommerceNet Business Information	http://www.commerce.net
Download Bookstore	http://dab.psi.net/DownloadBookstore/
Elvis Home Page	http://sunsite.unc.edu/elvis/elvishom.html
Fox Broadcasting	http://www.eden.com/users/my-html/fox.html
Games Domain	http://wcl-rs.bham.ac.uk/GamesDomain
GolfData Web	http://www.gdol.com
Internet Business Center	http://tig.com/IBC/index.html
Internet Shopping Network	http://www.internet.net/
Koblas Currency Converter	http://gnn.com/cgi-bin/gnn/currency
Library of Congress	http://lcweb.loc.gov/homepage/lchp.html
National Hockey League	http://maxwell.uhh.hawaii.edu/hockey/hockey.html
National Library of Medicine	http://www.nlm.nih.gov/
Quotecom Finacial Data	http://www.quote.com
Small Business Administration	http://www.sbaonline.sba.gov/
Sports Server	http://www.nando.net/sptsserv.html
Star Trek Generations	http://generations.viacom.com/
The Whitehouse	http://www.whitehouse.gov

Table W.1
Interesting Web Sites and Pages (continued)

Web Page or Site Name	Uniform Resource Locator (URL)
U.S. Government Information Sources	http://iridium.nttc.edu/gov_res.html
Virtual Tourist	http://wings.buffalo.edu/world
Web Wide World of Music	html://amrican.recordings.com/wwwofmusic/index.html
WebMuseum of Art	http://www.emf.net/louvre/
Whole Internet Catalog	http://www.digital.com/gnn/wic/index.html
Wine Page	http://augustus.csscr.washington.edu/personal/bigstar-mosaic/wine.html
World of Jazz Improvisation	http://www.wisc.edu/jazz/
World Wide Web Virtual Library	http://info.cern.ch/hypertext/DataSources/bySubject/Overview.html
World Wide Yellow Pages	http://www.yellow.com/
WWW Servers of the U.S. Federal Government	http://www.fie.com/www/us_gov.htm
Yahoo Page of What's on the Net	http://www.yahoo.com

XYZ

XBM IMAGES

XBM images are graphics files—specifically bitmap images—common to UNIX. They can be recognized by the extension .XBM. Air Mosaic, Quarterdeck Mosaic, and Netscape all have built-in XBM support, in that they can display an XBM file without the help of an external viewer.

See Also **GIF Images; Images; JPEG Images; Viewers**

YOUR E-MAIL: NETSCAPE

Netscape automatically inserts your e-mail address when you send messages with the Mail Document command. To enter your e-mail address in Netscape:

1. Choose Preferences from the Options menu.
2. Select Mail and News from the drop-down list.
3. Click in the Your Email text box and type your user name and address. For example, merrin@callamer.com.
4. Choose OK.

See Also **E-mail Address; Your Name**

YOUR NAME: NETSCAPE

Netscape automatically inserts your name when you send messages with the Mail Document command. To enter your name in Netscape:

1. Choose Preferences from the Options menu.
2. Select Mail and News from the drop-down list.
3. Click in the Your Name text box and type your real name.
4. Choose OK.

See Also **E-mail Address; Your E-mail**

Index

Note to the Reader

Boldfaced numbers indicate pages where you will find the principal discussion of a topic or the definition of a term. *Italic* numbers indicate pages where a topic is illustrated in a figure.

Symbols and Numbers

* wildcard
    for newsgroup searches, 225
    in Veronica search string, 277
(), in Veronica search string, 277
3D tables, in NCSA Mosaic, 261
32-bit applications, running under Windows, 37

A

Abort, as NCSA Mail window option, 236
accelerator keys, in NCSA Mosaic, **47–48**
Access the Internet (Peal), 15
Acrobat Reader, 279
Add Document dialog box (Air Mosaic), *54*
Add Folder dialog box (Air Mosaic), *80*
Add Item dialog box (NCSA Mosaic), 52, *53*, 81, *82*
address book, for QMC New Message window, 240
Air Mosaic, 4, **9–10**, *9*
    About command, 47
    accessing What's New, 24
    associating viewers, **280**, *281*
    canceling tasks in, 71, 253
    Configuration dialog box, **77–78**, *78*, 92, *93*, 244. *See also* Configuration dialog box (Air Mosaic)
    demo document, **90**
    document caching in, 92
    electronic mail in, **100**, **237**
    e-mail address for, **101**
    extensions in, **104**
    feature comparison, 7
    finding text in, **109–110**
    help for, 20, 21
    home page, 19
    internal support for sound cards, **273**
    launching, 16
    Load Automatically at Startup, 65
    NNTP server for, **195**
    opening local files, **199**
    proxy servers in, **215**
    reading news, **221**
    saving document as file, **172**
    SMTP server name for, **249**
    software for, 14
Air Mosaic console, 79
Air Mosaic hotlists, **142–143**, *143*
    adding document to, 50

changes in, 74
creating, 79
deleting, 86
exporting, **102–103**, *102*
importing NCSA menu as, **156–157**
modifying, **185**
multiple, 73–74
Air Mosaic Mail window, 237, *238*
Air Mosaic menus
adding cascading menu, **83**
adding item to SPRY menu, **55**
adding to, **52–54**
creating, **81–82**
deleting, **87**
modifying, **189**, 273
removing from menu bar, **87**
Air Mosaic screen display
animating logo, **56–57**
application window, *190*
button descriptions in, 265
color for links, **167–168**
customizing window, **83–84**
document title bar, *96*, 96
Document URL bar, 32
Font button, 76
fonts in, 73, **117**
history window, 27, **135–136**, *136*
Kiosk Mode, **165–166**, *166*
Open button, 200
program icon for, 210
setting window size and position, 231
toolbar for, *265*
toolbar style, **267**
turning off graphics, 28
turning off toolbar, 29
underlining links in, 269
URL bar, *270*, 270
URL text box in, 30
alt.culture.usenet newsgroup, 161

alt newsgroups, 162
anchors. *See also* hypertext links
changing cursor over, 72
to move between documents, 191
in NCSA Mosaic, **56**
and, in Veronica search string, 277
animated logo, in Air Mosaic, 56–57
Annotate menu (NCSA Mosaic), **57**
Delete this Annotation, 59
Edit this Annotation, 58
Annotation window (NCSA Mosaic), 57
annotations, **57–59**
deleting in NCSA Mosaic, **59**, 85
displaying in Quarterdeck Mosaic, **242**
Reload command for viewing, 227
viewing in NCSA Mosaic, **58**
viewing in Quarterdeck Mosaic, **58**
Anonymous FTP, **59**
user name as password, 273
Append Sig, as NCSA Mail window option, 236
application window in Air Mosaic, setting size and position, 231
Applications and Directories section (Netscape Preferences dialog box), **59–60, 259–260**
Bookmark File, 68
Temporary Directory, 262
Archie, **60**, 122
Archie Request form, **60–61**, *61*
Archie servers, selecting for searches, 61
Archives (Quarterdeck Mosaic), **62**, *62*, 112, *113*
Link Tree, **169–170**, *169*
articles, from newsgroups, 160
ASCII text files
HTML tags in, **149–150**
saving document as, **230**
AskERIC Virtual Library, 288

attachments
   to e-mail in Quarterdeck Message Center, 240
   sending documents as, 176
.au file extension, viewer for, 279
audio files, viewers for, 134
audio preferences, in NCSA Mosaic, **63**
Author, in Annotation window (NCSA), 57
Auto word wrap, as NCSA Mail window option, 236
Autoload Home Page (NCSA Mosaic), **64**
Autoload Images (Netscape), 28, 64
Autoload Inline Images (Air Mosaic), 28, 64
.avi file extension, viewer for, 279

B

Back button, 20
Back command, **67–68**, 121
background color
   in NCSA Mosaic, 126
   in Netscape, 76–77
   in Quarterdeck Mosaic, 68
Basic Authentication security, 233
bionet newsgroups, 162
bit.listserv.c+health newsgroup, 161
bit newsgroups, 162
biz newsgroups, 162
blue color bar, for secure document, 97, 233
Bookmark File text box (Netscape), 68
Bookmark List (Netscape), 181, *182*
   as home page, **139**
   opening, 278
Bookmark menu (Netscape), **69**
   Add Bookmark, 48–49
   View Bookmarks, 139, 181, 182, **278**
bookmarks in Netscape Navigator, 12, **48–49**, 69
   deleting, **182–183**
   displaying, **182**
   exporting to HTML document, 185
   modifying, **181**
   renaming, **183**
   reordering, **183–184**
Browse dialog box, 36, *43*
Browser as Viewer (Preferences dialog box), 48
browser window. *See also* Document View window
Browser window (Quarterdeck Mosaic), 69
   cascading, 72
   changing background color, 68
   closing current, 76
   tiling, **263**
browsers, **69**. *See also* Web browsers
browsing the Internet, **22–33**
browsing with Mosaic, 26
bugs, NCSA Mosaic list of, **69**
bullets, appearance in Quarterdeck Mosaic, **70**
business information, source for, 33, *34*
button anchors, 56
buttons. *See also* specific button names
   for frequently-used commands, 18

C

cache for documents, **91–94**
   in NCSA Mosaic, 71
canceling, **71**
Caps Lock key, 19
Cardiff Movie Database, 288
cascading menu, adding, **82–83**
cascading windows, 72
case-insensitive substring, in Archie searches, 60
case-sensitive substring, in Archie searches, 60

CBS Television Home Page, 288
Cdnow! The Internet Music Store, 288
CERN (European Center for Nuclear Research), **72**
Chameleon group window
    Custom icon, 16, 38
    NEWT icon, 16, 38
Chameleon Sampler, v, 5, **35–36**
    FTP program, 37
    installing, **36**
    PROVIDER.TXT file, 13
    TCP/IP protocol stack software, 14
    Telnet application, 262
Change Icon dialog box (Quarterdeck Mosaic), *211*
channels, for Internet Relay Chat, 161
CIA World Fact book, *32*, 32
City Net Guide to World Communities, 288
clarinet newsgroups, 162
Clean Slate, in Annotation window (NCSA), 57
Clear command, in Spyglass Mosaic, **76**
Clear Disk Cache Now button, 94
Clear Memory Cache Now button, 94
clipboard
    to copy URLs, 80
    copying text to, **79**
    cutting text to, **84**
    pasting text from, 202
    selecting text to copy to, **234**
color
    of anchors, 56
    changing background in Quarterdeck Mosaic, 68
    changing in Netscape, **76–77**
    of links, 167
    for links in Spyglass Mosaic after selecting, **283–284**
    for NCSA Mosaic tables, 261

Color dialog box (Air Mosaic), *168*
command line, displaying for DOS, 42
commands, menu bar for, 18
CommerceNet, home page, 33, *34*
CommerceNet Business Information, 288
Commit, in Annotation window (NCSA), 57
comp.infosystems.wais newsgroup, 285
comp newsgroups, 162
Compose button (Quarterdeck Message Center), 238
compressed files, 37
    unzipping, 41
CompuServe
    GIF images, **127**. *See also* GIF image files
    NetLauncher, *See* Air Mosaic
confidential information, 12
Configuration dialog box (Air Mosaic), **77–78**, *78*, 92, *93*, *244*
    Animate Logo, 56
    Documents in dropdown option, 97, *97*
    E-mail Address, 101
    Fonts button, 117
    Home Page, 140
    Hyperlinks, Underline, 269
    Load Automatically at Startup, 139
    News Server, 195
    Save Last Window Position, 231
    Show Document URL, **244–245**
    Show Status Bar, 246
    Show Toolbar, 29, 247
    Show URL in Status Bar, 248
    SMTP Server, 249
    Use 8-bit sound, 273
    Viewers, 104
    Viewers button, 263, 280–281
    When Loading Images, Redraw Every, 287
Configure File Type dialog box, 134
connect charges, 5, 10
Connect dialog box, 16

Connect menu (Quarterdeck)
    Check Mail, 219
    Send Messages, 238
connecting to the Internet, **13–15**
    before starting Mosaic, 16
    through networked computer, 14
console, in Air Mosaic, 79
context-sensitive online help, 6
control box, double-clicking to exit program, 101
Copy command, **79**, 80
Create Directory dialog box, *38*, 38
cursor
    appearance in NCSA Mosaic, 56
    changing over anchors, 72
    on hypertext link, 17
Custom window (Chameleon Sampler), 38, *39*
customizing Mosaic window, **83–84**
cutting text to clipboard, **84**
cyberspace, **84**
Cyberspace Sampler, 10

D

Data Engine tab, in Quarterdeck Mosaic Preferences dialog box, **85**, 105, *283*, 283
date, sorting by, in Archie searches, 60–61
days, setting number for Quarterdeck history, 128
DDE Service name, 135
Delete, in Annotation window (NCSA), 57
Delete command (Quarterdeck Mosaic), 85
deleting
    annotation in NCSA Mosaic, **59**
    bookmarks, **182–183**
    document from Spyglass Mosaic hotlist, 188
    font scheme in Quarterdeck Mosaic, **119**
    Hotlists, **85–86**
    items from Hotlist, **87–88**
    items from menu, **88–89**
    items from NCSA Hotlist, **147–148**
    menus, **86–87**
    Quarterdeck folders, **114–115**
    Quicklist items, **89**
Demo document, **89–90**
dial-up account, connecting to Internet & launching Mosaic, 16
Digest Authentication security, 233
directories
    for document caching, 92
    for extracted files, 42
    in Netscape, 59–60
    for storing annotations, 59
Directory buttons, in Netscape, **243–244**
Directory menu (Netscape), Go To Newsgroups, 223, 256
Dismiss, in Annotation window (NCSA), 57
Display Inline Images
    in NCSA Mosaic, 64, **91**
    in Quarterdeck Mosaic, **91**
dithering, for Netscape inline images, **153**, **155–156**
document caching, **91–94**
Document Information dialog box (Netscape), **94**, *95*
document retrieval, 28
    by reloading, 226
    canceling, 71
    from link, 91
    in Netscape, **198–199**
    stopping, **253**
    with URLs, **30–33**, **197**, **199–200**
Document Source command, **94–96**, *95*
Document Source window (NCSA Mosaic), *95*
Document Title list, controlling number in, 97
Document URL list (Air Mosaic), 174
    controlling number in, 97

document view windows, *18*, 18–19, **96–97**
   cascading, **72**
   closing current, 76
   size of, 9, 28
   tiling, **263**
documents
   adding to hotlist, **49–51**
   adding to Quarterdeck folders, 113
   annotating, **57–59**
   appearance in Quarterdeck Mosaic Hotlist, 63
   changes in, 29
   filenames for, 172
   gray border in Quarterdeck Mosaic, 242
   icon associated with, **210–211**
   images in, **153**
   moving between, 20, 191
   moving between with page turners, 245–246
   navigating in Netscape, 129
   print preview, **208–209**
   redisplaying while loading, **286–287**
   returning to previous, 20, **67–68**
   saving, **229–230**
   saving as ASCII text, **230**
   saving as file, 172
   selecting all text in, 233–234
   sending as e-mail, **175–176**
   title in title bar, **96**
domain name, 160
doorkey icon, in Netscape, **97**, 233
Down button, to reorder bookmarks, 183
Download Bookstore, 288
downloading
   display options for images, 156
   from FTP servers, 122
   Gopher for, **130**
   NCSA Mosaic, **35–41**
   NCSA Mosaic with Windows FTP, **37–41**
   unzipping after, 279
   viewers, **280**, *281*
   Win32s software, 41
drag and drop, 8, **265**
   to add documents to folder, 113
   to add documents to Quarterdeck Hotlist, 50, *51*
   to copy file to hard disk, 41
   to insert file in e-mail, 236
Duplicate command (Quarterdeck Window menu), **97**

E

Edit List Title dialog box (Air Mosaic), *187*
Edit menu, **99**
   Copy, **79**, 80
   Find, 232
   Paste, **202**
Edit menu (NCSA Hotlist Manager)
   Delete, 146
   Insert New Hotlist, 146
   Insert New Item, 146
Edit menu (NCSA Mosaic)
   Find, *108*, 108
   Preferences, 63
   Select All, **233–234**
Edit menu (Netscape)
   Cut, **84**
   Undo, **270**
Edit menu (Quarterdeck Mosaic)
   Annotation, 57, 58
   Cut, **84**
   Delete, **85**
   Find, *108*, 108
Edit menu (Spyglass Mosaic). *See also* Preferences dialog box (Spyglass Mosaic)
   Clear, **76**
   Cut, **84**

Find, 110
Helpers, 134, 279
Select All, **233–234**
View Source, 96, **278**
Edit Title-URL dialog box (Spyglass Mosaic), *188*
editing annotation
   in NCSA Mosaic, **58**
   in Quarterdeck Mosaic, **58**
electronic mail, **99–100**. *See also* e-mail
electronic payment system, 233
Elvis Home Page, 288
e-mail, **99–100**
   Air Mosaic to send, **237**
   for help, 5
   receiving in Quarterdeck Mosaic, **219**, **221**
   sending with Quarterdeck Mosaic, **237–239**
e-mail address, **100–101**, 160
   Finger to determine, 110
   in Netscape, **291**
   sending documents to, 175
empty cells, appearance in NCSA Mosaic tables, 261
enhanced forms, 6
Enhanced NCSA Mosaic for Windows (Spyglass), 4. *See also* Spyglass Mosaic
error messages, **101**
European Center for Nuclear Research (CERN), **72**
exact matches, in Archie searches, 60
Exit (File menu), **101**
Expanded News Listing option, 221
Expire Visited Anchors option, in NCSA Mosaic, 56
Export Hotlist to HTML dialog box (Air Mosaic), *102*

exporting
   hotlists, **102–103**
   Netscape bookmarks, **185**
Extensions text box, **104–105**
External Viewer Application (Preferences dialog box), 48
External Viewers Configuration dialog box (Air Mosaic), **104**, **263**, *263*, **264**, 280, *281*
extraction process, 41
   for NCSA Mosaic, 43
   for Win32s, 42

F

"Failed DNS Lookup" error message, 101
FAQ (Frequently Asked Questions), **107**
file extensions, and Web browser file handling, 180
File menu, **108**
   Exit, **101**
   Open Local File, 199
   Open URL, 200, 280
   Print, **206**
   Print Preview, 208
   Save As, 229
File menu (Air Mosaic)
   Document Source, 96
   Hotlists, 52, 74, *75*, 79, 83, 86, 87, 88, 142–143, 185, *186*
      Export, 102
   Open Local File, 173
   Open URL, 30, 221
   Print Margins, **207**
File menu (File Manager), Create Directory, 38
File menu (NCSA Hotlist Manager), Import, 148

File menu (NCSA Mosaic)
　Document Source, 96
　Exit, 33
　Open Local File, 173
　Open URL, 30, 54, 74, 143
　　Quicklist, 55
　Print Setup, 209
　Save As Text, 230
　Send E-mail, 99
　Send Mail, **234–236**
　Subscribed Newsgroups page, 222
File menu (Netscape)
　Document Info, 94
　Mail Document, 100, 175
　Open File, 173, **198**
　Open Location, 30, **199**
File menu (Program Manager), Run, 36
File menu (Quarterdeck Mosaic)
　Close, 76
　Open, 30, 197, *198*
　Open URL, 173, 217
　Print Setup, 209
　Properties, 210
　Reload, 226
File menu (Spyglass Mosaic)
　Close, 76
　Close All, 76
　Open Local, 173
　Open URL, 30, 224
　Page Setup, 201
File Properties dialog box (Quarterdeck Mosaic), *210*
filenames, of documents, 172
files. *See also* documents
　local, **172–173**
Find command, **108–110**
Finger command, **110–111**
firewall, **112**
　proxy server for, 212

software for file exchange, 250
First Virtual Holding company's Internet Payment System, 233
fixed fonts, changes in Netscape, 73
floating toolbar, in Quarterdeck Mosaic, 265, 266
folders in Quarterdeck Mosaic, 73, **112–115**
　adding document to, **113**
　adding from History to, **114**
　adding URL to, **113–114**
　appearance in Hotlist, 63
　creating, **114**
　deleting, **114–115**
　renaming, **115**
Followed Links Expire option, in Netscape, **115**
Font dialog box (NCSA Mosaic), 75
font schemes, in Quarterdeck Mosaic, **118–119**
Font Styles, in Quarterdeck Mosaic, **116**
fonts, **117–118**, 254
　changes in Netscape, 73
　in NCSA Mosaic, **74–76**
footers, for printing in Spyglass Mosaic, 201
forms, **119–120**, *120*
Forward button, 20
Forward command, 67, **121**
Fox Broadcasting Web site, 288
framed anchors, 56
Frequently Asked Questions (FAQ), **107**
ftp:://web/mosaic/windows/viewers, 192, 217
ftp://, accelerator key for, 48
FTP, **122**
　to download viewers, 280
FTP Connect dialog box, 39
FTP icon (Chameleon group window), 38
FTP Interface page (NCSA Mosaic), *123*
FTP server, displaying messages in Netscape, **245**

FTP sites, in NCSA Mosaic menu, **122–124**
FTP window, to select files for downloading, *40*, 40

G

Games Domain Web site, 288
gateway, **125**
GIF image files, **127**, 159
    interlaced display in Quarterdeck Mosaic, **160**
    viewers for, 279
    viewing, 134
global history, in Quarterdeck Mosaic, **127–128**
global Usenet newsgroups, 162
gnu newsgroups, 162
Go menu (Netscape), 129, 137
    Back, 68
    Forward, 121
    Home, 138
    Stop Loading, **253**
    View History, 27, 137, **278**
Go To Newsgroups command (Netscape), 129
Go To tool (Quarterdeck Mosaic), **129**
Go To URL dialog box (Quarterdeck Mosaic), *129*
GolfData Web, 288
gopher://, accelerator key for, 48
gopher://gopher.micro.umn.edu:70/11/Other%20Gopher%20and%20Information%20Servers, 132
gopher://Veronica.scs.unr.edu:70/11/veronica, 275
gopher://wx.atmos.uuic.edu:70/1, 131
Gopher, **130**
Gopher Menu, 275–276, *276*
    as starting point for Veronica search, *276*

gopher servers
    list in NCSA Mosaic, **130–131**
    searching with Veronica, **275–278**
GopherSpace Overview, in NCSA Mosaic, **131–132**
Graphic Interchange Format, 127
graphics. *See also* GIF image files; inline images
    JPEG images, 134, 155, **165**, 279
    turning off automatic display, 27, 63–64, **91**
    XBM images, 159, **291**
gray border, for Quarterdeck Mosaic documents, 242
gray color bar, for secure document, 97, 233
Group View, for newsgroup messages, 241
group window, *17*
    for Chameleon Sampler, 16, *36*, 36

H

hand icon, cursor as, 17, 72
hard disk
    local files on, **172–173**
    opening file saved on, 199
hard disk space
    for document caching, 71, 92
    for Mosaic install, 14
hardware, for Internet connection, **13–14**
hatched anchors, 56
headers, for printing in Spyglass Mosaic, 201
health, 161
Help menu, **133**
    About command, 47
Help menu (Air Mosaic)
    Contents, 21
    Send Mail to Spry, 100
Help menu (NCSA Mosaic)
    Bug List, **69**

FAQ page, 107
Feature Page, 107
Mail Technical Support, 99, **178**, *179*
Online Documentation, 22, 133, 189, 197
Help menu (Netscape)
    Frequently Asked Questions, **107**
    Handbook, 21, **133**
Help menu (Quarterdeck Mosaic), 21
Help menu (Spyglass Mosaic)
    Help Page, 21
    Mosaic Help Page, 133, 189
help online, **20–22**
Helpers command (Spyglass Mosaic), **134–135**, *134*
hepnet newsgroups, 162
highlighted text, in Mosaic window, 17
history, 5, **135–138**
    local, 127, **173**
    from Quarterdeck Mosaic, 8, **127–128**
history window, **26–27**, *26*
    adding document to Hotlist from, **51**
    adding to Quarterdeck folder from, **114**
    in Air Mosaic, 27, **135–136**, *136*
    finding by Mosaic version, 27
    in Netscape, *137*, 137
    in Spyglass Mosaic, **136–137**, *136*
Home command, 121, **137**
    loading for Quarterdeck Mosaic startup, **170**
home pages, 2, 3–4, **138–141**
    after launching Mosaic, 16
    for Air Mosaic, **140**
    autoloading in NCSA Mosaic, **64**
    autoloading in Netscape, 250
    canceling automatic display, 139–140
    CERN, 72
    changing, 140
    for CommerceNet, 33, *34*

displaying from different sites, 23
    for NCSA Mosaic, **16–19**, **140**
    in NCSA Mosaic, 64, 126
    in Netscape for, 19, 254, *255*
    redisplaying, **137–138**
    for Spyglass Mosaic, **140–141**
    for Web browsers, 19
Honolulu Community College, Home Page, 24, *25*
host, sorting by, in Archie searches, 60–61
Host text box, 38
.HOT extension, 146
Hotlist dialog box (Spyglass Mosaic), *188*
Hotlist Manager (NCSA Mosaic), **145–149**, *145*
    to delete items from Quicklist, 89
    to modify hotlists, **187**
Hotlists, **142–144**. *See also* bookmarks in Netscape Navigator
    adding document to, **49–51**, **231–232**
    changing, **73–74**
    creating, **79**
    deleting, **85–86**
    deleting document from Spyglass Mosaic list, 188
    deleting items from, **87–88**
    exporting, **102–103**
    importing NCSA menu to Air Mosaic as, **156–157**
    modifying, **185–188**
    modifying in Spyglass Mosaic, **187–188**
    from Quarterdeck Mosaic, 8
Hotlists dialog box (Air Mosaic), 52, *53*, *80*, 83, *186*
    to delete menu, 87
Hotlists menu (Quarterdeck Mosaic)
    Save To Current, 231–232
    Set As Current, **242**

Hotlists in NCSA Mosaic
    adding item in, **146–147**
    adding item to current, **147**
    creating, 146
    deleting, 146
    importing, **148**
    modifying, **187**
    multiple, 147
    placing on menu bar, **148**
    removing items from, **147–148**
HTML commands, **148–149**
HTML documents, **149**
    creating hotlist from links in, 148
    exporting bookmarks to, **185**
    from exporting hotlists, 102
    Font Scheme for, 118–119
    forms as, 119
    importing as bookmarks, **184**
    sending attachment as, 176
    to share home page, 139
    viewing, 134
HTML tags, 94, **149–150**
    customizing fonts in Air Mosaic for, **117**
    and font attributes in Quarterdeck Mosaic, **116**
    fonts associated with, 74
    saving text without, 230
    style sheets as collections of, 253
HTTP 1.0, 233
"HTTP: File/Directory Does Not Exist" error message, 101
http://, accelerator key for, 48
http://cs.indiana.edu/finger/gateway, 111
http://home.netscape.com/home/faq.html, 107
http://hoohoo.ncsa.uiuc.edu:80/ftp-interface.html, 123
http://info.cern.ch/hypertext/Products/WAIS/Overview.html, 285

http://iridium.nttc.edu/gov_res.html, 30
http://wings.buffalo.edu/world, 32
http://www11.w3.org/hypertext/DataSources/WWW/Servers.html, 33
http://www.fie.com/www/us_gov.htm, 30
http://www.ncsa.uiuc.edu/demowed.demo.htl, 90
http://www.ncsa.uiuc.edu/mosaic/archie.htl, 61
http://www.ncsa.uiuc.edu/SDG/Software/WinMosaic/FAQ.html, 107
http://www.ncsa.uiuc.edu/SDG/Software/WinMosaic/Features.html, 108
HTTP (HyperText Transport Protocol), **151**
HTTP/0.9 message, **151**
hypermedia, **151**
hypertext, **151**
hypertext links, 17, **152**
    to add document to folder, 114
    to add document to Hotlist, 50–51
    adding to bookmarks master list, 184
    appearance in Quarterdeck Mosaic, **152**
    color after selected in Spyglass Mosaic, **283–284**
    color for, **167–168**
    color in Netscape, 76–77, 115
    controlling display, 169
    displaying URL in Quarterdeck Mosaic for, **245**
    to move between documents, 191
    Netscape display options for, 254, *255*
    retrieving document from, 91
    underlined, **269**
Hypertext Markup Language, 148–149
HyperText Transport Protocol (HTTP), **151**

I

icons
    for NCSA Mosaic, 43
    viewing graphics displayed as, 63–64
ieee newsgroups, 162
Image View, 279
images, **153**
impact on other users, in Archie searches, 61
Import File, as NCSA Mail window option, 236
Import NCSA Menu as Hotlist (Air Mosaic), **156–157**, *157*
importing
    Hotlists to NCSA Mosaic, **148**
    HTML files as bookmarks, **184**
Include File, in Annotation window (NCSA), 57
Include Text, as NCSA Mail window option, 236
Include URL, as NCSA Mail window option, 236
indented lines, spacing in Quarterdeck Mosaic, 158
index, in NCSA Mosaic, 21
Inet/DDN newsgroups, 162
Info newsgroups, 162
inline images, **159**, *159*
    displaying, **91**, *154*
    loading in Spyglass Mosaic, **171–172**
    in Netscape, 153, 155–156, **170–171**
    setting preference in NCSA Mosaic, 126
Insert New dialog box (Air Mosaic), 185
installing
    Chameleon Sampler, 36
    NCSA Mosaic, **41–44**
    Win32s software, **42**
interlaced GIF file display, in Quarterdeck Mosaic, **160**

Internet
    browsing, **22–33**
    connecting to, **13–15**
    establishing account, **37**
    newsgroups, **160–161**
    what it is, **2**
Internet address, 99, **160**
Internet in a Box, 9
Internet Business Center, 288
Internet quotation style, 175
Internet Relay Chat (IRC), **161**
Internet Shopping Network, 288
Interrupt Current Operation button (Spyglass Mosaic), **253**
IP address, 160

J

Joint Photographic Experts Group, **165**
JPEG image files, 155, **165**
    viewer for, 279
    viewing, 134

K

k12 newsgroups, 163
Kiosk Mode, in Air Mosaic, **165–166**, *166*
Koblas Currency Converter, 288

L

Launch Application (Preferences dialog box), 48
launching Mosaic, 16
Library of Congress, 288
Link Tree, in Quarterdeck Mosaic Archives, **169–170**, *169*
links, 5, **167**. *See also* anchors; hypertext links

Load Automatically at Startup (Air Mosaic), 65
Load Home Page (Quarterdeck Mosaic), 65
Load Images Automatically (Spyglass Mosaic), 64, **171**
local files, **172–173**
Local History, in Quarterdeck Mosaic, 127, **173**
Location box, in Netscape application window, **173**
log in, as anonymous user for FTP, 59

M

Machine/Domain list, for NCSA Proxy tab preferences, 214
Macintosh, Mosaic for, 13
magnification, of print preview, 209
mail:, accelerator key for, 48
Mail Document command, e-mail address and name for, 291
Mail and News. *See also* Preferences dialog box (Netscape), Mail and News
Mail and News application, 8
Mail Technical Support (NCSA Help menu), 99
Mail window (NCSA Mosaic), options, 236
Mailbox window (Quarterdeck Message Center), *220*
mailing documents, in Netscape, **175–176**
margins for printing
   in Air Mosaic, **207**, *207*
   in Spyglass Mosaic, 201
menu bar, of Mosaic window, 17–18, *18*
menu bar (Air Mosaic), removing menu from, **87**
Menu bar (Chameleon Sampler), Connect, 38
Menu bar (NCSA Mosaic)
   Options, 84
   placing hotlists on, **148**
Menu Editor (NCSA Mosaic), 52, 74, 81, **179**

menus
   adding to in Air Mosaic, **52–54**
   adding to in NCSA Mosaic, **52**
   creating in Air Mosaic, **81–82**
   creating in NCSA Mosaic, **81**
   deleting, **86–87**
   deleting items from, **88–89**
   modifying, **189**, 273
   pop-up, **203**
Message window (Quarterdeck Message Center), 219, *220*
Microsoft Windows, 13, 14
Microsoft Word for Windows 6.0, WebAuthor and, 150
MIME (Multipurpose Internet Mail Extensions), **180**
misc newsgroups, 162
modem connection, SLIP or PPP account for, 15
MOS20BX.EXE file, 40
MOS20X.EXE file, 40
Mosaic. *See also* Air Mosaic; NCSA Mosaic; Netscape Navigator; Quarterdeck Mosaic; Spyglass Mosaic
   browsing with, 26
   changing options, **27–28**
   determining version, 47
   exiting, **33**, **35**
   forms of, **3–4**
   group windows for versions, *17*
   guided tour of, **16**
   limitations of, 3
   uses for, **3**
   what it is, **3**
   window components, 17–19
Mosaic Access to the Internet (Tauber and Kienan), 15
Mosaic in a Box, 6, 9, 10
   group window, *17*

Mosaic Help Page, in Spyglass Mosaic, **189**
MOSAIC.INI file, 57, 80, 81
    copying URLs from, 102
    editing annotations items in, **59**
    for NCSA Mosaic, **190–191**
Mosaic window, **190**
    customizing, **83–84**
.mov extension, 217
    viewer for, 279
movies, **191**
moving between documents, 20
MPEG format, **191–192**, 217
    viewer for, 279
MPEG Player, 279
MPEGPLAY viewer, 192
MS-DOS Prompt icon, 42
multimedia applications, associating file types with, 104–105
multimedia files, **192**
multimedia viewers, selecting, 85, 134
multiple folders, from Quarterdeck Mosaic, 8
Multipurpose Internet Mail Extensions (MIME), **180**

N

National Center for Supercomputing Applications (NCSA), 3, **193**
    e-mail for Tech support, 178
National Hockey League, 288
National Library of Medicine, 288
National Weather Service forecast page, 131
Navigate menu, **193**
Navigate menu (Air Mosaic)
    Add Document to Hotlist, 50
    Back, 67
    Cancel Current Task, 71, 253
    Forward, 121
    History, 27, 135–136
    Home, **138**
    Reload, 226
Navigate menu (NCSA Mosaic)
    Add Current to Hotlist, 50, 54
    Back, 67
    Forward, 121
    History, 26, 135–136
    Home, **138**
    Hotlist Manager, 143
    Menu Editor, 52, 74, 82
    Reload, 226
Navigate menu (Quarterdeck Mosaic)
    Go Back, 68
    Go Forward, 121
    Go To, 129, 198
    Home, **138**
    Stop Current Read, **253**
Navigate menu (Spyglass Mosaic)
    Add Current to Hotlist, 50
    Back, 67
    Forward, 121
    History, 27
    Home, **138**
    Hotlists, 103, 144
    Load Missing Images, **171–172**
    Reload, 226
navigating the Web, **193**
NCSA (National Center for Supercomputing Applications), 3, **193**
    e-mail for Tech support, 178
NCSA Documentation by Platform section, 21
NCSA icon, spinning, 24
NCSA Mosaic, 4, **5–6**
    About command, 47
    accelerator keys, **47–48**
    anchors in, **56**
    associating viewers, **282**

bug list for, **69**
as compressed file, 37
demo document in, **90**
development, 3
distribution of, 15
document caching in, **92**
downloading, 35–41
downloading with Windows FTP, **37–41**
editing annotation, **58**
electronic mail in, **99**
e-mail address for, **100–101**
FAQ page, **107**
feature comparison, 7
feature page, **107–108**
finding text in, 108
fonts in, **73**, **74–76**, **118**
FTP sites in menu, **122–124**
GopherSpace Overview, **131–132**
installing and configuring, **41–44**
internal support for sound cards, **273**
MOSAIC.INI file for, **190–191**
NNTP server for, **195**
Open URL button, 200
opening local files, **199**
Print button, 206
program icon for, 210
proxy servers in, **213–214**
reading news, **221–222**
Save As button, 229
saving document as file, **172**
Send E-mail, 236
SMTP server in, **249**
stopping document retrieval, 253
subscribing to newsgroups in, **256**
underlining links in, 269
User's Guide, 20, **21–22**
viewing annotation, **58**
NCSA Mosaic Demo Document link, 20

NCSA Mosaic home page, **16–19**, *18*, **140**, *141*
Starting Points, 21, 23–24, *25*, 144, **251–252**, *252*
adding item to, **54**
Archie Request Form, **60–61**, *61*
Finger Gateway, **111–112**
Gopher Servers, **130–131**
Gopher Servers, Veronica Search, 275
Home Pages, 24
NCSA Demo Document, 90
Other Documents, FTP Sites, 123–124
What's New ..., 22, *23*
World Wide Web Info, Information by Subject, 29
NCSA Mosaic hotlists, **143–144**
adding document to, 50
adding to Quicklist, **55**
deleting, **86**
deleting items from, **88**
Hotlist Manager, 51, 74
multiple, 50, 73–74
NCSA Mosaic menus
adding cascading menu, **82**
adding to, **52**
Annotate menu, **57**
creating, **81**
deleting, **86–87**
Menu Editor, 52, 74, 81, **179**
modifying, **189**, 273
pop-up, 203
NCSA Mosaic screen display
application window starting size and position, **158**
cursor changes over anchors, 72
customizing window, **84**
displaying inline graphics, **91**
Document Source window, *95*
group window, *17*

history window, **26–27**, *26*
icon for, 43
presentation mode, **205–206**, *206*
Print Preview window, *208*
table appearance in, **261**
toolbar in, *266*
URL bar, *270*, 270
NetLauncher (CompuServe), *See* Air Mosaic
NetManage, v
Netscape Handbook, **133**
NETSCAPE.INI file, 205
Netscape Navigator, 4, **11–12**, *12*
   About command, 47
   accessing What's New, 24
   Bookmark File text box, 68
   bookmarks, **48–49**. *See also* bookmarks in Netscape Navigator
   demo document, **90**
   displaying messages from FTP server, **245**
   document caching in, **92**, **94**
   document retrieval in, **198–199**
   electronic mail in, **100**
   extensions in, **105**
   FAQ (frequently asked questions) page, **107**
   feature comparison, 7
   finding text in, **109**
   Font button, 76
   fonts in, **73**
   Go To button, 129
   Go To Newsgroups command, 129
   home page, 19, 254, *255*
   images in, **153**
   Mail Document, 236
   MIME type list box, **180–181**
   NNTP server for, **195**
   online documentation, 21
   Print button, 206
   reading news, 222–224
   security alerts in, 233
   security in, 6, 11, **232–233**
   signature file for, **248–249**
   SMTP server for, 249
   Start With: Home Page, 65
   subscribing to newsgroups in, **256–257**
   supporting applications in, **259–260**
   temporary directory in, **262**
Netscape Navigator menus, pop-up, 203
Netscape Navigator screen display
   customizing window, 84
   Directory buttons in, **243–244**, *244*
   group window, *17*
   history window, 27, *137*, 137
   Location bar, 32, **173**, *244*
   program icon for, 210
   toolbar, *244*, *264*
   turning off graphics, 28
   turning off toolbar, 29
   underlining links in, 269
   URL bar, 30, 270, *271*
Network News Transfer Protocol-supported server, **195–196**
networked computer, connecting to Internet through, 14
networks
   access to annotations on, 59
   firewalls for security, 112
   gateway to connect, 125
New Message window (Quarterdeck Message Center), 238, *239*
   available function, 240
news:, accelerator key for, 48
news.announce.newusers newsgroups, 161
news newsgroups, 162
News RC File (Netscape), **194**
News Subscriptions dialog box, 256
newsgroups, **160–161**
   access with Air Mosaic Open URL command, 221

controlling sort for messages, 241
descriptions of, 104
displaying list of available, 221, 225
global, 162
list of subscribed, 194
in Netscape, 12
reading news, **221–225**
subscribing to, 194, **255–259**
Newsgroups dialog box (Quarterdeck Message Center), *258*, 258–259
NEWT icon, 16, 38
NNTP server, **195–196**
 as NCSA Mosaic preference setting, 241
not, in Veronica search string, 277
Number Lock key, 19
numbered lists, appearance in Quarterdeck Mosaic, 196

O

online documentation, 21
 Mosaic Help Page in Spyglass Mosaic, **189**
 for NCSA Mosaic, **197**
 in Netscape, 133
 for Spyglass Mosaic, 10
online forms, **119–120**, *120*
online group discussion, 161
Open command, 129
open technology, 233
Open URL dialog box, *30*, 74, 123, 197, *198*
Options menu (Air Mosaic), 200
 Autoload Inline Images, 28, 64
 Configuration, **77–78**, *78*. *See also* Configuration dialog box (Air Mosaic)
 Extended News Listing, **104**
 HTTP/0.9 command, 151
 Import NCSA Menu as Hotlist, **156–157**
 Kiosk mode, 165–166
 Load to Disk Mode, 172, 230
 Toolbar Style, **267**
Options menu (Hotlist Manager), On Menu Bar, 148
Options menu (NCSA Mosaic), 200. *See also* Preferences dialog box (NCSA Mosaic)
 Change Cursor over Anchors, 72
 Choose Font, 74–75
 Load to Disk, 172, 230
 Show Current URL, 28, 243
 Show Status Bar, 28, 246
 Show Toolbar, 28, 247
Options menu (Netscape), 200, **231**, 244. *See also* Preferences dialog box (Netscape)
 Autoload Images, 28, 64
 Show Directory buttons, 244
 Show FTP File Information, 245
 Show Toolbar, 29, 247
or, in Veronica search string, 277
O'Reilly and Associates books, Mosaic with, 6
Outbox folder, 238

P

Page Setup dialog box (Spyglass Mosaic), **201**, *202*
page turners, in Quarterdeck Mosaic, **245**, *246*
paragraph spacing, in Quarterdeck Mosaic, 201
password for Anonymous FTP, 59
 user name as, 273
Password text box, for FTP, 40
Paste command (Edit menu), **202**
pathname, in valid URL, 272
.pdf file extension, viewer for, 279
Personal Menus dialog box (NCSA Mosaic), 52, 74, 81, *82*, 82, 179, *180*
Pick of the Week, 23
placeholder, for graphics, 27
Point-to-Point Protocol (PPP), 15

pop-up menus, **203**
PPP account, closing connection, 101
preferences, **203–205**
Preferences dialog box (NCSA Mosaic), 78,
    203–204
  Anchors tab, 56
    Change Cursor over Anchors, 72
    Miscellaneous, Underlined, 269
    Show URL in Status Bar, 248
    Visually Age Visited Anchor, 284
  Apply Now button, 203
  Audio tab, **63**
  Cache tab, **71**
    Memory Cache, 92, 94
  Display Inline Images, 27, 91
  Fonts tab, 76
  General tab, 125, 126, 267
    Autoload Home Page, 64, 139
    Home Page, 140, *141*
    Use Internal 8-bit Sound, 273
  Initial Window Placement, 158
  Proxy tab, *213*
  Services tab, **239**, 240–241
    E-mail Address, 100–101, 235, 240
    News, 194
    NNTP Server text box, 195
    SMTP server name, 249
    Subscriptions button, 256, **259**
    Use Extended FTP, **272–723**
  Viewers tab, *282*, 282
Preferences dialog box (Netscape), 78, **204–205**
  Actions options, 48, *49*
  Applications and Directories, **59–60**, **259–260**
    Bookmark File, 68
    Directory & File Locations, **90**
    Temporary Directory, 262
  Browse button, **69**

Cache and Network, 92, *93*
Color, **76–77**
Fonts and Colors, 73
  Followed Links, 284
Helper Application, 279
  Use Browser as Viewer, **272**
Helper Applications, **134**, **180–181**
  Extensions, 105
Home Page Location, 140
Images and Security, *155*, 155–156
  Security Alerts, 242
Mail and News, 175, 194
  Mail Server, 178
  Mail (SMTP) Server, 249
  News (NNTP) Server, 195
  Signature File, 248
  Your Email, 291
  Your Name, 291
Proxies, 211, *212*
  Security Proxy, 233
Styles, 115, **254**, *255*
  Home Page Location, 142
  Link Style, 169
  Links: Underlined, 269–270
  Start With, 140, 250, *251*
  Window Styles, 247, **287**
Preferences dialog box (Quarterdeck Mosaic), 68, 78, **204**
  Actions options, 48, *49*
  Browse button, **69**
  Browser tab, 68, 69, *243*
    Show Annotations, 242
    Show Browser Margins, 242
    Show Page Turners, 245–246
    Show URL Field, **247**
    Show URL Helper, **248**
    Wipe Interval, **287**
  Data Engine tab, **85**, 105, *283*, 283
  Fonts tab, 116, 118–119

General tab, 125
   Home Page text box, 141
   Initial, 140
   Toolbar Icon Settings, 266–267
GIF Viewer tab, **127**, 160
Global History tab, 127
HTML Viewer tab, 70, **150–151**
   Anchor Visited Color, 284
   Change Cursor Over Anchors, **72**
   Display Inline Images, 28, 91
   Hypertext Link Style, 152
   Hypertext Links list, Underline, 269
   Indent Width, **158**
   Numbered Lists Style, 196
   Paragraph Spacing, 201
   Show Link URLs, 245
   Wait for Images, **285–286**
Load Home Page, **170**
Network tab, **194**
   Cache Enabled check box, 94
Preferences dialog box (Spyglass Mosaic), 78, **204**, *205*, *254*
   Home Page, 140, 141
   HTTP Proxy Server, 214
   Link Color, **168**
   Load Images Automatically, 28, **171**
   Show Toolbar, 29, 247
   Style Sheet, 253
   Underline Links, 269
   Visited Link Color, 284
Presentation mode, 84, **205–206**, *206*
previous document
   cache for, 92
   returning to, 20, **67–68**
Print dialog box, *207*
Print Margins, in Air Mosaic, **207**
print preview, **208–209**
printer, changing selected, **209**

printing, page setup in Spyglass Mosaic for, 201
priority, for Archie searches, 61
product logo, disabling movement, 56–57
program icons, **209–210**
Program Manager (Windows), Run dialog box, *44*
Properties command (Quarterdeck Mosaic), **210–211**
proportional fonts, changes in Netscape, 73
protocol, in valid URL, 272
PROVIDER.TXT file, on Chameleon Sampler, 13, 37
proxies, **212–214**
proxy servers
   in Air Mosaic, **215**
   in NCSA Mosaic, **213–214**
   in Netscape, **211**
   in Quarterdeck Mosaic, 194, **214**
   in Spyglass Mosaic, **214**

Q

QMOSAIC.INI file, 204
.qt extension, 217
Quarterdeck Enternet, 8
Quarterdeck Home Page, 19
   Internet Navigation System, NCSA What's New Page, 24
Quarterdeck Message Center, 161, **177**, *177*, 219, **224**, 237
   Compose button, 238
   Mailbox window, *220*
   subscribing to newsgroups in, **258**
Quarterdeck Mosaic, 4, **8**, *8*. *See also* folders in Quarterdeck Mosaic
   About command, 47
   Archives, **62**, *62*, 112, *113*
      Link Tree, **169–170**, *169*

associating viewers, **283**
bullet style, **70**
context-sensitive help, 20
demo document, **90**
document caching, **94**
electronic mail in, 99, **100**
extensions in, **104–105**
feature comparison, 7
finding text in, 108
Font button, 76
Font Scheme in, **118–119**
Font styles in, **116**
fonts in, 73, **118**
Go To tool, **129**
hypertext link style, **152**
interlaced GIF file display, **160**
Load Home Page, 65
NNTP server for, **195**
online documentation, 21
pop-up menus in, 203
Print button, 206
Properties command, **210–211**
proxy servers in, **214**
reading news, **224**
receiving e-mail, **219**, **221**
Save button, 229
to send e-mail, **237–239**
SMTP server in, **250**
tiling windows in, 263
Trash button, **268**
URL Helper, 48, **270–272**, *271*
URL text box in, 30
User Name in, **273**
Quarterdeck Mosaic annotations, **58**
   deleting, 59
   displaying, **242**
   editing, **58**
   viewing, **58**

Quarterdeck Mosaic hotlists
   adding document to, 50, *51*
   adding from history to, 51
   adding URL to, 50–51
Quarterdeck Mosaic screen display
   background color changes, 68
   cascading windows in, 72
   customizing window, 84
   group window, *17*
   history window, 27, 127
   moving toolbar, **265–266**
   numbered lists' appearance in, **196**
   page turners in, **245**, *246*
   program icon, 210
   status bar display, **252**
   toolbar for, *264*
   toolbar icon settings in, **266–267**
   turning off graphics, 28
   turning off toolbar, 29
   underlining links in, 269
   URL bar, 32, *270*, 270
Quarterdeck Viewer (Preferences dialog
   box), 48
Quarterdeck WebAuthor, **150**
Quicklist (NCSA Mosaic), **217**
   adding to, 55
   deleting items from, **89**
Quicktime movies, **217–218**
QuickTime viewer, 279
Quotecom Financial Data, 288

R

RAM, for documents in memory, 71
reading news, **221–225**
Readme file, for Chameleon Sampler, 36
rec.arts.sf.reviews newsgroup, 161
rec newsgroups, 162

recessed tables, in NCSA Mosaic, 261
relcom newsgroups, 163
Reload command, **226–227**
Rlogin, launching from Air Mosaic, 264

S

Save As command, **229–230**
Save As dialog box, 229, *230*
Save button, **229**
saving documents, 5, 172
sci newsgroups, 162
science fiction, review of, 161
Scroll Lock key, 19
Searchable Gopher Index page, *277*
searches, **232**
    with Archie, **60**
    with Veronica, **275–278**
secure documents, doorkey icon for, 97
security, **232–233**. *See also* firewall
    on Netscape, 6, 11, 242
security alerts, in Netscape, 233
selecting text for clipboard, **234**
self-extracting ZIP file, 37
Send Mail command, in NCSA Mosaic, **234–236**
Send Mail to Spry (Air Mosaic Help menu), 100
Send Mail/Post News dialog box, 175, *176*
Serial Line Internet Protocol (SLIP), 15
server
    directly logging into, **261–262**
    in valid URL, 272
service providers, 13
    establishing account with, 37
    list on Chameleon Sampler, 35
session, history for, 5, **135–138**
Set As Current, in Quarterdeck Mosaic, **242**

SETUP.EXE file, for Chameleon Sampler, 36
Setup program, for NCSA Mosaic, 41
shopping online, 6
    on Netscape, 12
Show Document URL (Air Mosaic Configuration dialog box), **244–245**
Show a Popup Alert Before option (Netscape), 233, **242**
Sig file, in NCSA Mosaic, 236, 241
signature file, in Netscape, **248–249**
Simple Mail Transport Protocol (SMTP) server, 178, **249–250**
SLIP account, closing connection, 101
SLIP/PPP software, 6, 14, **15**
    closing connection, 35
Small Business Administration, 288
SMOSAIC.INI file, 204
SMTP (Simple Mail Transport Protocol) server, 178, **249–250**
    in NCSA Mosaic Preferences, 241
soc newsgroups, 162
"SOCKET: Connection has been refused" error message, 101
SOCKS software, **250**
software. *See also* viewers
    from Sybex, 15
    Web browser requirements for, 14
sound cards, **273**
spacing in Quarterdeck Mosaic
    for indent lines, 158
    for paragraphs, 201
speed
    and animated logo, 56–57
    graphics display and, 27
    and NCSA Mosaic bullets, 126
Sports Server, 288
Spry, *See* Air Mosaic

Spry home page
  Spry City, *90*, 90
    Other Lists of Web sites, What's New to Visit?, 24
Spry Hotlist, 55
SPRY menu, adding item to, **55**
Spyglass Mosaic, **10–11**
  About command, 47
  accessing What's New, 24
  adding to menus, **51–55**
  demo document, **90**
  feature comparison, 7
  finding text in, **110**
  Go To button, 129
  home page, 19, **140–141**
  Interrupt Current Operation button, **253**
  Mosaic Help Page, **189**
  online documentation, 21
  Open button, 200
  opening local files, **199**
  page setup for printing, **201**
  Print button, 206
  proxy servers in, 214
  reading news, **224–225**
  Save button, 229
  security in, **233**
  style sheets in, 73, **253–254**, *254*
Spyglass Mosaic hotlist, **144**, *144*
  adding document to, 50
  exporting, **103**
  modifying, **187–188**
Spyglass Mosaic screen display
  automatic graphic display, **171**
  cascading windows in, 72
  color for links, **168**
  customizing window, 84
  history window, 27, **136–137**, *136*
  Load Images Automatically, 64
  program icon, 210
  tiling windows in, 263
  toolbar in, *266*
  turning off graphics, 28
  turning off toolbar, 29
  underlining links in, 269
  URL bar, 32, 270, *271*
  URL text box in, 30
Spyglass page, Welcome to Enhanced NCSA, Starting Points, Directories and Indexes, What's New, 24
Star Trek Generations, 288
Start With: Home Page (Netscape), 65
starting Mosaic, connecting to Internet before, 16
Starting Points (NCSA Mosiac), 20. *See also* NCSA Mosaic home page, Starting Points
status bar
  displaying in Quarterdeck Mosaic, **252**
  displaying URL on, 56
  on Mosaic window, *18*, 19
  toggling display, **246**
  URL in, **248**
Stop command, 253
Stop Current Read (Quarterdeck Navigate menu), 253
style sheets, in Spyglass Mosaic, **253–254**, *254*
subdirectories, *See* directories
Subscribed Newsgroups page (Netscape), 256, *257*
subscribing to newsgroups, **255–259**
  preference settings before, 194
supporting applications, in Netscape, **259–260**
Surfing the Internet with Netscape (Tauber and Kienan), 15
Sybex, software from, 15

T

tables, appearance in NCSA Mosaic, **261**
talk newsgroups, 162
TCP/IP protocol stack, 14
   NEWT icon and, 38
technical phone support, 5–6
Telnet, **261–262**
   launching from Air Mosaic, 264
   selecting in Netscape, 260
   setting NCSA Mosaic preference, 241
TEMP directory
   creating for downloaded files, 38
   deleting files in, 44
temporary directory, in Netscape, **262**
text
   color in Netscape, 76–77
   highlighted or underlined in Mosaic window, 17
   selecting all in document, 233–234
text files, viewing, 134
text string, searching document for, **232**
Thread View, for newsgroup messages, 241
tiling windows, **263**
title bar
   document title in, **96**
   of Mosaic window, 17, *18*
titles, for annotations, 57, 59
TN3270 application
   launching from Air Mosaic, 264
   selecting in Netscape, 260
toolbar, **264–265**
   in Air Mosaic, *265*
   displaying, **246**
   icon settings in Quarterdeck Mosaic, **266–267**
   moving in Quarterdeck Mosaic, **265–266**
   in Netscape, 254, *255*, *264*
   in Quarterdeck Mosaic, *264*
   in Spyglass Mosaic, *266*
   turning off, 29
toolbar (NCSA Mosaic), *18*, 18, *266*
   Home Page button, 20
   setting preference, 126, **267**
   turning display on and off, 28
Tools menu (Quarterdeck Mosaic). *See also* Preference dialog box (Quarterdeck Mosaic)
   Configure Network, 214, 273
      NNTP Server text box, 195
      SMTP Server, 250
   Mail/News, 100, 161, **177**, *178*, 219, 224, 237, 258
tour, of Mosaic capabilities, 90
Trash button, in Quarterdeck Mosaic, **268**
Tree View, for newsgroup messages, 241
.TXT extension, 230

U

u3b newsgroups, 163
underlined anchors, in NCSA Mosaic, 56
underlined hypertext links, **269**
underlined text, in Mosaic window, 17
Undo command (Netscape Edit menu), **270**
Uniform Resource Locator, 18
U.S. federal government, information about, 30
U.S. Government Information Sources, 30, *31*, 289
UNIX, 3
Unknown: Prompt User (Preferences dialog box), 48
unzipping files, 41
Up button, to reorder bookmarks, 183
URL bar
   in Mosaic window, *18*, 18, 32
   in Web browsers, **270**

URL box (Spyglass Mosaic), 174
URL Helper button (Quarterdeck Mosaic), **248**, **270–272**, *271*
URLs (Uniform Resource Locators), **272**
   accelerator keys for entering, 47–48
   to add menu items, 53
   adding to Quarterdeck folder, **113–114**
   adding to Quarterdeck Hotlist, 50–51
   for Archie Request Form, 61
   creating lists, **80–81**
   displaying in Quarterdeck Mosaic, 247
   displaying on status bar, 56, 248
   document retrieval with, 29, **30–33**, 173
   for FTP sites, 122
   for Gopher sites, 130
   history for current session, *136*
   in history window, 26
   for home page autoloading, 64
   lists, *See* Hotlists
   modifying for document in Hotlist, 188
   to move between documents, 191
   to open file in Netscape, 199
   organizing in Quarterdeck folder, 73, **112–115**
   for Quarterdeck Mosaic home page, 125
   for retrieved document, 24
   saving by Netscape, 48
   on status bar, 19
   for Web browser home pages, 138
Use Browser as Viewer option, in Netscape, 272
Use Extended FTP option, in NCSA Mosaic, **272–273**
Usenet newsgroups, **160–161**. *See also* newsgroups
User Name, in Quarterdeck Mosaic, **273**
User text box, for FTP, 40
users, finger to look for, 110

User's Guide, for NCSA Mosaic, 20, **21–22**
UUIC Weather Machine, 131

V

Veronica, 130, **275–278**
   introduction to, 276
   search string options, 277
version, determining for Mosaic, 47
Video Player, 279
videos, 191
   Quicktime movies, **217–218**
   viewers for, 134
View menu (Netscape)
   Load Images, 64, **170–171**
   Refresh, **225–226**
   Reload, 226
   Source, 96
View menu (Quarterdeck Mosaic)
   As Icon List, 63
   As Icons, 63
   As Text List, 63
   As Tree, 63
   Document source, 96
   Status bar, 252
   Toolbar, 29, 247
View Source
   selecting in Netscape, 260
   in Spyglass, 96, **278**
viewers, 153, **278–283**
   associating with application in Air Mosaic, **280**, *281*
   downloading, **280**, *281*
   locating shareware versions, 280
   for MPEG movies, 191–192
   unzipping after downloading, 279
Virtual Tourist, 289
   home page, 32, *33*

Visited Link Color (Spyglass Mosaic), **283–284**
vmsnet newsgroups, 163

W

W32OLE.EXE file, 37
WAIS (Wide Area Information Server), **285**
WAIS overview page, *286*
Wait for Images option, in Quarterdeck Mosaic, **285–286**
WAV files
    associating with NCSA Mosaic actions, **63**
    viewer for, 279
weather, 131
Web, *See* World Wide Web
Web browsers, xxvi, 2
    application window, **190**
    comparing, 6–8
    home pages for, 19
    software requirements for, 14
    URL bar in, **270**
    vs. Telnet, 262
Web document. *See also* documents
    as online documentation, 21
Web Wide World of Music, 289
WebAuthor (Quarterdeck), **150**
WebMuseum of Art, 289
Welcome to Netscape page, What's New, 24
WHAM, 279
What's New topic, **22–23**, *23*
    accessing, 24
When Loading Images, Redraw Every option, in Air Mosaic, **286–287**
Whitehouse, 288
Whole Internet Catalog, 289
Wide Area Information Server (WAIS), **285**

wildcards
    * for newsgroup searches, 225
    in Archie searches, 60
Win32s software, 5, 14, 37
    downloading, 41
    installing, **42**
Window menu (Quarterdeck Mosaic)
    Duplicate, **97**
    Global History, 127
    Local History, 27, 173
windows
    for Air Mosaic, *190*
    history list in Quarterdeck Mosaic for, 173, *174*
    starting size and position in NCSA Mosaic, 126, **158**
Windows FTP, to download NCSA Mosaic, **37–41**
Windows (Microsoft), 13, 14
    Browse File dialog box, 69
Windows NT, 37
WINDOWS\SYSTEM directory, 37
Wine Page, 289
Wipe Interval, in Quarterdeck Mosaic, **287**
World Fact book (CIA), *32*, 32
World of Jazz Improvisation, 289
World Wide Web, **2–3**
    interesting sites, 288–289
World Wide Web Virtual Library, 289
World Wide Yellow Pages, 33, *35*, 289
WWW. *See also* World Wide Web
WWW servers, alphabetic list by location, 33, *34*
WWW Servers of the U.S. Federal Government, 30, *31*, 289
WWW to Finger Gateway page, *111*, 111–112
WWW Virtual library, displaying, 29

X

X Windows, Mosaic for, 13
XBM images, 159, **291**

Y

Yahoo Page of What's on the Net, 289

Z

ZIP files, 37

Navigate the Internet

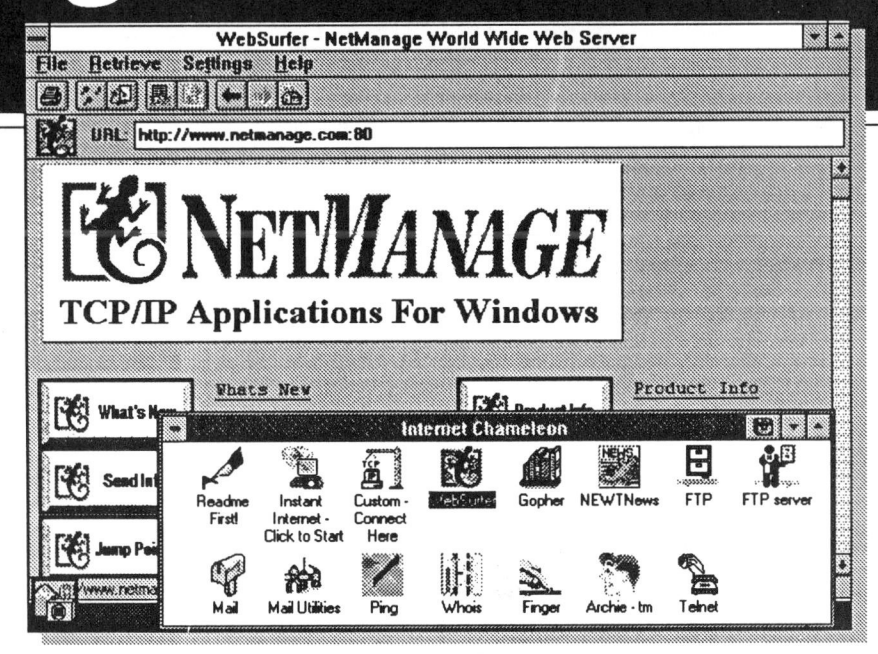

With Internet Chameleon™

Nothing makes cruising the Internet easier than Internet Chameleon. A Windows graphical user interface makes finding information resources easy.

- More Internet access tools than any other package
- Easy to use point-and-click interface
- Dial into the Internet
- Support for SLIP, CSLIP, PPP and ISDN Internet access up to 115.2 KBPS modem speed
- Instant Internet™ – signs you up for a new account in just minutes
- Easy 5 minute installation

Applications Included:

WebSurfer™ – World Wide Web browser, Electronic Mail (SMTP, POP) with MIME and Rules, Internet News Reader, Gopher Client, File Transfer: FTP and FTP Server, Archie, Telnet, and more.

Use Chameleon at Home and at the Office

For home or remote Internet Access you'll need **Internet Chameleon.** *For LAN TCP/IP access,* **Chameleon, Chameleon***NFS* **and ChameleonX** are the most widely used TCP/IP for Windows application suites in the world. Additional applications include: Dial-up and LAN (Ethernet, Token Ring, FDDI), 3270, 5250 & X-Window Emulation, NFS Client & Server, and much more.

SPECIAL UPGRADE OFFERS

Upgrade Your Chameleon Sampler Disk to Internet Chameleon for $99 *or* to full Chameleon for $125 – Call for "Book Upgrade."*

* Limit one per customer. A copy of this ad required for proof of purchase. Prices and terms subject to change without notice.

NETMANAGE™
(408) 973-7171
e-mail: sales@netmanage.com
World Wide Web: www.netmanage.com
10725 North De Anza Blvd., Cupertino, CA 95014 USA

MICROSOFT® WINDOWS™ COMPATIBLE

FOR EVERY COMPUTER QUESTION, THERE IS A SYBEX BOOK THAT HAS THE ANSWER

Each computer user learns in a different way. Some need thorough, methodical explanations, while others are too busy for details. At Sybex we bring nearly 20 years of experience to developing the book that's right for you. Whatever your needs, we can help you get the most from your software and hardware, at a pace that's comfortable for you.

We start beginners out right. You will learn by seeing and doing with our **Quick & Easy** series: friendly, colorful guidebooks with screen-by-screen illustrations. For hardware novices, the **Your First** series offers valuable purchasing advice and installation support.

Often recognized for excellence in national book reviews, our **Mastering** titles are designed for the intermediate to advanced user, without leaving the beginner behind. A **Mastering** book provides the most detailed reference available. Add our pocket-sized **Instant Reference** titles for a complete guidance system. Programmers will find that the new **Developer's Handbook** series provides a more advanced perspective on developing innovative and original code.

With the breathtaking advances common in computing today comes an ever increasing demand to remain technologically up-to-date. In many of our books, we provide the added value of software, on disks or CDs. Sybex remains your source for information on software development, operating systems, networking, and every kind of desktop application. We even have books for kids. Sybex can help smooth your travels on the **Internet** and provide **Strategies and Secrets** to your favorite computer games.

As you read this book, take note of its quality. Sybex publishes books written by experts—authors chosen for their extensive topical knowledge. In fact, many are professionals working in the computer software field. In addition, each manuscript is thoroughly reviewed by our technical, editorial, and production personnel for accuracy and ease-of-use before you ever see it—our guarantee that you'll buy a quality Sybex book every time.

To manage your hardware headaches and optimize your software potential, ask for a Sybex book.

FOR MORE INFORMATION, PLEASE CONTACT:

Sybex Inc.
2021 Challenger Drive
Alameda, CA 94501
Tel: (510) 523-8233 • (800) 227-2346
Fax: (510) 523-2373

Sybex is committed to using natural resources wisely to preserve and improve our environment. As a leader in the computer books publishing industry, we are aware that over 40% of America's solid waste is paper. This is why we have been printing our books on recycled paper since 1982.

This year our use of recycled paper will result in the saving of more than 153,000 trees. We will lower air pollution effluents by 54,000 pounds, save 6,300,000 gallons of water, and reduce landfill by 27,000 cubic yards.

In choosing a Sybex book you are not only making a choice for the best in skills and information, you are also choosing to enhance the quality of life for all of us.

[1698-1] The Mosaic Roadmap

GET A FREE CATALOG JUST FOR EXPRESSING YOUR OPINION.

Help us improve our books and get a **FREE** full-color catalog in the bargain. Please complete this form, pull out this page and send it in today. The address is on the reverse side.

Name _____   Company _____

Address _____   City _____ State ___ Zip _____

Phone ( ) _____

1. **How would you rate the overall quality of this book?**
   - ❏ Excellent
   - ❏ Very Good
   - ❏ Good
   - ❏ Fair
   - ❏ Below Average
   - ❏ Poor

2. **What were the things you liked most about the book? (Check all that apply)**
   - ❏ Pace
   - ❏ Format
   - ❏ Writing Style
   - ❏ Examples
   - ❏ Table of Contents
   - ❏ Index
   - ❏ Price
   - ❏ Illustrations
   - ❏ Type Style
   - ❏ Cover
   - ❏ Depth of Coverage
   - ❏ Fast Track Notes

3. **What were the things you liked *least* about the book? (Check all that apply)**
   - ❏ Pace
   - ❏ Format
   - ❏ Writing Style
   - ❏ Examples
   - ❏ Table of Contents
   - ❏ Index
   - ❏ Price
   - ❏ Illustrations
   - ❏ Type Style
   - ❏ Cover
   - ❏ Depth of Coverage
   - ❏ Fast Track Notes

4. **Where did you buy this book?**
   - ❏ Bookstore chain
   - ❏ Small independent bookstore
   - ❏ Computer store
   - ❏ Wholesale club
   - ❏ College bookstore
   - ❏ Technical bookstore
   - ❏ Other _____

5. **How did you decide to buy this particular book?**
   - ❏ Recommended by friend
   - ❏ Recommended by store personnel
   - ❏ Author's reputation
   - ❏ Sybex's reputation
   - ❏ Read book review in _____
   - ❏ Other _____

6. **How did you pay for this book?**
   - ❏ Used own funds
   - ❏ Reimbursed by company
   - ❏ Received book as a gift

7. **What is your level of experience with the subject covered in this book?**
   - ❏ Beginner
   - ❏ Intermediate
   - ❏ Advanced

8. **How long have you been using a computer?**
   _____ years
   _____ months

9. **Where do you most often use your computer?**
   - ❏ Home
   - ❏ Work
   - ❏ Both
   - ❏ Other _____

10. **What kind of computer equipment do you have? (Check all that apply)**
    - ❏ PC Compatible Desktop Computer
    - ❏ PC Compatible Laptop Computer
    - ❏ Apple/Mac Computer
    - ❏ Apple/Mac Laptop Computer
    - ❏ CD ROM
    - ❏ Fax Modem
    - ❏ Data Modem
    - ❏ Scanner
    - ❏ Sound Card
    - ❏ Other _____

11. **What other kinds of software packages do you ordinarily use?**
    - ❏ Accounting
    - ❏ Databases
    - ❏ Networks
    - ❏ Apple/Mac
    - ❏ Desktop Publishing
    - ❏ Spreadsheets
    - ❏ CAD
    - ❏ Games
    - ❏ Word Processing
    - ❏ Communications
    - ❏ Money Management
    - ❏ Other _____

12. **What operating systems do you ordinarily use?**
    - ❏ DOS
    - ❏ OS/2
    - ❏ Windows
    - ❏ Apple/Mac
    - ❏ Windows NT
    - ❏ Other _____

13. On what computer-related subject(s) would you like to see more books?

_____
_____
_____
_____

14. Do you have any other comments about this book? (Please feel free to use a separate piece of paper if you need more room)

_____
_____
_____
_____

- - - - - - - - - - - - - - - PLEASE FOLD, SEAL, AND MAIL TO SYBEX - - - - - - - - - - - - - - -

SYBEX INC.
Department M
2021 Challenger Drive
Alameda, CA
94501

Let us hear from you.

Talk to SYBEX authors, editors and fellow forum members.

Get tips, hints and advice online.

Download magazine articles, book art, and shareware.

Join the SYBEX Forum on CompuServe®

If you're already a CompuServe user, just type `GO SYBEX` to join the SYBEX Forum. If not, try CompuServe for free by calling 1-800-848-8199 and ask for Representative 560. You'll get one free month of basic service and a $15 credit for CompuServe extended services—a $23.95 value. Your personal ID number and password will be activated when you sign up.

Join us online today. Type `GO SYBEX` on CompuServe. If you're not a CompuServe member, call Representative 560 at `1-800-848-8199`.

SYBEX

(outside U.S./Canada call 614-457-0802)

SYBEX FORUM

WHAT'S ON THE DISK?

With the help of this disk, you can enjoy the Internet *immediately!*

Chameleon Sampler

NetManage's Chameleon Sampler software provides you with a powerful set of utilities you can use if you already have an account with an Internet service provider other than Netcom. You'll receive a fully functional SLIP or PPP connection to the Internet, allowing you to establish a high-speed connection that lets you download and use popular Web browsers like NCSA Mosaic or Netscape.

Chameleon Sampler also includes:

- TCP/IP software
- WinSock capability
- Four of the most useful Internet applications: e-mail, Telnet, FTP, and Ping

See Part 1 for instructions on installing and configuring Chameleon Sampler.

Customer Service and Support

For Chameleon Sampler technical support, call (408) 973-7171.

© 1995 SYBEX Inc.